Microeconomic Theory

Recent Economic Thought Series

Warren J. Samuels, Editor
Michigan State University
East Lansing, Michigan, U.S.A.

Other titles in the series:
Feiwel, G. R., *Samuelson and Neoclassical Economics*
Wade, L. L., *Political Economy: Modern Views*
Zimbalist, A., *Comparative Economic Systems: Recent Views*
Darity, W., *Labor Economics: Modern Views*
Jarsulic, M., *Money and Macro Policy*

This series is devoted to works that present divergent views on the development, prospects, and tensions within some important research areas of international economic thought. Among the fields covered are macromonetary policy, public finance, labor and political economy. The emphasis of the series is on providing a critical, constructive view of each of these fields, as well as a forum through which leading scholars of international reputation may voice their perspectives on important related issues. Each volume in the series will be self-contained; together these volumes will provide dramatic evidence of the variety of economic thought within the scholarly community.

Microeconomic Theory

edited by
Larry Samuelson
The Pennsylvania State University

Kluwer-Nijhoff Publishing
a member of the Kluwer Academic Publishers Group

Boston-Dordrecht-Lancaster

Distributors

for the United States and Canada: Kluwer Academic Publishers, 190 Old
Derby Street, Hingham, MA, 02043, USA

for the UK and Ireland: Kluwer Academic Publishers, MTP Press Limited,
Falcon House, Queen Square, Lancaster LA1 1RN, UK

for all other countries: Kluwer Academic Publishers Group, Distribution
Centre, P. O. Box 322, 3300 AH Dordrecht, The Netherlands

Library of Congress Cataloging in Publication Data
Main entry under title:

Microeconomic theory.

  (Recent economic thought)
  Includes index.
  I. Microeconomics—Addresses, essays, lectures.
I. Samuelson, Larry, 1953–   II. Series.
HB172.M59   1985   338.5   85–8072
ISBN 0-89838-170-3

Typeset by Macmillan India Ltd., Bangalore
Printed in the United States of America

Contents

Contributing Authors

Taradas Bandyopadhyay
Department of Economics
University of Hull
Hull, England HU6 7RX
    and
The Pennsylvania State University
University Park, PA 16802

Douglas H. Blair
Department of Economics
Rutgers University
New Brunswick, NJ 08903

Parkash Chander
Indian Statistical Institute
Delhi Center
7, S. J. S. Sansanwal Marg.
Delhi, India 110016

Kalyan Chatterjee
Division of Management Science
The Pennsylvania State University
University Park, PA 16802

Peter C. Fishburn
AT&T Bell Laboratories
Murray Hill, NJ 07974

Patricia A. Goering
Department of Economics
University of Florida
Gainesville, FL 32611

Klaus Hennings
Lehrstuhl VWLF
Universität Hannover
Wunstorfer Strasse 14
D-3000 Hannover 91
Federal Republic of Germany

Barry W. Ickes
Department of Economics
The Pennsylvania State University
University Park, PA 16802

Philip Mirowski
Department of Economics
Tufts University
Medford, MA 02155
        and
University of Massachusetts-Amherst
Amherst, MA 01003

Robert A. Pollak
Department of Economics
University of Pennsylvania
Philadelphia, PA 19104

Rafael Rob
Department of Economics
University of Pennsylvania
Philadelphia, PA 19104

Larry Samuelson
Department of Economics
The Pennsylvania State University
University Park, PA 16802

Joaquim Silvestre
Department of Economics
University of California-Davis
Davis, CA 95616
        and
Universitat Autònoma de Barcelona
Barcelona, Spain

It is often said that everyone understands precisely what is meant by the notion of probability—except those who have spent their lives studying the matter. Upon close scrutiny, the intuitively obvious idea of probability becomes quite elusive. Is it a subjective or objective concept? Are random variables simply improperly measured deterministic variables, or inherently random? What is meant by the phrase "other things held constant" that often appears in descriptions of probability? These questions involve fundamental philosophical and scientific issues, and promise to elude definitive answers for some time.

The same type of difficulty arises when attempting to produce a volume on microeconomic theory. The obvious first question—what is microeconomic theory?—defies immediate answer. If interpreted broadly, microeconomic theory expands to encompass virtually all of economics. Many "applied" fields might be described as bodies of microeconomic analysis characterized by a concern with some common topic. With the advent of the new microfoundations literature, the microeconomist may encroach upon the traditional territory of the macroeconomist. The boundary between microeconomic general equilibrium theory and macroeconomics is increasingly blurred. In addition, microeconomic theory (along with economics in general) has been encroaching upon various other social sciences. One quickly concludes that a broad view of microeconomic theory encompasses an unmanageably large collection of topics. On the other hand, however, one might be able to take such a narrow view of microeconomic theory as to leave the field with virtually no territory. Given the advent of mathematical economics, almost any exercise in microeconomic theory can be described as an endeavor in one of the topical fields of economics.

In the light of this dilemma, microeconomists must apparently be content to share the dilemma of probabilists, pursuing a subject whose boundaries appear obvious as long as one does not examine them too closely. This book accordingly refrains from offering a definition of microeconomics. However, some selectivity must be exercised if any hope is to remain of limiting the study to a single volume. Just as an art historian must implicitly serve as critic when deciding which works to include in a history of art, so must the choice of topics for this book reveal an image of microeconomic theory. Fortunately, the purpose here is not to produce a catalogue of current microeconomic theory, but to stimulate the interpretation and assessment of microeconomic theory. Accordingly, I have selected several typical topics within microeconomics for examination, eschewing an attempt at comprehensive coverage.

In addition to importance, the topics addressed in this book are characterized by extensive recent work and significant outstanding questions. The goal in each case is threefold, though the characteristics of the individual areas affect the degrees to which these three goals are pursued. An introduction to the basic questions and results in the area is provided. Intuition is often substituted for technical detail, in an effort to preserve accessibility to a wide audience. In addition, the gateways to the relevant literature are indicated. In addressing these two objectives, an exhaustive survey is generally not provided. Doing so would easily cause each topic's treatment to expand to the size of the volume. Instead, it is hoped that the treatment will be sufficiently extensive to pique the reader's curiosity, and provide the reader with the basic references required for further study. Finally, some interpretation of the status and prospects of further work in the area is offered. The result can be described as a critical introduction to selected topics in microeconomic theory.

While a definition of microeconomic theory is elusive, one easily identifies certain core areas of microeconomics. These include the theories of the consumer and the firm. These areas provide the building blocks of microeconomic inquiry, as well as much of economics. For example, economic models are commonly required to be based on the optimizing behavior of rational agents (generally, consumers or firms). The failure to adhere to this practice potentially subjects one to the charge of "ad hocery," one of the most feared criticisms in economics. Any discussion of microeconomic theory must accordingly begin with the theories of agents' behavior upon which microeconomics rests. Though theories of the consumer and firm have commanded the attention of scholars since the inception of economics as a recognized field (if not earlier), unanswered questions readily arise. These theories are said to be based on the optimizing behavior of rational agents. Can we specify what is meant by optimal? Do the agents in question optimize? Can we answer the same questions with respect to rationality? What are the constraints with which agents are faced, and what information do they have?

Two chapters address these questions. The traditional tool in the theory of the consumer is the maximization of expected utility. As Peter Fishburn demonstrates, it has become increasingly clear that expected utility theory may not be applicable in general, and the search for alternatives has begun.

The outcome of this search has the potential to affect virtually all aspects of economics. The second foundation of microeconomic theory is the theory of the firm. As Klaus Hennings' comments suggest, consumers are likely to have imperfect information about the products supplied by firms. The behavior of firms in such markets is an interesting issue, which recent work in micro-economics has addressed. Patricia Goering provides a sample of this work.

In introductory economics classes, economics is invariably characterized as the study of resource allocation. Traditionally, economics has accordingly concerned itself with how economies actually *do* allocate resources, with attention generally directed toward market economies. Recently, however, attention has been directed toward alternative resource allocation mechanisms. Several motivations for this interest arise. First, there is the increasing prominence of economies whose resource allocation mechanisms deliberately shun market forces. Secondly, there is the desire to address apparent failures in market allocation systems, such as the difficulties that arise in the face of externalities or public goods. Finally, the attempt to evaluate the performance of market directed allocation schemes naturally leads to a contemplation of alternative schemes. As a result, attention is directed to the study of how economies *might* be designed to allocate resources. This work initially appears to be somewhat removed from reality, with its notions of allocation mechanisms and mappings from economies into outcomes. Upon close examination, however, one finds the study of resource allocation mechanisms has much to contribute to our understanding of economics. Only with a thorough examination of alternatives and general resource allocation principles can a precise understanding be achieved of ideas which have occupied central places in economics throughout its history (such as the efficiency of a competitive market). Chapters by Rafael Rob and Parkash Chander address the issue of resource allocation mechanisms.

An alternative characterization of economics and frequent subtitle of introductory texts is that economics is "the science of choice." While economists have long examined individual choice, only recently has the problem been raised of transforming individual choices into social choices in some consistent way. In this endeavor, economists have been joined by political scientists, philosophers, and others. This issue is related to many other basic problems in economics. For example, attempts to construct theories of bargaining and political behavior encounter issues which arise in the social choice literature. However, the social choice literature is also somewhat atypical, in that it easily leads to normative statements, an activity obstentibly shunned by many economists. Douglas Blair and Robert Pollak provide an account of the social choice literature, and Taradas Bandyopadhyay provides a glimpse of some recent work in the area.

As microeconomic theories have become more sophisticated, so have they become more abstract. This abstraction has been subjected to increasing criticism, and a common stereotype of an economist includes a willingness to make any assumption, however incredible, that produces an elegant theory. Ultimately, microeconomic theory must be useful if it is to serve as anything other than a curiosity. It is then no surprise that activities in the field of microeconomics have included concerted attempts to expand the purview of the theory. For example, a convenient assumption in constructing micro-economic models is that the agents involved treat prices parametrically, assuming that their actions cannot affect the market price. Usually, this assumption is justified by appealing to the convention that there are a large number of agents in the market, with each individual agent being essentially insignificant. Unfortunately, this convention is in some cases clearly unac-ceptable. No major conceptual difficulties arise if the convention fails on only one side of a market. A rich collection of imperfect competition models addresses such cases. A greater challenge appears when neither side of a market is characterized by a large number of agents. For an extended period, the treatment of this case in economics textbooks consisted of describing it as bilateral monopoly (at least in the simplest case), and pronouncing it as outside the scope of economic inquiry. It was generally observed that some notion of bargaining strength would allow an analysis of the problem, and economists appeared to be of the opinion that this analysis might wisely be left to another discipline. Recently, however, economists have begun to explicitly address these cases, with the label of bilateral monopoly having been replaced by the more general description of bargaining. There is now an extensive literature on the theory and practice of bargaining. Kalyan Chatterjee discusses the theory of bargaining.

A second convention that has frequently been invoked by microeconomists is that markets clear, with prices adjusting so as to equate the quantities supplied and demanded. From the marginalist revolution onward, a basic concern of microeconomics involved the adjustment of prices to clear markets. However, it was presumably the apparent failure of this clearing process that inspired Keynesian macroeconomics. Upon the inception of the latter, macroeconomics found itself without a corresponding micro-foundation, as microeconomics had little to say about the failure of markets to clear. Economists have recently devoted considerable attention to developing theories of nonclearing markets. This work promises a potential micro-foundation for macroeconomics, as well as other insights. Joaquim Silvestre reports on such work.

An intention of this book is to provide some assessment of microeconomic theory. The crucial question is perhaps whether microeconomists are likely to make progress in fortifying strengths and addressing weaknesses in current theories. Of these two questions, one engenders less controversy in attempting to answer the former. There is little doubt that microeconomists will continue to improve and expand the collection of technical tools available to economists. However, criticism and controversy often surround microeconomics, generally involving the issue of the applicability of microeconomics to relevant economic problems. For example, it is partly dissatisfaction with contemporary microeconomics that motivates alternative points of view, such as institutional economics.

Four chapters provide opinions on the state of microeconomic theory. My introductory remarks and Barry Ickes' discussion of the usefulness of various seemingly esoteric areas of microeconomics provide optimistic assessments. In contrast, Phil Mirowski argues that serious shortcomings characterize contemporary microeconomics. Klaus Hennings suggests that many advances in microeconomic theory have been achieved only by significantly simplifying the objects of analysis.

The reader is invited to subject the various opinions offered to the test of a confrontation with the expositions of current work in microeconomics. Hence, Klaus Hennings' discussion of whether consumers optimize (given an exogenous preference structure) and how firms might behave in less than perfect markets should be compared with the essays of Peter Fishburn and Patricia Goering. Philip Mirowski's discussion of the role of institutions in economics should be compared with the exposition by Kalyan Chatterjee and Joaquim Silvestre of recent work (in bargaining and non-Walrasian theory) designed to capture features of actual economies. Barry Ickes' comments on the relevance of results in social choice and resource allocation theory for economic planning should be compared with the essays of Taradas Bandyopadhyay, Douglas Blair and Robert Pollak, Rafael Rob, and Parkash Chander. This confrontation provides the opportunity to form a first-hand assessment of the opinions offered in the book and of microeconomic theory.

This brief guide to the topics that follow leaves one painfully aware that important aspects of microeconomics have been excluded. If a discussion of potential microfoundations is to be provided, a treatment of general equilibrium theory with nonmarket clearing prices should be supplemented by a discussion of implicit contracts theories and rational expectations. For an examination of agreements when prices are not taken parametrically, a discussion of bargaining should be coupled with a discussion of recent work on auction theory, principle-agent problems, and signaling models. Discussion of social choice and resource allocation mechanisms could usefully be supplemented by examination of recent work in the theory of incentives, especially incentives under incomplete information. Other expanding areas of inquiry have been ignored completely. This list of omissions is itself incomplete, though it provides an indication of other interesting topics. Their exclusion can be justified only by appealing to the consideration of length, and the observation that while our selectivity has excluded some worthy topics, it has included no unworthy ones.

Throughout this preface, very little has been said about the content of the essays or about the authors. This omission is deliberate. Descriptions of the chapters' contents will be unable to match the contents themselves for clarity and insight, and no platitudes applied to the authors can impress as much as reading their works. It is accordingly the only appropriate choice to let any exposition beyond mere mention of the works emerge from the works themselves.

Acknowledgments

I am indebted to Warren Samuels, who provided encouragement and guidance throughout my work on the book. I also appreciate the cooperation and patience of Karen Knowles and David K. Marshall of Kluwer-Nijhoff. I have an obvious and overwhelming debt to the scholars whose work appears in these pages. Their generosity with their time and effort has been exemplary, and has made the production of this book possible.

Microeconomic Theory

1 INTRODUCTION:
An Affirmative View of
Microeconomic Theory

Larry Samuelson

It is often suggested that macroeconomics is in a period of crisis.[1] The disappointing economic performance of the world economy in recent years has brought the term stagflation into widespread use, and has caused economists to reexamine their theories of macroeconomics. The demise of Keynesian economics is often pronounced, though its proponents are not silent, and a variety of contenders have emerged to claim its place.

In comparison, one would expect microeconomics to be experiencing a state of relative tranquility. In the 1870s, Walras first explicity formulated a course of inquiry profound enough to be termed the fundamental problem of economics.[2] His goal was to characterize the determination of the equilibrium quantities and prices of an economy's goods and services. For the mere conception of this problem, Walras is accorded a prominent place in the history of economics. He was able to identify many of the issues surrounding the solution of the problem, though its complexity allowed it to defy a definitive solution for decades.

An important event in the recent history of economics has been the solution of the existence-of-equilibrium problem posed by Walras. In the 1930s, mathematicians and economists began to apply increasingly sophisticated analytical tools to the question.[3] The culmination of this effort was a precise statement of the conditions determining equilibrium prices and quantities in an economy, and of the circumstances in which a solution to these conditions will exist. This analysis has been summarized in Debreu [1959], Arrow and Hahn [1971], and Hildenbrand [1974]. The examination of this work now constitutes an important component of a graduate education in microeconomics, and in continuing microeconomic research.

Microeconomic theory thus appears to occupy the enviable position of an academic endeavor which has solved its fundamental problem. In spite of this, one frequently encounters criticisms of microeconomics.[4] These criticisms appear to have their origins in the methods by which microeconomists address their problems. As does all theory, microeconomic theory begins by abstracting from the object of its inquiry. The reward for such abstraction is the ability to apply powerful analytical tools to the analysis. The cost of the abstraction is that potentially important factors may be excluded from the analysis. One attempts to minimize the risk of such exclusion by retaining important features of the problem and eliminating less important ones. This is obviously a process fraught with pitfalls, and much of the criticism of microeconomics arises out of the suspicion that microeconomic theory has not been sufficiently successful in avoiding such pitfalls. In particular, the charge is often made that microeconomists are guided in their abstractions not by the principle of including important factors and excluding unimportant ones, but by the dictates of analytic tractability. Hence, the problems which microeconomic theory addresses are shaped by the methods it employs, while one would prefer to have the methods shaped by the problems which are of interest.

Though the assumptions encountered in microeconomics are frequently quite strong, it is not clear that this alone is cause for discontent. Instead, unrealistic assumptions have been defended by Milton Friedman [1953]. If the realism of assumptions were the only issue, microeconomics could perhaps construct an effective defense, though at the cost of some methodological debate. Notice, however, that Friedman reserves as the primary test of an internally consistent theory that its predictions be verified (or at least not falsified) by empirical testing. If one takes a skeptical view, it is not clear that much of contemporary microeconomics can pass such a test. The potential failure occurs not because the theory is falsified when tested, but because the questions answered by the theory do not have counterparts in the economy. Hence, rather than invoking unrealistic assumptions to examine realistic problems, microeconomic theory often examines unrealistic problems.[5] The difficulty is then not with potentially incorrect theory, but with potentially inapplicable theory. This is presumably the extreme form of allowing the analytic tools to shape the analysis, with questions chosen to fit the tools rather than the reverse.

This criticism provides a formidable challenge to microeconomic theory, and the latter must be assessed in light of the possible responses. In the remainder of this chapter some of these responses are illustrated. Our contention is that microeconomic theory has been continually developing new areas and methods of inquiry, and these developments have enhanced the ability of microeconomics to examine interesting problems. Microeconomic theory may not be immune to criticism, but is making progress in addressing potential deficiencies.

We begin by observing that microeconomic theory has responded to changing conditions in the economy. New subjects of examination have been prompted by economic conditions, and have flourished. One such area, the theory of exhaustible resources, is briefly explored in the next section. We find a rich body of microeconomic theory. This theory has been developed recently, in response to the increasing prominence of exhaustible resources in the economy, and has been useful in guiding thinking about economic events.

In addition to pursuing new areas of inquiry, microeconomic theory has consistently seen the development of new tools of analysis. Frequently, these techniques initially appear to be without obvious application, but subsequently reveal themselves to be useful. We may turn to the theory of exhaustible resources for one such example, as the calculus of variations techniques employed to examine resource markets were initially regarded with some skepticism, and have subsequently been widely embraced. We examine two additional examples, game theory and recent work in general equilibrium theory. In each case, new mathematical techniques have offered insights into the economy or into microeconomic theory.

These observations suggest that progress in microeconomics has occurred, and can be expected to continue. This chapter closes with a discussion of an area (disequilibrium theory) in which further progress in microeconomics appears to be especially needed, and notes preliminary efforts in this direction.

1. The Theory of Exhaustible Resources

A conventional motivation for studying economics is that resources are scarce, and this scarcity causes their allocation to be a complex problem. Within this conception of scarcity, one often finds the implicit presumption that resources are renewable. A typical analysis of the economy begins with a static model. An endowment of resources is posited and its allocation examined. Within this static model, resources are scarce. This model is then transformed into an intertemporal one by assuming that in each period, an endowment of resources appears and is allocated. Allowing for investment or other intertemporal links, the evolution of the economy can be examined.[6] The key to this analysis is that an endowment appears in *each* period, so that basic resource inputs are renewed from one period to the next. For many resources, such as labor, this is a reasonable assumption, and theories involving renewable resources will be generally applicable if these types of resources are of primary importance. In the 1970s, however, the inability to consider some important resources as renewable was clearly demonstrated. Significant resources are exhaustible, and the role of such resources in the economy cannot be examined with a conventional theory of scarce but renewable resources.

Microeconomic theory has quickly addressed this potential inapplicability. The 1970s produced a surge of activity in the economics of exhaustible resources. This provides an obvious example of a case in which microeconomic theory has been adapted to the pursuit of interesting economic problems. To examine this case more closely, we briefly outline the basic principles of an exhaustible resources model.[7]

Consider first a market composed of perfectly competitive resource extractors, who treat prices parametrically. Suppose that the period t market price is given by $p_t = f(R_t)$, where R_t is the quantity of resource extracted and sold in period t. For convenience, let the demand for resource curve be such that $\lim_{R_t \to \infty} f(R_t) = 0$ and $\lim_{R_t \to 0} f(R_t) = \infty$. Suppose also that costs of extraction are zero. Let the interest rate be r. The basic arbitrage result is that the price of resource must satisfy:

$$p_t = p_0 e^{rt}. \tag{1.1}$$

This indicates that the price of the resource must increase at the rate of interest, or that the present value price must be constant. If not, firms will be unwilling to extract and sell resource in some periods. For example, if $p_\tau > p_t e^{(\tau - t)r}$, then the present value of resource sales in period τ exceeds that of t, and no resource will be sold in the latter period, it being more profitable to sell in τ. The result is that no resource will be extracted or sold in period t, yielding an arbitrarily large p_t and vitiating the result of $p_\tau > p_t e^{(\tau - t)r}$. A market equilibrium can thus appear if and only if (1.1) holds, or iff prices grow at the rate of interest. Equivalently, we can establish this result by noting that the rate of growth of the resource price is the rate of return on holding the resource. If this rate is lower than the rate of return available on other assets (the rate of interest), competitive firms will be unwilling to hold any stock of resource. If it is higher than the interest rate, they will be unwilling to part with any resource. Neither result can hold in equilibrium.

The competitive price thus grows at the rate of interest. Competitive firms will then be indifferent as to when they extract and sell their resource, receiving equivalent present values from sales in all periods, and will be willing to adjust their extraction rates so that $p_t = f(R_t)$ is satisfied in each period (i.e., will be willing to satisfy the quantity demanded in each period). The initial price p_0 must adjust so that total quantity of resource extracted over the (infinite) horizon equals the initial stock of resource available to be extracted (X_0), or

$$\int_0^\infty R_t \, dt = X_0,$$

where $p_t = f(R_t)$ and $p_t = p_0 e^{rt}$. Notice that under our assumptions on $f(R_t)$, the quantity of resource extracted each period gradually falls, with the resource stock asymptotically exhausted.

This basic model is easily extended in a number of directions. For example, extraction costs may be nonzero. Let a constant extraction cost of c per unit of resource extracted exist, so that at time t extraction costs are cR_t. Then the magnitude which must increase at the rate of interest is the price of extraction net of extraction costs, or

$$(p_t - c) = (p_0 - c)e^{rt},$$

giving ($\cdot$ designates a time derivative):

$$\dot{p}_t = r(p_t - c).$$

Again, we find that the price of the resource increases over time, though in this case at a rate less than the rate of interest.

One easily invokes conventional arguments to demonstrate that these competitive solutions are efficient. What can we conclude? The (efficient) allocation of an exhaustible resource, attained by a competitive market, exhibits the following features:

(1)　The price of resource increases over time.
(2)　The price of resource is based on a scarcity rent consideration, and may be significantly higher than the cost of production.
(3)　The overall level of the price path adjusts so that total quantity of resource demanded throughout the horizon equals the initial stock of resource.

These observations constitute an important contribution of microeconomic theory. To illustrate this, consider the following example of an analysis which is apparently not guided by a familiarity with the theory of exhaustible resources:[8]

> (OPEC supporters) . . . seem to be rejecting the play of free market forces in determining prices. In such a market the price of a product is closely related to the

cost of producing the last unit of supply that is demanded by a buyer. No one anywhere in the world is pumping oil that cost $10 a bbl. to 'produce'. The cost of bringing up a barrel ranges from 10¢ in Saudi Arabia to 60¢ in Venezuela to $3 or so in the US. OPEC's defenders seem to have the notion that somehow market forces have never properly recognized the value of oil, that its price always should have been higher. This tosses rational economic analysis out the window.

In light of this statement, it is apparent that microeconomic theory has much to contribute to our understanding of exhaustible resources.[9]

A second illustration is in order. Suppose again that a resource stock of fixed size exists, extracted by perfectly competitive firms, but that an alternative technology also exists, such as solar power or shale oil, capable of producing a perfect substitute for the resource. Let the alternative source also be owned by perfect competitors, and let there be no restrictions on its capability to produce the output. Let the unit cost of extracting the resource be c_1, and the unit cost of producing resource substitute via the alternative technology be $c_2 > c_1$. We can derive some characteristics of an equilibrium in this market. As long as some resource remains, the alternative technology will not be used, since $c_2 > c_1$ ensures that the competitive resource extractors can undercut the price of the substitute. Similarly, no resource use will persist once the alternative technology is brought into production. The cost of the substitute limits the price of the resource, so that the latter could not grow over time. Competitive resource sellers will be unwilling to hold a resource whose price is not increasing, and will accordingly exhaust the resource before the alternative technology comes into use. Hence, we will have two intervals, the first (say $[0, T]$)), in which the resource is extracted and the alternative technology is idle; and the second $((T, \infty))$ in which only the alternative is employed, the resource being exhausted and hence no further resource being extracted. The price of the resource substitute will be constant over the second interval, and will be given by c_2. In the first interval, the price of the resource will increase from an initial value of p_0 to a terminal value of c_2. This increase in price is required to induce the competitive resource owners to offer resource for sale throughout the interval. A terminal resource price greater than c_2 clearly cannot occur, and a terminal resource price less than c_2 will cause some resource to be held until after the alternative technology is brought into use, which is not an equilibrium. Hence, the price must rise to the level c_2. The initial value p_0 and the date of the switch from resource to alternative technology (T) will be set so the resource is exactly exhausted at time T.

Hence, when the resource is in use, its price is less than that of the substitute produced by the alternative technology, and increases until it achieves the price of the latter. In light of this observation, consider the following:[10]

Nearly every OPEC member . . . rejects the notion that the price of oil is now too high. 'What do they mean by high?' asks Iran's Minister of Interior . . . incredulously. He reasons that the price is about equal to what it would cost to obtain an alternative form of energy, such as gas produced from coal. Thus he . . . insist(s) that \$9.70 per bl is a fair price.

We again have a case in which casual intuition fails, since the argument in the preceding quotation is apparently not guided by the microeconomic theory of exhaustible resources. A solid foundation of microeconomic analysis is required to usefully address interesting exhaustible resource questions.

The exhaustible resource models that we have presented are rudimentary. However, they can easily be expanded to encompass important features of resource markets, and such expansion produces frequent surprises. For example, the formation of OPEC and its impact in the 1970s directs attention to the case of a monopolized resource market. In conventional economic theory, the basic effect of a monopoly is to increase price and reduce output. In the case of an exhaustible resource monopoly, this strategy may take an unexpected form.

Let a single firm exercise a monopoly over the resource stock. For convenience, assume that extraction costs are zero. The firm's objective is

$$\max_{R_t} \int_0^\infty f(R_t) R_t e^{-rt}\, dt, \tag{1.2}$$

subject to

$$\int_0^\infty R_t\, dt = X_0. \tag{1.3}$$

This problem can be solved by standard control theory techniques, with a Hamiltonian given by

$$H(R_t, X_t, \lambda_t) = f(R_t) R_t e^{-rt} - \lambda_t X_t$$

with equation of motion $\dot{X}_t = -R_t$ and first order conditions for an interior solution of (1.3) and

$$\left(\frac{\partial f(R_t)}{\partial R_t} R_t + f(R_t)\right) e^{-rt} - \lambda_t = 0, \qquad \frac{\partial \lambda_t}{\partial t} = 0.$$

This yields

$$p_t(1 + 1/\eta_t) = \lambda e^{rt}, \tag{1.4}$$

where η_t is the period t elasticity of demand. The monopoly's optimization condition thus requires that the marginal revenue from resource sales grow at the rate of interest. As expected, the monopoly is concerned with marginal revenue rather than price.

The implications of this result are intriguing. First, consider the simplest case of a constant elasticity of resource demand. Then (1.4) becomes

$$p_t = \lambda' e^{rt}, \tag{1.5}$$

where λ' is a constant. Hence, the price grows at the rate of interest, as it does in the competitive market. In the constant elasticity case, the monopoly and competitive markets then yield the same growth rate of price. Do they yield the same price level? The answer is that they must. If the monopoly sets a higher price in some periods than the perfect competitor, then it must set a higher price in every period if the optimality condition of a price which grows at the rate of interest is to be preserved. This will reduce the total quantity of resource demanded over the horizon, causing the monopoly to sell less than its endowment of resource. It cannot be optimal for the firm to sell less than its endowment, and hence the optimal monopoly price can be no higher than the competitive price. Similarly, the monopoly cannot set a price lower than the competitive price. This would require the resource price to be lower than the competitive price in every period, and would hence involve an attempt to sell more resource than is available. The conclusion is that if the elasticity of demand is constant, the competitive and monopoly solutions coincide. This contrasts with the results of conventional monopoly theory.

If the elasticity of demand is not constant, two interesting possibilities arise. Suppose that the demand becomes more elastic as the quantity of resource sold decreases. Then $(1 + 1/\eta_t)$ increases over time (as the quantity of resource extracted decreases), and the optimality condition given by (1.4) requires that the resource price grow at a rate slower than the rate of interest. As we have seen, the monopoly cannot adopt a price which is either always higher or always lower than the competitive price, since doing so would entail selling too little total resource or violating the resource constraint. A growth rate of the resource price less than the interest rate must then be accomplished by setting the price higher than the competitive price in initial periods, with the price growing more slowly than the competitive price and eventually falling below the latter. The monopoly thus matches the intuitive expectation of raising the resource price above the competitive level in initial periods, but only in these periods. Eventually, the monopoly supplies the resource more cheaply than the competitive market. This outcome is reversed if demand becomes less ealstic as the quantity of resource sold decreases. Arguments similar to those we have just presented reveal that in this case, the monopoly initially charges a lower price than the competitive market, with the price growing faster than the rate of interest and eventually exceeding the competitive price.

We might also inquire whether the monopoly depletes the resource more or less rapidly than a competitive market. This result can be inferred from the respective price levels, since a higher period t price corresponds to a smaller period t quantity sold, and hence again depends upon the elasticity of demand. The monopoly depletes the resource more rapidly than a competitive market if elasticity decreases as quantity sold decreases; and less rapidly if elasticity increases as quantity sold decreases. A monopoly may thus be either the friend or foe of a conservationist.[11]

A comparison of monopoly and competitive pricing can obviously yield a variety of outcomes, depending upon the nature of the demand curve. These outcomes may not match an expectation guided by a familiarity with conventional monopoly theory.

In addition to these examples, a host of exhaustible resource problems arise which are easily misdiagnosed if casual intuition is applied, and which can be usefully examined only with the help of microeconomic theory. For example, it is commonly contended that the owners of a common property resource deposit, in an effort to realize the profits of extraction before other owners deplete the stock, will deplete the stock too rapidly. This phenomenon has been described as the "tragedy of the commons" (cf. Hardin [1968]). Only recently has this intuitive statement been subjected to a rigorous examination (see Eswaran and Lewis [1984] for a guide to work in this area). Whether the resource is depleted too rapidly depends crucially on the equilibrium concept adopted by the firms in computing their profit maximizing extraction patterns, with a particularly important role played by the conjectures that each firm forms regarding the reactions prompted by changes in the firm's strategy. The issue is accordingly more complex then intuition suggests.

In general, a solid grasp of exhaustible resource fundamentals is provided only by employing the appropriate microeconomic analysis to the problem, including superficially esoteric control theoretic (or calculus of variations) techniques. We can conclude that in the case of exhaustible resources, microeconomic theory has successfully addressed itself to a new area of inquiry, with powerful results.

2. Techniques of Microeconomic Theory

Microeconomic theory has been characterized not only by new objects of inquiry, but also by the development of new analytic tools. It is evident that the expansion into new areas has been fruitful, as the previous section indicated, but the new analytic tools have occasionally drawn more skeptical responses. Upon examination, however, many such tools are found to allow important contributions to our understanding of both the economy and economics. In this section, we provide two examples of abstract analytical developments which have permitted the analysis of previously inaccessible questions.

We begin by considering noncooperative game theory. Game theory initially found only sporadic application in economic analysis, in spite of its practitioners' belief that it was ideally suited for economic analysis. Recent years have witnessed an explosion in the use of game theory to examine economic problems, and game theory has become a standard tool even for the nonspecialist.

The foundation of noncooperative game theoretic applications in economics is the notion of a Nash equilibrium, formalized by Nash [1951] and anticipated by Cournot [1897].[12] A game can be characterized by a set of n players, indexed by $i = 1, \ldots, n$; a set of actions or strategies available to each player, denoted X_i; and a payoff or utility function $u_i: \Pi_{j=1}^n X_i \to R$ for each player. An important aspect of the latter is that agent i's utility is a function not only of agent i's strategy, but also of the strategies chosen by the other agents in the game. It is this interdependence, so often found in economic interactions, that endows the game with its interesting features. Let $x_i \in X_i$ denote an element of player i's strategy set, and hence a choice of strategy, and let $x_{-i} \in X_1 x X_2 x \cdots x X_{i-1} x X_{i+1} x \cdots x X_n$ denote a choice of strategies on the part of each of the other $n - 1$ agents. A Nash equilibrium is a collection of strategies $x_1^*, \ldots, x_n^*$ with the following property:

$$u_1(x_1^*, x_{-1}^*) \geq u_1(x_1, x_{-1}^*) \quad \forall x_1 \in X_1$$

$$\vdots \qquad\qquad \vdots$$

$$u_n(x_n^*, x_{-n}^*) \geq u_n(x_n, x_{-n}^*) \quad \forall x_n \in X_n.$$

Hence, a Nash equilibrium is such that each agent's offer is optimal, given the offers of other agents. Restated, no agent can gain by unilaterally choosing a different strategy.

This is a seemingly abstract notion, and has no apparent connection to the economy. However, economists have found the concept indispensible in several areas.[13] We consider one example, presented by the problem of an established monopoly faced with the threat of potential entry by another firm. Suppose that the monopoly has a two period planning horizon. The monopoly (hereafter referred to as firm one) is a monopoly in period one, but a second firm (firm two) may enter the market in period two, yielding a duopoly. Firm one will naturally prefer that entry does not occur. An intuitive expectation is that firm one will engage in limit pricing to deter entry. Hence, the firm will charge a lower price than the pure monopoly price in period one, reducing its period one profits. The potential entrant, upon observing the low profits of the established firm, will reduce its estimate of the duopoly profits it will earn if it enters in the second period, and hence may decide not to enter. The benefits to the existing firm of deterring entry may exceed the foregone period one profits, making it optimal to limit price.

The difficulty with this scenario lies in explaining why the monopolist's period one price affects the entrant's decision.[14] The profits to be earned by the potential entrant in period two depend upon the demand conditions in the market, the cost conditions of both firms, and the duopoly solution which emerges, but does not depend upon the price charged by firm one in period one. If firm two is fully informed about demand and cost conditions, firm one's period one price cannot affect firm two's entry decision. Hence, there is no incentive for the monopoly to limit price in period one, and in the absence of some uncertainty, limit pricing will not appear.

If limit pricing is to occur, then some uncertainty must arise. To capture this possibility, let there be two possible types of monopoly. With probability p, the monopoly has the relatively high unit cost of $\bar{c}_1$; with probability $1 - p$, it has relatively low cost $\underline{c}_1 < \bar{c}_1$. Similarly, there are two types of entrants, a high cost entrant ($\bar{c}_2$) with probability q; and a low cost entrant ($\underline{c}_2 < \bar{c}_2$) with probability $1 - q$. Let $\pi_2 (\cdot, \cdot)$ be the profits earned by the entrant in the period two duopoly solution given that the entrant enters, where $(\cdot, \cdot)$ identifies the types of firms one and two. We assume that $\pi_2 (\cdot, \cdot)$ includes a fixed cost-of-entry fee. Let[15]

$$\pi_2(\bar{c}_1, \underline{c}_2) > \pi_2(\bar{c}_1, \bar{c}_2) > 0,$$

$$\pi_2(\underline{c}_1, \bar{c}_2) < \pi_2(\underline{c}_1, \underline{c}_2) < 0.$$

Notice that both types of firm two would like to enter against a high cost firm one, and neither would like to enter against a low cost firm one. It is clear that either type of firm one earns highest period two profits if no entry occurs, and lowest if entry occurs and the entrant is low cost.

What is the optimal strategy for firm one? To answer this, we first specify a strategy for each of the possible types of firm one. This method of analysis requires a subtle interpretation. We must determine what firm one will do if it actually is a high cost firm, as well as what it will do if it actually is a low cost firm. We shall accordingly speak of the strategy of the high cost firm one and of the low cost firm one. This may appear to imply that two of "firm one" exist, one of each type. This is not the case. Instead, there are two possible types of firm one, only one of which actually exists. We examine two strategies, one of which will be optimal for each type of firm one.

One quickly discovers that the choice of strategies in this market is a complex issue. The high cost firm one may be able to successfully deter entry by charging a price lower than its pure monopoly price. This tactic potentially deters entry not because the entrant's period two duopoly profits depend upon firm one's period one price, but because the period one price may reveal or conceal information about the identity of firm one, about which the entrant is uncertain. Hence, the high cost firm one may attempt to masquerade as a low cost firm by adopting the same price as would the latter. Two complications arise, however. First, the potential entrant, realizing that the high cost firm has an incentive to disguise its type, will realize that observing the pure monopoly price of a low cost firm does not necessarily signal that the existing firm is of low cost. The entrant may or may not find it profitable to enter in such a case, depending upon p. Furthermore, if entry would still occur in this case, then if the monopoly were a low cost monopoly, it would have an incentive to reveal that it really is low cost, so as to preclude entry. It may accordingly adopt a price other than its pure monopoly price, sacrificing some first period profit in order to banish all doubts as to its type and hence deter entry. Whether it will be profitable to do so depends upon how much lower the price will have to be set to render it unprofitable for a high cost firm one (if it existed) to match the price, and also on the strategies of the potential entrants. The latter specify ranges of observed firm one prices for which entry will occur, and hence clearly can affect the profitability of various firm one prices.

This delicate interplay of forces presents a formidable challenge, but is easily examined through the use of game theory. Milgrom and Roberts [1982] apply game theoretic techniques to the problem and find that, for reasonable values of the game's parameters:

(1) Both pooling and separating equilibria exist. In a pooling equilibrium, the two possible types of existing firms would adopt the same price, so that the price reveals no information. In a separating equilibrium, they would adopt different prices, so that the price reveals unambiguously the type of existing firm in the market.

(2) In a separating equilibrium, entry occurs in precisely the circumstances in which it does without limit pricing. (We say that limit pricing does not occur if, of the two types of firm one, each would charge their pure monopoly price in period one.) Hence, entry occurs with probability p in this case.

(3) In a separating equilibrium, limit pricing occurs (at least one firm would not adopt its period one pure monopoly price). This occurs because the low cost firm would adjust its price so as to make it sufficiently unattractive for the high cost firm to imitate the low cost firm and subject the latter to the threat of entry.

(4) In a pooling equilibrium (which must involve limit pricing, since the two types of firm one would adopt the same price), entry may occur either

more often, less often, or equally as often as in the case with no limit pricing. In particular, entry may occur with probability $1 - q$, with only the low cost type two firm entering.

We thus have a somewhat surprising conclusion: limit pricing occurs, but may not limit entry. We can think of the two types of potential firm ones (high cost and low cost) as being locked in a struggle, with the high cost firm one attempting to imitate the low cost firm and the latter attempting to distinguish itself; and this struggle induces limit pricing. However, the entrant is aware of this struggle and may infer the information contained in various outcomes, so that entry may not be deterred.

This rudimentary model has been expanded in a number of directions.[16] Our interest lies in the role that game theory has played in the analysis of limit pricing. It is an intuitive suspicion that limit pricing will occur. The practice may have policy implications as well, so that an economic analysis of the problem is important. However, a model simple enough to be addressed by conventional techniques, involving two firms and no uncertainty, does not yield limit pricing. A more complex model can be constructed of limit pricing, based on uncertainty. However, the analysis of the model and derivation of the results is conveniently accomplished only through the use of game theory. This model not only potentially features limit pricing, but reveals that the limit pricing may have surprising effects. We again have an example of a question which is posed by events in the economy, and which frustrates an analysis based on inspection and intuition alone. The application of recent developments in microeconomic theory to the question produces rewarding results. In this case, it is the development of new tools of analysis rather than areas of inquiry which enables the investigation to proceed. Game theory has allowed progress in many other areas of inquiry. For example, Schotter [1981] and Shubik [1982] demonstrate that game theoretic techniques may be employed to incorporate institutional considerations into economic analysis. This possibility allows economists to address new issues of major importance.

We can offer a second example of the insights to be gained from sophisticated analytic analysis. In this case, it is the structure of economic theory rather than the economy that is illuminated. One of the oldest ideas in economic theory is that of perfect competition.[17] The convenience of perfect competition in model construction preserves a central place in economics for the concept. The frequency with which perfect competition appears in economic analysis naturally directs one's attention to the theoretical foundations of the concept.

For convenience, we initially consider exchange economies. We also adopt a restricted notion of perfect competition, taking it to mean price taking behavior on the part of the economy's agents. This is the behavior presumed in Walrasian general equilibrium theory. However, it excludes considerations of entry and exit of agents in markets, which appear in many treatments of perfect competition.

Assume that agents in exchange economies choose the quantities they will trade, being potentially cognizant of any effect their actions may have on prices. It is known that price taking behavior, or perfect competition, is not ensured if the number of agents in the economy is finite.[18] However, if the economy is modeled as containing an infinite number of agents, any individual agent will literally be insignificant in the market, and price taking behavior will occur.[19]

When employing a model involving perfect competition, the claim is obviously not made that there are an infinite number of agents in the economy, but rather that perfect competition provides a good approximation of the behavior of economies with large numbers of agents. Two responses are in order. First, empirical tests can be conducted to determine if agents in the economy exhibit price taking behavior. The second response concerns the internal structure of economic theory. The importance of this issue arises out of the observation that logical consistency is a necessary condition for an acceptable theory. Models of economies with finite numbers of agents have been constructed, as well as models with infinite numbers of agents. Are the equilibria of the latter good approximations of the equilibria of the former? If not, the conventional justification for models employing perfect competition is inconsistent with economic theory, and microeconomics is plagued by logical flaws. If so, the approximation justification for perfect competition is theoretically sound (though the empirical issue remains). Clearly, this is a question of the utmost importance.

Only recently has this question been investigated. The first requirement in such an investigation is a formal model of an economy with an infinite number of agents, so that perfectly competitive behavior will appear. This is accomplished by taking the real numbers in the unit interval, $[0, 1]$, to represent the agents in the economy.[18] A function associates with each element of $[0, 1]$ a consumption set (generally taken to be the nonnegative orthant), an endowment, and a preference relation. The offers of the agents to trade good x are represented by a function $f_x: [0, 1] \to R$, where $f_x(\alpha)$ is the offer of agent $\alpha \in [0, 1]$. The equilibrium condition is given by $\int_0^1 f_x(\alpha)\, d\alpha = 0$. Each agent is literally insignificant in this economy, since an individual is a subset of $[0, 1]$ of (Lebesgue) measure zero, and altering $f_x(\alpha)$ on a set of measure zero cannot affect $\int_0^1 f_x(\alpha)\, d\alpha$. Hence, the actions of an individual agent cannot affect prices.

The next step in the investigation is the modelling of an economy with a finite number of agents. An economy of size n, represented by $\mathscr{E}_n$, consists of a specification of a consumption set (again generally taken to be the nonnegative orthant), an endowment, and a preference relation for each of n consumers. Call the infinite or continuum economy $\mathscr{E}$. A sequence of finite economies can be constructed so that $\lim_{n \to \infty} \mathscr{E}_n = \mathscr{E}$, with a suitable definition of convergence. Since the economy $\mathscr{E}$ necessarily features price taking or perfectly competitive behavior, its equlibria are described as Walrasian equilibria. To distinguish them, the equilibria of the economies $\mathscr{E}_n$ are often referred to as Cournot equilibria, presumably because the quantity setting behavior is reminiscent of models examined by Cournot.

The key question is then the following. If x^* is a Walrasian equilibrium for economy $\mathscr{E}$, is there a sequence x_n^* of Cournot equilibria of economies such that $\lim_{n \to \infty} x_n^* = x^*$? If so, we can confidently assert that x^*, the equilibrium of the competitive economy, approximates the equilibrium of an economy with a finite number of agents. The larger is this number, the closer is the approximation. If no such sequence x_n^* could be found, then some Walrasian equilibria would exist which are not good approximations of any equilibrium of finite economies. In this case, we cannot place too much credence in results gained from examining Walrasian equilibria.[21] Fortunately, recent results indicate that this question can be answered in the affirmative (cf. Mas-Collel [1982]) if the economy is regular. Regularity is a property satisfied by almost all economies (cf. Debreu [1970] and Dierker [1977]), so its imposition need not cause concern.

Discussions of perfect competition are often carried on in terms of the actions of firms and not consumers, raising the question of whether the result reported above generalizes to economies with production. Models of economies with a finite number of agents, including consumers and producers, have been developed by Gabszewicz and Vial [1972] and Roberts [1980], among others. It is again found that under certain conditions, including regularity, that a Walrasian equilibrium of the infinite economy is the limit of a sequence of equilibria of finite economies. The sufficient conditions for this result to hold are generally innocuous, with one potential exception: firms' production sets must be convex.

The assumption that production sets be convex is often considered quite restrictive. It ensures that increasing returns to scale do not occur. It is somewhat unnatural to preclude increasing returns in a model of perfect competition. The familiar undergraduate treatment of the firm abounds in U-shaped cost curves, and hence includes the possibility of increasing returns. If increasing returns are excluded, it is not clear that the theory can explain the number of firms in the market. Variations in the number of firms in a market are an important feature of many formulations of perfect competition, and one would like the theory to be capable of expansion to include such factors.

Nonconvexities have been incorporated in examinations of perfect competition. The results in this case depend upon the formulation of the problem. The important characteristics of the model formulation include whether the agents are allowed to play mixed strategies and whether the aggregate returns to scale are constant or decreasing. If mixed strategies are allowed and aggregate returns are decreasing, then a result similar to the one reported above obtains. Under reasonably innocuous conditions, Walrasian equilibria of the infinite economy are limits of sequences of equilibria in finite economies. If mixed strategies are allowed but the aggregate returns to scale are constant, or if aggregate returns are decreasing but only pure strategies allowed, then this result obtains if and only if the Walrasian equilibrium of the limit economy satisfies a condition termed downward sloping demand.[22] This condition requires that the profit of each firm of any given type vary inversely with the mass (the infinite economy counterpart of the number of firms) of firms of that type which are active in the market. This condition is readily applied in partial equilibrium analysis and has an appealing name, but is quite restrictive in a general equilibrium analysis (cf. Novshek and Sonnenschein [1983a]). This raises some question as to the applicability of standard theories of perfect competition.

Two conclusions can be drawn. First, the results concerning whether a Walrasian equilibrium of an infinite economy is a good approximation of a finite economy's equilibrium depends upon what kind of model and equilibrium concept is adopted for the latter. The choices involve such issues as whether mixed strategies are to be allowed and the returns to scale, and also the more basic question of whether quantity setting is the proper conception of how agents interact in such models. Additional work is required to characterize more completely the relationship between Walrasian equilibria of infinite economies and the equilibria of finite economies for a variety of formulations of the latter.[23]

The more general observation to be made is that the idea of perfect competition has long played a central role in economics. In spite of this, the logical status of the idea has centered around rather vague assertions to the effect that price taking behavior approximates the behavior of large economies. The logical relationship between this assertion and other aspects of economic theory has only recently been examined, and requires sophisticated, mathematical general equilibrium analysis. Mas-Collel [1983], for example, develops a fixed point theorem tailor made for his examination, while measure theoretic techniques are required to examine the infinite economy. The conclusion is that newly developed, sophisticated mathematical techniques can make a contribution to economics. In the case of perfect competition, their use is required if economists are to know whether they hold consistent or contradictory theories.

3. Disequilibrium Economics

The previous sections presented some recent accomplishments in microeconomic theory. This section examines an area in which further important work is likely to occur. We begin by recalling that the "fundamental problem" of economics, as posed by Walras, involved the determination of the prices and quantities traded of an economy's goods. The principles which are invoked to determine these prices and quantities are equilibrium conditions, requiring that the quantity of each good supplied equals the quantity demanded.

A common response to equilibrium models of the economy is to note that no account is provided of how the economy achieves an equilibrium. A conventional explanation is that a Walrasian auctioneer conducts a tâtonnement process (cf. Arrow and Hahn [1971]), successively announcing hypothetical prices and soliciting hypothetical offers to trade from the economy's agents. This process continues until the announced offers to trade balance on all markets, at which point trade is conducted and an equilibrium appears. In practice, market arrangements may not approximate such adjustment processes, and trade may occur at disequilibrium prices. Markets do not always achieve an equilibrium, or "clear." The failure of the labor market to clear is the most frequently cited example, and efforts to bring the labor market into equilibrium play a prominent role in economic policy formation. While macroeconomists have long struggled with the problem of nonclearing markets, or disequilibrium market outcomes, a microeconomic theory of why such disequilibrium outcomes appear and how markets behave in disequilibrium has only recently begun to emerge.

An obvious point of departure for constructing such a theory is to adopt a convention diametrically opposed to that of the auctioneer, and assume that prices are fixed. These prices are not likely to be fixed at equilibrium levels, so that trading at disequilibrium prices may be unavoidable. If agents proceed as if they are in a Walrasian model when formulating their offers to trade, the quantities supplied and demanded of various goods will not balance. Some agents will then be unable to complete desired trades. This causes agents to be faced with constraints on the quantities which can be traded, and it is the presence of such quantity constraints or rationing which endows this model with its unique features. We shall refer to this model as a fixed-price model. It is a member of a class of models which we refer to as non-Walrasian.[24] These models are characterized by the prospect that trades may occur at prices which do not yield a Walrasian equilibrium.

A well-known fixed-price model has been offered by Drèze [1975]. We present a simplified version.[25] For convenience, consider a pure exchange economy of m agents and n goods. The fixed vector of prices is given by

$p \in R^n_{++}$. A typical consumer is characterized by an initial endowment $w \in R^n_+$, identifying an amount of each of the n goods which the consumer holds; a preference relation $\succsim$ on R^n_+ satisfying suitable assumptions; and a collection of perceived constraints $\ell \in R^n_-$ and $\mathscr{L} \in R^n_+$. The vector ℓ contains n nonpositive elements, with each element corresponding to one of the economy's n goods, and identifying a limit on the quantity of each good which the agent can sell (negative numbers identify quantities sold). Similarly, the vector $\mathscr{L}$ identifies limits on the amounts of each quantity that the agent can buy. The agent chooses an optimal trade subject to these constraints. Hence, the agent chooses that $x^* \in R^n$ which satisfies $px^* \leq 0$ and:[26]

$$x^* + w \succsim x + w \tag{1.6}$$

for all $x \in R^n$ which satisfy

$$px \leq 0, \tag{1.7}$$

$$\ell \leq x \leq \mathscr{L}. \tag{1.8}$$

Condition (1.6) requires that no feasible alternative be preferred to x^*, and (1.7)–(1.8) identify the set of feasible alternatives. The first of these conditions specifies that the agent be able to finance purchases. Condition (1.8) requires that the agent not violate the constraints on trades posed by ℓ and $\mathscr{L}$. The first condition is familiar from Walrasian theory, while the constraints in the second presumably arise because prices are not set at Walrasian equilibrium levels.

The question then arises of whether the trades chosen by the economy's agents in solving (1.6)–(1.8) will be consistent. In a Walrasian general equilibrium model, prices adjust to ensure consistency. This cannot occur in a model with fixed prices, and it is the perceived constraints which must adjust to ensure consistency. Hence, an equilibrium is a set of constraints ℓ_i^*, $\mathscr{L}_i^*$, and offers x_i^* (where i indexes the agents in the economy, and hence $i = 1, \ldots, m$), such that $\Sigma_{i=1}^{\infty} x_i^* = 0$. Given the achievement of such an equilibrium, the trades offered by agents will balance, in that quantities supplied and demanded will be equal on all markets. Agents might prefer to conduct trades at existing prices other than those actually offered (unlike a Walrasian general equilibrium), but such trades are rendered infeasible by the quantity constraints.

This fixed-price model allows a wide variety of potential applications, including the possibility of constructing a microfoundation for macroeconomics. The perceived quantity constraints are reminiscent of the expectations which play a prominent role in macroeconomics. For example, one easily constructs cases in a simple production economy in which firms perceive a constraint on their ability to sell their outputs, and accordingly restrict purchases of labor. Consumers are then faced with constraints on labor sales and hence incomes, and may reduce consumption accordingly. This may cause the firm's expectations to be fulfilled, yielding an equilibrium. This equilibrium features an effective demand failure, and suggests that fixed-price theories may be useful in examining macroeconomics. Policy applications of fixed-price models have been offered by Hool [1980], Malinvaud [1977], and Benassy [1982], who present additional references to fixed-price policy examinations.

Under appropriate assumptions, it can be shown that a set of equilibrium quantity constraints and offers exists for the Drèze model. However, the question again arises of how this set of constraints and offers comes into being. An obvious mechanism for achieving an equilibrium does not exist. Agents may hold perceptions of quantity constraints which induce an incompatible set of trades, with adjustment of perceived constraints required before an equilibrium can be achieved. This last remark suggests that we must again appeal to a tâtonnement mechanism to motivate the existence of an equilibrium. The tâtonnement process would involve adjustments in constraints rather than prices, with an auctioneer repeatedly positing constraints and soliciting hypothetical offers until an equilibrium is achieved. The non-Walrasian model has then altered the nature of the Walrasian tâtonnement, but retained the process.

In light of this observation, an interesting issue arises. Walrasian general equilibrium theory is built around a tâtonnement process in prices. An implication of this construction is that trade will always occur at market clearing prices, and it is dissatisfaction with this implication that prompts the search for a non-Walrasian theory. Two possibilities present themselves in constructing the latter. One might construct a theory involving a tâtonnement process in something other than prices, such as perceived quantity constraints. This yields the type of fixed-price theory presented above, and is the most common approach. The second alternative is to eliminate the reliance on a tâtonnement process.

These alternatives can be illuminated by revising our terms. Walrasian models are often characterized as "equilibrium" models, and non-Walrasian models as "disequilibrium" ones. However, the standard analysis of the disequilibrium model is to demonstrate, via an appropriate fixed point argument, the existence of equilibrium quantity constraints. Hence, we have the equilibrium of a disequilibrium model, a rather convoluted expression.[27] The point is that the equilibrium nature of the Walrasian model rests on two principles, those being that efficient adjustment (i.e., tâtonnement) occurs, and occurs in prices. The disequilibrium model disposes with one of these conventions, but retains the other. The interesting issue then involves the implications of this choice of non-Walrasian modelling convention. What would be the result if the other pillar of Walrasian theory, the tâtonnement process, were abandoned?

Whether this issue is an interesting one depends upon whether a theory without a tâtonnement process enables one to model the economy more effectively than a theory with such a process. An initial inspection suggests that a model without a tâtonnement process might allow significant insights into the economy. For example, an immediate difficulty which fixed-price models encounter is the question of why prices are fixed. In spite of such impressive theoretical achievements as the construction of implicit contracts models,[28] a completely satisfactory account of price rigidities of the severity found in fixed-price models has not appeared. The basic difficulty lies in explaining why optimizing agents, whose plans are not confounded by miscalculation or lack of adjustment, can fail to secure the mutually beneficial gains available from adjusting prices. A theory which deletes the tâtonnement process has the potential to address such issues, and in the process potentially produce useful insights into the economy. Models which are not characterized by tâtonnement processes may thus provide economics with a useful technique.

We can explore some of the issues which arise in connection with a non-tâtonnement model. This question cannot be examined in the context of a conventional Walrasian model or in the fixed-price model outlined above, since neither case is able to specify the outcome of potentially incompatible offers. We accordingly offer a reformulation of the fixed price model.[29] Let $y_i \in R^n$, $i = 1, \ldots, m$; be agent i's offer to trade the n goods in the economy. Then let $F_i : R^{nm} \rightarrow R^n$ be a function which associates with any collection of offers $y_1, \ldots, y_m$ a realized trade x_i for agent i. The functions $F_1, \ldots, F_m$ are referred to as rationing schemes.[30] Let prices be fixed. Given a collection of offers for all agents except i (denoted $y^*_{-i} = y^*_1, \ldots, y^*_{i-1}, y^*_{i+1}, \ldots, y^*_m$), agent i chooses $y_i^* \in R^n$ which satisfies

$$F_i(y_i^*, y^*_{-i}) \succsim F_i(y_i, y^*_{-i}) \quad \forall y_i \in R^n \quad \text{such that } pF_i(y_i, y^*_{-i}) \le 0 \quad (1.9)$$

and

$$pF_i(y_i^*, y^*_{-i}) \le 0. \quad (1.10)$$

An equilibrium is a collection of offers $y_1^*, \ldots, y_m^*$ such that each agent's offer solves the relevant version of (1.9)–(1.10). This is the familiar Nash equilibrium concept. Notice that we have said nothing about trades balancing in defining the equilibrium. This balance is implicit in the properties of the rationing scheme. The key to an equilibrium is that the offers must be optimal, given the offers of other agents and hence the relationship between offers and trades induced by the rationing scheme.

We can readily compare this non-Walrasian model with a Walrasian version.

Following Dubey [1982], we achieve a Walrasian model by allowing agents' strategies to include not only offers of quantities to trade but also of prices at which they would like to trade. The rationing scheme converts these offers into quantities traded at various prices. Provided that a significantly severe penalty is imposed on agents whose strategies induce bankruptcy, the Nash equilibrium of this game yields a Walrasian equilibrium. The statement that a Walrasian equilibrium is built around a tâtonnement process in prices is equivalent to the statement that the rationing scheme determines prices as well as quantities (this allows price adjustment), and that a Nash equilibrium obtains (the tâtonnement process). We obtain a conventional non-Walrasian model, deleting the adjustment of prices (and allowing quantity constraints) but retaining the tâtonnement process, by altering the specification of the agents' strategy spaces and rationing scheme to include only quantities, but retaining interest in the game's Nash equilibria.

The functional equivalent in this model of abandoning the tâtonnement construction is to allow the possibility of outcomes which are not Nash equilibria. We can think of a Nash equilibrium as being achieved by an adjustment process which ensures that all offers are best replies. The absence of an adjustment process then raises the possibility of non-Nash outcomes. In such outcomes, some agents, upon observing the strategies played by other agents, will be disappointed with their own strategies; in that they will discover that their strategies are not the best replies available to the strategies of others.

The type of disequilibrium property in which we are interested is then based on the observation that economies generally cannot accommodate a period of adjustment before trading occurs. Agents may accordingly be incompletely informed of the strategies of others when offers are made. Upon the realization of offers, many agents will find that their offers are not optimal given the offers of others. If a next stage of trading occurs, it is likely to involve revisions in offers. The functions ordinarily reserved for a tâtonnement process are then (perhaps imperfectly) accomplished as the economic activity proceeds.

It is clear that the types of outcomes described in the previous paragraphs, involving imperfect adjustment processes, may include cases in which markets do not clear. If this approach is to be interesting, however, we must explain why agents may fail to achieve a Nash equilibrium. Presumably, some explanation more convincing than the ineptness of economic agents is required. Two possibilities arise. First, suppose that agents are uncertain as to some characteristics of the economy (and that a complete set of contingent claims markets does not exist). Agents may then formulate offers which are ex ante optimal, in expected utility terms, but yield outcomes which are not ex post optimal, given the realization of the uncertain characteristics. Implicit contracts models are an example of this approach. Agents strike wage and employment bargains which are ex ante optimal, given some uncertainty as to the state of the price of the output produced by a firm. Upon a realization of that price, the particular wage and employment levels are unlikely to be market clearing.[31] Models with various other types of uncertainty have also been constructed.[32]

Imperfect information models may not yield ex post Nash equilibria, but generally do yield ex ante Nash equilibria (or involve some notion of ex ante adjustment, if not formulated in game theoretic terms). Hence, a strong tâtonnement flavor persists. We might dispense with this completely by examining cases in which Nash equilibria do not arise, even in ex ante terms. The obvious initial reaction to this statement is that Nash equilibria should not fail to appear. Agents can deduce the optimal or equilibrium strategies of their opponents, and hence can arrive at a Nash equilibrium without communication or adjustment processes.[33] Notice, however, that this argument encounters difficulties in some cases, the most obvious one being cases of multiple Nash equilibria. For example, models with potential quantity constraints typically yield multiple equilibria. Cases may then arise in which an unambiguous deduction of other agents' strategies is impossible. In such cases, the examination of outcomes which are not Nash equilibria is potentially important.

Some initial forays into the construction of such models have been attempted. Bernheim [1984] and Pearce [1984] introduce the concept of rationalizable behavior. Their point of departure is an explicit rejection of the Nash equilibrium notion, for reasons similar to those cited in the preceding discussion. Rationalizable behavior includes the possibility that agents may be unable to so fortuitiously coordinate actions as to always achieve mutual best replies. The apparent difficulty with the concept is that in many cases it appears to allow too wide a variety of action, and in some familiar games virtually everything is rationalizable. Additional work in this area is required.

An extensive treatment of disequilibrium economics is offered by Franklin Fisher [1983]. Fisher constructs a general equilibrium model in which agents are aware that trading proceeds in spite of potential disequilibrium outcomes, and hence are aware of both potential quantity constraints and disequilibrium-induced price adjustment. The model is an explicitly dynamic one, unlike much of our previous discussion. Agents form expectations about the economy which may be revised in light of experienced economic outcomes. Fisher derives fairly general conditions under which such an economy will converge to an equilibrium state. His analysis thus provides insight into the behavior of the economy in disequilibrium, as well as an analytic foundation for the study of the economy's equilibrium. This last observation arises because the interest which can be placed in an equilibrium analysis depends upon the efficiency with which an economy in disequilibrium converges to equilibrium. Fisher's analysis is much more general then conventional fixed-price theories, and accordingly appears to indicate a promising path for future research. As he notes, there is considerable work in this area, including basic modelling questions and applications, yet to be done.

The conclusion is that existing non-Walrasian models have pursued one possible formulation of a "disequilibrium" model, but not the only one. The alternative, which essentially involves relaxing the assumption that a tâtonnement process exists and is efficient enough to secure equilibrium offers, may also have important contributions to make. This may especially be the case in addressing the issue of why prices do not adjust. Whether this approach is useful or not can be determined only with further work in the area, but it appears to be an important area of investigation.

4. Conclusion

This essay has examined some selected areas of microeconomic theory. The conclusions to be drawn are threefold. First, as the economy presents new questions, microeconomic theory has expanded into new areas of inquiry. In many such areas, such as the theory of exhaustible resources, microeconomic theory has made valuable contributions to our understanding of the economy. Secondly, microeconomics has been characterized by the continual application of new analytical tools, primarily new mathematical techniques. These techniques may initially appear quite removed from reality, but have permitted substantial gains in the ability of economists to address problems of direct interest and to understand the structure of economic theories. Finally, there is undoubtedly much to be done in microeconomic theory. We have suggested one area which is likely to be an important topic of future work, involving the construction of disequilibrium theories.

The ultimate conclusion is that microeconomic theory is not in such dire shape as some critics would suggest. Work on the more theoretical frontiers of the discipline may not appear immediately applicable to practical problems. However, microeconomic theory has a consistent record of exploiting new techniques to examine interesting issues in the economy and in economic theory. The expectation is that this development will continue.

Notes

1. For a discussion of current macroeconomic theory, see Perry [1984], Sargent [1984], and the ensuing discussion (Barro, Blinder, and Nordhaus [1984]).

2. For example, Schumpeter [1954, p. 242] indicates that the discovery of the fundamental problem "was not fully made until Walras, whose system of equations, defining (static) equilibrium in a system of interdependent quantities, is the Magna Carta of economic theory . . . ". See also Walras [1954].

3. Weintraub [1983] provides a history of general equilibrium theory.

4. The suspicion that conventional economics has not always been addressing the appropriate questions has sustained alternative schools of thought, including that of Cambridge, England (see Robinson [1975] for an assessment of the usefulness of one large body of microeconomic literature) and that of the institutionalists (see Fusfeld [1977] and Mirowski [1981]).

5. There is some danger of becoming entangled in semantic issues here, since a theory which has no counterpart in the economy is presumably an extreme form of a theory based on unrealistic assumptions. The basic point is that regardless of the terms used to characterize a theory, increasing abstraction may push unrealistic theory into inapplicable theory, making it more difficult to defend the theory.

6. Economic growth models typically fit this description, with labor being the renewable input. See Jones [1976] for examples.

7. The theory of exhaustible resources originates with papers by Gray [1914] and Hotelling [1931]. The literature remained sparse until 1974, in which Solow [1974] and the *Review of Economic Studies* Symposium issue appeared, the latter containing ten papers addressing a variety of resource topics. The literature has subsequently grown rapidly. A useful guide to exhaustible resource issues and results is given by Dasgupta and Heal [1979], which provides the basis for much of the following presentation.

8. This quotation is from Dasgupta and Heal [1979, p. 59], who in turn take it from *Time* magazine [October 14, 1976].

9. The objection might be raised that in the case of oil, prices have not increased at the rate of interest in recent years, with the two price shocks of the 1970s surrounded by periods of relatively constant or even falling prices. The failure of prices to increase steadily is presumably caused by features not captured in the simple model just outlined. One obvious excluded factor is the possession of market power by resource sellers, which we consider shortly. However, the prediction that prices increase over time is quite robust, and appears in markets characterized by imperfect competition. The culprits in the relative constancy of oil prices include the discovery of new resource deposits and decreases in demand. These have the effect of decreasing the entire (increasing) price path of the resource. Oil prices then increase along a given equilibrium price path, but decrease as new discoveries and demand conditions continually depress the entire path. The result can be a price which is relatively constant over some period of time. The contribution of microeconomic theory is the provision of an analytic apparatus in which to isolate and examine these factors.

10. This quotation is also from Dasgupta and Heal [1979, p. 178], who again take it from *Time* magazine [October 14, 1976].

11. By conservationist, we mean one who would like to see the resource depleted less rapidly. It is not immediately obvious why a depletion pattern less rapid than the efficient depletion pattern would be desired, though one might appeal to an argument such as an improperly set market rate of discount.

12. Game theory has its origins in the work of von Neumann [1959] and von Neumann and Morgenstern [1944]. The title of the latter work reveals the author's conviction that game theory would prove to be particularly useful in the study of economics. Additional game theory sources include Luce and Raiffa [1957] and Shubik [1982].

13. See Schotter and Schwödiauer for a survey of game theoretic applications in economics. Our analysis of limit pricing is based on Milgrom and Roberts [1982], who provide a guide to the limit pricing literature.

14. The argument in this paragraph follows Friedman [1979].

15. One could easily derive profit relationships of this type from a standard duopoly model, beginning with demand and cost functions and solving for profits.

16. The idea that period one prices might convey information about the state of the market has been obtained by letting the entrant entertain some uncertainty about the (stochastic) market demand curve, and this extension of the model yields additional interesting insights (as well as avoiding difficulties with multiplicity of equilibria encountered in the original model). See Matthews and Mirman [1983].

17. It has been suggested that Adam Smith's concept of a self-regulating competitive market is the primary reason for the eminent position accorded to Smith in the history of economics. See Mirowski [1982].

18. Roberts and Postlewaite [1976] observe that the agents in such an economy will generally have an incentive to deviate from price taking behavior if the economy is of finite size, and offer an investigation of the conjecture that these incentive disappear as the economy becomes arbitrarily large.

19. Models with an infinite number of agents have been examined by Aumann [1964] and Hildenbrand [1974], who employ a continuum to represent the agents in the economy.

20. See Novshek and Sonnenschein [1978, 1983a, 1983b], Mas-Collel [1982, 1983], the *Journal of Economic Theory* Symposium of 1980 (especially Roberts [1980]), and Gabszewicz and Vial [1972].

21. The details of these arguments are sufficiently technical as to preclude their reproduction here. Mas-Collel [1982] offers a useful survey and derives the results we present. We might also inquire whether a converse property holds, i.e., whether it is the case that if x_n^* is a sequence of equilibria of $\mathscr{E}_n$ and $\lim_{n \to \infty} x_n^* = x^*$, then x^* is a Walrasian equilibrium of $\mathscr{E}$. The answer is again affirmative.

22. The first result is due to Mas-Collel [1983], the second to Novshek and Sonnenschein [1978, 1983a]. A reliance on mixed strategies is often considered unacceptable, on the grounds that economic agents do not employ such strategies. It can be shown that the amount of mixed strategies which appears in the equilibria described in these results is minimal (in a precise mathematical sense).

23. Novshek and Sonnenschein [1983b] probe the implications of allowing free entry in a general equilibrium model, thus incorporating another element of microeconomic theory that is pervasive in undergraduate treatments and missing from much of general equilibrium theory.

24. Surveys of the non-Walrasian literature are given in Benassy [1982], Drazen [1980], and Grandmont [1977]. The first generation of fixed-price models include Benassy [1973, 1975], Drèze [1975], Younès [1975]. Grandmont and Laroque [1976] and Silvestre [1982, 1983] provide useful examinations of these models.

25. In addition to the following specification, we might add a condition specifying that if some agent faces a binding constraint on purchases of good i, then no agent faces a binding constraint on sales of good i, and vice versa. This requirement ensures that constraints appear on only one side of a market, and suggests a minimum degree of market coordination. If we add such a condition, we have essentially the version of the Drèze model presented by Grandmont and Laroque [1976]. For a comparison with the original Drèze model, see Silvestre [1982, section 2].

26. The restriction of the preference relation $\succeq$ to R_+^n and a corresponding consumption set specification ensures that the agents will not attempt to consume negative amounts of a good.

27. It is ambiguity which surrounds the terms equilibrium and disequilibrium that prompts our use of the terms Walrasian and non-Walrasian.

28. See Hart [1983] and the *Quarterly Journal of Economics* Supplement [1983] for an introduction to the implicit contracts literature. This literature provides one approach to wage rigidities, which are the most visible form of price rigidities.

29. Our reformulation of the fixed-price model is a simplified version of models offered by Gale [1979], Heller and Starr [1979], and Böhm and Lévine [1979].

30. The properties of rationing schemes have been examined by Benassy [1977], Green [1980], and Svensson [1980].

31. Notice that the resulting unemployment may be interpreted as voluntary, since the contracts were voluntarily constructed. This raises complex classification issues.

32. The literature in this area is too vast to be surveyed here. Two interesting examples are Woglom [1982] and Bryant [1983].

33. See Bernheim [1984] and Pearce [1984] for an examination of the rationale for a Nash equilibrium.

References

Arrow, K. and F. Hahn, *General competitive analysis*. New York: North-Holland, 1971.

Aumann, R., "Markets with a continuum of traders." *Econometrica* 32 (1964), 39–50.

Barro, R., A. Blinder, and W. Nordhaus, "Discussion." *American Economic Review* 74(2) (1984), 416–421.

Benassy, J.-P., "Disequilibrium theory." Doctoral Dissertation, University of California, Berkeley, 1973.

Benassy, J.-P., "NeoKeynesian disequilibrium theory in a monetary economy." *Review of Economic Studies* 42 (1975), 503–524.

Benassy, J.-P., "On quantity signals and the foundations of effective demand." *Scandinavian Journal of Economics* 79 (1977), 147–168.

Benassy, J.-P., *The economics of market disequilibrium*. New York: Academic Press, 1982.

Bernheim, B., "Rationalizable strategic behavior." *Econometrica* 52 (1984), 1007–1028.

Böhm, V. and P. Lévine "Temporary equilibria with quantity rationing." *Review of Economic Studies* 46 (1979), 361–378.

Bryant, J., "A simple rational expectations Keynes-type model." *Quarterly Journal of Economics* 98 (1983), 525–528.

Cournot, A., *Researches into the mathematical principles of the theory of wealth* (translated by N. T. Bacon). New York: Macmillan, 1897.

Dasgupta, P. S. and G. M. Heal, *Economic theory and exhaustible resources*. Cambridge: Cambridge University Press, 1979.

Debreu, G., *Theory of value*. New Haven: Yale University Press, 1959.

Debreu, G., "Economies with a finite set of equilibria." *Econometrica* 38 (1970), 387–392.

Dierker, E., "Regular economies: A survey." In *Frontiers of quantitative analysis* (edited by M. Intriligator), Amsterdam: North-Holland, 1977.

Drazen, A., "Recent developments in macroeconomic disequilibrium theory." *Econometrica* 48 (1980), 283–305.

Drèze, J., "Existence of an exchange equilibrium under price rigidities." *International Economic Review* 16 (1975), 301–320.

Dubey, P., "Price-quantity strategic games." *Econometrica* 50 (1982), 111–126.

Eswaran, M. and T. Lewis, "Appropriability and the extraction of a common property resource." *Economica* 51 (1984), 393–400.

Fisher, F. M., *Disequilibrium foundations of equilibrium economics.* Cambridge: Cambridge University Press, 1983.

Friedman, J., "On entry preventing behavior and limit price models of entry." In *Applied game theory* (edited by S. Brams, A. Schotter, and G. Schwödiauer), Wurzburg: Physica-Verlag, 1979, pp. 236–253.

Friedman, M., "The methodology of positive economics." In *Essays in positive economics* (by M. Friedman), Chicago: University of Chicago Press, 1958, 3–43.

Fusfeld, D., "The development of economic institutions." *Journal of Economic Issues* 11 (1977), 742–783.

Gabszewicz, J. and Vial, J., "Oligopoly 'a la Cournot' in a general equilibrium analysis." *Journal of Economic Theory* 4 (1972), 381–400.

Gale, D., "Large economies with trading uncertainty." *Review of Economic Studies* 46 (1979), 319–338.

Grandmont, J., "Temporary equilibrium theory." *Econometrica* 45 (1977), 535–572.

Grandmont, J. and G. Laroque, "On temporary Keynesian equilibria." *Review of Economic Studies* 43 (1976), 53–68.

Gray, L., "Rent under the assumption of exhaustibility." *Quarterly Journal of Economics* 28 (1914), 466–489.

Green, J., "On the theory of effective demand." *Economic Journal* 90 (1980), 341–353.

Hardin, G., "The tragedy of the commons," *Science* 162 (1968), 1243–1247.

Hart, O., "Optimal labor contracts under asymmetric information: An introduction." *Review of Economic Studies* 50 (1983), 3–36.

Heller, W. and R. Starr, "Unemployment equilibrium with myopic complete information." *Review of Economic Studies* 46 (1979), 339–360.

Hildenbrand, W., *Core and equilibria of a large economy.* Princeton: Princeton University Press, 1974.

Hool, B., "Monetary and fiscal policies in short run equilibria with rationing." *International Economic Review* 21 (1980), 301–316.

Hotelling, H., "The Economics of exhaustible resources." *Journal of Political Economy* 39 (1931), 137–175.

Jones, H., *An introduction to modern theories of growth.* New York: McGraw Hill, 1976.

Journal of Economic Theory. Symposium on noncooperative approaches to the theory of perfect competition 22 (1980).

Luce, R. and H. Raiffa, *Games and decisions.* New York, John Wiley, 1957.

Malinvaud, E., *The theory of unemployment reconsidered.* Oxford: Blackwell, 1977.

Matthews, S. and L. Mirman, "Equilibrium limit pricing: The effects of private information and stochastic demand." *Econometrica* 51 (1983), 981–996.

Mas-Collel, A., "The Cournotian foundations of Walrasian equilibrium theory: An exposition of recent theory." In *Advances in economic theory* (edited by Werner Hildenbrand), Cambridge: Cambridge University Press, 1982, pp. 183–224.

Mas-Collel, A., "Walrasian equilibrium as limits of noncooperative equilibria. Part I: Mixed strategies." *Journal of Economic Theory* 30 (1983), 153–170.

Milgrom, P. and J. Roberts, "Limit pricing and entry under incomplete information: An equilibrium analysis." *Econometrica* 50 (1982), 443–460.

Mirowski, P., "Is there a mathematical neoinstitutional economics?" *Journal of Economic Issues* 15 (1981), 593–613.

Mirowski, P., "Adam Smith, empiricism, and the rate of profit in eighteenth-century England." *History of Political Economy* 14 (1982), 178–198.

Nash, J., "Noncooperative games, " *Annals of Mathematics* 45 (1951), 286–295.

Novshek, W. and H. Sonnenschein, "Cournot and Walras equilibrium." *Journal of Economic Theory* 19 (1978), 223–266.

Novshek, W. and H. Sonnenschein, "Walrasian equilibria as limits of noncooperative equilibria, Part II: Pure strategies." *Journal of Economic Theory* 30 (1983a), 171–187.

Novshek, W. and H. Sonnenschein, "General equilibrium with free entry: A synthetic approach to the theory of perfect competition." California Institute of Technology Social Science Working Paper 497, 1983b.

Pearce, D., "Rationalizable strategic behavior and the problem of perfection." *Econometrica* 52 (1984), 1029–1050.

Perry G., "Reflections on macroeconomics." *American Economic Review* 74(2) (1984), 401–407.

Quarterly Journal of Economics. Supplement 98 (1983).

Review of Economic Studies. Symposium on the economics of exhaustible resources, 41 (1974).

Roberts, J. and A. Postlewaite, "The incentives for price taking behavior in large exchange economies." *Econometrica* 44 (1976), 115–127.

Roberts, K., "The limit points of monopolistic competition." *Journal of Economic Theory* 22 (Symposium) (1980), 256–279.

Robinson, J., "The unimportance of reswitching." *Quarterly Journal of Economics* 89 (1975), 32–39.

Sargent, T., "Autoregressions, expectations, and advice." *American Economic Review* 74(2) (1984), 408–415.

Schotter, A., *The Economic Theory of Social Institutions.* Cambridge: Cambridge University Press, 1981.

Schotter, A. and G. Schwödiauer, "Economics and game theory: A survey." *Journal of Economic Literature* 18 (1980), 479–527.

Schumpeter, J., *History of economic analysis* (edited from manuscript by Elizabeth Boody Schumpeter). New York: Oxford University Pres, 1954.

Shubik, M., *Game theory in the social sciences.* Cambridge: MIT Press, 1982.

Silvestre, J., "Fixprice analysis in exchange economies." *Journal of Economic Theory* 26 (1982), 28–58.

Silvestre, J., "Fixprice analysis in productive economies." *Journal of Economic Theory* 30 (1983), 401–409.

Solow, R., "The economics of resources or the resources of economics." *American Economic Review* 64(2) (1974), 1–14.

Svensson, L., "Effective demand and stochastic rationing." *Review of Economic Studies* 47 (1980), 339–355.

Von Neumann, J., "On the theory of games of strategy." In *Contributions to the Theory of Games* (edited by A. Tucker and R. D. Luce), Princeton: Princeton University Press, Vol. 4, 1959, 13–42.

Von Neumann, J. and O. Morgenstern, *Theory of games and economic behavior.* Princeton: Princeton University Press, 1944.

Walras, L., *Elements of pure economics* (translated by W. Jaffe). Homewood, Illinois: Richard D. Irwin, Inc., 1954.

Weintraub, E., "On the existence of a competitive equilibrium: 1930–1954." *Journal of Economic Literature* 21 (1983), 1–39.

Woglom, G., "Underemployment equilibrium with rational expectations." *Quarterly Journal of Economics* 97 (1982), 89–108.

Younes, Y., "On the role of money in the process of exchange and the existence of non-Walrasian equilibrium." *Review of Economic Studies* 42 (1975), 489–502.

2 ALTERNATIVES TO EXPECTED UTILITY THEORY FOR RISKY DECISIONS

Peter C. Fishburn

Expected utility theory says that a rational agent's preferences over risky alternatives can be ordered by the mathematical expectations of utilities for the possible outcomes of the alternatives. Moreover, a rational agent will choose among risky alternatives so as to maximize expected utility.

Formulated in the early 1940s by John von Neumann and Oskar Morgenstern [1944] to facilitate strategic analyses of conflict situations, expected utility theory has become the dominant theory of rational behavior for situations in which the outcomes of decisions are probabilistically related to actions taken. It has been widely used in all areas of economic analysis that involve agents' choices among risky alternatives, and has left an indelible mark on microeconomic theory.

Despite its widespread acceptance and use, expected utility theory has not gone unchallenged as the normative guide for decision making under risk. Critical examinations of the theory that owe much to the pioneering research of Maurice Allais [1953] and Ward Edwards [1954] have led to a growing belief that certain tenets of expected utility rest on very shaky ground, or, more severely, are systematically contradicted by the declared preferences and choices of reasonable people. Over the years, defenders of expected utility have rebutted its critics in various ways, such as through charges of faulty experimental method and by invoking the idol of the rational economic agent whose preference patterns should not be dictated by the reasoned choices of mere mortals. On the other hand, it is the considered opinion of some that relevant normative economic theory ought to be based on ways that thoughtful people choose among risky alternatives, and that the evidence against certain facets of expected utility in this regard is overwhelming and can no longer be dismissed.

Consequently, new efforts have been mounted to reexamine the utility-theoretic foundations of decision making among risky alternatives. A major thrust of this work has been to modify or weaken the assumptions of expected utility that have been most vulnerable to experimental refutation. This has resulted in several new theories of preference and choice for risky situations that accommodate some of the more prevalent violations of expected-utility behavior. At the same time, attention has been devoted to the implications of these new theories for economic analysis in areas that have relied on expected utility theory. Although much remains to be done, results obtained in economic analysis appear promising for two main reasons. First, many of the consequences or conclusions based on expected utility also obtain, at least in a qualitatively similar form, under the new and weaker theories. Second, because of their greater flexibility, the new theories can account for economic phenomena that cannot be explained by expected utility theory.

Ensuing sections of this chapter describe aspects of the new utility theories and illustrate their effects on economic analysis. The next section begins with a few words on the history of expected utility, describes its basic form, and then discusses seemingly reasonable behaviors that it cannot accommodate.

The following section notes early modifications of expected utility that weaken its axioms but retain its essential linear or expectational form. We then go on to more recent modifications that characterize the new theories alluded to above. All of these abandon the independence or linearity axiom of von Neumann and Morgenstern that gives rise to their simple expectational form, and one departs radically from their assumption that preferences are transitive.

We, then, illustrate the fact that much of the power of expected utility theory in economic analysis is retained by the new theories despite their abilities to model behavior patterns that are inconsistent with expected utility.

We initially focus on situations in which the probabilities of outcomes, given alternatives, are assumed to be known. The penultimate section drops this assumption and comments briefly on recent work in the foundations of decision making under uncertainty within the states-of-the-world formulation promoted by Savage [1954].

The chapter concludes with remarks on possible future directions for utility theory in decision making under risk and uncertainty.

1. Expected Utility Violations

The roots of expected utility extend back to Daniel Bernoulli [1738] and Gabriel Cramer [1738, pp. 33–35], who recognized that prudent individuals in risky monetary situations often depart from the principle of maximizing expected profit or wealth, especially when sizable sums are at stake. Thus, a small businessman may prefer a sure gain of $20,000 to a risky venture that loses $10,000 with probability 0.2 and gains $30,000 with probability 0.8 even though its expected gain is $22,000.

Bernoulli suggested that an individual's utility for wealth level x is approximately proportional to the logarithm of x, and Cramer proposed the square root of x as a utility function. Both espoused the principle of comparing risky options, or lotteries, by comparing their expected utilities.

von Neumann and Morgenstern

More than two centuries later, von Neumann and Morgenstern [1944] put forth a set of intuitively plausible axioms for an individual's preferences between risky alternatives that imply the expected utility principle of Bernoulli and Cramer. In particular, if P is a convex set of probability distributions on an outcome set X, so that the convex combination $\lambda p + (1 - \lambda)q$ is in P whenever $0 \leq \lambda \leq 1$ and p and q are in P [the probability that $\lambda p + (1 - \lambda)q$ assigns to x is $\lambda p(x) + (1 - \lambda)q(x)$], and if the von Neumann–Morgenstern axioms hold for a preference relation $\succ$ on P [read $p \succ q$ as "p is preferred to q"], then there is a real valued function u on P such that, for all p and q in P and all $0 \leq \lambda \leq 1$,

$$p \succ q \quad \text{if and only if} \quad u(p) > u(q),$$
$$u(\lambda p + (1 - \lambda)q) = \lambda u(p) + (1 - \lambda)u(q).$$

Moreover, another real valued function v on P satisfies these properties in place of u for the same preference relation $\succ$ on P if, and only if, there are numbers $a > 0$ and b such that

$$v(p) = au(p) + p \quad \text{for all } p \text{ in } P.$$

This is the essence of the von Neumann–Morgenstern utility theorem.

Although it may not seem to have anything to do with *expected* utility, appearances can be deceiving. The key to expected utility is the *linearity property*

$$u(\lambda p + (1 - \lambda)q) = \lambda u(p) + (1 - \lambda)u(q).$$

It is important to bear in mind that p and q are functions, not numbers, and that $\lambda p + (1 - \lambda)q$ is another function in the same set as p and q.

Linearity says that the utility of the convex combination $\lambda p + (1 - \lambda)q$ equals the similar convex combination of the utilities of p and q. Suppose that P contains every probability distribution that assigns probability 1 to a particular outcome in X. These are the sure-thing distributions. Because P is assumed to be convex, it then contains every simple probability distribution on X, where p is *simple* if its total probability of 1 is confined to a finite subset of X. Let

$$u(x) = u(p) \quad \text{when} \quad p(x) = 1,$$

so that utilities of outcomes are defined from the utilities of the sure-thing distributions. It then follows from induction on the number of outcomes that are assigned positive probabilities in a distribution that, for all simple p in P,

$$u(p) = \sum_x p(x)u(x).$$

In other words, the utility of a risky alternative, as described by its probability distribution over the outcome set X, equals the expected value with respect to that probability distribution of the utilities of the outcomes.

When this result is combined with the *ordering property* $p \succ q \Leftrightarrow u(p) > u(q)$, we get

$$p \succ q \quad \text{if and only if} \quad \sum_x p(x)u(x) > \sum_x q(x)u(x),$$

for all simple probability distributions p and q. Hence the preference relation orders the risky alternatives, or their corresponding probability distributions, by their expected utilities.

Four additional remarks are needed before we consider preference patterns that cannot be represented in the preceding manner. First, preferences, not utilities, are taken as primitive in the von Neumann–Morgenstern formulation. The utility function u on P, or its specialization u on X, is derived from an individual's preferences. The task of utility assessment is to measure u efficiently on the basis of $\succ$ and its associated *indifference relation* $\sim$, where $p \sim q$ if neither $p \succ q$ nor $q \succ p$. Since $p \sim q \Leftrightarrow u(p) = u(q)$ for their representation, expected utility equations based on indifference offer one way of assessing outcome utilities from other outcome utilities. For example, if \$10,000 as a sure thing is indifferent to a 50–50 lottery for either \$0 or \$30,000, then

$$u(\$10,000) = \tfrac{1}{2}u(\$0) + \tfrac{1}{2}u(\$30,000).$$

Thus, if any two of the three outcome utilities in this equation have been scaled, then the third can be obtained from the equation.

Second, if u on X is one von Neumann–Morgenstern utility function that satisfies their expected utility representation $p \succ q \Leftrightarrow \Sigma p(x)u(x) > \Sigma q(x)u(x)$, then v on X also serves this purpose if and only if v is a positive affine transformation of u, i.e., $v = au + b$ for numbers $a > 0$ and b. If v on X is any other transformation of u, then there will be p and q with $p \succ q$ and $\Sigma p(x)v(x) \leq \Sigma q(x)v(x)$. The uniqueness character of von Neumann–Morgenstern utilities is sometimes summarized by saying that they are unique up to the choice of an origin and a scale unit. If $x \succ y$ and we assign $u(x)$ and $u(y)$ any values so long as $u(x) > u(y)$, then the rest of u on X is uniquely determined.

Third, outcomes in X can be anything we take them to be since the formulation is entirely abstract. They could be commodity bundles, magazines, vacation resorts, vegetables, or whatever. Monetary amounts are often used in examples to connect with intuition and economic situations, but there is nothing in the basic von Neumann–Morgenstern theory about decreasing marginal utility or risk aversion and other attitudes towards risk, which appeared later in the work of Pratt [1964] and Arrow [1965].

Finally, we have noted that *expected* utility via von Neumann and Morgenstern applies only to simple probability distributions on X. Extensions of their theory for nonsimple measures, where in general $u(p) = \int u(x)\,dp(x)$, are discussed in Fishburn [1970, chapter 10; 1982, chapter 3].

Violations of Ordering

We shall focus on two main classes of violations of expected utility, namely violations of ordering or transitivity, and violations of linearity or independence. We begin with the ordering violations.

The ordering property of expected utility implies that $\succ$ on P satisfies

asymmetry: if $p \succ q$ then not $(q \succ p)$,

negative transitivity: if $p \succ q$ then for any r in P, either $p \succ r$ or $r \succ q$.

These two properties characterize $\succ$ as a *weak order* (asymmetric type) on P. It is easily seen that they require both $\succ$ and its indifference relation $\sim$ to be transitive, so that

$$(p \succ q,\ q \succ r) \Rightarrow p \succ r, \qquad (p \sim q,\ q \sim r) \Rightarrow p \sim r.$$

Moreover, $(p \succ q,\ q \sim r) \Rightarrow p \succ r$ and $(p \sim q,\ q \succ r) \Rightarrow p \succ r$. These implications also follow directly from the ordering property.

There is no quarrel with asymmetry since it is little more than an explication of the notion of strict preference. Transitivity, however, is another matter.

The simplest violations of transitivity are violations of transitive indifference. An individual who is indifferent between \$3410 as a sure thing and a

50–50 gamble between $0 and $10,000, is also indifferent between the gamble and $3400 as a sure thing, yet prefers $3410 to $3400, violates transitive indifference. As a second example, suppose

$$x = (9.75, 11.30, 12.00),$$
$$y = (10.00, 11.00, 12.00),$$
$$z = (10.25, 11.00, 11.80),$$

where each of x, y, and z is a proposed union wage contract showing dollars per hour in each of the next three years. It is not unreasonable to suppose that $x \sim y$, $y \sim z$, and $x \succ z$ from the viewpoint of the union negotiator. Although x pays a nickle more over the three years, it starts out below y, and this just balances out the x versus y comparison. Contract z also pays a nickle more than y, and it starts out better than y, but all this is balanced out by y's greater third-year amount, which is important for future negotiations. Finally, x is preferred to z because they have the same total and x gives a better position for the future. These aspects outweigh the 50 cent advantage of z over x in the first year, which is recovered under x in the next two years.

More flagrant violations of transitivity arise when there are strict preference cycles. Examples based on multiple criteria appear in May [1954] and Tversky [1969]. Consider

$$x = (\text{excellent, satisfactory, good}),$$
$$y = (\text{good, excellent, satisfactory}),$$
$$z = (\text{satisfactory, good, excellent}),$$

where each triple characterizes a job opportunity by ratings of salary, work location, and perceived quality of work. If the individual prefers one opportunity to another when it is clearly better than the other on at least two of the three criteria and is not unsatisfactory on any, then preferences are cyclic with $x \succ y \succ z \succ x$.

A somewhat different violation of transitivity is known as the *preference reversal phenomenon*. This occurs in the monetary setting when p and q are lotteries, x and y are sure things, and

$$p \succ q, \quad p \sim x, \quad q \sim y, \quad \text{and} \quad y > x,$$

where $y \succ x$ is presumed to follow from $y > x$. If preferences were fully transitive, then $x \sim p$, $p \succ q$, and $q \sim y$ require $x \succ y$, which contradicts $y > x$. When $p \sim x$, it is usual to refer to x as the *certainty equivalent* of p. Thus a preference reversal occurs when one lottery is preferred to another but has a *smaller* certainty equivalent than the other.

A number of experiments, cited by Slovic and Lichtenstein [1983] and Fishburn [1985], have demonstrated the pervasiveness of preference reversals. They seem most likely to obtain when p (called the *probability lottery*) has a high probability of yielding a modest gain and q (the *money lottery*) has a low probability of yielding a large gain, as when

$$p(\$200) = 0.7, \qquad p(\$0) = 0.3;$$
$$q(\$1200) = 0.1, \qquad q(\$0) = 0.9.$$

If $p \succ q$, and if p has certainty equivalent \$100 and q has certainty equivalent \$110, then a preference reversal obtains.

Violations of Linearity

Suppose p, q, and r are in P and $0 < \lambda < 1$. The linearity property of expected utility then says that

$$u(\lambda p + (1-\lambda)r) = \lambda u(p) + (1-\lambda)u(r),$$
$$u(\lambda q + (1-\lambda)r) = \lambda u(q) + (1-\lambda)u(r).$$

Hence if $u(p) > u(q)$ or $p \succ q$, the von Neumann–Morgenstern theory requires $\lambda p + (1-\lambda)r \succ \lambda q + (1-\lambda)r$. The implication $p \succ q \Rightarrow \lambda p + (1-\lambda)r \succ \lambda q + (1-\lambda)r$ is one type of independence or linearity axiom for expected utility. Another, used by Herstein and Milnor [1953], is $p \sim q \Rightarrow \frac{1}{2}p + \frac{1}{2}r \sim \frac{1}{2}q + \frac{1}{2}r$. In both cases, independence asserts that the addition of identical parts $[(1-\lambda)r$ or $\frac{1}{2}r]$ to other lotteries shall not change the original preference or indifference between them.

Systematic violations of independence were first established by Allais [1953, 1952] in the early 1950s and have been subsequently verified by Morrison [1967], MacCrimmon and Larsson [1979], and Kahneman and Tversky [1979]. We consider two examples of the type used by Allais and others.

First, suppose

$$p(\$500,000) = 1.00, \qquad q(\$2,500,000) = 0.10,$$
$$q(\$500,000) = 0.89,$$
$$q(\$0) = 0.01.$$

The general preference here is $p \succ q$ since p guarantees a large gain but q might yield nothing. Now let

$$p'(\$500,000) = 0.11, \qquad q'(\$2,500,000) = 0.10,$$
$$p'(\$0) = 0.89, \qquad q'(\$0) = 0.90.$$

In this case most people prefer q' to p' since q' has a much larger prize with only slightly less probability than p'. However, $p \succ q$ and $q' \succ p'$ violate linearity since the first preference reduces to

$$(0.11)u(\$500{,}000) > (0.10)u(\$2{,}500{,}000) + (0.01)u(\$0)$$

under linearity, and the second reduces to the opposite inequality. The two cases are related by the lotteries p and r, where $r(\$2{,}500{,}000) = 10/11$ and $r(\$0) = 1/11$. We have

$$p = \lambda p + (1 - \lambda)p, \qquad q = \lambda r + (1 - \lambda)p$$

and

$$p' = \lambda p + (1 - \lambda)s, \qquad q' = \lambda r + (1 - \lambda)s,$$

where $\lambda = 0.11$ and $s(\$0) = 1$. The independence axiom requires the preference (or indifference) between p and q and between p' and q' to be the same as between p and r.

Second, consider the comparison between $\lambda p + (1 - \lambda)r$ and $\lambda q + (1 - \lambda)r$ as λ varies over $[0, 1]$ with

$$p(\$3{,}000) = 1,$$
$$q(\$4{,}000) = 0.9, \qquad q(\$0) = 0.1,$$
$$r(\$0) = 1.$$

At $\lambda = 1$ the choice is between p and q, and the prevalent preference is $p \succ q$. As λ decreases toward 0, the original attractiveness of p over q diminishes and a reversal may occur. For example, at $\lambda = 1/10$, $\lambda p + (1 - \lambda)r$ yields \$3,000 with probability 0.10 and \$0 otherwise, and $\lambda q + (1 - \lambda)r$ yields \$4,000 with probability 0.09 and \$0 otherwise. In this case, many people prefer the second lottery.

2. Alternatives to Expected Utility

As a point of departure for our discussion of alternatives to expected utility, we first list three axioms that are necessary and sufficient for the basic expected utility model. The following apply to all p, q, and r in P, and all λ strictly between 0 and 1.

AXIOM 1. $\succ$ on P is a weak order.

AXIOM 2. If $p \succ q$ then $\lambda p + (1 - \lambda)r \succ \lambda q + (1 - \lambda)r$.

AXIOM 3. If $p \succ q \succ r$ then $\alpha p + (1 - \alpha)r \succ q \succ \beta p + (1 - \beta)r$ for some α, β strictly between 0 and 1.

We have already considered the ordering and independence axioms in some detail. The third axiom is a continuity condition that seems plausible in most situations. Its main effect is to ensure that no lottery is "infinitely more desirable" than another lottery. Situations in which it might fail are noted by Chipman [1960].

Modifications that Preserve Linearity

Early modifications of the von Neumann–Morgenstern axioms that were aimed at generalizing their theory tended to focus on axioms 1 and 3, ordering and continuity, but left the independence axiom untouched or weakened only slightly. Hausner [1954], and later Chipman [1960], showed that if axiom 3 is dropped, then expected utility takes on a lexicographically ordered vector-valued form rather than a real valued form. The simplest example is

$$p \succ q \Leftrightarrow u_1(p) > u_1(q) \quad \text{or} \quad [u_1(p) = u_1(q), u_2(p) > u_2(q)],$$

where each u_i, as u previously, is linear on P.

On the other hand, Aumann [1962 and 1964] retained continuity but weakened axiom 1 by not assuming that indifference is transitive. His representation includes the one-way implication

$$p \succ q \Rightarrow u(p) > u(q),$$

with u linear.

Fishburn [1979] attempted to capture the essence of the von Neumann–Morgenstern linearity feature by weakening axiom 1 to asymmetry, dropping axiom 3, and replacing axiom 2 by

AXIOM 2'. *If $p \succ q$ and $r \succ s$, then*

$$\lambda p + (1 - \lambda)r \succ \lambda q + (1 - \lambda)s.$$

Asymmetry of $\succ$ and axiom 2' imply that $\succ$ is acyclic, but they do not imply that $\succ$ is transitive. Fishburn observes that if X is finite with $m > 1$ outcomes, and if $\succ$ is asymmetric and satisfies axiom 2', then there are $n < m$ linear functions $u_1, \ldots, u_n$ on P such that, for all p and q in P,

$$p \succ q \Rightarrow (u_1(p), \ldots, u_n(p)) \neq (u_1(q), \ldots, u_n(q))$$
$$\text{and } u_i(p) > u_i(q) \text{ for the smallest } i$$
$$\text{at which } u_i(p) \neq u_i(q).$$

This is a very weak version of one-way lexicographic expected utility.

Additional discussions of weakenings of axioms 1–3 that preserve a sense of linearity appear in Fishburn [1982a].

Alternatives without Linearity

Apart from Allais [1953, 1952], alternatives to expected utility that accommodate the violations of linearity discussed in the preceding section are quite recent. For expository convenience, these alternatives are classified according to whether they assume that preferences are transitive, whether outcomes other than money are subsumed by the theory, and whether an explicit axiomatic characterization has been provided. Although these three dichotomies allow eight classes, only five classes contain existing theories. They are identified by their authors as follows:

Preferences assumed to be transitive
    (1)   Money outcomes, not fully axiomatized: Allais [1953, 1952]; Machina [1982a].
    (2)   Money outcomes, axiomatized: Kahneman and Tversky [1979].
    (3)   Arbitrary outcomes, axiomatized: Chew and MacCrimmon [1979]; Chew [1983, 1982]; Fishburn [1983a].

Preferences not assumed to be transitive
    (4)   Money outcomes, not fully axiomatized: Loomes and Sugden [1982]; Bell [1982].
    (5)   Arbitrary outcomes, axiomatized: Fishburn [1982b, 1984a].

We shall consider the transitive theories first, then comment on aspects of the others.

Alternatives with Transitive Preferences

Allais's counterproposal to expected utility assumes that utilities are fully ordered and can be represented by a real valued function, so that he subscribes to assumptions like axioms 1 and 3. In addition, he assumes that preferences for monetary lotteries satisfy the "axiom of absolute preference," which others (see Whitmore and Findlay [1978]) would refer to as agreement with first-degree stochastic dominance. We say that p *first-degree stochastically dominates* q, and write $p >_1 q$, if $p \neq q$ and, for every real x, the probability that p yields a return of x or more is as great as the probability that q yields a return of x or more. Then Allais's axiom of absolute preference says that, for all p and q in P, $p >_1 q \Rightarrow p \succ q$. This is a very appealing assumption that no one takes issue with as a principle of rational choice in the monetary context.

Allais also discusses other aspects of decision making under risk, including the utility-scaling of money apart from probability considerations, and subjective distortion of given probabilities. The reader is referred to Allais [1953, 1952, 1979] for details.

Machina [1982a] presumes assumptions of transitivity, continuity, and agreement with $>_1$ in working with probability distributions whose wealth outcomes x lie in a bounded interval $[0, M]$. He assumes in addition that the real valued function u on P that represents $>$ is differentiable or smooth in an appropriate sense. This implies that, for distributions within a small neighborhood containing p, preferences are nearly identical to those generated by an expected utility model. However, preferences between distributions that are farther apart need not mimic expected utility behavior.

The last of the transitive theories geared explicitly to monetary outcomes is Kahneman and Tversky's [1979] prospect theory. They view outcomes as increments to present wealth and confine their attention to lotteries that have at most two nonzero outcomes. Explicitly, $(x, \alpha; y, \beta)$ is a risky prospect that yields x with probability α, y with probability β, and 0 with probability $1 - \alpha - \beta \geq 0$. Preferences among such lotteries adhere to a real valued function u in the usual sense: $p > q \Leftrightarrow u(p) > u(q)$.

Unlike the other theories discussed in this section, prospect theory allows subjective distortion of given probabilities. In addition, the form of u varies in different regions. If either $\alpha + \beta < 1$, or $x \geq 0 \geq y$, or $x \leq 0 \leq y$, then

$$u(x, \alpha; y, \beta) = \pi(\alpha)v(x) + \pi(\beta)v(y),$$

where $v(0) = \pi(0) = 0$, $\pi(1) = 1$, and both v and π are increasing functions. On the other hand, if $p + q = 1$ and either $x > y > 0$ (a sure minimum gain of y) or $x < y < 0$ (a sure minimum loss of y), then

$$u(x, \alpha; y, \beta) = v(y) + \pi(\alpha)[v(x) - v(y)].$$

Explicit axioms for the first form are given in the appendix of Kahneman and Tversky [1979]. They do not axiomatize the second form. As with other alternatives, their theory accounts for violations of linearity. Moreover, it can describe behaviors attributed to subjective distortion of probabilities; for example, overvaluation of very small probabilities.

The other transitive theories mentioned above allow arbitrary outcomes and have been fully axiomatized. Fishburn [1983a, Theorem 1] uses axiom 1, a technical boundedness condition, and assumptions of continuity and convexity to obtain u on P that satisfies the ordering conditions and has $u(\lambda p + (1 - \lambda)q)$ continuous and increasing [constant] in λ when $p > q$ [$p \sim q$]. His continuity axiom is

AXIOM 3'. *If $p > q$ and $q > r$ then $q \sim \alpha p + (1 - \alpha)r$ for at least one α in $(0, 1)$,* and his convexity axiom is, for all $0 < \lambda < 1$,

AXIOM 4.   *If* $(p \succ q, \; p \succsim r)$ *then* $p \succ \lambda q + (1 - \lambda)r$; *if* $(q \succ p, \; r \succsim p)$ *then* $\lambda q + (1 - \lambda)r \succ p$; *if* $(p \sim q, \; p \sim r)$ *then* $p \sim \lambda q + (1 - \lambda)r$.

The latter axiom retains vestiges of axiom 2, but makes all comparisons against a fixed distribution p. In terms familiar to many economists, axiom 4 asserts that the preference relation is both quasi-concave and quasi-convex. In axiom 4, $\succsim$ means either $\succ$ or $\sim$.

Our final theory in the transitive category was initially discussed by Chew and MacCrimmon [1979] and has since been refined by Chew [1983, 1982] and Fishburn [1983a]. It is due primarily to Chew. I shall follow the presentation in Fishburn [1983a] for expositional continuity. Chew's [1982] axioms are quite similar and are equivalent to those noted here. One more axiom is needed.

AXIOM 5.   *If* $p \succ q \succ r$ *and* $q \sim \frac{1}{2}p + \frac{1}{2}r$, *then* $\lambda p + (1 - \lambda)r \sim \frac{1}{2}p + \frac{1}{2}q \Leftrightarrow \lambda r + (1 - \lambda)p \sim \frac{1}{2}r + \frac{1}{2}q$.

Axiom 5 is a symmetry or balance condition that is a specialized version of the following proposition: if q lies midway in preference between p and r, then an indifference statement in p, q, and r will be preserved at indifference when p and r are interchanged throughout. Together, axioms 1, 3', 4, and 5 are necessary and sufficient for the existence of *linear* functions u and w on P with w nonnegative such that, for all p and q in P,

$$p \succ q \Leftrightarrow u(p)w(q) > u(q)w(p),$$

with w positive everywhere except perhaps when P has a most-preferred or a least-preferred distribution, but not both, in which case w may vanish at the extreme. Admissible transformations for the linear functions used in the representation are described in the aforementioned papers.

If w is constant in this representation, then we obtain the von Neumann–Morgenstern model since u is linear. More generally, if $w > 0$, then $\succ$ is represented by a ratio of linear functions since

$$u(p)w(q) > u(q)w(p) \Leftrightarrow u(p)/w(p) > u(q)/w(q).$$

The weighting function w clearly allows departures from expected utility behavior. Because of the ratio form, Chew's theory is sometimes referred to as a ratio theory of (expected) utility.

Alternatives without Transitive Preferences

Although the nontransitive utility theories of Loomes and Sugden [1982], Bell [1982], and Fishburn [1982b, 1984a] were developed independently, they share a common underlying theme. This theme says that an individual's comparison of two risky alternatives may involve interdependencies between the two that cannot be separated in the sense presumed by theories discussed earlier. Thus, while other theories attach a utility $u(p)$ or $u(p)/w(p)$ separately to each p in P, the nontransitive theories do not. Instead, they adopt an interactive functional form $\phi(p,q)$ such that

$$p \succ q \Leftrightarrow \phi(p,q) > 0.$$

Thus preference corresponds to the part of $P \times P$ on which ϕ is positive, and indifference holds when ϕ vanishes. The function ϕ is taken to be *skew-symmetric*, which means that $\phi(q,p) = -\phi(p,q)$. This implies that $\phi(p,p) = 0$, or $p \sim p$, and that $\phi(q,p)$ is negative when $\phi(p,q)$ is positive.

The nontransitive theories hold that, when p is compared to q, p may be viewed differently than when it is compared to r. In other words, the evaluation of p depends crucially on what it is being compared to.

The interactive feature of ϕ allows preference cycles such as $p \succ q \succ r \succ p$ since there is nothing to prevent $\phi(p,q) > 0$, $\phi(q,r) > 0$, and $\phi(r,p) > 0$. It can also account for fully transitive behavior, which would be the case when $\phi(p,q)$ can be decomposed as the difference $u(p) - u(q)$. When $\phi(p,q) = u(p) - u(q)$, we have $p \succ q \Leftrightarrow u(p) > u(q)$, as before.

Roughly speaking, $\phi(p,q)$ can be thought of as a measure of the individual's preference for p versus q, or as a measure of the intensity of preference for p over q. Notions of psychological regret may also be involved in ϕ, and I shall say more about this in a later section. However interpreted, it is not presumed that the ϕ values are naturally additive in the sense that $\phi(p,r) = \phi(p,q) + \phi(q,r)$. This would be the case if $\phi(p,q) = u(p) - u(q)$, but not otherwise.

Although the theories of Loomes and Sugden [1982] and Bell [1982] have restricted interpretations in the risky decision format used in this section, they were originally designed for the states-of-the-world format, and I shall defer their discussion. The rest of this section summarizes Fishburn's [1982b, 1984a] nontransitive theory.

The axioms used by Fishburn have already been stated. They are axioms 3', 4, and 5 for continuity, convexity, and symmetry. These three axioms are necessary and sufficient for the existence of a real valued skew-symmetric function ϕ on $P \times P$ that is linear separately in each argument and satisfies $p \succ q \Leftrightarrow \phi(p,q) > 0$, for all p and q in P. Linearity in each argument means that

$$\phi(\lambda p + (1-\lambda)q, r) = \lambda\phi(p,r) + (1-\lambda)\phi(q,r),$$

and that

$$\phi(p, \lambda q + (1-\lambda)r) = \lambda\phi(p,q) + (1-\lambda)\phi(p,r).$$

Because ϕ is a skew-symmetric bilinear function in this representation,

Fishburn's theory is referred to as the SSB theory of utility. The uniqueness property of SSB utilities is very simple: if ϕ is an SSB function that represents $\succ$ in the manner indicated, then so does another SSB function ϕ' if and only if there is a number $a > 0$ such that $\phi'(p, q) = a\phi(p, q)$ for all p and q in P.

A version of expected utility arises from $\phi(p, q)$ in the following way. If p and q are simple probability distributions on an arbitrary outcome set X, and if we extend ϕ to $X \times X$ by the natural definition

$$\phi(x, y) = \phi(r, s) \quad \text{when } r(x) = s(y) = 1,$$

then bilinearity implies that

$$\phi(p, q) = \sum_x \sum_y p(x)q(y)\phi(x, y).$$

When additional axioms, given in Fishburn [1984a], are adopted for more general probability measures, we obtain

$$\phi(p, q) = \int \int \phi(x, y) \, dp(x) \, dq(y).$$

Hence $\phi(p, q)$ equals the expected value of ϕ on $X \times X$ with respect to the product measure $p \times q$.

A few of the theories mentioned earlier are special cases of the SSB theory. If, in addition to axioms 3′, 4, and 5, we assume that $\sim$ is transitive on P, then axiom 1 also holds and ϕ can be decomposed as

$$\phi(p, q) = u(p)w(q) - u(q)w(p),$$

with u and w linear and $w \geq 0$. This yields Chew's ratio theory discussed at the end of the preceding subsection.

If, instead of assuming that $\sim$ is transitive, we add the independence axiom of Herstein and Milnor [1953], $p \sim q \Rightarrow \frac{1}{2}p + \frac{1}{2}r \sim \frac{1}{2}q + \frac{1}{2}r$, and drop axiom 5, which becomes redundant, then we get the von Neumann–Morgenstern expected utility model. In other words, axioms 3′, 4, and independence imply that ϕ can be decomposed as $\phi(p, q) = u(p) - u(q)$, with u linear. This particular axiomatization of expected utility assumes neither asymmetry nor transitivity explicitly. These properties follow from the other assumptions.

3. Applications

Many of the papers cited in the preceding section as well as others include examples of expected utility violations that can be accommodated by the new theories. The purpose of the present section is to note papers that give examples of functions consistent with violations and several others, to illustrate a few such cases, and to mention other concerns in economic analysis that have been addressed by the new theories.

Transitivity Violations

We consider first the SSB theory since it and the similar theories of Loomes and Sugden [1982] and Bell [1982] are the only ones designed to accommodate cyclic preferences and preference reversals.

Plausible examples of cyclic preferences are illustrated previously and in Fishburn [1984a, 1984d]. Specific cases of SSB functions that generate preference reversals appear in Loomes and Sugden [1983], Bell [1982], and Fishburn [1984d, 1985]. An especially simple example from the last of these for nonnegative monetary outcomes is

$$\phi(x, y) = (x - y)f(y) \quad \text{for } x \geq y \geq 0,$$

where f is positive and strictly decreasing. This says that the degree of preference for x over y is a weighted difference of the two outcomes. If the difference $x - y$ remains fixed while the base point y increases, then the "utility differential" of the difference decreases. As shown in Fishburn [1985], this form in the SSB model gives rise to preference reversals in some abundance.

Additional aspects of preference reversals that relate to risk attitudes are noted in Loomes and Sugden [1983] and Fishburn [1984b]. For example, the latter paper shows that if $\phi(x, y)$ is increasing in x, which is expected in the monetary context and is required for agreement with first-degree stochastic dominance, then preference reversals of the type illustrated previously must occur if indifference is not transitive.

Linearity Violations

Allais-type violations of linearity or independence are shown by Machina [1982a], Kahneman and Tversky [1979], Chew [1983], Loomes and Sugden [1982], Bell [1982], and Fishburn [1984d] to be consistent with all of the new theories.

For an illustration, again let $\phi(x, y) = (x - y)f(y)$ for $x \geq y \geq 0$ with f positive and decreasing. Suppose y has $f(y) = \frac{1}{2}f(0)$. Set $x = 2y$, and consider

$p(\lambda)$: probability λ for y, $1 - \lambda$ for 0,

$q_\alpha(\lambda)$: probability $\alpha\lambda$ for $2y$, $1 - \alpha\lambda$ for 0,

where $0 < \alpha < 1$. The SSB model implies that $p(1) \succ q_\alpha(1)$ for each $\alpha < 2/3$. That is, y as a sure thing is preferred to a gamble with probability α for $2y$ (nothing otherwise) so long as $\alpha < 2/3$. Moreover, given fixed α with $1/2 < \alpha < 2/3$, as λ decreases from 1 toward 0, $p(\lambda) \succ q_\alpha(\lambda)$ changes to indifference at $\lambda = 4 - 2/\alpha$ and then to $q_\alpha(\lambda) \succ p(\lambda)$ for smaller values of λ.

Insurance and Gambling

Several authors, including Machina [1982a], Chew [1983], Loomes and Sugden [1982], and Bell [1982], show that combinations of insurance buying and gambling that are simultaneously incompatible with expected utility can be consistent with nonlinear utility theories. A simple example from Chew notes that people who uniformly avoid 50–50 bets in favor of their actuarial expectations may purchase lottery tickets at unfavorable odds over the same range of outcomes. This is inconsistent with expected utility since the first behavior implies that $u(x)$ is concave, or risk averse, which rules out gambling behavior. However, it is consistent with Chew's ratio theory and other nonlinear models.

Risk Attitudes

The theory of risk attitudes in expected utility, due to Pratt [1964] and Arrow [1965], has been generalized for nonlinear utility by Machina [1982b], Fishburn [1984b], and Chew [1984], among others. Because of the greater flexibility of the new theories, familiar notions of risk aversion, risk seeking, and so forth are being replaced by more intricate patterns of risk attitudes. Work cited in the preceding paragraph provides specific examples.

Stochastic Dominance

Stochastic dominance is an important aspect of risk analysis in expected utility theory. Recently, Machina [1982a], Chew [1983], and Fishburn [1984a, 1984b] have observed that stochastic dominance implications for expected utility also hold for more general theories.

To illustrate this, let $\succ_1$ and $\succ_2$ denote the first-degree and second-degree stochastic dominance relations on P:

$$p \succ_1 q \text{ if } p \ne q \quad \text{and} \quad \sum_{x \le y} p(x) \le \sum_{x \le y} q(x) \quad \text{for all } y;$$

$$p \succ_2 q \quad \text{if } p \ne q$$

and

$$\int_{y \le z} \left(\sum_{x \le y} p(x) \right) dy \le \int_{y \le z} \left(\sum_{x \le y} q(x) \right) dy \quad \text{for all } z.$$

In expected utility theory, $p >_1 q \Leftrightarrow u(p) > u(q)$ for all $u(x)$ that increase in x, and $p >_2 q \Leftrightarrow u(p) > u(q)$ for all $u(x)$ that are increasing and concave in x. In SSB utility theory, $p >_1 q \Leftrightarrow \phi(p, q) > 0$ for all $\phi(x, y)$ that increase in x, and $p >_2 q \Leftrightarrow \phi(p, q) > 0$ for all $\phi(x, y)$ that are increasing and concave in x.

Choice Theory

Basic choice theory in expected utility says to choose an alternative from a feasible set that maximizes expected utility within that set. A similar prescription applies to nonlinear utility theories which assume that preferences are transitive. Maximum elements will always exist unless the supremum is not achieved within the feasible set.

The same idea applies to nontransitive theories so long as mixtures of feasible alternatives are also considered to be available for choice. Suppose for example that Q is a finite set of probability distributions in the SSB context. Let $H(Q)$ denote the convex hull of Q, i.e., all distributions $\lambda_1 q_1 + \cdots + \lambda_n q_n$ with q_i in Q, $\lambda_i \ge 0$, and $\lambda_1 + \ldots + \lambda_n = 1$. Then, as proved in Fishburn [1984a], there is a p^* in $H(Q)$ such that $\phi(p^*, p) \ge 0$ for all p in $H(Q)$. Hence $H(Q)$ contains a distribution that is preferred or indifferent to every other distribution in $H(Q)$.

Social Choice and Income Inequality

The relevance of nonlinear utility for social choice theory and income inequality theory have been discussed by Fishburn [1984c] and Chew [1983], respectively.

For the social choice setting, let $\phi(x, y)$ denote the number of voters who express a preference for x over y minus the number who express a preference for y over x in a paired-comparison voting situation with three or more candidates in a set X. Consider probability distributions $p, q, \ldots$ on X as social choice lotteries, and let $\phi(p, q)$ be defined by bilinear extension from $\phi(x, y)$. As just observed, there will be a p^* such that $\phi(p^*, p) \ge 0$ for all social choice lotteries p. Fishburn [1984c] shows that if the winner is selected on the basis of p^* then: (1) if X can be partitioned into nonempty subsets A and B such that every candidate in A has a majority over every candidate in B, $p^*(b) = 0$

for every b in B; and (2) if every voter can be assigned a weak order on X such that sincere voting would be consistent with the observed $\phi(x, y)$ data, then no candidate who is strongly Pareto dominated in those orders can be elected. Thus choice by p^* adheres both to a majority-choice rule and to Pareto optimality.

Chew's [1983] discussion of income inequality views p as an income distribution, with $p(x)$ the relative frequency of individuals who have income x. He interprets x for which $u(x)/w(x) = u(p)/w(p)$ as the income level such that a society in which all people have income x is equally as well off in the aggregate as a society with income distribution p. He then argues that his ratio-model interpretation provides a richer and more suitable framework for the analysis of alternative income distributions than does the model based on a single linear function u.

4. Decisions under Uncertainty

We complete our review of recent developments with comments on the states formulation for decision making under uncertainty (Savage [1954], Fishburn [1970, 1982a]). It will be assumed that there are n exclusive and exhaustive states. The decision maker's preference relation $\succ$ is defined on a set F of uncertain alternatives or acts, where each *act* is a function f that assigns an outcome f_i in X to state i for $i = 1, \ldots, n$. The usual subjective expected utility model in this setting consists of a probability distribution π on the states ($\pi_i \geq 0, \Sigma \pi_i = 1$) and a utility function u on X such that, for all acts f and g in F,

$$f \succ g \Leftrightarrow \sum_{i=1}^{n} \pi_i u(f_i) > \sum_{i=1}^{n} \pi_i u(g_i).$$

Various axiomatizations of this and closely related representations are reviewed in Fishburn [1981].

The model developed by Loomes and Sugden [1982] and Bell [1982] replaces u on X by a skew-symmetric function ϕ on $X \times X$, with

$$f \succ g \Leftrightarrow \sum_{i=1}^{n} \pi_i \phi(f_i, g_i) > 0.$$

As in Fishburn's SSB model, this allows preference cycles. It also accommodates certain violations of independence in the traditional subjective expected utility model. Both Loomes and Sugden [1982] and Bell [1982] interpret ϕ in the monetary context as

$$\phi(x, y) = v(x) - v(y) + r[v(x) - v(y)] - r[v(y) - v(x)],$$

where v is a value function on X and r is a function that measures degrees of regret or rejoicing associated with value differences.

An axiomatization of the basic model of Loomes, Sugden, and Bell is given in Fishburn [1984e] along with axioms for more general models in the states formulation. Rather than working only with acts as defined above, Fishburn bases his axioms on lottery acts, which are functions that assign a lottery in P to each state. The decision maker's probability distribution π and his "utility" function ϕ on $X \times X$ are deduced from the axioms.

The preceding model is a significant generalization of the traditional model, but is nevertheless unable to accommodate violations of the traditional model uncovered by Ellsberg [1961]. Consider an urn that contains 30 red balls and 60 others that are solid yellow and solid black in an unknown proportion. Ellsberg observed that many people have the following preferences:

[win \$1,000 if a red ball is chosen at random]
$\succ$ [win \$1,000 if a yellow ball is chosen at random];

[win \$1,000 if yellow or black is chosen]
$\succ$ [win \$1,000 if red or black is chosen];

where in each case nothing is won if the complementary event obtains. Let $\phi(\$1,000,0) = 1$. Then the first preference implies that $\pi(\text{red}) > \pi(\text{yellow})$, and the second gives $\pi(\text{yellow or black}) > \pi(\text{red or black})$, which reduces to $\pi(\text{yellow}) > \pi(\text{red})$.

Three ways have been suggested to incorporate Ellsberg phenomena into models for decisions under uncertainty. Fishburn [1983b] and Schmeidler [1984] propose somewhat different weakenings of the traditional view of subjective probability. The first of these shows how replacement of π by a biadditive function of two arguments can account for the observed behavior when only two outcomes are involved. However, as noted in Fishburn [1984e], this approach runs into difficulties when there are many possible outcomes. Schmeidler's approach applies to any number of outcomes and replaces π by a monotonic but not necessarily additive set function on subsets of states. His treatment of utility retains most of the flavor of the von Neumann–Morgenstern model, and his representation assumes that preferences are transitive and that Allais-type independence violations cannot arise among p lotteries within a state.

The third way to accommodate Ellsberg phenomena is based on intuitive notions of disappointment and elation in Bell [1985], where it is argued that a preference for one-stage over two-stage resolution of an uncertain lottery can generate the kind of preferences observed by Ellsberg.

5. Prospectus

The theory of von Neumann and Morgenstern took a decade or two to become
established as a basic component of microeconomic theory. Since then, it has
been the preeminent theory of individual preference and choice for decision
making under risk.

An obvious fact about the new theories of utility for risky situations is their
multiplicity. All accommodate standard violations of linearity, but only a few
allow nontransitive preferences. Because of the multiplicity of new proposals to
replace expected utility, there is likely to be some confusion and debate as time
goes on about their relative merits.

It seems certain that the new theories will be developed well beyond their
present state, especially for applications in economic analysis, and other new
proposals may arise. I would guess that at least another decade or two will pass
before one or more of the new theories finds its way into the mainstream of
economic theory, if indeed this happens at all in the near future. Expected
utility is firmly entrenched even though its inadequacies are manifest to some
who have done research in the field, and familiar ideas that have convinced
many people of their claim to rationality or reasonableness are not easily
supplanted.

Alternatives to Savage's theory of subjective expected utility appear a bit less
well developed than alternatives to the von Neumann–Morgenstern theory,
perhaps because of their added feature of subjective probability. I anticipate
substantially more work on the axiomatic foundations in this area during the
next few years, along with exploratory applications in economics and statistics.

References

Allais, M., "Le comportement de l'homme rationnel devant de risque: critique des
    postulats et axiomes de l'ecole Americaine". *Econometrica* 21 (1953), 503–546.
——, "The foundations of a positive theory of choice involving risk and a criticism of
    the postulates and axioms of the American school." (1952), pp. 27–145 in Allais and
    Hagen, 1979.
——, "The so-called Allais paradox and rational decisions under uncertainty." In
    Allais and Hagen, 1979, pp. 437–681.
Allais, M., and O. Hagen (eds.), *Expected Utility Hypotheses and the Allais Paradox.*
    Dordrecht, Holland: Reidel, 1979.
Arrow, K. J., *Aspects of the Theory of Risk Bearing.* Helsinki: Yrjö Jahssonin Säätiö,
    1965.
Aumann, R. J., "Utility theory without the completeness axiom." *Econometrica* 30
    (1962), 445–462, and 32 (1964), 210–212.
Bell, D. E., "Regret in decision making under uncertainty." *Operations Research* 30
    (1982), 961–981.

————, "Disappointment in decision making under uncertainty." *Operations Research* 33 (1985), 1–27.

Bernoulli, D., "Specimen theoriae novae de mensura sortis." *Commentarii Academiae Scientiarum Imperialis Petropolitanae* 5 (1738), 175–192. Translated by L. Sommer, *Econometrica* 22 (1954), 23–36.

Chew, S. H., "A generalization of the quasilinear mean with applications to the measurement of income inequality and decision theory resolving the Allais paradox." *Econometrica* 51 (1983), 1065–1092.

————, "A mixture set axiomatization of weighted utility theory." Discussion paper 82-4, revised, College of Business and Public Administration, University of Arizona, 1982.

————, "Weighted utility theory and risk aversion." Unpublished manuscript, 1984.

Chew, S. H., and K. R. MacCrimmon, "Alpha-nu choice theory: a generalization of expected utility theory." Working paper 669, Faculty of Commerce and Business Administration, University of British Columbia, 1979.

Chipman, J. S., "The foundations of utility." *Econometrica* 28 (1960), 193–224.

Edwards, W., "The theory of decision making." *Psychological Bulletin* 51 (1954), 380–417.

Ellsberg, D., "Risk, ambiguity, and the Savage axioms." *Quarterly Journal of Economics* 75 (1961), 643–669.

Fishburn, P. C., *Utility Theory for Decision Making.* New York: Wiley, 1970. Reprinted, Krieger, 1979.

————, "On the nature of expected utility." In Allais and Hagen, 1979, pp. 243–257.

————, "Subjective expected utility: a review of normative theories." *Theory and Decision* 13 (1981), 139–199.

————, *The Foundations of Expected Utility.* Dordrecht, Holland: Reidel, 1982. a

————, "Nontransitive measurable utility." *Journal of Mathematical Psychology* 26 (1982), 31–67. b

————, "Transitive measurable utility." *Journal of Economic Theory* 31 (1983), 293–317. a

————, "Ellsberg revisited: a new look at comparative probability." *Annals of Statistics* 11 (1983), 1047–1059. b

————, "Dominance in SSB utility theory." *Journal of Economic Theory* 34 (1984), 130–148. a

————, "Elements of risk analysis in nonlinear utility theory." *INFOR* 22 (1984), 81–97. b

————, "Probabilistic social choice based on simple voting comparisons." *Review of Economic Studies* 51 (1984), 683–692. c

————, "SSB utility theory: an economic perspective." *Mathematical Social Sciences* 8 (1984), 63–94. d

————, "SSB utility theory and decision making under uncertainty." *Mathematical Social Sciences* 8 (1984), 253–285. e

————, "Nontransitive preference theory and the preference reversal phenomenon." *International Review of Economics and Business* 32 (1985), 39–50.

Hausner, M., "Multidimensional utilities." In *Decision Processes* (R. M. Thrall, C. H. Coombs, and R. L. Davis, eds.). New York: Wiley, 1954, pp. 167–180.

Herstein, I. N., and J. Milnor, "An axiomatic approach to measurable utility."
    Econometrica 21 (1953), 291–297.

Kahneman, D., and A. Tversky, "Prospect theory: an analysis of decision under risk."
    Econometrica 47 (1979), 263–291.

Loomes, G., and R. Sugden, "Regret theory: an alternative theory of rational choice
    under uncertainty." *Economic Journal* 92 (1982), 805–824.

———, "A rationale for preference reversal." *American Economic Review* 73 (1983),
    428–432.

MacCrimmon, K. R., and S. Larsson, "Utility theory: axioms versus 'paradoxes.'"
    In Allais and Hagen, 1979, pp. 333–409.

Machina, M. J., "'Expected utility' analysis without the independence axiom."
    Econometrica 50 (1982), 277–323. a.

———, "A stronger characterization of declining risk aversion." *Econometrica* 50
    (1982), 1069–1079. b

May, K. O., "Intransitivity, utility, and the aggregation of preference patterns."
    Econometrica 22 (1954), 1–13.

Morrison, D. G., "On the consistency of preferences in Allais' paradox." *Behavioral
    Science* 12 (1967), 373–383.

Pratt, J. W., "Risk aversion in the small and in the large." *Econometrica* 32 (1964),
    122–136.

Savage, L. J., *The Foundations of Statistics*. New York: Wiley, 1954. Second edition,
    Dover, 1972.

Schmeidler, D., "Subjective probability and expected utility without additivity."
    Unpublished, 1984.

Slovic, P., and S. Lichtenstein, "Preference reversals: a broader perspective." *American
    Economic Review* 73 (1983), 596–605.

Tversky, A., "Intransitivity of preferences." *Psychological Review* 76 (1969), 31–48.

von Neumann, J., and O. Morgenstern, *Theory of Games and Economic Behavior*.
    Princeton, New Jersey: Princeton University Press, 1944. Second edition, 1947; third
    edition, 1953.

Whitmore, G. A., and M. C. Findlay (eds.), *Stochastic Dominance*. Lexington,
    Massachusetts: Heath, 1978.

3 CONSUMER LEARNING AND OPTIMAL PRICING STRATEGIES FOR PRODUCTS OF UNKNOWN QUALITY

Patricia A. Goering

Economic agents frequently make decisions without complete information about the relevant variables (see Hirshleifer and Riley [1979]). In particular, consumers are typically uncertain about the quality of products with which they are unfamiliar and thus make decisions without complete information about the relevant variables. Recent research (Cremer [1984], Goering [1985a, 1985b], Grossman, Kihlstrom and Mirman [1977], Shapiro [1983], and Smallwood and Conlisk [1979]) has examined the effect of incomplete information and consumer learning about product quality through product usage on the optimal decision making of consumers and firms. This chapter will suggest a model of consumer purchasing decision making with incomplete information about product quality and learning through personal experience. The implications of this model of consumer behavior on product demand and on the pricing decisions of firms will then be explored.

In a similar model, Shapiro [1983] has studied the optimal pricing strategy of a single firm when product quality is unknown to consumers in an infinite time horizon model. Purchasing decisions are based on the firm's reputation, known by all consumers, and individual tastes for quality. The higher an individual's taste for quality, the higher the price the individual is willing to pay for the product.

Product quality is perfectly revealed to purchasers through usage. Quality is assumed to be invariant among individual units of the product and over time. Hence, purchasers acquire perfect information about the quality of future purchases. Their future purchasing decisions are then based on this private information and their individual tastes. Although the purchasing decisions of non-purchasers continue to be based on the firm's reputation, learning by purchasers shifts demand for the product.

Shapiro shows how the optimal prices of a product with given quality are affected by the firm's reputation and consumer learning. If the firm's reputation is lower than the quality of the product, then the firm should set its initial price low enough to induce at least its target sales level even though demand is based entirely on its reputation. Although this price may be lower than that which maximizes initial profits, the number of purchasers who learn that the product has high quality and are, therefore, willing to pay higher future prices is increased. A higher price can then be set in future periods without reducing sales.

If, however, the firm has a higher reputation for quality than the true quality of the product, then the firm should initially set a high price, inducing consumers with relatively high tastes for quality to make purchases. In this case, purchasers learn that the product has low quality and, therefore, lower their reservation prices. However, by gradually lowering the price in subsequent periods, consumers with lower tastes for quality continuously enter the market. In doing so, the firm is able to "price discriminate" among consumer tastes over time. After exploiting its reputation, however, the optimal price is the same as the full information price.

Thus, Shapiro's model shows how incomplete information and consumer learning through personal experience can lead to prices which do not necessarily maximize current profits and to price changes over time. In addition, although Shapiro uses a partial equilibrium analysis, his results suggest that incomplete information and consumer learning may explain why firms producing identical products but with different reputations, or firms with the same reputations who produce products with different quality, may use different pricing strategies.

Shapiro examines the case in which consumers acquire information about product quality only through personal experience as a starting place for a more complete analysis of the effects of incomplete information and consumer learning on the optimal decision making of firms. In general, consumers are able to acquire information about product quality from sources in addition to personal experience such as advertising, word-of-mouth reports, published quality ratings, signals such as warranties and prices, and so on. Although Shapiro's model could be extended to analyze optimal advertising strategies, the optimal provision of warranties, etc., the results obtained may be limited since consumers acquire perfect information about product quality after a single purchase. Hence, any information acquired from these sources can only influence consumers' purchasing decisions prior to their initial purchase.

Often, however, information acquired from these various sources continues to affect purchasing decisions after an initial purchase. In particular, this will occur if consumers are unable to acquire perfect information about product quality. In this chapter, a model similar in spirit to Shapiro's but which allows for the continuing influence of imperfect information on consumer purchasing decisions is explored. The optimal pricing strategies derived here are consistent with Shapiro's but are generated from a model which differs from Shapiro's in three respects: the time horizon considered, the source of consumer heterogeneity, and the information acquired by consumers through product usage. First, for simplification, a two period model rather than an infinite time horizon model is considered.

Second, expectations about product quality rather than tastes for quality are allowed to vary among consumers. Individual expectations are not generally based upon all of the information potentially available to consumers. If the information used by individuals is not consistent, then their expectations will differ. In addition, individual expectations may be influenced differently by the same piece of information.[1] The higher an individual's expectation about product quality, the higher the price the individual will be willing to pay for the product. The distribution of consumer expectations then determines the demand faced by a firm.

Finally, the notion of imperfect rather than perfect learning about product quality through product usage due to quality variation among individual units of a product suggested by Smallwood and Conlisk [1979] is incorporated in this model. Variable quality is particularly characteristic of services. Although an entree at a restaurant may generally be quite good, it may be of lower quality if, for example, fresh produce was unavailable on a particular occasion. Similarly, the quality of service at a repair store may depend on the particular repairman working or on the number of repairs to be completed on that day.

Thus, many products have a distribution of quality levels. Consumers who have expectations sufficiently high in order to make a purchase observe the quality of the purchased unit. As in Shapiro [1983], it is assumed that consumers are able to perfectly evaluate the quality of individual units.[2] A single observation, however, generally does not enable a purchaser to infer the distribution of quality. Although perfect learning does not, in general, occur, purchasers do acquire some information about the distribution. This information is used to revise their previous expectations. Since different consumers observe different samples, they revise their expectations differently. A Bayesian model of consumer learning similar, although less sophisticated, to that in Grossman, Kihlstrom and Mirman [1977] is hypothesized.

As consumer learning occurs and expectations are revised, the demand for the product shifts. Given consumers' prior beliefs, the shift is determined by the number of consumers who update their expectations and the manner in which they are revised. The distribution of revised expectations depends on the information acquired by consumers: the actual distribution of product quality. Because it is assumed as in Shapiro's model that the distribution of product quality has been determined previously, the producer is unable to control the *type* of learning that occurs. However, if the firm is a price setter, it is able to control the *amount* of learning that occurs in any period by adjusting that period's price. The number of consumers who sample the product in a period is determined by the current price.

A rational producer takes the effect of its current prices on consumer learning and future demand into consideration in choosing prices. For example, by setting a price lower than that which maximizes current profits, a firm can induce consumers with lower expectations to make purchases. If the average quality of the product is generally higher than consumer expectations, then these consumers will, on average, raise their expectations and future demand will be increased. Similarly, if consumer expectations about the quality of the product are, on average, higher than its actual quality, then producers can reduce the number of purchasers who will, on average, lower their expectations by setting a price higher than that which maximizes current profits. Demand is thus less reduced by consumer learning.

Thus, a producer is able to influence future demand with its current price. Notice, however, that it does so only by increasing or decreasing the *rate* of consumer learning. It is unable to manipulate the information consumers acquire, thereby, *misleading* them. Over time, the distribution of expectations of consumers who purchase the product converges to the actual average quality of the product. By increasing the rate of learning, a firm producing a high average quality product is able to charge a high price consistent with the product's high quality at an earlier point in time. Similarly, a firm producing a low average quality product can postpone the point at which it must charge a low price consistent with the product's low quality by decreasing the rate of learning. By gradually lowering its price, the firm is able to "price discriminate" among consumer expectations over time.

A formal model is developed to capture the main behavioral relationships in the next section. As in Shapiro's model, it is assumed that product quality, here a distribution, is exogenously determined and known to the producer. In particular, it is assumed that quality levels are uniformly distributed. Consumers know that the average quality of the product is either high or low. The purchasing decisions of otherwise identical consumers are based on individual expectations about the probability of each being actual average quality. After making a purchase, some consumers are able to infer the product's average quality. Perfect learning then occurs. The remaining purchasers, however, acquire no new information with which to revise their previous expectations. For a more general treatment of this problem, see Goering [1985a, 1985b].

The following two sections derive the optimal pricing strategies. In order to isolate the effect of consumer learning on the firm's optimal prices from the effects of the pricing strategies of competing firms, a partial equilibrium analysis is used. Because the effect of learning depends on the information acquired, i.e., on whether the actual average quality of the product is high or low, the next two sections examine each of these possibilities. The case in which the firm produces a high average quality product is first explored and then the low average quality case is examined.

The optimal pricing strategy of a rational firm which takes the effect of consumer learning on future demand into consideration in choosing its current prices is derived in each case. It is shown that if the product has high average quality, the firm will set a price in the first period lower than the optimal myopic first period price. In doing so, second period demand is increased, allowing for a second period price higher than the optimal price had the firm ignored the effect of consumer learning.

If the product has low average quality and if the proportion of purchasers who are able to infer the product's quality is sufficiently small, then a rational firm will initially set a higher price than the optimal myopic price, thereby, increasing second period demand. As in the high average quality case, the optimal second period price is higher than the optimal myopic second period price. If, however, the proportion of purchasers who learn product quality is sufficiently large, then a rational firm will extract maximum profits before learning occurs, i.e., charge the optimal myopic price initially. The price is then lowered in the second period to be consistent with the product's low average quality.

1. The Model

Suppose a single firm produces a product in each of two periods. Within each period, however, the firm is unable to produce individual units of the product with constant quality. Specifically, the quality of the product $\tilde{q}$ varies in each period as follows:

$$\tilde{q} = \mu + \tilde{\varepsilon},$$

where $\tilde{\varepsilon}$ is uniformly distributed on $[-1, 1]$. Then, $\tilde{q}$ is uniformly distributed on $[\mu - 1, \mu + 1]$ with mean μ.

Consumers know the distribution of $\tilde{\varepsilon}$, but know only that the average quality is either high or low, i.e., $\mu \in \{\underline{q}, \bar{q}\}$, where $\bar{q} > \underline{q} > 0$. It is assumed that quality is always positive, i.e., $\underline{q} - 1 > 0$, and that the distribution of quality when average quality is high and low overlap, i.e., $\bar{q} - \underline{q} < 2$. If the distributions do not overlap, then consumers can always infer the average quality of the product by observing the quality of any individual unit. Thus, this assumption guarantees that some consumers will receive units with quality levels such that they are unable to infer the product's average quality, i.e., $\bar{q} - 1 < q < \underline{q} + 1$.

Each consumer believes that the product has high average quality with probability ρ and low average quality with probability $(1 - \rho)$. Let $g(\rho)$ represent the density function of prior probabilities among consumers which is known to the producer.

Assume that consumers purchase only one unit of x per period. Consumers have utility over the quality of the purchased unit and other goods, y, purchased with their remaining income. Although the basic results of this model can be derived from a general utility function, for simplicity it is assumed that a consumer's marginal utility for quality is independent of the quantity of other goods consumed. Specifically, let $u(q, y) = q + y$, where $q = 0$ if no good is purchased. Expected utility for each consumer is

$$E[u(q, y)|\rho] = \rho\bar{q} + (1 - \rho)\underline{q} + y.$$

Each consumer faces a budget constraint $p + y = I$, where p is the price of the firm's product, I is the identical income received by all consumers and the price of y, $p_y = 1$.

First Period Demand

A purchase is made if the expected utility of the purchase is as great as the utility of making no purchase. In the first period, purchases are made by consumers with expectations such that

$$\rho\bar{q} + (1 - \rho)\underline{q} \geq p_1,$$

where p_1 is the first period price. Let $\hat{\rho}(p)$ be the marginal consumer whose beliefs are such that he is indifferent between making a purchase at a given price and making no purchase, i.e.,

$$\hat{\rho}(p) = \begin{cases} 0, & \text{when } 0 < p < \underline{q}, \\ \dfrac{p - \underline{q}}{\bar{q} - \underline{q}}, & \text{when } \underline{q} \leq p \leq \bar{q}, \\ 1, & \text{when } \bar{q} < p. \end{cases}$$

Since

$$\frac{\partial E[u(q, I-p)|\rho]}{\partial \rho} = \bar{q} - \underline{q} > 0,$$

all consumers with $\rho \geq \hat{\rho}(p_1)$ make a purchase in the first period, while those with $\rho < \hat{\rho}(p_1)$ remain out of the market. Given p_1, only consumers who believe the product has high average quality with sufficiently high probability will buy the product.

The demand facing the firm $x^1(p_1)$ is

$$x^1(p_1) = \int_{\hat{\rho}(p_1)}^1 g(\rho)\, d\rho. \tag{3.1}$$

Since

$$\hat{\rho}'(p_1) = \frac{1}{\bar{q} - \underline{q}} > 0$$

implies

$$x^{1'}(p_1) = -g(\hat{\rho}(p_1))\hat{\rho}'(p_1) < 0,$$

the higher the price, the fewer consumers there are who believe that the product has high average quality with high enough probability to make a purchase.

Second Period Demand

Demand for the firm's product in the second period comes from two sources. The first source is consumers whose second period purchasing decisions are based on their original expectations because they chose not to make a purchase and have not observed the quality of a sample of the product in the first period.

The second source is first period purchasers who have observed a sample of the product. Some of those purchasers learn the product's average quality with certainty. If the quality of the good purchased by a consumer is less than the lower bound of the distribution of quality when average quality is high, i.e., $q < \bar{q} - 1$, the consumer knows for sure that average quality is low. Similarly, a consumer knows average quality is high if the good received has quality above the upper bound of the distribution when average quality is low, i.e., $q > \underline{q} + 1$. Let $(1 - k)$ be the proportion of first period purchasers who learn average quality with certainty, i.e.,[3]

$$(1 - k) = \tfrac{1}{2}(\bar{q} - \underline{q}).$$

The remaining first period purchasers receive a product with quality $\bar{q} - 1 \leq q \leq \underline{q} + 1$. These $kx^1(p_1)$ consumers are unable to infer the product's average quality. Since it is assumed that q is uniformly distributed, these consumers receive no new information with which to revise their prior beliefs. Any quality level such that $\bar{q} - 1 \le q \le \underline{q} + 1$ is equally likely to have been generated by either distribution. Given q, prior probabilities are updated using Bayes rule as follows:

$$\Pr(\bar{q}|q) = \frac{\Pr(\bar{q})\Pr(q|\bar{q})}{\Pr(\bar{q})\Pr(q|\bar{q}) + \Pr(\underline{q})\Pr(q|\underline{q})}$$

$$= \frac{\rho(\frac{1}{2})}{\rho(\frac{1}{2}) + (1 - \rho)(\frac{1}{2})}$$

$$= \rho.$$

Similarly, $\Pr(\underline{q}|q) = (1 - \rho)$. Thus, their posterior probability beliefs are identical to their prior probability beliefs.

Demand in the second period, then, comes from three groups of potential purchasers: consumers who did not make a purchase in the first period, first period purchasers who acquired no information about the product's average quality, and first period purchasers who know the product's average quality. Second period demand and, hence, the optimal pricing strategy, is dependent on the average quality of the product. Therefore, the cases in which the firm produces a high and low average quality product are considered separately.

2. High Average Quality

Suppose the firm produces a high average quality product, i.e., $\mu = \bar{q}$. In this case, consumers who purchase a product either learn the product has high average quality or acquire no information. Consumer expectations are either raised or remain unchanged.

If the firm is aware of consumer learning, then there is an incentive to use the first period price to influence second period demand. By setting a price lower than a myopic firm and sacrificing some first period profits, the firm induces a larger number of consumers to buy its product. Due to this larger group of first period purchasers, a larger number of "loyal" consumers are created. With more loyal consumers, the firm maximizes second period profits by setting a price higher than that of a myopic firm.

The larger the proportion of consumers who learn in the first period that the product has high average quality, i.e., the shorter the overlap of the distributions, the lower the first period price and the higher the second period price. The larger this proportion, the more loyal consumers are created with any given price reduction and, thus, the greater the return in terms of second period profits from a given sacrifice of first period profits. The more learning that occurs, the larger the incentive for the firm to use its first period price to influence demand and, hence, the larger the difference between the myopic and rational optimal prices.

Consumers who purchased a good in the first period and learned that the product has high average quality buy the product in the second period if the expected utility of purchasing a high average quality product at a given price is at least as large as that from making no purchase, that is, if $\bar{q} \geq p_2$. As long as the price is less than the high level of average quality, all of these consumers make a purchase. There are $(1-k)\int_{\hat{\rho}(p_1)}^{1} g(\rho)d\rho$ of these consumers.

There are $k\int_{\hat{\rho}(p_1)}^{1} g(\rho)\,d\rho$ consumers who made a purchase in the first period but remain uncertain about the product's average quality. Since these consumers acquired no information in the first period, their expectations remain unchanged. Only those who believe that the product has high average quality with sufficiently high probability, $\rho \geq \hat{\rho}(p_2)$, make a purchase in the second period. If $\hat{\rho}(p_2) \leq \hat{\rho}(p_1)$, i.e., $p_2 \leq p_1$, all of the consumers are repeat purchasers. If however, $\hat{\rho}(p_2) > \hat{\rho}(p_1)$, i.e., $p_2 > p_1$, only $k\int_{\hat{\rho}(p_2)}^{1} g(\rho)\,d\rho$ consumers who are still uncertain about quality are repeat purchasers.

New consumers will enter the market if the price is lower in the second period. These consumers did not believe the firm's product had high average quality with sufficiently high probability given p_1 in order to make a purchase, i.e., $\rho < \hat{\rho}(p_1)$. Given a lower price, however, their expectations are high enough to buy the product, i.e., $\rho \geq \hat{\rho}(p_2)$. Then, if $p_2 \leq p_1$, $\int_{\hat{\rho}(p_2)}^{\hat{\rho}(p_1)} g(\rho)d\rho$ new consumers enter the market. If, however, $p_2 > p_1$, no new consumers enter the market.

Total demand in the second period when the firm produces a high average quality product $x^2(p_1, p_2; \bar{q})$ is

$$x^2(p_1, p_2; \bar{q}) = \begin{cases} x^1(p_2), & \text{when } 0 \leq p_2 \leq p_1, \\ \bar{x}^2(p_1, p_2), & \text{when } p_1 < p_2 \leq \bar{q}, \\ 0, & \text{when } \bar{q} < p_2, \end{cases}$$

where $x^1(p)$ is defined in (3.1) and

$$\bar{x}^2(p_1, p_2) = \int_{\hat{\rho}(p_2)}^{1} g(\rho)\,d\rho + (1-k)\int_{\hat{\rho}(p_1)}^{\hat{\rho}(p_2)} g(\rho)\,d\rho.$$

Notice that $x^{1'}(p_2) < 0$ and

$$\bar{x}_2^2(p_1, p_2) = -kg(\hat{\rho}(p_2))\hat{\rho}'(p_2) < 0,$$

where subscripts refer to partial derivatives, imply that demand is inversely related to the price set by the firm in the second period.

Second period demand is also a function of the first period price. Specifically,

$$x_1^2(p_1, p_2; \bar{q}) = \begin{cases} 0, & \text{when } 0 \le p_2 \le p_1, \\ \bar{x}_1^2(p_1, p_2), & \text{when } p_1 < p_2 \le \bar{q}, \end{cases}$$

where

$$\bar{x}_1^2(p_1, p_2) = -(1-k)g(\hat{\rho}(p_1))\hat{\rho}'(p_1) < 0.$$

Notice that, if the price is lower in the first period than in the second, then p_1 is inversely related to second period demand. First period purchasers who learned the product has high average quality and, consequently, make a purchase in the second period can be divided into two groups. The first group is consumers whose initial expectations are high enough given p_2 to make a purchase, i.e., $\rho \ge \hat{\rho}(p_2) > \hat{\rho}(p_1)$.

The second group is consumers whose initial expectations would not induce a purchase at price $p_2 (\hat{\rho}(p_2) > \rho \ge \hat{\rho}(p_1))$. However, since they learned in the first period that the product has high average quality, they make purchases in the second period. By lowering p_1, the firm increases the number of first period purchasers and consumers in the second group. At a lower p_1, consumers with lower expectations make purchases, some of whom learn that the product has high average quality. They, then, make purchases in the second period only because of the information acquired in the first period. Thus, the learning process has increased second period demand.

If, however, the price is lower in the second period than in the first, then the first period price has no effect on second period demand. In this case, all first period purchasers' initial expectations are high enough given p_2 to buy the product, i.e., $\rho \ge \hat{\rho}(p_1) \ge \hat{\rho}(p_2)$. There are, therefore, no consumers who would be unwilling to make purchases in the second period given period p_2 had they not learned in the first period that the product has high average quality. Since the learning process has not changed the purchasing decisions of consumers, changing p_1 has no effect on second period demand.

Given $x^1(p_1)$ and $x^2(p_1, p_2; \bar{q})$, the firm chooses a price in each period. A "rational" firm takes the effect of its first period price on future demand into consideration and chooses its prices to maximize the sum of discounted profits. A dynamic programming approach is used to model the firm's decision making process. First, consider the optimal second period price given any first period price.

Since the firm's second period demand function is segmented, the profit function $\pi^2(p_1, p_2; \bar{q})$ is composed of segments of two functions; one if $p_1 < p_2$, the other if $p_2 \leq p_1$. If $p_2 \leq p_1$, then $x^1(p_2)$ is the relevant segment of the demand function. Let $\pi^1(p_2)$ be the corresponding profit function where

$$\pi^1(p_1) = (p_1 - c)x^1(p_1) \tag{3.2}$$

and c is the constant marginal cost of production. Let $\hat{p}$ maximize $\pi^1(p)$[4], i.e.,

$$\pi^{1'}(\hat{p}) = 0. \tag{3.3}$$

If $p_1 < p_2 \leq \bar{q}$, then $\bar{x}^2(p_1, p_2)$ is the relevant segment of the demand function. Let $\bar{\pi}^2(p_1, p_2)$ be the corresponding profit function, i.e.,

$$\bar{\pi}^2(p_1, p_2) = (p_2 - c)\bar{x}^2(p_1, p_2). \tag{3.4}$$

Let $\bar{p}_2(p_1)$ maximize $\bar{\pi}^2(p_1, p_2)$, i.e.,

$$\bar{\pi}_2^2(p_1, \bar{p}_2(p_1)) = 0. \tag{3.5}$$

Then, in general, the second period profit function is

$$\pi^2(p_1, p_2; \bar{q}) = \begin{cases} \pi^1(p_2), & \text{when } 0 \leq p_2 \leq p_1, \\ \bar{\pi}^2(p_1, p_2), & \text{when } p_1 < p_2 \leq \bar{q}. \end{cases} \tag{3.6}$$

The optimal second period price $p_2^*(p_1; \bar{q})$ is either $\hat{p}$ or $\bar{p}_2(p_1)$. Lemma 1 states that $\bar{p}_2(p_1)$ is greater than $\hat{p}$ as long as $p_1 \leq \hat{p}$.

LEMMA 1. *For all $p_1 \leq \hat{p}$ and $0 \leq k < 1$, $\bar{p}_2(p_1) > \hat{p}$, where $\hat{p}$ and $\bar{p}_2(p_1)$ are defined in (3.3) and (3.5), respectively.*

Proof. Differentiating $\bar{\pi}^2(p_1, p_2)$ and $\pi^1(p_2)$ with respect to p_2 yields

$$\bar{\pi}_2^2(p_1, p_2) = -(p_2 - c)k\, g(\hat{\rho}(p_2))\hat{\rho}'(p_2)$$

$$+ \int_{\hat{\rho}(p_2)}^1 g(\rho)\, d\rho + (1 - k)\int_{\hat{\rho}(p_1)}^{\hat{\rho}(p_2)} g(\rho)\, d\rho \tag{3.7}$$

and

$$\pi^{1'}(p_2) = -(p_2 - c)g(\hat{\rho}(p_2))\hat{\rho}'(p_2) + \int_{\hat{\rho}(p_2)}^1 g(\rho)\, d\rho. \tag{3.8}$$

Equations (3.7) and (3.8) imply

$$\bar{\pi}_2^2(p_1, p_2) = \pi^{1'}(p_2)$$

$$+ (1 - k)\left\{ (p_2 - c)g(\hat{\rho}(p_2))\hat{\rho}'(p_2) + \int_{\hat{\rho}(p_1)}^{\hat{\rho}(p_2)} g(\rho)\, d\rho \right\}. \tag{3.9}$$

$\pi^{1'}(\hat{p}) = 0$ and (3.9) imply

$$\bar{\pi}_2^2(p_1, \hat{p}) = (1-k)\left\{ (\hat{p} - c)g(\hat{\rho}(\hat{p}))\hat{\rho}'(\hat{p}) + \int_{\hat{\rho}(p_1)}^{\hat{\rho}(\hat{p})} g(\rho)\, d\rho \right\}.$$

$p_1 < \hat{p}$ and, therefore, $\hat{\rho}(p_1) \leq \hat{\rho}(\hat{p})$, and $0 \leq k < 1$ imply $\bar{\pi}_2^2(p_1, \hat{p}) > 0$. $\bar{\pi}_2^2(p_1, \bar{p}_2(p_1)) = 0$ and $\bar{\pi}_{22}^2(p_1, p_2) < 0$ imply $\bar{p}_2(p_1) > \hat{p}$. □

If the firm considers the effect of its prices on future demand, then it chooses p_1 to maximize the sum of discounted profits $\Pi(p_1, p_2^*(p_1; \bar{q}); \bar{q})$, where $p_2^*(p_1; \bar{q})$ is the optimal second period price for any p_1 when the firm produces a product of high average quality. Since the second period profit function is segmented, $\Pi(p_1, p_2^*(p_1; \bar{q}); \bar{q})$ is likewise. Suppose that $p_1^*(\bar{q}) < p_2^*(p_1^*(\bar{q}); \bar{q})$, where $p_1^*(\bar{q})$ is the optimal first period price when the product has high average quality. From (3.6), $\bar{\pi}^2(p_1, p_2)$ is the relevant portion of the second period profit function and $p_2^*(p_1; \bar{q}) = \bar{p}_2(p_1)$. Let $\bar{\Pi}(p_1, \bar{p}_2(p_1))$ be the corresponding total profit function, i.e.,

$$\bar{\Pi}(p_1, \bar{p}_2(p_1)) = \pi^1(p_1) + \delta\bar{\pi}^2(p_1, \bar{p}_2(p_1)). \tag{3.10}$$

Let $\bar{p}_1$ maximize $\bar{\Pi}(p_1, \bar{p}_2(p_1))$, i.e.,

$$\frac{\partial \bar{\Pi}(\bar{p}_1, \bar{p}_2(\bar{p}_1))}{\partial p_1} = 0.$$

In this case, the optimal prices are $\bar{p}_1$ and $\bar{p}_2(\bar{p}_1)$.

From Lemma 1, $\bar{p}_2(p_1) > \hat{p}$ for all $p_1 < \hat{p}$. Lemma 2 which follows states that $\bar{p}_1 < \hat{p}$. Hence, $\bar{p}_1 < \bar{p}_2(\bar{p}_1)$ and the condition that $p_1^*(\bar{q}) < p_2^*(p_1^*(\bar{q}); \bar{q})$ is satisfied.

LEMMA 2.   *For all $p_2 > c$ and $0 \leq k < 1$, $\bar{p}_1 < \hat{p}$.*

Proof.   Differentiating $\bar{\Pi}(p_1, \bar{p}_2(p_1))$ with respect to p_1 and using the envelope theorem yields

$$\frac{\partial \bar{\Pi}(p_1, \bar{p}_2(p_1))}{\partial p_1} = \pi^{1'}(p_1) - \delta(\bar{p}_2(p_1) - c)(1-k)g(\hat{\rho}(p_1))\hat{\rho}(p_1). \tag{3.11}$$

$\pi^{1'}(\hat{p}) = 0$ and (3.11) imply

$$\frac{\partial \bar{\Pi}(\hat{p}, \bar{p}_2(\hat{p}))}{\partial p_1} = -\delta(\bar{p}_2(\hat{p}) - c)(1-k)g(\hat{\rho}(\hat{p}))\hat{\rho}'(\hat{p}) < 0.$$

$$\frac{\partial^2 \bar{\Pi}(p_1, \bar{p}_2(p_1))}{\partial p_1^2} < 0 \quad \text{and} \quad \frac{\partial \bar{\Pi}(\bar{p}_1, \bar{p}_2(\bar{p}_1))}{\partial p_1} = 0$$

imply $\bar{p}_1 < \hat{p}$. □

On the other hand, suppose that $p_1^*(\bar{q}) \geq p_2^*(p_1^*(\bar{q}); \bar{q})$. Then, $\pi^1(p_2)$ is the relevant portion of the second period profit function and $p_2^*(p_1; \bar{q}) = \hat{p}$. Since the firm chooses p_1 to maximize $\pi^1(p_1) + \delta\pi^1(p_2)$ and $\partial\pi^1(p_2)/\partial p_1 = 0$, the optimal first period price is $\hat{p}$. In this case, the optimal first and second period prices are identical.

Thus, two pricing strategies exist: $\langle \hat{p}, \hat{p} \rangle$ and $\langle \bar{p}_1, \bar{p}_2(\bar{p}_1) \rangle$. The optimal pricing strategy, however, is such that the first period price is lower than the second period price. These results are summarized in Theorem 1.

THEOREM 1. *When $\mu = \bar{q}$, the optimal prices are $\langle \bar{p}_1, \bar{p}_2(\bar{p}_1) \rangle$.*

Proof. Assume the contrary, i.e., the optimal prices are $\langle \hat{p}, \hat{p} \rangle$. Given $p_1 = \hat{p}$, $\pi^2(\hat{p}, p_2; \bar{q})$ as defined in (3.6) is shown in figure 3-1. Lemma 1 guarantees that $\bar{p}_2(\hat{p}) > \hat{p}$. From (3.2) and (3.4), if $p_1 = p_2 = \hat{p}$, $\bar{\pi}^2(\hat{p}, \hat{p}) = \pi^1(\hat{p})$. $\pi^{1''}(p) < 0$, $\bar{\pi}_{22}^2(p_1, p_2) < 0$, $\pi^{1'}(\hat{p}) = 0$, and $\bar{\pi}_2^2(\hat{p}, \bar{p}_2(\hat{p})) = 0$ then imply $\pi^1(\hat{p}) < \bar{\pi}^2(\hat{p}, \bar{p}_2(\hat{p}))$. Equation (3.10) then implies $(1 + \delta)\pi^1(\hat{p}) = \bar{\Pi}(\hat{p}, \bar{p}_2(\hat{p}))$. Since $\bar{p}_1$ is a maximizer, $\bar{\Pi}(\bar{p}_1, \bar{p}_2, (\bar{p}_1)) > \bar{\Pi}(\hat{p}, \bar{p}_2(\hat{p}))$. Hence, $\bar{\Pi}(\bar{p}_1, \bar{p}_2(\bar{p}_1)) > (1 + \delta)\pi^1(\hat{p})$ and $\langle \hat{p}, \hat{p} \rangle$ is not an optimal pricing strategy. $\square$

Thus, the optimal rational first period price is lower than the optimal myopic first period price. That is, equations (3.1–3.3) imply that the optimal myopic first period price is $\hat{p}$. Some first period purchasers learn the product has high average quality and, therefore, make purchases in the second period at a higher price than they would without this information. A group of "loyal" consumers is created. With the addition of the loyal consumers, the firm maximizes profits in the second period by charging a higher price. Specifically, it is shown in the

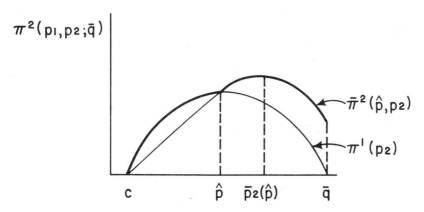

Figure 3-1.

proof of Theorem 1 that given $p_1 = \hat{p}$, the optimal second period price is $\bar{p}_2(\hat{p})$. A rational firm, however, will use its first period price to influence second period demand. A lower first period price increases the number of first period purchasers and, hence, the number of consumers who learn that the product has high average quality. With a larger number of loyal consumers, the rational firm charges a higher price. Thus, the second period price is not only higher than the first period price but higher than the myopic profit maximizing price. Lemma 1 implies $\bar{p}_2(\hat{p}) > \hat{p}$. Then, $\bar{p}_1 < \hat{p}$ and $d\bar{p}_2(p_1)/dp_1 < 0$[5] imply $\bar{p}_2(\hat{p}) < \bar{p}_2(\bar{p}_1)$. The larger the proportion of purchasers who learn that the product has high average quality, the larger the difference between the myopic and rational optimal prices.[6]

3. Low Average Quality

Now suppose that the firm produces a product of low average quality, i.e., $\mu = \underline{q}$. In this case, first period purchasers who learn the product has low average quality revise their expectations downward. The learning process by consumers reduces future demand when the product's average quality is low. Thus, the optimal pricing strategy in this case differs from the high average quality case in which the learning process increases future demand.

If the proportion of first period purchasers who learn about the product's average quality is sufficiently small, then the learning process has a relatively small negative effect on second period demand. Since second period demand is reduced by consumer learning, the optimal myopic second period price is lower than the first period price. A rational firm can reduce the negative effect of consumer learning, however, by charging a higher price in the first period. Fewer consumers learn about the product's low average quality, increasing second period demand. Although some first period profits are sacrificed, second period profits increase. A lower second period price induces consumers with lower expectations to make purchases. Such a pricing strategy enables the firms to "price discriminate" among consumer expectations over time.

If, however, the proportion of purchasers who learn is sufficiently large, then second period demand is so adversely affected by the learning process that the optimal pricing strategy is to charge the myopic profit maximizing price in the first period. In doing so, the firm extracts the maximum profits before any consumers learn that the product has low average quality. Since a significant number of consumers learn average quality in the first period, the optimal second period price is sufficiently low to compensate these consumers for the product's low average quality. All consumers make a purchase in the second period.

Here, as in the high average quality case, second period demand comes from three groups of consumers: consumers who did not make a purchase in the first period, first period purchasers who acquired no additional information after observing a sample of the product, and first period purchasers who learned the product's quality.

Consumers who know that the product's average quality is low are repeat purchasers in the second period only if the expected utility from purchasing a low average quality product at a given p_2 is at least as large as the utility from making no purchase, that is, if $\underline{q} \geq p_2$. In order to induce these consumers to buy the product, the firm must charge a price low enough to compensate them for the low average quality of the product. There are $(1-k)\int_{\hat{\rho}(p_1)}^1 g(\rho)\,d\rho$ of these consumers.

The remaining $k\int_{\hat{\rho}(p_1)}^1 g(\rho)\,d\rho$ first period purchasers who received no additional information with which to revise their expectations make a purchase if their initial expectations are sufficiently high given p_2, i.e., $\rho \geq \hat{\rho}(p_2)$. If $p_2 \leq p_1$ and, therefore, $\hat{\rho}(p_2) \leq \hat{\rho}(p_1)$, all of these consumers are repeat purchasers. If, however, $p_2 > p_1$ and $\hat{\rho}(p_2) > \hat{\rho}(p_1)$, only $k\int_{\hat{\rho}(p_2)}^1 g(\rho)\,d\rho$ of these consumers make a purchase, while the remaining $k\int_{\hat{\rho}(p_1)}^{\hat{\rho}(p_2)} g(\rho)\,d\rho$ consumers leave the market.

Here, as in the previous case, if the price is lower in the second period than in the first, $\int_{\hat{\rho}(p_2)}^{\hat{\rho}(p_1)} g(\rho)\,d\rho$ new consumers enter the market. If, however, $p_2 \geq p_1$, no new consumers make purchases.

The demand function in the second period $x^2(p_1, p_2; \underline{q})$ is

$$x^2(p_1, p_2; \underline{q}) = \begin{cases} 1, & \text{when } 0 \leq p_2 \leq \underline{q}, \\ \underline{x}^2(p_1, p_2), & \text{when } \underline{q} < p_2 < p_1, \\ kx^1(p_2), & \text{when } p_1 \leq p_2 \leq \bar{q}, \\ 0, & \text{when } \bar{q} < p_2, \end{cases}$$

where $x^1(p)$ is given in (3.1) and

$$\underline{x}^2(p_1, p_2) = k\int_{\hat{\rho}(p_1)}^1 g(\rho)\,d\rho + \int_{\hat{\rho}(p_2)}^{\hat{\rho}(p_1)} g(\rho)\,d\rho.$$

$kx^{1\prime}(p_2) < 0$ and $\underline{x}^2_2(p_1, p_2) = -g(\hat{\rho}(p_2))\hat{\rho}'(p_2) < 0$ imply that the second period demand is inversely related to p_2.

Here, as in the high average quality case, second period demand is also a function of the first period price. Specifically,

$$x^2_1(p_1, p_2) = \begin{cases} 0, & \text{when } 0 \leq p_2 \leq \underline{q}, \\ \underline{x}^2_1(p_1, p_2), & \text{when } \underline{q} < p_2 < p_1, \\ 0, & \text{when } p_1 \leq p_2, \end{cases}$$

where
$$\underline{x}_1^2(p_1, p_2) = (1 - k)g(\hat{\rho}(p_1))\hat{\rho}'(p_1) > 0.$$

Notice that, the relationship between the first period price and second period demand is symmetrical to that in the high average quality case. Here, if the price is lower in the second period than in the first but not as low as the low level of average quality, then p_1 is directly related to the second period demand. If $\underline{q} < p_2 < p_1$, all first period purchasers had initial expectations high enough to buy a product in the second period, i.e., $\rho \geq \hat{\rho}(p_1)$ and $\hat{\rho}(p_1) > \hat{\rho}(p_2)$ imply $\rho > \hat{\rho}(p_2)$. Some first period purchasers, however, learned that the product has low average quality and are unwilling to make a purchase when $p_2 > \underline{q}$. A higher p_1 reduces the number of first period purchasers and, hence, number of consumers who know the product has low average quality and leave the market. All of the consumers who no longer make a purchase in the first period due to a higher p_1 are now willing to buy the product, since all of their purchasing decisions are based on their initial expectations. Thus, second period demand is increased.

If, however, the second period price is higher than the first period price, then second period demand is unaffected by p_1. In the high average quality case, a lower p_1 increases the number of first period purchasers, some of whom revise their expectations upward and are then willing to pay a higher price in the future. In this case, however, consumers' expectations either remain unchanged or are lowered. A lower p_1 increases the number of consumers who lower their expectations. As long as $p_1 < p_2$, increasing p_1 has no effect on second period demand even though it reduces the number of consumers who learn the product's average quality and leave the market. Those consumers who no longer buy the product in the first period due to a higher p_1 are unwilling to buy the product in the second period based on their initial expectations, i.e., $\rho < \hat{\rho}(p_1)$ and $\hat{\rho}(p_1) < \hat{\rho}(p_2)$ imply $\rho < \hat{\rho}(p_2)$. Hence, second period demand is not increased.

In order to determine the optimal pricing strategy, first consider the optimal second period price given any first period price. Since the second period demand function $\pi^2(p_1, p_2; \underline{q})$ is composed of independent segments of three functions, the profit function is likewise: one if $0 \leq p_2 \leq \underline{q}$, a second if $\underline{q} < p_2 \leq p_1$, and a third if $p_1 < p_2 \leq \bar{q}$. If $0 \leq p_2 \leq \underline{q}$, then all consumers including those who know the product's low average quality make a purchase, i.e., $x^2(p_1, p_2; \underline{q}) = 1$. Let $\underline{\pi}(p_2)$ be the corresponding profit function, i.e.,

$$\underline{\pi}(p_2) = p_2 - c. \tag{3.12}$$

Since no new consumers are induced into the market at a price below $\underline{q}$, $\underline{\pi}(p_2)$ is maximized when $p_2 = \underline{q}$.

Let $\underline{\pi}^2(p_1, p_2)$ be the profit function corresponding to the demand function when $\underline{q} < p_2 \leq p_1$, $\underline{x}^2(p_1, p_2)$. That is,

$$\underline{\pi}^2(p_1, p_2) = (p_2 - c)\left\{k \int_{\hat{\rho}(p_1)}^1 g(\rho)\,d\rho + \int_{\hat{\rho}(p_2)}^{\hat{\rho}(p_1)} g(\rho)\,d\rho\right\}. \tag{3.13}$$

Let $\underline{p}_2(p_1)$ maximize $\underline{\pi}^2(p_1, p_2)$, i.e., $\underline{\pi}_2^2(p_1, \underline{p}_2(p_1)) = 0$.

Suppose that the second period price is so high that not only do consumers who know the product's low average quality leave the market but no new consumers enter the market, i.e., $p_1 < p_2 \leq \bar{q}$. Then, $kx^1(p_2)$ is the relevant segment of the demand function. The corresponding profit function $k\pi^1(p_2)$ is maximized when $p_2 = \hat{p}$, where $\pi^1(p)$ and $\hat{p}$ are defined in (3.2) and (3.3), respectively. Here, the second period profit function is proportional to the first profit function, since some proportion of first period purchasers have left the market and the remaining consumers have not changed their expectations.

The second period profit function is

$$\pi^2(p_1, p_2; q) = \begin{cases} \underline{\pi}(p_2), & \text{when } 0 \leq p_2 \leq \underline{q}, \\ \underline{\pi}^2(p_1, p_2), & \text{when } \underline{q} < p_2 < p_1, \\ k\pi^1(p_2), & \text{when } p_1 \leq p_2 \leq \bar{q}, \\ 0, & \text{when, } \bar{q} < p_2. \end{cases} \tag{3.14}$$

From (3.2) and (3.13), if $p_1 = p_2$, then $\underline{\pi}^2(p_1, p_2) = k\pi^1(p_2)$, i.e., the profit function is continuous at $p_1 = p_2$. The profit function is not, however, continuous at $p_2 = \underline{q}$. If p_2 is slightly larger than $\underline{q}$, all consumers who know the product's low average quality leave the market. Specifically,

$$\underline{\pi}(\underline{q}) = \underline{q} - c$$

$$> (\underline{q} - c)\left\{k \int_{\hat{\rho}(p_1)}^1 g(\rho)\,d\rho + \int_0^{\hat{\rho}(p_1)} g(\rho)\,d\rho\right\}$$

$$= \underline{\pi}^2(p_1, \underline{q}).$$

The optimal second period price is either $\underline{q}, \underline{p}_2(p_1)$ or $\hat{p}$. Lemma 3 states that $\underline{p}_2(p_1)$ is less than the optimal myopic first period price $\hat{p}$.

LEMMA 3. *For all $0 \leq k < 1$, $\underline{p}_2(p_1) < \hat{p}$.*

Proof. Differentiating $\underline{\pi}^2(p_1, p_2)$ with respect to p_2 yields

$$\underline{\pi}_2^2(p_1, p_2) = -(p_2 - c)g(\hat{\rho}(p_2))\hat{\rho}'(p_2)$$

$$+ k\int_{\hat{\rho}(p_1)}^1 g(\rho)\,d\rho + \int_{\hat{\rho}(p_2)}^{\hat{\rho}(p_1)} g(\rho)\,d\rho. \tag{3.15}$$

Rewriting (3.15) and substituting (3.8) yields

$$\underline{\pi}_2^2(p_1, p_2) = \pi^{1'}(p_2) - (1-k)\int_{\hat{\rho}(p_1)}^{1} g(\rho)\,d\rho.$$

$\pi^{1'}(\hat{p})$ implies

$$\underline{\pi}_2^2(p_1, \hat{p}) = -(1-k)\int_{\hat{\rho}(p_1)}^{1} g(\rho)\,d\rho < 0.$$

Since $\underline{\pi}_2^2(p_1, \underline{p}_2(p_1)) = 0$ and $\underline{\pi}_{22}^2(p_1, p_2) < 0$, $\underline{p}_2(p_1) < \hat{p}$ for all $0 \le k < 1$. □

Here, as in the high average quality case, a rational firm chooses $p_1^*(\underline{q})$ to maximize the sum of discounted profits given $p_2^*(p_1; \underline{q})$. First, suppose $p_2^*(p_1^*(\underline{q}); \underline{q}) \le \underline{q}$. From (3.9), $\underline{\pi}(p_2)$ is the relevant segment of the profit function and $p_2^*(p_1; \underline{q}) = \underline{q}$. Let $\underline{\underline{\Pi}}(p_1, \underline{q})$ be the corresponding total profit function, i.e.,

$$\underline{\underline{\Pi}}(p_1, \underline{q}) = \pi^1(p_1) + \delta\underline{\pi}(\underline{q}). \tag{3.16}$$

Since

$$\frac{\partial \underline{\underline{\Pi}}(p_1, \underline{q})}{\partial p_1} = \pi^{1'}(p_1),$$

and $\pi^{1'}(\hat{p}) = 0$, $p_1^*(\underline{q}) = \hat{p}$. Therefore, if $p_2^*(p_1; \underline{q}) \le \underline{q}$, the firm charges the optimal myopic price in the first period, thereby extracting maximum profits before any consumers learn that the product has low average quality. The second period price is low enough to compensate those consumers who learn average quality. Thus, all consumers make a purchase in the second period.

Now suppose that $\underline{q} < p_2^*(p_1^*(\underline{q}); \underline{q}) < p_1^*(\underline{q})$. Then, $\underline{\pi}^2(p_1, p_2)$ is the relevant segment of the second period profit function and $p_2^*(p_1; \underline{q}) = \underline{p}_2(p_1)$. Let $\underline{\Pi}(p_1, \underline{p}_2(p_1))$ be the corresponding total profit function, where

$$\underline{\Pi}(p_1, \underline{p}_2(p_1)) = \pi^1(p_1) + \delta\underline{\pi}^2(p_1, \underline{p}_2(p_1)). \tag{3.17}$$

Let $\underline{p}_1$ maximize $\underline{\Pi}(p_1, \underline{p}_2(p_1))$, i.e.,

$$\frac{\partial\underline{\Pi}(p_1, \underline{p}_2(p_1))}{\partial p_1} = 0.$$

In this case, the optimal prices are $\underline{p}_1$ and $\underline{p}_2(\underline{p}_1)$. Lemma 3 guarantees that $\underline{p}_2(\underline{p}_1) < \hat{p}$. Lemma 4 which follows states that $\underline{p}_1 > \hat{p}$. Therefore, $\underline{p}_2(\underline{p}_1)$ and $\underline{p}_1$ satisfy the condition that $p_2^*(p_1^*(\underline{q}); \underline{q}) < p_1^*(\underline{q})$.

LEMMA 4.   For all $0 \le k < 1$, $\underline{p}_1 > \hat{p}$.

Proof.   Differentiating $\underline{\Pi}(p_1, \underline{p}_2(p_1))$ with respect to p_1 yields

$$\frac{\partial\underline{\Pi}(p_1, \underline{p}_2(p))}{\partial p_1} = \pi^{1'}(p_1) + \delta(\underline{p}_2(p_1) - c)(1-k)g(\hat{\rho}(p_1))\hat{\rho}'(p_1). \tag{3.18}$$

$\pi^{1'}(\hat{p}) = 0$ and (3.18) imply

$$\frac{\partial \underline{\Pi}(\hat{p}, \underline{p}_2(\hat{p}))}{\partial p_1} = \delta(\underline{p}_2(\hat{p}) - c)(1 - k)g(\hat{\rho}(\hat{p}))\hat{\rho}'(\hat{p}) > 0.$$

$$\frac{\partial \underline{\Pi}(p_1, \underline{p}_2(p_1))}{\partial p_1} = 0 \quad \text{and} \quad \frac{\partial^2 \underline{\Pi}(p_1, \underline{p}_2(p_1))}{\partial p_1^2} < 0$$

imply $\underline{p}_1 > \hat{p}$ for all $0 \le k < 1$. $\square$

In this case, a rational firm scarifices some first period profits by charging a price higher than the optimal myopic price. In doing so, the number of first period purchasers is reduced and fewer consumers learn about the product's low average quality. Still, some first period purchasers learn that the product has low average quality and will only make a purchase at a very low second period price. Hence, second period demand decreases. In response to this reduction in demand, the firm lowers the price below its optimal first period price, thereby, inducing new consumers with lower expectations into the market.

The second period price reduction, however, is less than the price reduction by a myopic firm. $\underline{p}_1 > \hat{p}$ and $(d\underline{p}_2(p_1))/dp_1 > 0$[7] imply $\underline{p}_2(\underline{p}_1) > \underline{p}_2(\hat{p})$. By setting a price in the first period higher than the myopic firm, the rational firm reduces the negative effect of the learning process by consumers on second period demand. Although the rational firm is able to charge a second period price higher than the myopic firm, it is still lower than the optimal myopic first period price, i.e., $\underline{p}_2(\hat{p}) < \underline{p}_2(\underline{p}_1) < \hat{p}$.

Finally, suppose $p_1^*(\underline{q}) \le p_2^*(p_1^*(\underline{q}); \underline{q}) \le \bar{q}$. Then $k\pi^1(p_2)$ is the relevant segment of the second period profit function and $p_2^*(p_1, q) = \hat{p}$. Since second period profits are not affected by p_1 when $p_1 < p_2$, the optimal first period price is $\hat{p}$. In this case, the optimal prices are identical to the optimal prices when no learning occurs, i.e., $p_1^*(\underline{q}) = p_2^*(p_1^*(\underline{q}); \underline{q}) = \hat{p}$. Theroem 2 implies, however, that this pricing strategy is never profit-maximizing when consumer learning occurs.

Two possibly optimal pricing strategies remain. In the first case, the firm charges the optimal myopic price in the first period. The second period price is low enough so that all consumers, including those who are aware of the product's low average quality, make a purchase. In the second case, the firm sets a price higher than that of the myopic firm in the first period. The second period price, although lower than the optimal first period price, is higher than that of the myopic firm. The optimal pricing strategy depends on the proportion of first period consumers who learn average quality.

If no learning occurs in the first period, i.e., $k = 1$, then the firm sets $p_1 = \hat{p}$ and maintains that price in the second period. When some consumers learn that the product has low average quality in the first period, however, i.e., $k < 1$, the optimal rational prices differ from the optimal myopic prices. In order to determine the optimal pricing strategy, let

$$\beta(k) = \underline{\underline{\Pi}}(\hat{p}, \underline{q}, k) - \underline{\Pi}(\underline{p}_1, \underline{p}_2(\underline{p}_1), k). \tag{3.19}$$

If there exists a $\bar{k}_L$ such that

$$\beta(\bar{k}_L) > 0, \tag{3.20}$$

then there exists a unique $\bar{k}$ such that

$$\beta(\bar{k}) = 0. \tag{3.21}$$

If the proportion of consumers who remain uncertain about the product's average quality after observing a sample is sufficiently small, i.e., $0 \le k \le \bar{k}$, then the optimal prices are $\hat{p}$ and $\underline{q}$. If, however, this proportion is sufficiently large, i.e., $\bar{k} < k \le 1$, then the optimal prices are $\underline{p}_1$ and $\underline{p}_2(\underline{p}_1)$. If $\bar{k}_L$ does not exist, then $\underline{p}_1$ and $\underline{p}_2(\underline{p}_1)$ are the optimal prices for all k. These results are summarized in Theorem 2.

THEOREM 2. *If there exists a $\bar{k}_L$ defined in (3.20), then there exists a unique $\bar{k}$ defined in (3.21). If $0 \le k \le \bar{k}$, then the optimal rational prices are $\langle p_1^*(\underline{q}), p_2^*(p_1^*(\underline{q}); \underline{q}) \rangle = \langle \hat{p}, \underline{q} \rangle$. If, however, $\bar{k} < k \le 1$, then $\langle p_1^*(\underline{q}), p_2^*(p_1^*(\underline{q}); \underline{q}) \rangle = \langle \underline{p}_1, \underline{p}_2(\underline{p}_1) \rangle$. If $\bar{k}_L$ does not exist, then $\langle p_1^*(\underline{q}), p_2^*(p_1^*(\underline{q}); \underline{q}) \rangle = \langle \underline{p}_1, \underline{p}_2(\underline{p}_1) \rangle$ for all k.*

Proof. The optimal prices are either $\langle \hat{p}, \hat{p} \rangle$, $\langle \hat{p}, \underline{q} \rangle$, or $\langle \underline{p}_1, \underline{p}_2(\underline{p}_1) \rangle$. Suppose that the optimal prices are $\langle \hat{p}, \hat{p} \rangle$. Given $p_1 = \hat{p}$, $\pi^2(\hat{p}, p_2; \underline{q})$ which is defined in (3.14) is shown in figure 3-2. Lemma 3 guarantees that $\underline{p}_2(\hat{p}) < \hat{p}$

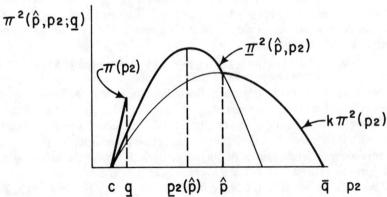

Figure 3-2.

if $0 \le k < 1$. From (3.2) and (3.13), at $p_1 = p_2 = \hat{p}$, $k\pi^1(\hat{p}) = \underline{\pi}^2(\hat{p}, \hat{p})$. Then, $\pi^{1''}(p) < 0$, $\underline{\pi}^2_{22}(p_1, p_2) < 0$, $\pi^{1'}(\hat{p}) = 0$, and $\underline{\pi}^2_2(\hat{p}, p_2(\hat{p})) = 0$ imply $k\pi^1(\hat{p}) < \underline{\pi}^2(\hat{p}, p_2(\hat{p}))$. Equation (3.17) then implies $(1 + \delta k)\pi^1(\hat{p}) < \underline{\Pi}(\hat{p}, \underline{p}_2(\hat{p}))$. Hence, $\langle \hat{p}, \hat{p} \rangle$ is not an optimal pricing strategy.

The optimal prices then are either $\langle \hat{p}, \underline{q} \rangle$ or $\langle p_1, \underline{p}_2(p_1) \rangle$. Suppose no learning occurs, i.e., $k = 1$. Equations (3.11) and (3.3) imply $\underline{p}_1 = \hat{p}$. Profits in the second period are either $\underline{\pi}(\underline{q})$ or $\underline{\pi}^2(\hat{p}, \underline{p}_2(\hat{p}))$. Since $\hat{\rho}(\underline{q}) = 0$, (3.14) implies $\underline{\pi}(\underline{q}) = \underline{\pi}^2(\hat{p}, \underline{q})$ when $k = 1$. Since $\underline{p}_2(p_1)$ is a maximizer, $\underline{\pi}^2(\hat{p}, \underline{p}_2(\hat{p})) > \underline{\pi}^2(\hat{p}, \underline{q})$. Equations (3.16) and (3.17) then imply $\underline{\underline{\Pi}}(\hat{p}, \underline{q}) < \underline{\underline{\Pi}}(\hat{p}, \underline{p}_2(\hat{p}))$, i.e., $\beta(1) < 0$, where $\beta(k)$ is defined in (3.19).

Differentiating $\beta(k)$ with respect to k yields

$$\beta'(k) = -\delta(\underline{p}_2(\underline{p}_1) - c) \int_{\hat{\rho}(\underline{p}_1)}^{1} g(\rho)\, d\rho < 0.$$

$\beta'(k) < 0$ implies that if $\bar{k}_L$ exists, where $\beta(\bar{k}_L) > 0$, then there exists a unique $\bar{k}$ such that $\beta(\bar{k}) = 0$. See figure 3-3.

Since $\beta'(k) < 0$, if $k > \bar{k}$, then $\underline{\underline{\Pi}}(\hat{p}, \underline{q}, k) \le \underline{\underline{\Pi}}(\underline{p}_1, \underline{p}_2(\underline{p}_1), k)$ and $\langle p_1^*(\underline{q}), p_2^*(p_1^*(\underline{q}), \underline{q}) \rangle = \langle \underline{p}_1, \underline{p}_2(\underline{p}_1) \rangle$. If, however, $k \le \bar{k}$, then $\underline{\underline{\Pi}}(\hat{p}, \underline{q}, k) \le \underline{\underline{\Pi}}(\underline{p}_1, \underline{p}_2(\underline{p}_1), \bar{k})$ and $\langle p_1^*(\underline{q}), p_2^*(p_1^*(\underline{q}), \underline{q}) \rangle = \langle \hat{p}, \underline{q} \rangle$. If $\bar{k}_L$ does not exist then $\beta'(k) < 0$ and $\beta(1) \le 0$ imply $\beta(k) \le 0$, i.e., $\underline{\underline{\Pi}}(\hat{p}, \underline{q}, k) \le \underline{\underline{\Pi}}(\underline{p}_1, \underline{p}_2(\underline{p}_1), k)$, for all k. Hence, $\langle p_1^*(\underline{q}), p_2^*(p_1^*(\underline{q}), \underline{q}) \rangle = \langle \underline{p}_1, \underline{p}_2(\underline{p}_1) \rangle$ for all k. $\square$

As the proportion of purchasers who learn about the product's low average quality increases, second period demand and profits are reduced.[8] Given p_1, the firm's optimal second period price tends to fall in response to the reduction in demand.[9] Then, as k decreases, $\underline{p}_2(\hat{p}, k)$ becomes a less profitable

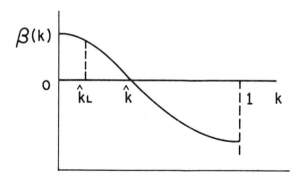

Figure 3-3.

pricing strategy. If the proportion of consumers who learn average quality is sufficiently large, the optimal second period price is $\underline{q}$ which is low enough so that all consumers are willing to make a purchase. According to Lemma 5, $\langle \hat{p}, \underline{q} \rangle$ becomes an optimal pricing strategy for the myopic firm when less consumer learning occurs than for the rational firm. In order to state Lemma 5, let

$$\hat{\beta}(k) = \underline{\pi}(\underline{q}) - \underline{\pi}^2(\hat{p}, \underline{p}_2(\hat{p}), k). \tag{3.22}$$

It can be shown in a manner similar to the proof of Theorem 2 that a unique $\hat{k}$ exists such that $\hat{\beta}(\hat{k}) = 0$.

LEMMA 5. $\hat{k} \geq \bar{k}$.

Proof. $k \leq \bar{k}$ implies $\overline{\Pi}(\hat{p}, \underline{q}) \geq \underline{\Pi}(\underline{p}_1, \underline{p}_2(\underline{p}_1))$. Since $\underline{p}_1$ is a maximizer, $\underline{\Pi}(\underline{p}_1, \underline{p}_2(\underline{p}_1)) \geq \underline{\Pi}(\hat{p}, \underline{p}_2(\hat{p}))$. Then, $k \leq \bar{k}$ implies $k \leq \hat{k}$, i.e., $\underline{\Pi}(\hat{p}, \underline{q}) \geq \underline{\Pi}(\hat{p}, \underline{p}_2(\hat{p}))$.

Similarly, $k \geq \hat{k}$ implies $\underline{\Pi}(\hat{p}, \underline{p}_2(\hat{p})) \geq \underline{\Pi}(\hat{p}, \underline{q})$. Since $\underline{\Pi}(\underline{p}_1, \underline{p}_2(\underline{p}_1)) \geq \underline{\Pi}(\hat{p}, \underline{p}_2(\hat{p}))$, $k \geq \hat{k}$, implies $k \geq \bar{k}$, i.e., $\underline{\Pi}(\underline{p}_1, \underline{p}_2(\underline{p}_1)) \geq \underline{\Pi}(\hat{p}, \underline{q})$. Hence, $\bar{k} < \hat{k}$. $\square$

As long as $k > \bar{k}$, however, $\langle \underline{p}_1, \underline{p}_2(\underline{p}_1) \rangle$ remains a profitable pricing strategy for the firm. As the negative effect of the learning process on second period demand increases, the incentive to set a high price in the first period so as to reduce the negative effect of consumer learning increases. Consequently, the optimal first period price tends to rise.[10] The smaller k, the larger the return in terms of increased second period profits from any increase in p_1 and sacrifice in first period profits. However, since as k decreases, $p_2(p_1, k)$ decreases, the value of any increased second period demand decreases. This indirect effect of increased consumer learning on the optimal first period price reduces the incentive to set a higher first period price. Thus, the net effect of an increase in consumer learning on the optimal first period price depends on the relative strengths of the above direct and indirect effects.[11]

If the proportion of first period purchasers who learn average quality is sufficiently large, i.e., $k \leq k$, it is no longer profitable for the rational firm to attempt to "hide" the product's low average quality. In this case both the rational and myopic firms maximize profits when $\langle p_1^*(\underline{q}), p_2^*(p_1^*(\underline{q}); \underline{q}) \rangle = \langle \hat{p}, \underline{q} \rangle$.

4. Concluding Remarks

This chapter has examined the effect of consumer learning about product quality on optimal pricing strategies when product quality varies uniformly.

Since consumers are uncertain whether the average quality is high or low, their purchasing decisions are based on their individual expectations.

It was shown that demand for the product depends on the distribution of expectations among consumers. Since expectations are revised as consumers acquire private information from product usage, demand and, hence, the price which maximizes current profits changes over time. Since consumer learning in each period is, in general, incomplete, it has a continuing effect on prices over time.

In addition, it was shown that a firm can use its price to influence the rate of consumer learning and, hence, future demand. Future profits are thus increased. The incentive to use current prices to influence the rate of learning depends on the actual distribution of product quality relative to the distribution of consumer expectations. A rational firm which produces a high (low) average quality product has an incentive to initially set a price lower (higher) than the price which maximizes initial profits. By increasing (decreasing) the rate of consumer learning, future demand is increased.

Although the specific pricing strategies derived from this model depend on the assumptions of product quality and prior expectations, the implications of these results are more general (see Goering [1985b]). In particular, these results imply that the effect of current prices on future demand due to consumer learning about quality from product usage is one factor, among others, to be considered in determining optimal pricing strategies. An investigation of the effect of information acquired from sources other than product experience such as advertising, prices, warranties, etc., as well as the effect of the existence of substitute products on the optimal decision making of consumers and firms is left for future research.

Notes

1. See Goering (1985a), pp. 75–76 for a discussion of the sources of variation in expectations.

2. See Goering (1985a), pp. 76–77 for a discussion of the applicability of this model to products with imperfectly observable quality and inaccurate perceptions of quality.

3. When $\mu = \bar{q}$, $(1-k) = \int_{q+1}^{\bar{q}+1} \frac{1}{2} dp = \frac{1}{2}(\bar{q}-\underline{q})$. Similarly, when $\mu = \underline{q}$, $(1-k)\int_{\underline{q}-1}^{\bar{q}-1} \frac{1}{2} dq = \frac{1}{2}(\bar{q}-\underline{q})$.

4. It is assumed throughout this chapter that the second-order conditions for a unique maximum are satisfied. This is essentially an assumption on the density function of consumer expectations. Specifically, it assumes $g'(\rho)$ is sufficiently small or positive.

5. Specifically,

$$\frac{d\bar{p}_2(p_1)}{dp_1} = \frac{(1-k)g(\hat{\rho}(p_1))\hat{\rho}'(p_1)}{\pi_{22}^2(p_1, \bar{p}_2(p_1))} < 0.$$

6. Specifically,

$$
\begin{aligned}
\frac{d\bar{p}_1(k)}{dk} &= \frac{-\delta(1-k)g(\hat{\rho}(p_1))\hat{\rho}'(p_1)\left[k(p_2-c)g(\hat{\rho}(p_2))\hat{\rho}'(p_2)+k\int_{\hat{\rho}(p_1)}^{\hat{\rho}(p_2)}g(\rho)\,d\rho\right]}{\kappa(p_1,p_2)} \\
&\quad -\frac{\delta k(p_2-c)g(\hat{\rho}(p_1))\hat{\rho}'(p_1)\{k(p_2-c)g'(\hat{\rho}(p_2))\hat{\rho}'(p_2)^2+k2g(\hat{\rho}(p_2))\hat{\rho}'(p_2)\}}{\kappa(p_1,p_2)}>0,
\end{aligned}
$$

and

$$
\begin{aligned}
\frac{d\bar{p}_2(\bar{p}_1(k),k)}{dk} &= \frac{[(p_1-c)g'(\hat{\rho}(p_1))\hat{\rho}'(p_1)^2+2g(\hat{\rho}(p_1))\hat{\rho}'(p_1)-\delta(1-k)(p_2-c)g'(\hat{\rho}(p_1))\hat{\rho}'(p_1)^2]}{\kappa(p_1,p_2)} \\
&\quad \cdot\left[k(p_2-c)g(\hat{\rho}(p_2))\hat{\rho}'(p_2)+k\int_{\hat{\rho}(p_1)}^{\hat{\rho}(p_2)}g(\rho)\,d\rho\right] \\
&\quad -\frac{(1-k)g(\hat{\rho}(p_1))^2\hat{\rho}'(p_1)^2k\delta(p_2-c)}{\kappa(p_1,p_2)}<0,
\end{aligned}
$$

where

$$
\begin{aligned}
\kappa(p_1,p_2) &= \delta(1-k)^2g(\hat{\rho}(p_1))^2\hat{\rho}'(p_1)^2 \\
&\quad -[k(p_2-c)g'(\hat{\rho}(p_2))\hat{\rho}'(p_2)^2+2g(\hat{\rho}(p_2))\hat{\rho}'(p_2)] \\
&\quad \cdot[(p_1-c)g'(\hat{\rho}(p_1))\hat{\rho}'(p_1)^2+2g(\hat{\rho}(p_1))\hat{\rho}'(p_1)+\delta(1-k)(p_2-c)g'(\hat{\rho}(p_1))\hat{\rho}'(p_1)^2]<0.
\end{aligned}
$$

7. Specifically,

$$
\frac{dp_2(p_1)}{dp_1}=\frac{(1-k)g(\hat{\rho}(p_1))\hat{\rho}'(p_1)}{-\pi_{22}^2(p_1,p_2)}>0.
$$

8. In particular,

$$
\frac{d\underline{\Pi}(\underline{p}_1(k),\underline{p}_2(\underline{p}_1(k),k),k)}{dk}=\delta(\underline{p}_2(\underline{p}_1(k),k)-c)\int_{\hat{\rho}(\underline{p}_1(k))}^{1}g(\rho)\,d\rho>0.
$$

9. Specifically,

$$
\frac{\delta p_2(p_1,k)}{\partial k}=\frac{-\int_{\hat{\rho}(p_1)}^{1}g(\rho)\,d\rho}{\pi_{22}^2(p_1,p_2,k)}>0.
$$

10. Given p_2,

$$
\frac{d\underline{p}_1(k)}{dk}=\frac{\delta(p_2-c)g(\hat{\rho}(p_1))\hat{\rho}'(p_1)}{(\delta^2\underline{\Pi}(p_1,\underline{p}_2(p_1)))/\delta p_1^2}<0.
$$

11. Specifically,

$$\frac{dp_1(k)}{dk} = \frac{-\delta(1-k)g(\hat{\rho}(p_1))\hat{\rho}'(p_1)\int_{\hat{\rho}(p_1)}^1 g(\rho)\,d\rho}{o(p_1,p_2)}$$
$$+ \frac{\delta(p_2-c)g(\hat{\rho}'(p_1))\hat{\rho}'(p_1)[(p_2-c)g'(\hat{\rho}(p_2))\hat{\rho}'(p_2)^2 + 2g(\hat{\rho}(p_2))\hat{\rho}'(p_2)]}{o(p_1,p_2)},$$

and

$$\frac{dp_2(\underline{p}_1(k),k)}{dk} = \frac{-(1-k)g(\hat{\rho}(p_1))^2\hat{\rho}'(p_1)^2\delta(p_2-c)}{o(p_1,p_2)}$$
$$+ \left(\int_{\hat{\rho}(p_1)}^1 g(\rho)\,d\rho[-(p_1-c)g'(\hat{\rho}(p_1))\hat{\rho}'(p_1)^2 - 2g(\hat{\rho}(p_1))\hat{\rho}'(p_1) \right.$$
$$\left. + \delta(1-k)(p_2-c)g'(\hat{\rho}(p_1))\hat{\rho}'(p_1)^2] \right) \Big/ o(p_1,p_2),$$

where

$$o(p_1,p_2) = \delta(1-k)^2 g(\hat{\rho}(p_1))^2\hat{\rho}'(p_1)^2 + \delta(p_2-c)g(\hat{\rho}(p_2))\hat{\rho}'(p_2)[(p_2-c)g'(\hat{\rho}(p_2))\hat{\rho}'(p_2)^2$$
$$+ 2g(\hat{\rho}(p_2))\hat{\rho}'(p_2)] < 0.$$

References

Cremer, J., "On the Economics of Repeat Buying." *The Rand Journal of Economics*, 15 (1984), 396–403.

Goering, P. A., "Effects of Product Trial on Consumer Expectations, Demand and Prices." *Journal of Consumer Research*, 12 (1985a), 74–82.

Goering, P. A., "Learning Quality and Prices." *Information Economics and Policy* (forthcoming), 1985b.

Grossman, S. J., Kihlstrom, R. E. and Mirman, L. J., "A Bayesian Approach to the Production of Information and Learning by Doing." *Review of Economic Studies*, H44 (1977), 533–547.

Hirshleifer, J. and Riley, S. G., "The Analytics of Uncertainty and Information — An Expository Survey." *Journal of Economic Literature*, 17 (1979), 1421–1575.

Shapiro, C., "Optimal Pricing of Experience Goods." *The Bell Journal of Economics*, 14 (1983), 497–507.

Smallwood, D. E. and Conlisk, J. "Product Quality in Markets Where Consumers are Imperfectly Informed." *Quarterly Journal of Economics*, 93 (1979), 1–23.

4 RATIONALITY AND SOCIAL CHOICE

Douglas H. Blair
and
Robert A. Pollak

Are there "consistent" procedures for aggregating individuals' preferences into collective judgments? This question was first posed formally more than thirty years ago by the economist Kenneth J. Arrow, now of Stanford University. After listing intuitively appealing properties that any preference aggregation procedure should satisfy, Arrow proved that these properties were incompatible: no procedure satisfying all of Arrow's axioms can be found, not for lack of ingenuity, but because none exists. Consistency is impossible.[1]

Over the last 15 years philosophers, economists, and political scientists have reexamined Arrow's axioms seeking to circumvent his "impossibility theorem" by relaxing his requirements. The problem has attracted widespread interest because it is closely linked with central questions in each of these disciplines. Philosophers face it, for example, when operationalizing the ethical doctrine of utilitarianism, which holds that the rightness of actions depends on their consequences for people's happiness. Political scientists encounter it when

This paper is an extended and more technical version of Blair and Pollak [1983].

evaluating or designing voting rules for committees or legislatures. Economists confront it when analyzing rationing and other nonmarket resource allocation or planning mechanisms. This task is an important one in normative economics, since in determining the appropriate scope for governmental intervention in the operations of the free market, it is crucial to have an understanding of the potential performance of its alternatives. Arrow's work has also attracted the attention of game theorists and other mathematicians and represents one of the first uses of the techniques of formal logic in economics or social science. In part for this theorem Arrow shared the Nobel prize in economics in 1972.

Majority rule deserves first consideration among preference-aggregation procedures, based on considerations of simplicity, equality, and tradition. But when more than two alternatives must be ranked, majority rule encounters a difficulty, as the philosopher Condorcet recognized nearly two hundred years ago.[2] The problem, the "paradox of voting," is easily illustrated. Consider a three-member committee that must collectively rank three candidates, A, B, and C. The first member prefers A to B to C, the second B to C to A, and the third C to A to B. Then candidate A defeats candidate B (two votes to one), B defeats C (two votes to one), but C defeats A (two votes to one). In this case the ranking based on majority voting is cyclic, even though each member's preferences are internally consistent. Numerous historical and contemporary cases of preference configurations yielding voting cycles have been found. For example, William H. Riker argues that the passage of the Seventeenth Amendment, providing for the direct election of senators, was delayed for ten years by parliamentary maneuvers that depended on voting cycles involving two versions of the Amendment and the status quo.[3]

When the feasible set contains more than two alternatives, some new principle is needed for generating choices from pairwise rankings. The preferences that induce the paradox of voting create difficulties for each natural method for making this transition. The simplest method, originally proposed by Condorcet, chooses from the feasible set the alternative that defeated all others. However, when the paradox of voting occurs, no such alternative exists, since each alternative (e.g., candidate) is defeated by another. A second method for proceeding from pairwise rankings to choices is to specify an agenda, listing the sequence in which pairs of alternatives are taken up and compared. For example, an agenda might call for an initial vote on A and B, followed by a second stage in which the winner of the first ballot is compared with C. Under this agenda, on the first ballot A defeats B, and on the second C defeats A; thus the ultimate winner is C. It is easy to verify, however, that under each of the three possible agendas of this form, the candidate taken up last will emerge the victor. Which of the three candidates is chosen thus depends on which of the three agendas is used. This sensitivity suggests that voting cycles pose substantive as well as aesthetic difficulties: when cycles occur the choice of an ultimate winner is at best arbitrary (if the agenda is selected randomly) and at worst determined by an agenda-setter's machinations.[4]

Further opportunities for strategic behavior arise if a voter can alter the agenda by introducing new candidates or alternatives for consideration. Suppose that alternative C represents the status quo and that alternative B is a motion that has been introduced. Since B will defeat C (two votes to one) individual 3, who prefers C to B, will be disappointed. But if individual 3 can introduce the amendment A, then the amendment A will defeat the motion B on the first ballot. Then, on the second ballot, the amendment will lose to the status quo, C, and individual 3 will have secured enactment of his most-preferred alternative.

Even if new alternatives or candidates cannot be introduced and the agenda cannot be manipulated, opportunities may still exist for voters to profit by misrepresenting their preferences. Consider the agenda in which C is taken up last. If all individuals vote sincerely on each ballot, then C, who is individual 1's least-preferred candidate, will be selected. Suppose, however, that individual 1 votes for B on the first ballot; in that case B prevails, going on to defeat C in the second round. By "sophisticated" voting individual 1 has secured the election of his preferred candidate.

Arrow's question was this: Is the problem of inconsistent "group preferences" peculiar to majority rule, or is it inherent in all voting systems? To answer this question, he might have assembled a list of procedures and checked to see whether there exist configurations of individual preference rankings that result in ill-behaved collective rankings. Such a list might include rank-order voting (the mechanism used in wire-service rankings of collegiate athletic teams), weighted majority rule in which individuals are assigned varying numbers of votes (the mechanism used by corporations — one share, one vote), and two-stage procedures like the U. S. Electoral College. The difficulty with this approach is that Arrow would have had to consider an immense number of aggregation procedures. To be precise, consider the set of mechanisms Arrow called constitutions — rules assigning to each configuration of individuals' rankings a collective ranking of the alternatives. That is, a constitution specifies whether each alternative is preferred, indifferent, or inferior to every other alternative. With three alternatives there are 13 possible preference orderings. Thus, with two individuals there are $13^2 = 169$ possible configurations of individual preferences. Since a constitution associates a preference ranking with each of these configurations, there are, even if we limit our attention to constitutions yielding consistent orderings in the trivial two-person three alternative case, 13^{169} distinct constitutions to evaluate.

Of necessity Arrow chose an axiomatic route to answer the question. He narrowed the field by imposing requirements that he argued were necessary properties of any reasonable aggregation method, and then characterized the class of constitutions that remained.

The first of Arrow's five conditions might be called Universal Scope. It requires that an acceptable constitution be capable of aggregating every logically possible configuration of voters' preferences. Since the choice of a constitution is a long-run decision, predicting which patterns of conflict will arise is impossible. Hence, Arrow argued, we should not adopt a constitution that will break down when certain configurations of voters' preferences arise; rather, we should insist on one sufficiently general to resolve all possible controversies. This long-run perspective rejects majoritarian claims that in practice troublesome preference configurations (e.g., those corresponding to the paradox of voting) are unlikely to occur. Universal Scope requires a constitution capable of aggregating even the most intractable preference configurations.

Arrow's second requirement, often called Unanimity, is a weak condition governing the operation of a constitution when there is no disagreement among voters. It specifies that for configurations of preferences in which every individual prefers alternative A to B, the collective ranking must rank A above B. This condition rules out codes of behavior such as those with religious or traditional origins that determine the collective ranking of two alternatives independently of individuals' preferences, since such codes would remain unaltered even when every individual prefers to violate its commandments. If we accept the view that the social ranking should reflect individuals' preferences, it is difficult to quarrel with the Unanimity condition; it resolves what are surely the easiest problems of preference aggregation.

Arrow's third condition, Pairwise Determination, is the most subtle.[5] It requires that the social ranking of any pair of alternatives depend only on individuals' preferences between those two alternatives. No matter how individuals' preferences concerning other alternatives change, as long as each individual's ordering of A and B remains invariant, then the group ranking of A and B also remains invariant. For example, this condition implies that collective ranking of Ronald Reagan and Jimmy Carter is independent of how individuals rank Edward Kennedy relative to them or to Walter Mondale. Thus, when the set of currently available alternatives is relatively small, a constitution satisfying Pairwise Determination requires little information about individuals' preferences to determine the collective ranking of these feasible alternatives. In particular, information about individuals' preferences for unavailable options is irrelevant to the group's ranking of the feasible alternatives, an advantage when eliciting individuals' preferences is difficult or costly. Without the Pairwise Determination condition, the constitution must specify which other alternatives are relevant to determining the collective ranking of A and B and how individuals' preferences for these other alternatives should affect the ranking of A and B.

One commonly used procedure, rank-order voting, violates Pairwise Determination. One version of this constitution assigns each individual's first-place candidate three points, his second two points, and his third one. The collective ranking is then generated by summing candidates' scores over all voters. When the three-person "paradox of voting" configuration of preferences occurs, the committee is indifferent among the three candidates, since each of the three candidates receives six votes. Suppose, however, that the preferences of the first voter change from A over B over C to A over C over B. Although no voter has changed his ordering of A and B, rank-order voting now yields a collective ranking in which A is preferred to B, since A still receives 6 votes, while B now receives 5. Thus, with rank-order voting, the collective ranking of A and B depends not only on individuals' rankings of A and B but also on the relative position of some third alternative such as C.

Before describing Arrow's final two requirements, it is useful to introduce notation for binary relations. The expression $x\,R\,y$ represents the ranking statement "x is collectively at least as good as y." Just as the binary relations of equality ($=$) and strict inequality ($>$) among real numbers can be defined in terms of the relation "is at least as large as," ($\geq$) the relations of strict collective preference (P) and collective indifference (I) can be derived from the weak preference relation R.

Arrow's fourth condition is Completeness: for every pair of alternatives x and y it must be true that $x\,R\,y$ or $y\,R\,x$ (or both, in which case x and y are indifferent). This axiom compels the aggregation procedure to rank every pair of alternatives. As long as the constitution has the option of declaring any pair of alternatives indifferent, completeness seems a relatively innocuous requirement.

The fifth axiom requires that weak collective preference be transitive: if $x\,R\,y$ and $y\,R\,z$, then $x\,R\,z$. Completeness and transitivity are conventional consistency conditions in economic models, and economic actors whose preferences are complete and transitive are said to be "rational." By extension, Arrow used the term "Collective Rationality" to describe constitutions satisfying both completeness and transitivity. In imposing these conditions on constitutions, he was not suggesting the existence of a "collective will" independent of individual preferences; Arrow explicitly rejected such personification as illegitimate. Instead, he imposed these conditions to ensure that the chosen alternative would be independent of the agenda or path by which it is reached.

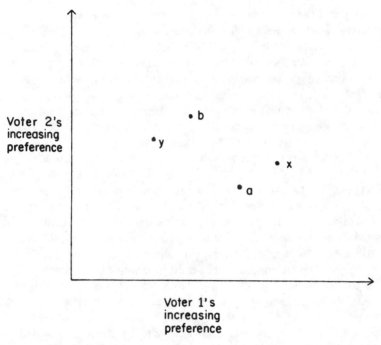

Voter 2's
increasing
preference

Voter 1's
increasing
preference

Figure 4-1.   P-transitive Arrow constitutions treat alternatives in a neutral manner. To
see this, suppose voter 1 prevails over 2's opposition when he prefers a to b. For the
configuration of rankings illustrated above,

$$x P a \quad \text{by Unanimity,}$$
$$a P b \quad \text{by Assumption,}$$
$$b P y \quad \text{by Unanimity,}$$

$$x P y \quad \text{by P-transitivity.}$$

By Pairwise Determination, $x P y$ whenever 1 prefers x to y and 2 prefers y to x, regardless
of their preferences concerning a and b. When there are at least five alternatives, as
Julian Blau has noted, this argument extends 1's decisiveness over one pair (a, b) to every
pair. It takes two applications of the argument to show that the result holds for
"overlapping" pairs such as (a, c) and (b, a).

Having defined and defended this set of five desirable properties for
constitutions, Arrow demonstrated that the only procedures satisfying all of
them share a particularly simple and unappealing form. Under every such
constitution there must exist a dictator, that is, an individual with the power to
impose on the group his strict preference over any pair of alternatives. In fact,

Arrow stated his theorem in a slightly different way. He added a sixth axiom, Nondictatorship, and proved that there were no constitutions obeying all six axioms; hence, his result is often described as an "impossibility theorem" (see Figures 4-1 and 4-2).

Thus the prospective designer of voting procedures for clubs, committees, or governments who accepts these conditions as necessary properties of constitutions is simply out of luck. Arrow's apparently weak assumptions have powerful and unpalatable implications. As Arrow's impossibility theorem makes evident, his requirements are not weak; although singly they are attractive, in combination they are pernicious. The last three decades have seen an extensive reexamination of the axioms by collective choice theorists seeking to circumvent Arrow's unhappy conclusion.

Abandoning the Unanimity condition has generated little enthusiasm. On reconsideration, Unanimity still seems an extraordinarily weak requirement to impose on mechanisms for aggregating individuals' preferences into group rankings. Furthermore, Robert Wilson of Stanford University has shown that the only additional constitutions satisfying Arrow's remaining axioms but violating Unanimity are even less appealing than dictatorships.[6] There are two new possibilities. The first is universal indifference, a rule making every pair of alternatives perpetually indifferent, regardless of individuals' rankings. The second is inverse dictatorship, a rule under which some given individual's preferences over pairs of alternative are reversed to form the collective ranking. No such procedure is likely to be adopted, since a voter with the requisite infallibly bad judgment is unlikely to be found.

Pairwise Determination drew heavy fire in the first decade after Arrow published his work, but criticism of this condition has subsided. Nondictatorial procedures satisfying the remaining conditions do exist: rank-order voting is the most prominent example. Arrow's original defense of Pairwise Determination, based on the informational economy it affords, remains compelling for many investigators. Constitutions that violate this axiom are generally cumbersome, at least when the number of alternatives is fairly large. A powerful additional argument for Pairwise Determination arises when the possibility of individual indifference is assumed away, a case in which Arrow's theorem continues to hold. It is easy to show that every constitution not satisfying Pairwise Determination must, for some configuration of individual preferences, be susceptible to the advantageous misrepresentation of preferences by some individual. More specifically, without Pairwise Determination there must be two configurations of individuals' preferences in which each individual's ranking of some pair of alternatives, say, x and y, is the same (i.e., each individual who prefers x to y in the first configuration also prefers x to y in the second), yet which correspond to different collective

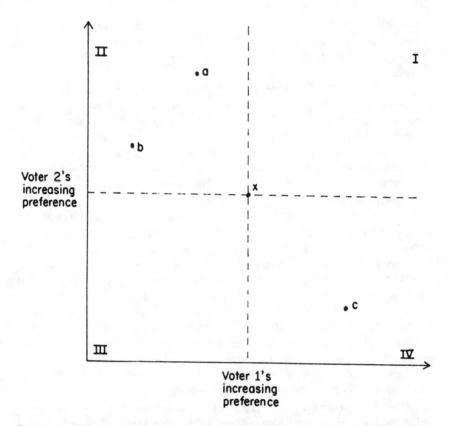

Figure 4-2. To prove a two-person version of Arrow's theorem, choose an alternative x and divide the other alternatives into four quadrants according to whether (I) both voters prefer the alternative to x, (II) voter 2 prefers it to x, while voter 1 does not, (III) neither voter prefers the alternative to x, or (IV) voter 1 prefers it to x, while voter 2 does not. The neutrality property of P-transitive constitutions implies that all the alternatives in a particular quadrant must be ranked in the same way with respect to x. The Unanimity condition implies that quadrant I is preferred to x and quadrant III inferior. Quadrants II and IV could not both be preferred (or both be inferior) to x, since the neutrality property requires that if $a P x$, then $x P c$; hence, if one of these quadrants is preferred to x, then the other must be inferior. Neither quadrant II nor IV can be indifferent to x without violating Unanimity: if, for instance, II were indifferent, then $a I x$ and $x I b$; but by I-transitivity, $a I b$, and this violates Unanimity, since both voters prefer a to b. Arrow's conditions are thus consistent with only two types of constitutions: (1) those which quadrant II is preferred to x and quadrant IV inferior, and (2) those in which quadrant IV is preferred to x and quadrant II inferior. But constitutions satisfying one of these conditions, together with the requirements that quadrant I is preferred to x and quadrant II inferior, are dictatorial. This proof is due to Charles Blackorby, David Donaldson, and John Weymark of the University of British Columbia.

rankings of x and y. When this is true, there must exist two such configurations which differ in the preference ranking of only one individual. One of these configurations corresponds to a collective ranking that is closer to this individual's rankings of x and y. When x and y are the only feasible candidates this individual can report that his preferences for the other alternatives are such as to cause the collective ranking of x and y to be closer to his own ranking of them.

A plausible argument can be made that Universal Scope is too ambitious a requirement: since not every logically possible configuration of preferences is equally likely and since some may be extremely unlikely, requiring a constitution capable of consistently aggregating every logically possible configuration of preferences seems unnecessarily strong. Much effort, however, has failed to find a weakened version of Universal Scope which provides an attractive escape from Arrow's result. The most common research strategy has been to choose a particular aggregation procedure, usually majority rule, and to look for restrictions on the admissible configurations of preferences that rule out combinations implying intransitive collective preferences. For this strategy to be fruitful, the restrictions must be plausible in terms of a theory of preference formation or preference structure, but social scientists have generally been unsuccessful in modeling formally the origins or structure of preferences. The best known of these restrictions, single-peaked preferences, was discovered in the 1940s by the Welsh economist Duncan Black.[7] Ordinarily, single-peaked preferences occur when individuals rank alternatives according to some single criterion: for example, each voter might order candidates according to their proximity to his ideological position in the liberal-conservative spectrum. When all individuals perceive the same spectrum and rank alternatives in this way, preferences are single-peaked, and the majority preference relation does not cycle. If single-peakedness were a plausible restriction on preferences, one which we could confidently expect to hold in practice, then the case for majority rule would be compelling. Unfortunately, when individuals evaluate candidates according to multiple criteria, there appears to be no natural and appealing generalization of single-criterion ranking that gives rise to single-peakedness. Since the multiple criteria case is presumably the more common one, the absence of an appealing generalization of single peakedness to this case argues for retaining Universal Scope.

Arrow's least defensible requirement is probably Transitivity. Collective choice theorists have examined the consequences for collective choice rules of several rationality conditions weaker than the transitivity of group preferences. It is not difficult to show that R-transitivity, the transitivity of weak collective preference, is equivalent to the conjunction of P-transitivity and I-transitivity, so one straightforward weakening of Arrow's requirement is to abandon I-transitivity. Since studies by mathematical psychologists have shown that individuals frequently exhibit intransitive indifference in experimental situations, I-transitivity is particularly vulnerable to criticism. And since individuals often fail to satisfy I-transitivity, there is no compelling reason to demand it of collective preference. The economist and philosopher Amartya Sen of Oxford University first noticed the sensitivity of Arrow's dictatorship conclusion to the requirement of transitive group indifference; he offered an example of a nondictatorial constitution satisfying Arrow's remaining axioms and P-transitivity.[8] The procedure Sen proposed, which might be called the rule of consensus, gives $x P y$ if and only if every individual ranks x as at least as good as y and at least one individual strictly prefers x to y. To see that collective indifference need not be transitive, consider a group of two individuals, one preferring y to x to z and the other x to z to y: the rule of consensus gives $x I y$ and $y I z$, but $x P z$.

The phenomenon of intransitive individual indifference may reflect the inability of individuals to distinguish among alternatives that are "close together" (for example, in dimensions such as sweetness, heaviness, or political conservatism). That is, x and y may be indifferent for an individual because they are indistinguishably close, as may y and z; yet x and z may be sufficiently far apart that the individual strictly prefers one to the other. The psychologist R. Duncan Luce of Harvard University has proposed a notion of preference consistency called the semiorder to model situations entailing such perception thresholds. Semiorders exhibit P-transitivity but permit intransitive indifference. If we interpret collective choice as a process of aggregating individuals' policy judgments to form collective policy judgments, then it is plausible to suppose that the group cannot discriminate perfectly between "similar" alternatives. Thus the notion of imperfect discrimination can be applied to collective as well as individual preferences.

The semiorder, however, is a stronger rationality requirement than P-transitivity alone, a fact which has important consequences for preference aggregation procedures. As we have shown elsewhere, requiring that collective preferences be semiorders still implies dictatorship in the presence of the other Arrow axioms. Thus the perception-threshold justification for weakening transitivity, while appealing and plausible, does not avoid Arrow's dismal conclusion.

It is remarkable that one of Arrow's justifications for R-transitivity— independence of the preferred alternatives from the agenda or path by which they are reached — leads directly to an argument for P-transitivity alone as the appropriate rationality requirement for collective preferences. Charles Plott of the California Institute of Technology has proposed a formal definition of path independence and has shown that a constitution satisfies this condition if and only if collective preferences are P-transitive.[9] Thus, while Arrow's original Collective Rationality condition is sufficient for path independence, it is unnecessarily strong.

Sen's rule of consensus shows that nondictatorial P-transitive constitutions exist. But, as Sen recognized, the rule of consensus is not a particularly appealing solution to Arrow's problem because it is often indecisive. Whenever any two individuals have opposing strict preferences over a pair of alternatives — surely a ubiquitous form of conflict of interest — the rule of consensus declares the two alternatives socially indifferent. A constitution that yields social indifference whenever individual preferences conflict is of limited usefulness for guiding choices.

But perhaps there are more attractive P-transitive constitutions. Allan Gibbard, a philosopher at the University of Michigan, has shown that there are not.[10] Gibbard proved that under every P-transitive procedure obeying Arrow's remaining requirements there exists a set of individuals he called an oligarchy, having two privileges. First, the oligarchy can impose on the entire group its unanimous strict preference over every pair of alternatives. Second, each member of the oligarchy has a "veto" over strict social preference opposite his own: whenever any member of the oligarchy strictly prefers some x to y, it cannot be true that yPx. Thus, an oligarchy is a kind of multimembered dictatorship. A dictator is an oligarchy of one, while the rule of consensus implies an oligarchy consisting of the entire group.

The presence of oligarchs need not imply an unequal distribution of power, as the rule of consensus shows; the more members the oligarchy has, the more equal, in some sense, is the distribution of power. Yet the more individuals belong to the oligarchy, the greater is the probability that the rule will be indecisive, since conflicts between oligarchs imply collective indifference. Since path independence requires P-transtivity, Gibbard's theorem implies that path independence, though undeniably an attractive consistency property for collective choice, can only be purchased at great cost. We must weaken Collective Rationality beyond P-transitivity to escape the dilemma of choosing between indecisive and inegalitarian constitutions.

A less restrictive requirement than P-transitivity is acyclicity, the absence of cycles of strict collective preference, such as the one encountered in the paradox of voting. Acyclicity is an attractive property to demand of a constitution, especially when the procedure adopted for converting pairwise rankings to choices is to select those alternatives that are undefeated by all others. Acyclicity guarantees that at least one such alternative always exists: it is a necessary and sufficient condition for every finite feasible set to contain at least one undefeated alternative.

Acyclic constitutions satisfying Arrow's axioms — a phrase we use hence forth to refer to Arrow's axioms other than Transitivity—differ from R-transitive or P-transitive constitutions in two ways that make their structure somewhat complicated (see Figure 4-3). First, under acyclic constitutions all pairs of alternatives need not be treated in a similar way. An individual or coalition with the power to impose its will over one pair of alternatives may lack that power over another pair. Similarly, an individual or coalition with veto power over some pair of alternatives may not have that power over every other pair. Under P-transitive or R-transitive constitutions satisfying Arrow's axioms, this asymmetry is not possible: if a particular configuration of individual preferences between x and y implies that x is collectively preferred to y (Pairwise Determination guarantees that no additional information about individual preferences plays a role in determining the collective ranking of x and y), then the same configuration of individual preferences between z and w implies that z is collectively preferred to w. Under acyclicity, all pairs of alternatives need not be treated in such a neutral fashion.

Nonneutral procedures are widely used. In the U.S. Senate, to take one (sometimes cyclic) example, an ordinary bill passes with a simple majority, a motion to limit debate requires a three-fifths majority, and a constitutional amendment needs a two-thirds majority. Whether neutrality is an appealing feature of a constitution depends on the nature of the alternatives. When candidates for office are being ranked, a neutral rule is usually more appealing than one favoring a particular candidate. But when alternatives have asymmetric consequences, nonneutral rules biased against more drastic outcomes may be appealing. Thus, a jury trial is guaranteed only in serious cases, and, at the other extreme, death sentences are automatically reviewed by appellate courts.

Acyclic constitutions are complicated in a second way, in that additional support for x relative to y may actually worsen x's position relative to y in the group preference relation. That is, acyclic collective preferences need not be positively associated with individual preferences. Since positive association is an attractive condition, and since under acyclicity it does not follow from Arrow's axioms, many political theorists would be willing to impose it as an additional requirement.

Veto power is an essential feature of acyclic constitutions satisfying Arrow's axioms (see Figure 4-4).[11] Because of the complexity of the full class of acyclic procedures, we begin by considering the ones satisfying the additional requirements of neutrality and positive association. This class of constitutions has been studied by Julian Blau of Antioch College, Donald Brown of Yale University, and Rajat Deb of Southern Methodist University. With these additional requirements, relaxing P-transitivity to acyclicity broadens the menu of available preference aggregation methods. Typical of these additional constitutions is the voting rule used by the United Nations Security Council until 1965. The Security Council then consisted of five permanent and seven nonpermanent members. A motion succeeded if it received at least seven affirmative votes, and no negative vote from any permanent member.

Under acyclicity a new aspect of the collective decision problem, the ratio of the number of alternatives to the number of voters, becomes critical: the smaller this ratio, the more attractive the range of acyclic constitutions. To understand the role this ratio plays, consider why the paradox of majority voting requires at least three alternatives. Suppose, for concreteness, that there are five individuals. When there are only two alternatives, x and y, a collective ranking cycle — that is, both $x P y$ and $y P x$ — could occur only if at least three individuals (a majority) prefer x to y and at least three prefer y to x. But this means that at least one individual prefers x to y and prefers y to x, contradicting our assumption that individual preferences are rational. When there are three alternatives, however, cycles can occur without contradicting individual rationality. For example, a cycle occurs when we assign the three orderings that generated the three-person paradox of voting to five persons, with no more than two sharing the same ordering. Majority rule does have an acyclic variant in the five person-three alternative case, however. Suppose we require four affirmative votes for strict collective preferences rather than three. Under this constitution, a cycle such as $x P y$, $y P z$, $z P x$ would contradict individual rationality: for each pair of alternatives in the cycle, at least four individuals must have pairwise preferences that agree with the collective ranking. With five individuals, however, at least one of them must agree with all three collective rankings, and thus must himself have cyclic preferences.

Although the four-fifths majority rule constitution has no oligarchy, acyclicity has been purchased at a price: any set of two voters can block a social ranking that stands opposite their own. Such minority coalitions have veto power much like the members of an oligarchy. Constitutions that grant veto power to a large number of small coalitions are likely to lead to social deadlock rather than social decisions.

The larger the ratio of alternatives to individuals, the smaller is the smallest coalition with veto power under acyclic constitutions satisfying neutrality and positive association. With five voters and five or more alternatives, some individual must have veto power, just as in an oligarchy: the negative vote of such an individual can block strict social preference over any pair of alternatives. But the unanimous support of those with veto power need not be sufficient for collective preference; in rules for which it is sufficient, the vetoers constitute an oligarchy and group preferences are P-transitive. For example, while each permanent member of the Security Council had a veto, the permanent members did not jointly constitute an oligarchy, since additional

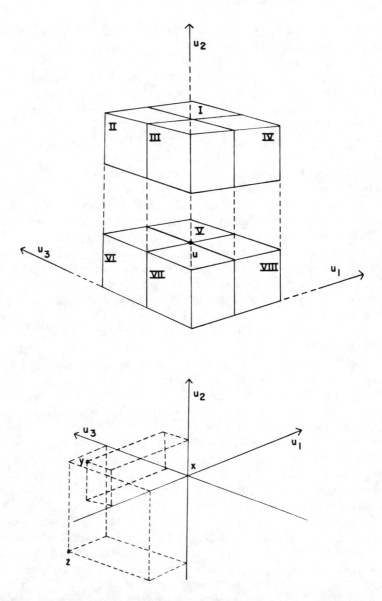

Figure 4-3 and Figure 4-4. R-transitive, P-transitive, and acyclic constitutions begin to differ interestingly when there are three persons. Given an alternative x, the remaining alternatives can be assigned to the eight numbered octants above on the basis of individuals' preferences over those alternatives relative to x. As in the two-person case, the neutrality property of P-transitive constitutions implies that all alternatives in a

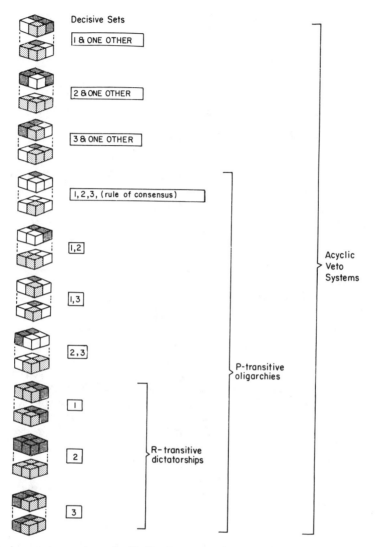

Decisive Sets

| 1 & ONE OTHER |

| 2 & ONE OTHER |

| 3 & ONE OTHER |

| 1, 2, 3, (rule of consensus) |

1,2

1,3

2,3

1

2

3

Acyclic
Veto
Systems

P-transitive
oligarchies

R-transitive
dictatorships

particular octant must be ranked in the same way relative to x; the same must be true of neutral acyclic constitutions. Once again, if one octant (e.g., II) is preferred to x, then its opposite (e.g., VIII) must be inferior. Without I-transitivity, nothing prevents opposite octants from both being indifferent to x; indeed, neutrality requires that if one is indifferent to x then the other is also, because one octant bears the same relation to x in individuals' rankings as x does to the opposite octant. Since the Unanimity condition compels a constitution to prefer octant I to x and x to octant VII, all possible constitutions are covered by considering the possible choices for collective preferences of three support from nonpermanent members was necessary for collective preference.

Dropping the simplifying assumption of neutrality enlarges and complicates the menu of available rules, but does not make it significantly more palatable. Without neutrality an individual may have veto power over some pairs of alternatives but not over others. We have recently shown that when the ratio of alternatives to individuals is large, at least one individual must be able to veto a large number of pairs of alternatives. More precisely, when there are more alternatives than individuals, then someone must have veto power over at least some critical fraction of the ordered pairs of alternatives. This critical fraction increases as the ratio of alternatives to voters increases, and approaches one as that ratio increases without limit. Thus, when the number of alternatives is large relative to the number of individuals, there must exist at least one person who can veto almost all pairs of alternatives (see Figure 4-5).

Of course, it may well be true that many individuals may possess veto power.

---

octants, no two of which are opposite each other, say II, III, and IV. Suppose that III is preferred to x. Then both II and IV must also be preferred to x since each can include points that everyone prefers to points in III. Thus voter 2 is a dictator, (i.e., the oligarchy contains a single-member). The three possible dictatorships are illustrated in Figure 4-4. The dark shaded octants are collectively preferred, the light shaded ones are inferior, and the clear ones are indifferent to x.

To prove a three-person version of Gibbard's oligarchy theorem, we need only show that P-transitivity implies that the two octants II and IV cannot both be preferred to x if III is not. Assume that they are both preferred. We need only consider the case in which III is indifferent. (If III were inferior, then V would be preferred to x. Then either II and V, would both be preferred or else IV or V would both be preferred. But that is exactly the case being considered, except for a renumbering of the individuals.) Now consider the alternatives y and z in the diagram shown on p. 92. Alternative z is in VI, which is opposite the preferred octant IV, so x P z. By P-transitivity, y P z. But y bears the same relation to z as (the indifferent) octant III bears to x, contradicting neutrality. It follows that the only P-transitive constitutions satisfying Arrow's conditions are the oligarchic ones illustrated on the previous page.

Neutral acyclic constitutions satisfying positive association must have an individual with veto power; that is, no octant can be collectively preferred to x unless the individual in question prefers that octant to x. In view of the fact that opposite any preferred octant must be an inferior octant, the only three-person constitution that must be ruled out is majority rule, under which octants I, II, IV, and V are preferred. Since V is now preferred, III must be inferior. This constitution violates acyclicity, since y P x (because y is in II), x P z (because z is in VI), and z P y (since z bears the same relation to y as V does to x). Thus the only acyclic constitutions satisfying neutrality and positive association are the veto systems illustrated in figure 4-4.

1	2	3	4	5
x_2	x_4	x_6	x_8	x_{10}
x_3	x_5	x_7	x_9	x_1
x_4	x_6	x_8	x_{10}	x_2
x_5	x_7	x_9	x_1	x_3
x_6	x_8	x_{10}	x_2	x_4
x_7	x_9	x_1	x_3	x_5
x_8	x_{10}	x_2	x_4	x_6
x_9	x_1	x_3	x_5	x_7
x_{10}	x_2	x_4	x_6	x_8
x_1	x_3	x_5	x_7	x_9

Figure 4-5. We have shown elsewhere that acyclic constitutions obeying Arrow's other conditions, regardless of whether they treat alternatives in a neutral fashion, must give at least one individual veto power over many pairs of alternatives. Computing the exact number of vetoes is complex, but a simple argument shows that someone must veto a smaller but still large number of pairs — large in the sense that the fraction of veto pairs tends to one as the number of alternatives grows large.

We show that, in a society with 5 individuals and A alternatives, an acyclic constitution obeying Arrow's other conditions and positive association must give some individual veto power over at least $A(A-1) - 16(A-1)$ ordered pairs of alternatives. Since the total number of ordered pairs is $A(A-1)$, the fraction of pairs which such an individual can veto approaches one as the number of alternatives grows large. Suppose, contrary to our claim, that no individual can veto $A(A-1) - 16(A-1)$ pairs. Then for each individual, there are at least $16(A-1)+1$ ordered pairs which he cannot veto. We use these sets of "nonveto" pairs to construct a cycle of strict social preference. First choose a nonveto pair for the first individual, say (x_1, x_2); that is $x_1 P x_2$ can occur even when the first individual prefers x_2 to x_1. Next select a nonveto pair (x_3, x_4) for the second individual, choosing a pair not involving either of the two previously used alternatives, x_1 and x_2. (This is possible since at most $4(A-1)$ of the second individual's nonveto pairs involve x_1 or x_2.) Continue through the set of individuals in this manner, disqualifying pairs involving previously used alternatives. For the fifth individual, at least one eligible nonveto pair (x_9, x_{10}) remains, since no more than $16(A-1)$ of his $16(A-1)+1$ nonveto pairs could have been disqualified at earlier stages.

Under positive association, no individual who is unanimously opposed on an ordered pair which he cannot veto can prevail over that pair. Joining positive association with Arrow's other axioms, the preference configuration above implies the collective preference cycle $x_1 P x_2, x_2 P x_3, \ldots, x_9 P x_{10}, x_{10} P x_1$. Each pair beginning with an odd

An egalitarian would argue that all individuals should be granted the veto power that acyclicity and the Arrow axioms require granting to some. But the larger the set of vetoers, the more frequent the incidence of collective indifference, since indifference occurs whenever two individuals with veto power in the appropriate directions rank x and y in opposite ways.

As in the special case of acyclic rules satisfying neutrality and positive association, the palatability of acyclic constitutions in the general case depends on the ratio of alternatives to individuals. When the number of alternatives is only slightly smaller than the number of individuals, "small" coalitions must be endowed with extensive veto power, though individuals need have no vetos at all. As the number of alternatives increases, the size of the smallest necessary vetoing coalition grows larger.

The "impossibility theorems" that began with Arrow's famous proposition define constraints on our choices of collective decision-making rules, and these constraints are severe. Three widely shared objectives stand in irreconcilable conflict with each other: collective rationality, decisiveness, and equality of power. If we forgo collective rationality, thereby accepting the necessary arbitrariness and manipulability of irrational procedures, then majority rule is likely to be our choice, since it attains the remaining goals. If we insist on retaining a degree of collective rationality, then we can achieve equality by adopting the rule of consensus, but only at the price of extreme indecisiveness. We can increase decisiveness by concentrating veto power in fewer and fewer hands: the most decisive rule, dictatorship, is the least egalitarian. For any collective decision problem, this menu offers a truly Hobbesian choice.

Notes

1. See Arrow [1963]. Kelly [1978], Fishburn [1973] and Sen [1970, 1982] provide guides to much of the collective choice literature.

2. See Condorcet [1785]; and see Black [1958, part 2] for a history of these issues.

3. See Riker [1965] for this and other examples of similar issues as well as chapter 4 of Riker and Ordeshook [1973] and the references cited therein.

---

alternative is preferred to its successor because the only individual opposed to that ranking lacks veto power over that pair. Each pair beginning with an even alternative is unanimously preferred to its successor. Hence, acyclicity, the Arrow axioms, and positive association imply that some individual must veto at least $A(A-1)$ '16$(A-1)$ pairs. A further refinement of this argument dispenses with positive association.

4. For examinations of agenda manipulation and strategic behavior with sincere and strategic voting, see Farquharson [1969], McKelvey [1976, 1979], Schofield [1978], and Shepsle and Weingast [1984].

5. This condition is also commonly referred to as the independence of irrelevant alternatives, though the label pairwise determination is more descriptive.

6. See Wilson [1972].

7. The single-peakedness condition was developed by Black [1948, 1958], and is discussed by Arrow [1963]. The basic examination of the multiple-criteria case is Plott [1967].

8. See Sen [1970].

9. See Plott [1973].

10. See Gibbard [1969]. A similar result is presented by Mas-Colell and Sonnenschein [1972].

11. For a discussion of acyclic constitutions and the role of vetoers in such constitutions, see Blair and Pollak [1979, 1982], who also provide a guide to the literature on this subject.

References

Arrow, K. J., *Social choice and individual values*, New Haven: Yale University Press, 1963.

Black, D., "On the rationale of group decision-making." *Journal of Political Economy* 56 (1948), 23–34.

Black, D., *The theory of committees and elections*, Cambridge: Cambridge University Press, 1958.

Blair, D. H. and R. A. Pollak, "Collective rationality and dictatorship: The scope of the Arrow theorem." *Journal of Economic Theory* 21 (1979), 186–194.

Blair, D. H. and R. A. Pollak, "Acyclic collective choice rules." *Econometrica* 50 (1982), 931–944.

Blair, D. H. and R. A. Pollak, "Rational collective choice." *Scientific American* 249 (1983), 88–95.

Condorcet, Marquis de, "Essai sur l'Application de l'Analyse à la Probabilité des Decisions Rendues à la Pluralité des Voix." Paris, 1785.

Farquharson, R., *Theory of voting*, New Haven: Yale University Press, 1969.

Fishburn, P. C., *The theory of social choice*, Princeton: Princeton University Press, 1973.

Gibbard, A., "Social choice and the Arrow conditions." unpublished, 1969.

Kelly, J. S., *Arrow impossibility theorems*, New York: Academic Press, 1978.

Mas-Colell, A. and H. Sonnenschein, "General possibility theorems for group decision functions." *Review of Economic Studies* 39 (1972), 185–192.

McKelvey, R. D., "Intransitivities in multidimensional voting models and some implications for agenda control." *Journal of Economic Theory* 12 (1976), 472–482.

McKelvey, R. D., "General conditions for global intransitivities in formal voting models." *Econometrica* 47 (1979), 1085–1111.

Plott, C. R., "A notion of equilibrium and its possibility under majority rule." *American Economic Review* (1967), 787–806.

Plott, C. R., "Path independence, rationality and social choice." *Econometrica* 41 (1973), 1075–1091.

Riker, W. H., "Arrow's theorem and some examples of the paradox of voting." *Mathematical Applications in Political Science*, vol. I, Dallas: Southern Methodist University Press, 1965, pp. 41–60.

Riker, W. H. and P. C. Ordeshook, *An introduction to positive political theory*, Englewood Cliffs, Prentice-Hall, Inc., 1973.

Schofield, N., "Instability of simple dynamic games." *Review of Economic Studies* 45 (1978), 575–594.

Sen, A. K., *Collective choice and social welfare*, San Francisco: Holden-Day, 1970.

Sen, A. K., *Choice, welfare and measurement*, Cambridge: MIT Press, 1982.

Shepsle, K. A. and B. R. Weingast, "Uncovered sets and sophisticated voting outcomes with implications for agenda institutions." *American Journal of Political Science*, 28, 1984, pp. 49–74.

5 RESOLUTION OF PARADOXES IN SOCIAL CHOICE

Taradas Bandyopadhyay

Arrow's celebrated general possibility theorem essentially shows that certain value judgments which we might find fair to incorporate in a social choice mechanism are logically inconsistent. Since the Pareto condition (which simply says that given two alternative social states, a and b, if every individual strictly prefers a to b, then they collectively also strictly prefer a to b), is ethically a compelling normative condition especially in the framework where social choice is based only on the individual's utility information, one must look at the remaining criteria, i.e., independence of irrelevant alternatives (what Blair and Pollak in the previous chapter called pairwise determination) and transitive rationality. It is now well established that in the absence of the condition of independence of irrelevant alternatives an aggregation procedure is vulnerable to the strategic manipulation, that is, an individual by mis-revealing his true or sincere preferences can influence the social outcome in his own advantage. Hence, the relaxation of the transitive rationality requirement becomes the central aspect of the social choice literature.

The line of investigation concerned with exploring the weakening of transitive rationality requirement of social preference relation does not take us very far from what is established in the previous chapter. Impossibility theorems in this framework essentially indicate that when an aggregation procedure satisfies the Pareto principle, the condition of independence of irrelevant alternatives, and a collective rationality condition, the distribution of power in a society is required to be asymmetric. To be specific, given the independence condition and the Pareto principle, the transitivity requirement implies the existence of a dictator while quasi-transitivity yields an oligarchy. If, in addition, one assumes the restriction that the number of alternatives must be greater than the number of individuals, then acyclic social strict preference implies the existence of an individual who has veto power over a large number of pairs of alternatives.

As a consequence of impossibility results involving various collective rationality requirements of a social preference relation; investigation focused on the study of social choice directly in terms of choice functions without having a binary preference relation. An aggregation procedure in this set up specifies a nonempty choice set for every profile of individual preference orderings and for every set of alternative social states actually presented for choice. Now for a given pair of alternative social states $\{a, b\}$, if the aggregation procedure picks a, one can argue that the society considers "as if" a is at least as good as b. Blair et al. [1976] have shown that even in the choice theoretic framework, given the independence condition and the pareto criterion, the transitivity of "as if" social weak preference relation implies the existence of a dictator, while transitivity of "as if" social strict preference relation implies the existence of an oligarchy.

These negative results raise a question about the justification of introducing a rationality condition which relates pairwise choice to an overall choice with some sort of maximization criteria. In defence of the requirement of transitive rationalization of a social choice rule, Arrow [1951] cited the integrability controversy in the field of consumer's demand theory and argued that the basic problem is the independence of final choice from the sequence in which the smaller set comparisons are made. To make this point more clear, Arrow [1959] axiomatized the transitive rationalization by introducing a consistency condition, known as the weak axiom of revealed preference.

In this chapter, we factorize the weak axiom of revealed preference and show that any constituent part of this consistency condition (which does not ensure collective rationality of "as if" social preference relations) ensures a power structure similar to Arrow, Gibbard, and others, whenever a nontrivial decision mechanism is required to satisfy the other Arrow conditions. It is shown that the critical factor in all impossibility results that indicate unacceptable power structure in a society is some criterion of exclusion. This exclusion is ensured either directly, or by the consistency conditions, or by some normative requirement such as Pareto optimality. However, in the absence of any requirement of exclusion, the social choice procedure would be vitiated, since in that case a finally chosen alternative could be the one which is unanimously rejected in some pairwise contest. In other words, in the presence of a unanimously preferred alternative social state, a society could end up with a unanimously rejected one. We conclude that in the framework where the individuals' utility information is the only input the paradoxes in social choice cannot be resolved.

1. Basic Framework

The basic elements in any study of social decision process are the set of alternatives among which a group must choose, and the set of individuals making up the group itself. Let X be the finite set of all possible social alternatives which *may* be presented for choice. For example, in the problems of consumers' choice, X is usually the set of all possible commodity bundles obtainable in the economy. We assume that this set is feasible. All elements of X must be mutually exclusive. Only one social state or alternative can prevail at the end of the choice procedure. We assume that the number of alternatives is greater than two ($|X| > 2$). The set of alternatives *actually* presented before a group for making a choice will be called an *issue*, denoted by A. A is any nonempty subset of X. Let $\underline{X}$ be the set of all issues. The number of alternatives in $\underline{X}$ is equal to $2^{|X|} - 1$. A social choice rule will serve the role of picking out some element(s) from an issue; the set of "chosen" elements is called a choice set.

A society denoted by L, is the set of those individuals involved in the group decision process. In this study, L will always be assumed to be finite with cardinality $|L| = N$. For instance, in problems of consumers' choice, L is the set of economic agents. In game theory, L is the set of players. Any subset of L is called a coalition.

For all individuals $i \in L$, we assume that there is a binary weak preference (at least as good) relation R_i defined over X. For all $x, y \in X$, $[x P_i y$ iff $(x R_i y$ & $\sim y R_i x)]$, $[x I_i y$ iff $(x R_i y$ & $y R_i x)]$. Intuitively, P_i and I_i are, respectively, the strict preference relation and indifference relation corresponding to R_i. In the following definition we introduce some properties of R_i.

DEFINITION 2.1.   Let Q be a binary relation defined over X. Q is
(2.1.1)   *reflexive* over X iff for all $x \in X$, $x Q x$;
(2.1.2)   *connected* over X iff for all distinct $x, y \in X$, $x Q y$, or $y Q x$;
(2.1.3)   *acyclic* over X iff there does not exist $x_1, x_2, \ldots, x_n \in X$, such that $(x_1 Q x_2$ & $x_2 Q x_3$ & $\cdots$ & $x_{n-1} Q x_n$ & $x_n Q x_1)$;
(2.1.4)   *a quasi-transitive* over X iff for all $x, y, z \in X$, $[(x_1 Q x_2$ & $x_2 Q x_3$ & $\ldots$ & $x_{n-1} Q x_n$ & $x_n Q x_1)$ and $(y Q z$ & $\sim z Q y) \to (x Q z$ & $\sim z Q x)]$;

(2.1.5) *transitive* over X iff for all x, y, $z \in X$, $[(x Q y \ \& \ y Q z) \to x Q z]$;

(2.1.6) *an ordering* over X iff Q is reflexive, connected, and transitive over X.

Throughout this chapter we assume that the weak preference relation of every individual is an ordering over X. Thus for all $i \in L$, R_i satisfies reflexivity, connectedness, and transitivity over X. For all $i \in L$, let S_i be the set of preference orderings over X which individual i can express. In game theory, S_i would be the set of all strategies available to individual i. Let $S = S_1 \times S_2 \times \cdots \times S_N$. An element of S, a profile of individual orderings, will be called a situation, and will be indicated by s, s', etc. That is, $s = (R_1, R_2, \ldots, R_N)$, $s' = (R'_1, R'_2, \ldots, R'_N)$; and so on. Note that two preference profiles are distinct whenever $R_i \neq R'_i$ for some $i \in L$. In our study S_i is to be interpreted as the set of all possible preference orderings R_i over X.

Given any individual preference profile (situation) $s \in S$ and an issue A, our problem is to find out a set of chosen elements for the society. The relationship between the choice set and the individual preferences is made clear in the following definition. The method of deriving a social choice set from a preference profile, s, is called a social choice rule. Formally,

DEFINITION 2.2. A social choice rule is a function f which for every situation s and every issue A specifies exactly one nonempty subset $f(s, A)$ of A.

If $f(s, A)$ has exactly one element, that element emerges as the final outcome given the issue A and the situation s. If on the other hand $f(s, A)$ has more than one element, then we assume that the final outcome is chosen from these elements and each element of $f(s, A)$ has a positive probability of being chosen. For example, a lottery assigning equal probabilities to all elements of $f(s, A)$ could be used to make the final choice. Also, note that the social choice rule must generate a choice for any given set of individual preference orderings. This property is known as the condition of "unrestricted domain."

Before proceeding further, we introduce some additional notation. Given f and $s \in S$, a base relation R is defined as follows: for all x, $y \in X$; $[x R y$ iff $x \in f(s, \{x, y\})]$; $(x P y$ iff $\{x\} = f(s, \{x, y\})]$; and $[x I y$ iff $\{x, y\} = f(s, \{x, y\})]$. Intuitively, for a given pair of alternatives $\{x, y\}$ if a social choice rule picks one alternative, say x, then the relation R says that for society "as if" x is at least as good as y. Similarly, the asymmetric components P, and the symmetric components I, can be interpreted. Note that from a definition of a social choice rule, the relation R must be reflexive and connected.

Following Edgeworth, in economics, a choice (whether individual or social) is considered rational if it is obtained in the process of some sort of maximization. A social choice rule f on $\underline{X}$ is *rational* if and only if there is a binary relation R on X such that

$$f(s, A) = \{x \in A \mid x R y \text{ for all } y \in A\}.$$

Thus a rational social choice rule selects the R-best elements in an issue for every profile of individual preference orderings. One may also say that R rationalizes f. Consequently, a rational decision-making procedure reduces the problem of making a choice to that of comparing two at a time.

We introduce first the conditions that provide invaluable guidance to make a social choice from a pair of alternatives.

Let $L_{xy} = \{i \in L \mid x\,R_i\,y\}$, $L_{(xy)} = \{i \in L \mid x\,P_i\,y\}$, and $L_{\overline{xy}} = \{i \in L \mid x\,I_i\,y\}$ be the set of individuals in a society for whom the indicated preference holds, given the profile of individual preference orderings s. For example, L_{xy} denotes the set of individuals who consider x is at least as good as y; similarly, every member of $L_{(xy)}$ strictly prefers x over y, and every member of $L_{\overline{xy}}$ is indifferent between x and y. Similarly, for a different preference profile s' we use L'_{xy}, $L'_{(xy)}$, and $L'_{\overline{xy}}$, etc. Further, $|L_{xy}|$, $|L_{(xy)}|$, and $|L_{\overline{xy}}|$ stand for the number of individuals, respectively; in L_{xy}, $L_{(xy)}$, and $L_{\overline{xy}}$.

We are interested in social choice in a democratic society, and the democratic values impose certain restrictions on the social choice rule. We can capture the democratic values, while setting up the desirable rules to govern the social choice process, by introducing two sets of conditions on the social choice rule. The first set of conditions are desirable, i.e., we would like the social choice rule to satisfy these conditions. The second set of conditions are undesirable, and we are interested in a social choice rule which violates these conditions. All these conditions provide guidance in making a choice from a pair of alternatives.

The desirable set of properties are defined below:

DEFINITION 2.3. Let A be any issue and let f be the social choice rule,

(2.3.1) *Pareto Optimality.* For all $s \in S$, for all $x, y \in A$, if $\left| L_{(xy)} \right| = N$ then $\sim y \in f(s, A)$.

(2.3.3) *Strict Pareto Optimality.* For all $s \in S$, for all $x, y \in A$, if $|L_{xy}| = N$ and $|L_{(xy)}| \geq 1$ then $\sim y \in f(s, A)$.

(2.3.4) *Absence of veto* (AV). For all $s \in S$, for all $x, y \in A$, if $|L_{(xy)}| \geq N - 1$ then $\sim y \in f(s, A)$.

Corresponding to the condition of Pareto optimality we have the *weak Pareto principle* (as defined by Arrow) when $|A| = 2$. Similarly for $|A| = 2$, we have the property of strict Pareto principle. The weak Pareto principle stipulates that if an alternative x is unanimously (strictly) preferred over y, then x must be chosen and y must be rejected. If we choose from more than a two-element set then under the Pareto optimality in this case one can simply say that y must be rejected. The strict Pareto optimality requires that when an alternative x is unanimously weakly preferred to y and strictly preferred by some individual then y must be rejected. AV is essentially an almost unanimity condition. The definition 2.3 introduces conditions which require certain types of power to be invested in certain bodies.

The next set of desirable properties imposes restrictions on the choice set when the situation changes, given the issue. We first consider what is known as the independence of irrelevant alternatives. Intuitively, the independence property requires that if individual preferences with respect to "relevant" alternatives remain the same as between two situations, then the choice set remains the same.

DEFINITION 2.4. *Independence of Irrelevant Alternatives*: Let $A \in \underline{X}$ and f be a social choice rule. For all $s, s' \in S$, if for all $x, y \in A$ and all $i \in L$, $[(L_{xy} = L'_{xy})$ & $(L_{yx} = L'_{yx})]$ then $[(x R y \leftrightarrow x R' y)$ & $(y R x \leftrightarrow y R' x)]$.

The independence condition stipulates that individual rankings with respect to alternatives belonging to the issue under consideration are relevant for choice from that issue; information regarding individual rankings with respect to alternatives outside the issue does not influence the social choice. For example, consider an election involving the Democratic Party Candidate (D) and the Republican Party Candidate (R), this choice should depend on voters ordering of D vis-a-vis R, and not on how the voters rank the Liberal Party Candidate vis-a-vis the Conservative Party Candidate, or the Conservative Party Candidate vis-a-vis the Ecology Party Candidate. This condition ensures that a social choice is determined by individual orderings only and is not influenced by their preference intensities independent of their orderings. This is the "irrelevant" aspect of the condition noted by Sen [1970]. In other words, the individual rankings over the alternative social states that belong to the issue under consideration are relevant for choice; the information regarding individual rankings with respect to social states outside the issue does not influence the social choice. In short, this condition ensures the economic use of information. Furthermore, a social choice function that violates the condition of pairwise determination is vulnerable to strategic misrevelation of preferences, i.e., there exists an individual who by misrepresenting his true preferences can influence the social outcome in his favor. It follows that if one is interested to get truthful revelation of preferences for the purpose of social choice, the pairwise determination will be an appealing property of the social choice procedures.

The independence condition is somewhat technical. The relationship between democracy and the following conditions, is rather straight forward.

DEFINITION 2.5. Let f be the social choice rule that satisfies independence of irrelevant alternatives. Let s and s' be any two situations in S, and let $\{x, y\}$ and $\{z, w\}$ be any two ordered pairs of alternatives. Let A be any issue.

(2.5.1)   *Anonymity* (AN): If $[(| L_{xy} | = | L'_{xy} |)$ & $(| L_{yx} | = | L'_{yx} |)]$ then $(x R y \rightarrow x R' y)$.

(2.5.2)   *Neutrality* (NT): If $[(L_{xy} = L'_{zw})$ & $(L_{yx} = L'_{wz})]$ then $(x R y \rightarrow z R' w)$.

(2.5.3) *Duality* (D): If all individuals' preference orderings in $s' \in S$ are the inverse of situation $s \in S$ then $f(s, A) \cap f(s', A)$ either is $\varnothing$ or A.

(2.5.4) *Monotonicity* (M): If $(L_{xy} \subseteq L'_{xy} \& L'_{yx} \subseteq L_{yx})$ then $[(x P y \rightarrow x P' y) \& (x R y \rightarrow x R' y)]$.

(2.5.5) *Strict Monotonicity* (SM): If $(L_{xy} \subseteq L'_{xy} \& L'_{yx} \subseteq L_{xy})$ and if at least one of these is the proper subset, then $(x R y \rightarrow x P' y)$.

The condition of anonymity requires that if a given set of preferences is permuted among the individuals, social choice should remain invariant. Anonymity clearly has a strong appeal insofar as it emphasizes the quality of different individuals. However, it is a demanding condition not fulfilled by several social choice rules often used in real life. Most forms of representative democracy, as distinguished from direct democracy, violate this condition. Neutrality requires that the rule of choice should not discriminate between alternatives, and whatever criterion permits us to say that x is socially as good as y should also be sufficient for declaring x' to be as good as y' after replacing x and y by x' and y', respectively. Essentially, neutrality rules out any special treatment of any particular alternative as compared to other alternatives.

Like neutrality, duality also prohibits favoritism for one of the two alternatives for social choice.[1] In terms of x and y, the dual of a preference profile is obtained by reversing each individual's preferences. Duality says that $x P y$ iff $y P' x$ and $x I y$ iff $x I' y$. In other words, over one ordered pair of alternatives if there is a permutation over alternatives then neutrality becomes identical with duality. In general, however, these two properties are different. For example, the Borda Rule violates duality, whereas it satisfies neutrality. Monotonicity requires that if an alternative, say x, is chosen at the beginning and if the individual orderings remain the same except that x "moves up" in some individuals' preferences, then x should continue to be chosen. This is a compelling property from the ethical point of view; and most social choice rules satisfy this property. Strict monotonicity requires that if some individual's preference shifts relatively in favor of x vis-a-vis y with everyone else's preference between x and y remaining the same, then social choice should shift positively in favor of x, and if the society was previously indifferent, now it must strictly prefer x. This property is not widely satisfied by the social choice rules in real life.

Next we discuss some properties that impose restrictions on the choice set without referring to any change in the situation or the issue.

First we introduce a set of conditions related to asymmetric power structure of individuals. These conditions, e.g., dictatorship of single individual or oligarchic power of a small group of individuals, are undesirable in democracy. To introduce these sets of undesirable properties of a social choice rule we shall use the following definition.

DEFINITION 2.6.   Let A be an issue and let x, $y \in A$. A coalition $\tilde{L}$ is:

(2.6.1)   Decisive for x against y iff for all $s \in S$, if $x P_i y$ for all $i \in \tilde{L}$ then $x P y$.

(2.6.2)   Weakly decisive for x against y iff for all $s \in S$, if $x P_i y$ for all $i \in \tilde{L}$ then $x R y$.

We now define the undesirable properties.

DEFINITION 2.7.   An individual $i \in L$ is said to be a *dictator* iff i is decisive over every pair of alternatives; *weak dictator* iff i is weakly decisive over every pair; almost dictator iff i is a weak dictator and for all pairs x, $y \in X$, $x P_i y$ & $x R_j y$ for any $j \in (L - \{i\})$ implies $x P y$. A coalition of individuals $\tilde{L} \subseteq L$ is said to be *oligarchic* iff $\tilde{L}$ is decisive over every pair, and all $i \in \tilde{L}$ are weak dictators. A dictator is said to be a *global dictator* if the choice set contains only the R-best alternatives of his preference ordering.

By dictator we mean that for all pairs of alternatives if an individual prefers x to y, society must prefer x to y, irrespective of the preferences of other individuals in the society. Weak dictatorship gives somebody a veto power: whenever a weak dictator strictly prefers x over y, x must be an element of the choice set. Oligarchy is a unique group of individuals such that if any one of them strictly prefers x to any y, x must be chosen from that pair, and if all members of the group strictly prefer x to y then y must be rejected in that pairwise contest. A weak dictator is said to be an almost dictator if in the absence of opposition from at least one member of the society he becomes decisive over every pair of alternatives. The properties of dictator, oligarchy, weak dictator, almost dictator are the characterization of various power structures in terms of pairwise choice, i.e., an individual or a coalition of individuals is decisive or weakly decisive over every pair of alternatives. These conditions do not say anything about the final choice set. However, by a global dictator we mean an individual who is decisive over every pair of alternatives and the final choice set containing only his most preferred alternatives.

2. Rationality, Consistency and Impossibility

We are looking for a social choice rule that satisfies desirable properties of a democratic society and in the process does not produce an undesirable distribution of power. It is well known that if the choice is only over a pair then there is a solution to the problem. When we consider the problem of choice from three or more alternatives, we can take two alternatives at a time and make our choice, and then using the information about pairwise choice we make our final choice. This process of making a final choice on the basis of choice over the pairs of alternatives requires choice to be logically consistent. For example, in the theory of revealed preference, consistency of choice requires that if x is chosen while y is available and y is chosen while z is available then between x and z, x must be chosen. This logical consistency of choice in the context of a social aggregation procedure imposes some restrictions on social choice rules. This type of restriction is known as the collective rationality condition. Since X is finite, a social choice rule satisfying acyclicity of relation P (over the set of alternatives from which a choice is to be made) guarantees the existence of a maximal set.

In this chapter we are not looking for an aggregation procedure for welfare comparison, but merely for decision-making based on democratic principles.[2] An acyclic social strict preference (in the base) relation is not necessary for the existence of a choice set, since acyclicity is a condition on choice over pairs, it does not tell us anything about the relationship between choice over pairs and a choice from a larger set. To make such comparisons we need consistency conditions. One such condition is introduced by Arrow [1959].[3]

Weak Axiom of Revealed Preference. For all profiles of individual preference orderings $s \in S$, all issues $A \in \underline{X}$, and all pairs of alternatives $x, y \in A$, if $f(s, A) \cap \{x, y\} \neq \varnothing$ then $f(s, A) \cap \{x, y\} = f(s, \{x, y\})$.

Arrow has shown that the weak axiom of revealed preferences is a necessary and sufficient condition for a social choice rule to have transitive rationalization, i.e., the (base) relation R is transitive and it is as if society were choosing best alternatives in the issue defined in terms of the weak preference relation R. Consequently, we have the following results.

THEOREM 1. *Let a social choice rule satisfy*
  (i) *independence of irrelevant alternatives,*
  (ii) *the weak Pareto principle,*
  (iii) *weak axiom of revealed preference.*
Then there exists an individual who is a global dictator.

For every preference profile and every agenda (issue), the weak axiom of revealed preference says that whenever $f(s, A) \cap \{x, y\} \neq \varnothing$, $f(s, A) \cap \{x, y\} = f(s, \{x, y\})$. Factorizing the equality of the two sets into (a) $f(s, A) \cap \{x, y\} \subseteq f(s, \{x, y\})$ and (b) $f(s, A) \cap \{x, y\} \supseteq f(s, \{x, y\})$, two independent conditions can be obtained. The part (a) is known as Chernoff condition,[4] and the part (b) is called the Strong Dominance condition (see Bordes [1976]). The Chernoff condition says that all alternatives rejected in a pairwise comparison must be excluded in a larger set comparison; the strong dominance condition requires that an alternative being chosen in a pairwise comparison cannot be excluded in a larger set comparison while the other alternative in that pair is chosen. The above theorem shows that if we accept both (a) and (b) we are in trouble. In defending the weak axiom of revealed preference, Arrow cited the integrability problem in the field of consumer's demand theory, and argued that those familiar with the controversy would observe that the basic issue in any choice problem is the independence of the final choice from the path in which comparisons are made over the pairs. An intransitive social choice mechanism may produce decisions that are clearly unsatisfactory. A satisfactory choice procedure is one that ensures that if the problem of choosing over an issue A (which contains more than two alternatives) is broken up into choosing over pairs and then choosing over the remaining alternatives, the final choice from this procedure should still be in the choice set from A.[5] In other words, the final choice should not be affected because of the way the issue was manipulated. This objective can be achieved by the following condition:[6]

Weak Path Independence. For all profiles of individual preference orderings $s \in S$, and all issues A, $A^t \in \underline{X}$ where $|A^t| \leq 2$ such that $\bigcup_t A^t = A$, $f(s, \bigcup_t f(s, A^t)) \subseteq f(s, A)$.

Note that the strong dominance condition implies the weak path independence criterion. While the weak path independence condition provides the criterion of inclusion of some alternatives in the overall choice set which have survived at the end of pairwise comparisons, the Chernoff condition offers the criterion of exclusion of some alternatives from the overall choice set given the information about the exclusion of the alternatives in the pairwise comparisons. Plott [1972] has shown that if the weak path independence condition is combined with the Chernoff condition then the final choice based on pairwise comparisons will be the same as the choice which is based on superset comparison. This is what he called the property of path independence. Formally, this property can be defined as follows:

Path Independence. For all profiles of individual preference orderings $s \in S$ and all issues A, $A^t \in \underline{X}$ where $|A^t| \leq 2$ such that $\bigcup_t A^t = A$, $f(s, \bigcup_t f(s, A^t)) = f(s, A)$.

Parks [1971] has proved that $f(s, \bigcup_t f(s, A^t)) \supseteq f(s, \bigcup_t A^t)$ is equivalent to the Chernoff condition. In other words, factorizing the path independence condition one obtains the weak path independence condition and the Chernoff condition. Since the weak path independence condition is implied by the strong dominance condition, while converse is not true, it is obvious that the path independence condition is also implied by the weak axiom of revealed preference. This moves Plott to argue that if one is interested in getting a choice rule based on pairwise comparisons, so that the final choice remains invariant from the sequence in which pairwise comparisons are made, then the requirement of satisfying the weak axiom of revealed preference is unnecessarily restrictive. The consequences of introducing a less restrictive consistency condition is stated below.[7]

THEOREM 2. *Let a social choice rule satisfy*
  (i) *independence of irrelevant alternatives,*
  (ii) *the weak Pareto principle,*
  (iii) *path independence.*
Then there exists an oligarchy.

Although every path independent social choice rule which satisfies the independence condition and the pairwise weak Pareto criterion does not necessarily give decisive power over every pair of alternatives to an individual, it gives decisive power to a unique group of individuals, each member of which is weakly decisive in the pairwise contests. The path independence condition is a combination of the Chernoff condition and the weak path independence condition. Now what happens if any one of these two constituent parts of the path independence condition is considered?

THEOREM 3. *Let a social choice rule satisfy*
  (i) *independence of irrelevant alternatives,*
  (ii) *the weak Pareto principle,*
  (iii) *the Chernoff condition.*
Then someone is weakly decisive over $(|X| - N - 1)(|X| - 1)$ *pair of alternatives.*[8]

Note that the number of pairs over which an individual has weak decisive power (or veto power) increases as the ratio of alternatives to voters increases. This shows that when the number of alternatives is large relative to the number of individuals, there must exist at least one person who is weakly decisive over almost all pairs of alternatives. However, considering the other part of path independence condition, i.e., the weak path indepencence condition, Ferejohn and Grether [1977] have established the following possibility result.

THEOREM 4. *Let* $|X| > 3$ *and* $N > 4$. *Then there exists a social choice rule which satisfies*
  (i) *independence of irrelevant alternatives,*
  (ii) *the weak Pareto principle,*
  (iii) *weak path independence,*
  (iv) *strict monotonicity,*
  (v) *anonymity, and either*
  (vi) *neutrality or duality.*

May [1952] has shown a social choice rule which satisfies independence, strict monotonicity, anonymity and either neutrality or duality is necessarily a rule that chooses alternatives in the pairwise contests on the basis of majority decision.[9] This possibility theorem with the requirement of weak path independence and the impossibility results with the Chernoff condition led the social choice theorists to conclude that any consistency condition related to the Chernoff property is the main culprit for paradoxes in social choice, while the consistency property like weak path independence causes no problem at all. However, a close observation of the positive results reveals that in this case a social choice rule may end up with a choice set that contains more than one alternative, including the one which is unanimously rejected in a pairwise comparison with the other. In the choice theoretic framework, where a social choice procedure specifies a multivalued choice set, the final choice is made by some random mechanism. But when a multivalued choice set contains an alternative that is rejected by all members of the society, and as a result of random process if that alternative is finally chosen, the purpose of making a social decision on the basis of information about the preferences of its members would then be vitiated. Such an aggregation procedure would violate even a minimal concept of efficiency. An economist would ask, "Why should a society accept one alternative when another alternative exists which would make everyone better off?" Almost all social philosophers agree that all concepts of sovereignty require that the people unanimous should not be ignored. In fact, the entire edifice of economic theory as we know it today is built on Paretian value judgments, and so the rejection of these value judgments would raise the question of relevance of a significant part of modern economic theory. Thus the requirement that the social choice rules must satisfy Pareto optimality is clearly a compelling one; and it is more so in the analytical framework where social choice is based only on the individuals' preferences.

Since the Chernoff condition ensures exclusion of all pairwise rejected alternatives from the choice set, it is obvious that whenever a social choice rule satisfies the weak Pareto principle and the Chernoff condition it excludes all alternatives from the choice set which are rejected in the pairwise contests by every member of the society, i.e., the Pareto optimality is satisfied. Now the dilemma is that while the Chernoff condition together with weak path independence and other Arrow conditions generate an oligarchical power structure, in its absence one may end up with a Pareto suboptimal outcome. This suggests the introduction of the Pareto optimality criterion. Ferejohn and Grether have shown that once the weak Pareto principle is replaced by the Pareto optimality criterion, their possibility results break down, i.e., every social choice rule which satisfies the independence condition, the Pareto optimality, duality and the weak path independence condition gives decisive power to a minority group of individuals. The social decision based on minority opinion is indeed very common in real life in every 'democratic' society. The question is to what extent the decision making power is concentrated.

THEOREM 5. *Let* $|X| > 3$. *Let a social choice rule satisfy*
  (i) *independence of irrelevant alternatives,*
  (ii) *the Pareto optimality criterion,*
  (iii) *duality,*
  (vi) *weak path independence.*
Then there exists an individual who is a dictator.

The last two results show that for $|X| > 3$, every social choice rule which satisfies independence, the weak Pareto principle, duality and weak path independence is either dictatorial (i.e., gives someone decisive power in every pairwise contests) or violates Pareto optimality. The Pareto optimality is a combination of the weak Pareto principle (i.e., the unanimity in the pairwise contests) and some kind of rejection condition which simply requires the exclusion of all alternatives from the choice set that are rejected unanimously in the pairwise contests. While Chernoff condition suggests the exclusion of all pairwise rejected alternatives from the overall choice set, Pareto optimality requires exclusion of all unanimously rejected alternatives from the final choice set. Since the Chernoff condition is identified as the source of the problem, the Pareto optimality requirement may be appealing but can be argued as the cause of the problem. We now propose to consider the following weak condition.

Reward for unanimity. A social choice function is said to satisfy the reward for unanimity if and only if for all profiles of individual preference orderings $s \in S$, and for any pair $\{x, y\} \subseteq A \subseteq X$, $|L_{(xy)}| = N$ implies $f(s, A) \neq A$.

The reward for unanimity condition says that if, in a pairwise contest some alternative is rejected by every member of the society, then for the same preference profile it must make a nontrivial decision by excluding at least one alternative in a larger set comparison. Note that the excluded alternative is not necessarily one of the alternatives rejected in the pairwise contests. In the presence of unanimously rejected alternative social state the requirement of a minimally resolute social decision is certainly a very weak condition. It is obvious that the Pareto optimality requirement implies both the weak Pareto principle and the reward for unanimity condition but the latter two together do not imply the former.

Now introducing this extremely weak exclusion criterion, we obtain the following impossibility result which shows how fragile is the possibility result that has been obtained by Ferejohn and Grether.

THEOREM 6.   *Let* $|X| > 3$. *Every social choice rule which satisfies*

(i)   *independence of irrelevant alternatives,*
(ii) *the weak Pareto principle,*
(iii) *duality,*
(iv) *weak path independence,*

is dictatorial if and only if it satisfies the reward for unanimity condition.[10]

The weak axiom of revealed preference and its constituents, the Chernoff condition and the strong dominance condition, are the criteria for making a consistent choice, both for an individual and a society. The reward for unanimity condition is a criterion which can be used only in the context of a social choice. A condition stated below is very similar in spirit with the reward for unanimity criterion, but is applicable both in individual choice and in social choice.

Minimum Rejection.   A social choice rule, f, is said to satisfy minimum rejection if and only if for any pair $\{x, y\} \subseteq A \subseteq X$ if $\{x\} = f(s, \{x, y\})$ then $f(s, A) \neq A$.

This condition, originally introduced by Bandyopadhyay [1984], says that given a configuration of individual preferences if some alternative is rejected in a pairwise comparison then for the same preference configuration at least one alternative must be rejected in a superset comparison. In other words, this condition requires that if a society can be decisive over a pair then it must not end up with the entire agenda as a choice set. Note that the minimum rejection condition does not impose any regularity on choice in the sense the Chernoff condition does. The Chernoff condition or its various weaker versions, as proposed by Fishburn [1973] and Sen [1977], imposed restrictions on the pairwise choice from the information on what alternatives are chosen from larger sets. Strengthening the exclusion criterion to the minimum rejection condition one can obtain the dictatorial theorem similar to the theorem 6 without the structural restriction that the number of alternatives must be at least four. In other words, every social choice rule which satisfies conditions (i) to (iv) of theorem 6 is dictatorial if and only if it satisfies the minimum rejection condition.

In introducing the weak path independence condition, Ferejohn and Grether argued that this condition guarantees that *one* of the best alternatives will be chosen independent of the sequence in which pairwise comparisons are made. However, a close observation reveals that the weak path independence condition is more demanding than what they are intended to achieve, since it requires that *all* best alternatives will be chosen independent of path. In the presence of a cycle of social strict preference relations (of any length), it is immediate that the weak path independence would suggest that all alternatives involved in the cycle must be contained in the choice set. A cycle may contain alternatives that are unanimously rejected in the pairwise contests. Now to avoid this problem we propose the following weak consistency conditions.

Minimum Path Independence. Let f be a social choice rule. For all A^t, $A \in \underline{X}$, where $\bigcup_t A^t = A$, $|A^t| \leq 2$, $f(s, \bigcup_t f(s, A^t)) \cap f(s, A) = \varnothing$.

The minimum path independence condition requires that at least one of the elements of the final choice set based on pairwise comparison must belong to the final choice set based on superset comparison, irrespective of the sequence in which pairwise comparisons are made. This condition is "quite close to" what Ferejohn and Grether's motivation suggests. Alternatively, the weak path independence condition can be weakened into:

Weak Nondominance. Let f be a social choice rule. For all $\{x, y\} \subseteq A \in \underline{X}$, $f(s, \{x, y\}) = \{x, y\}$ implies $f(s, A) \neq \{y\}$.

The weak nondominance says that if in a pairwise comparison both are chosen then in a super set comparison one of them cannot be the only element in the choice set.[11] Although both minimum path independence and weak nondominance are implied by weak path independence, the converse is not true.

The consequences of relaxing weak path independence into the minimum path independence and weak nondominance is that in this case there exists a nondictatorial social choice which satisfies all other conditions stated in theorem 5; however the characterization of all such nondictatorial social choice rules are stated below.

THEOREM 7. *Every social choice rule which satisfies*
  (i)   *independence of irrelevant alternatives,*
  (ii) *the weak Pareto principle,*
  (iii) *duality,*
  (iv) *minimum path independence,*
  (v)   *weak nondominance,*
is oligarchical if and only if it satisfies the minimum rejection condition.[12]

All conditions stated in the above theorem except duality are clearly appealing. When choice is making over a pair, duality is identical with the (pairwise) neutrality which is not satisfied by many real life decision making procedures, e.g., constitutional amendment rules frequently require that status quo can be changed only if the proposed amendment receives a special majority (say two-thirds) over the status quo. The consequences of introducing neutrality instead of duality is given below. This result should be compared with the theorem 7.

THEOREM 8. *Let* $|X| > N$. *Every social choice rule which satisfies*
 (i)   *independence of irrelevant alternatives,*
 (ii)   *the weak Pareto principle,*
 (iii) *neutrality,*
 (iv)   *weak path independence,*
is weakly dictatorial if and only if it satisfies the minimum rejection condition.

Furthermore a comparison with theorem 5 is illuminating. What we have shown is that for $|X| > N$ every social choice rule which satisfies the independence condition, the weak Pareto principle, the weak path independence condition and the minimum rejection condition is dictatorial if it satisfies the duality condition, and weakly dictatorial if it satisfies the neutrality property. An individual is said to be weakly decisive if he has veto power in every decision over the pairs. If someone has a veto power over a pair, the neutrality property makes him a weak dictator. A veto power over one pair of alternatives may be acceptable to many people depending upon the nature of the alternative social states. In fact Sen [1970] argues that if the alternatives are different on the private affairs of an individual, e.g., whether one should eat a sirloin steak or roast beef for his dinner, then that individual should have decisive power (not just veto power) over that pair of alternatives. But once the neutrality property is imposed then it makes that individual decisive over every pair of alternatives, i.e., a dictator. Now what happens when the requirement of neutrality is dropped and instead the strict monotonicity condition, another characteristic of a majority decision rule, is considered.

THEOREM 9. *Let* $N > 3$. *Every social choice rule which satisfies*
 (i)   *independence of irrelevant alternatives,*
 (ii)   *the weak Pareto principle,*
 (iii) *strict monotonicity,*
 (iv)   *minimum path independence*
is almost dictatorial if and only if it satisfies the minimum rejection condition.

The strict monotonicity condition is an appealing condition when a choice is made by a small number of individuals. For example, when $N = 3$ the sensitivity of social choice due to change in preferences by some individual is clearly desirable. However, its appeal diminishes when N becomes larger and larger. Theorems 5 to 9 show that a weakly path independent social choice rule satisfying other very reasonable conditions ensures unacceptable power structures whenever it is required to satisfy some of the properties of a majority decision rule. It is pointed out before that even in the absence of any such conditions like duality, neutrality, and strict monotonicity a weakly path independent social choice rule satisfying other conditions gives someone veto power if the number of alternatives are restricted to be at least as large as the number of individuals. The following result shows that this structural restriction is not critical in general to establish a veto theorem.

THEOREM 10. *There is no social choice rule which satisfies together*
  (i) *independence of irrelevant alternatives,*
 (ii) *the absence of veto condition, and*
(iii) *minimum path independence.*

Note that the absence of veto condition is playing a crucial role in two ways. First, it says that whenever all but one individual member of a society (strictly) prefer an alternative a over an alternative b, the society should choose a over b. This part has the same spirit as the weak Pareto principle. The second part says that since b is rejected by all but one individual in some pairwise contest, b must be excluded from the final choice set. The requirement of excluding some alternatives from the final choice set having the information about the pairwise choice is the critical factor in all impossibility theorems. The exclusion of an alternative from the final choice set is ensured sometimes by invoking a consistency condition, e.g., the Chernoff condition and other times by considering some version of Pareto optimality condition. In the absence of any exclusion criterion one can obtain a possibility result (see theorem 4), but in the process one may end up in choosing finally an alternative which is considered to be inferior to some other alternative by every member of the society. The exclusion criterion essentially restricts the image set of the social choice rules. In fact, if one insists that the social choice rule must be a singleton then almost all consistency conditions related to the weak axiom of revealed preference in the literature would be identical. For example, Chernoff condition, strong dominance, weak path independence, minimum path independence are all equivalent to the weak axiom of revealed preference. However, in the absence of any restriction on the image set of the social choice rules, the whole exercise of making a decision on the basis of individual's preferences would turn out to be trivial. So long as the decision procedures are based only on the utility information of the individuals there is no resolution of paradoxes in social choice.

3. Proofs

Let us start with some definitions. Let $A = \{x_1, x_2, \ldots, x_n\}$. Also let f be a social choice rule. Then for all $s \in S$, f is

Pseudo transitive iff $(x_1 R x_2, x_2 R x_3, \ldots, x_{n-1} R x_n, x_n R x_1) \rightarrow f(s, A) = A$.
Pseudo Quasi-transitive iff $(x_1 P x_2, x_2 P x_3, \ldots, x_{n-1} P x_n, x_n R x_1) \rightarrow f(s, A) = A$.
Pseudo Acyclic iff $(x_1 P x_2, x_2 P x_3, \ldots, x_{n-1} P x_n, x_n P x_1) \rightarrow f(s, A) = A$.

LEMMA 1. (1.1) *If a social choice rule satisfies minimum path independence then it satisfies pseudo acyclicity over triples.*

(1.2) *If a social choice rule satisfies minimum path independence, weak nondominance and duality then it satisfies pseudo quasi-transitivity.*

(1.3) *If a social choice rule satisfies weak path independence and duality then it satisfies pseudo transitivity.*

Proof. (1.1) To the contrary suppose not. Suppose for $A = \{x, y, z\}$, we have $x P y$, $y P z$, $z P x$ and $f(s, A) \neq A$. Without loss of generality suppose $\sim z \in f(s, A)$. Since

$$\{z\} = f(s, [f(s, \{z\}) \cup f(s, \{x, y\})]);$$

therefore by the condition of minimum path independence $\{z\} \cap f(s, A) \neq \varnothing$. Hence $z \in f(s, A)$, a contradiction.

(1.2) To the contrary suppose not. Suppose for $A = \{x, y, z\}$, we have $x P y$, $y P z, z R x$, and $f(s, A) \neq A$. Since we have already shown for $z P x, f(s, A) \neq A$ leads to a condition, what we need to show is that for $z I x, f(s, A) \neq A$ would also lead to a contradiction. By supposition $f(s, A) \neq A$. Given minimum path independence and weak nondominance it is obvious that $f(s, A)$ is either $\{x, z\}$ or $\{x, y\}$. Let $s' \in S$ be a profile of individual preference orderings such that every individual's preference in s' is the inverse of their preferences in s. By duality and independence of irrelevant alternatives we must have $z P' y$, $y P' x$, and $x I' z$. Once again, given minimum path independence and weak nondominance we have either $f(s', A) = \{x, z\}$ or $f(s', A) = \{y, z\}$. Hence $f(s', A) \cap f(s, A)$ is neither $\varnothing$ nor A; a contradiction with duality.

(1.3) This part is very similar to the proof of (1.2) and therefore is omitted.

For a pair of alternatives $\{x, y\} \subseteq X$ if all individuals preferred x over y we simply write $x P_L y$. By the weak Pareto principle in the pairwise contest y must be rejected.

LEMMA 2. *If a social choice rule satisfies*
(i) *reward for unanimity,*
(ii) *weak path independence,*
(iii) *duality,*
then its (base) relation must be Pareto transitive:

For all $x, y, z \in X$, $(x R y \& y P_L z \rightarrow x P z) \& (x P_L y \& y R z \rightarrow x P z)$.

Proof. Let f be a social choice rule.

We first show that given the hypothesis $x R y$ & $y P_L z \rightarrow x P z$. To the contrary suppose not. Suppose $x R y$, $y P_L z$, and $z R x$. Since f satisfies weak path independence and duality, by lemma (1.3), $f(s, A) = A$. This violates reward for unanimity.

Similarly $x P_L y$ & $y R z \rightarrow x P z$ can be established.

LEMMA 3 (BANDYOPADHYAY [forthcoming]). *If a social choice rule satisfies*
   (i)   *independence of irrelevant alternatives,*
   (ii) *the weak Pareto principle,*
   (iii) *Pareto transtivity,*
then someone is a dictator.

Now the proof of theorem 6 follows from lemma 2, lemma 3, and theorem 4.[13]

LEMMA 4. *If a social choice rule satisfies*
   (i)   *minimum rejection,*
   (ii) *minimum path independence,*
   (iii) *weak nondominance,*
   (iv) *duality,*
then its (base) relation must be quasi-transitive.

Proof. Suppose not. Then given the hypothesis, by lemma (1.2), its base relation must be pseudo quasi-transitive. A contradiction with minimum rejection.

LEMMA 5 (BLAIR ET AL [1976]). *If a social choice rule satisfies*
   (i)   *independence of irrelevant alternatives,*
   (ii) *the weak Pareto principle,*
   (iii) *quasi-transitivity (in the base relation),*
then there exists an oligarchy.

The proof theorem 7 is immediate from lemma 4, lemma 5, and theorem 4.[14]

The proof of theorem 8 is very similar to theorem 6 of Bandyopadhyay [1984] and therefore is omitted.

LEMMA 6. *If a social choice rule satisfies*
   (i)   *minimum rejection,*
   (ii) *minimum path independence,*
then its (base) relation must be acyclic over triples.

Proof. Suppose not. Then given minimum path independence the (base) relation must be pseudo acyclic, which contradicts minimum rejection.

LEMMA 7 (BLAIR ET AL. [1976]).   Let $N > 3$. *If a social choice rule satisfies*
   (i)   *independence of irrelevant alternatives,*
   (ii) *the weak Pareto principle,*
   (iii) *strict monotonicity,*
   (iv) *acyclicity over triples,*
then someone is a weak dictator.

Now the rest of the proof of theorem 9 follows from the following lemma and theorem 4.[15]

LEMMA 8 (BORDES AND SALLES [1978]).   *Let $N \geq 3$. If a social choice rule satisfies strict monotonicity, a weak dictator, if he exists at all, must be an almost dictator.*

The proof of theorem 10 is very similar to theorem 9 of Bandyopadhyay [1984] and therefore is omitted.

Notes

1.   Fishburn [1973] introduced the notion of duality in social choice. (See Fishburn [1973] for details).

2.   For detailed discussion on this point see Sen [1977].

3.   In Arrow [1959] this condition is called C4.

4.   Chernoff [1954] first introduced such a condition.

5.   This description of a satisfactory choice procedure is due to Ferejohn and Grether [1977].

6.   The weak path independence condition was introduced by Ferejohn and Grether [1977].

7.   Independently Gibbard [1977], Guha [1972], and Mas-Collel and Sonnenschein [1972] have shown that an aggregation procedure which for every profile of individual preference orderings specifies a quasi-transitive social preference relation is oligarchical if it is required to satisfy independence of irrelevant alternatives and the weak Pareto principle. This result was proved in the choice theoretic framework by Blair et al [1976]. Since path independence implies quasi-transitivity (in the base) relation, hence theorem 2 follows. (See Kelly [1978]).

8.   This result is due to Blair et al. [1982].

9.   According to the majority decision a unique alternative is chosen from a pair whenever that alternative is preferred to the other by more than fifty percent members of the society.

10.   So this theorem is a generalisation of theorem 5.

11.   This condition was introduced by Sen [1977].

12.   Without assuming any version of path independence condition Bandyopadhyay has shown impossibility results with duality, weak nondominance and strict Pareto optimality (See Bandyopadhyay [1983], theorems 6 and 7.).

13.   Theorem 4 is an example to prove the necessity part, and the sufficiency part follows from lemmas 2 and 3.

14.   The lemmas complete the proof of sufficiency part, and the necessity part is established by theorem 4.

15.   Once again the proof of necessity part follows from theorem 4. Lemmas 7 and 8 proves that given the hypothesis there exists a weak dictator, and the sufficiency part completes by lemma 9.

References

Arrow, K. J., "Social Choice and Individual Values." Ist ed., Wiley: New York, 1951.

Arrow, K. J., "Rational Choice Functions and Orderings." *Economica* 26 (1959) pp. 121–127.

Bandyopadhyay, T., "On a Pareto Optimal and Rational Choice in a Democratic Society." *Economic Journal*, Supplementary Issue (1983) 114–121.

Bandyopadhyay, T., "On the Frontier Between Possibility and Impossibility Theorems in Social Choice." *Journal of Economic Theory* 32 (1984), 52–66.

Bandyopadhyay, T., "Pareto Optimality and the Decisive Power Structure with Expansion Consistency Conditions." *Journal of Economic Theory* 35, (1985), 366–375.

Batra R. and P. K. Pattanaik, "On some suggestions for having non-binary social choice functions. *Theory and Decision* 3 (1972), 1–11.

Blair, D. H., G. Bordes, J. S. Kelly and K. Suzumura, "Impossibility Theorems without Collective Rationality." *Journal of Economic Theory* 13 (1976), 361–379.

Blair D. H. and R. A. Pollak, "Acyclic Collective Choice Rules." *Econometrica* 50 (1982), 931–943.

Blau J. and R. Deb, "Social Deicision Functions and the Veto." *Econometrica* 45 (1977), 871–879.

Bordes, G., "Consistency, Rationality and Collective Choices." *Review of Economic Studies* 43 (1976), 451–457.

Bordes G. and M. Salles, "Sur les fonctions de decision collective: un commentaire et un resultat." *Rev. Econ. Pol.* 88 (1978), 442–448.

Chernoff, H., "Rational Selections of Decision Functions." *Econometrica* 22 (1954), 423–443.

Ferejohn J. A. and D. H. Grether, "Weak Path Independence." *Journal of Economic Theory*, 14 (1977), 19–31.

Fishburn, P., "The Theory of Social Choice." Princeton, N.J.: Princeton University Press, 1973.

Gibbard, A., "Intransitive Social Indifference and the Arrow Dilemma." unpublished manuscript, 1969.

Guha, A. S., "Neutrality, Monotonicity and the Right of Veto." *Econometrica* 40 (1972), 821–826.

Kelly, J. "Arrow Impossibility Theorems." New York: Academic Press.

May, K. O., "A Set of Independent Necessary and Sufficient Conditions for Simple Majority Decision." *Econometrica* (1952), 680–684.

Mas-Collel, A. and H. Sonnenschein, "General Possibility Theorems for Group Decisions." *Rev. Econ. Stud.* 39 (1972), 185–192.

Parks, R. P., "Rationalizations, Extensions and Social Choice Paths." Ph.D. Dissertation, Purdue University, 1971.

Plott, C. R., "Path Independence, Rationality and Social Choice." *Econometrica* 41 (1972), 1075–1091.

Plott, C. R., "Axiomatic Social Choice Theory: An Overview and Interpretation." *American Journal of Political Science* 20 (1976), 511–596.

Richelson, J. "Some Further Results on Consistency, Rationality and Collective Choice." *Rev. Econ. Stud.* 45 (1978), 343–346.

Schwartz, T., "Rationality and the Myth of the Maximum." *Nous* 6 (1972), 97–118.

Sen, A. K., "Collective Choice and Social Welfare." San Francisco: Holden-Day, 1970.

Sen, A. K., "Social Choice Theory: A Re-examination." *Econometrica*, 45 (1977), 53–87.

Sen, A. K., "Social Choice Theory." *Hand Book of Mathematical Economics* (K. J. Arrow and M. Intriligator, eds.), Amsterdam: North-Holland, 1981.

6 THE DEMAND REVEALING
MECHANISM

Rafael Rob

The failure of the price system to achieve an efficient resource allocation of public goods has long been recognized. One can analytically dissect this market failure within the Lindahl structure. As it is well known, the latter is an attempt to mimic the Walrasian model to the case of public goods. In the Lindahl framework, individual agents act as conventional utility maximizers, choosing the levels of public services they desire *given* their tax shares (responding passively, that is, to parametrically given prices). The "auctioneer" adjusts prices ensuring that individual choices are mutually consistent. In equilibrium, tax shares are set at the individualized marginal valuations.

On the one hand then, the Lindahl scheme requires the adjustment of as many parameters as there are individuals. Literally understood, this means there is one agent per "market." Clearly, such markets are noncompetitive. On the other hand, the determination of tax-shares (prices) behooves the planner

This work was supported by National Science Foundation grant SES84-16191.

to collect information about individuals' willingness to pay. But when the environment is so noncompetitive, the incentives to correctly transmit this information are obviously lacking.

Realizing the impact of valuations on tax liabilities, each individual would be inclined to distort or misrepresent information about his own utility. Admittedly, this problem is not unique to the case of allocating public services. Sophisticated individuals can and, in fact, do manipulate (private good) market outcomes to their benefit. Customarily, it is accomplished by secret or proxy trading, delaying purchases, withholding or destroying outputs, and so on. The success of such maneuvers hinges, however, on one's being in a superior market position. For example, there might be dominant traders (size wise) on one side of the market; or a small number of individuals might possess valuable "inside information," etc. Nonetheless, when there are many nonatomic agents, competition among them eliminates market power. As a result, the expected gains associated with strategic behavior are practically nil. Price taking behavior and Walrasian outcomes are then predicted to emerge (see Gresik and Satterthwaite [1983], Wilson [1977], and Wilson [1982] for a formal treatment of this process).

Moving to the case of public goods, a recommendation to implement the Lindahl scheme could hardly be justified along the same lines. A large number of agents is certainly not going to promote competition. As we saw, adding an individual means opening a new market. Consequently, the degree of rivalry is, at best, unchanged and the problem of "free riding" still exists. If collective decisions need to be made in sizable communities, there is thus a need for an alternative procedure. The demand revealing mechanism (DRM henceforth) is one such scheme.

1. Terminology and Notation

A mechanism is a group decision-making procedure. In order for a mechanism to possess desirable properties, it must respond to individual characteristics. That is, the decision must vary with underlying conditions. In the case at hand, the decision is over levels of public goods and tax burdens. So we can symbolically write $x(v_1 \ldots, v_n)$, $\{t_i(v_1, \ldots, v_n)\}_{i=1}^n$. $v_i(\cdot)$ is individual i's willingness to pay for varying levels of public services $(i = 1, \ldots, n)$ and x is the quantity of public goods selected given that the configuration of preferences is $v \equiv (v_1, \ldots, v_n)$. t_i is the tax liability assessed to individual i. This formulation suppresses the obvious dependence on the cost of providing collective goods. We proceed therefore under the presumption that this cost is easily verifiable (in comparison with the verification of private information about the valuation v_i).

Assume that we live in a world with transferable utility (and this assumption is crucial to everything that follows). There are two commodities — one private which we call money and denote by m. The other is a public good which we denote by x. The utility of a representative individual is given by $u_i(m_i, x) = m_i + v_i(x)$. The initial endowments of money possessions are $(m_1^0, m_2^0, \ldots, m_n^0)$. The cost of producing the public good is constant, c, per unit. v_i's are assumed to belong to the class of increasing, concave valuations (this restriction is unnecessary — see Green and Laffont [1979]). Finally, the objective of the social planner is to provide a Pareto-optimal level of public services. Under the above assumptions, the decision he faces can be summarized as:

$$\text{Max}_x\, w(x, n) = \text{Max}_x \sum v_i(x) - cx \qquad (6.1)$$

such that

$$\frac{\sum m_i^0}{c} \geq x \geq 0.$$

The determination of the optimal x^* [denoted hereafter by $x^*(v)$] is via the marginal[1] conditions

$$\sum v_i'(x^*) = c. \qquad (6.2)$$

Within this simplified structure, the Lindahl mechanism prescribes that individual i should be assessed the tax share $\tau_i = v_i'(x^*)$. He should then choose any x level he desires, considering τ_i an exogeneous parameter beyond his control. The utility maximization program he faces is thus:

$$\underset{0 \,\leq\, x \,\leq\, (m_i^0/\tau_i)}{\text{Max}}\ v_i(x) - \tau_i x. \qquad (6.3)$$

By construction, the solutions to these n problems are consistent and optimal, i.e., $x_i^* = x_2^* = \cdots = x_n^* = x^*$.

All this is fine so long as the "auctioneer" (planner, center, government, etc.) knows the valuations v_i's. In practice, though, v_i's vary from person to person and we can safely assume that only individual i knows his v_i. But the operation of the Lindahl scheme requires that we *first* compute x^*, evaluate $v_i'(\cdot)|_{x^*}$ and only *then* announce τ_i. That is, it requires that we centralize information about the n-tuple $(v_i, \ldots, v_n)$. So let us now think about this as a game where v_i is a choice variable. In other words, where each agent can transmit any $\tilde{v}_i$ he desires while the center continues to adopt the Lindahl rules.

These rules specify [see Arrow (1979)] that each individual can enforce certain x choices so long as he makes up for the difference between the cost of the project and what his fellow citizens are paying. Specifically, if the first $n-1$ individuals announce $\tilde{v}_1, \ldots, \tilde{v}_{n-1}$ and if x is the desired level (by n), then

$\tau = c - \Sigma_{i=1}^{n-1} \tilde{v}_i'(x)$, where τ is the professed marginal valuation of the nth individual $(\tau = \tilde{v}_n'(x))$. This dependence between the level of public services $- x$ and the tax share $-\tau$, determines the "feasible set" for individual n. Having chosen an (x, τ) pair with $\tau \geq 0$ he can always "fit" a suitable valuation $\tilde{v}_n(\cdot)$ consistent with this choice. Mathematically,

$$\underset{(x,\,\tau)\,\geq\,0}{\text{Max }} v_n(x) - \tau x, \tag{6.4}$$

such that

$$\sum_1^{n-1} \tilde{v}_i'(x) + \tau = c \qquad (\tilde{v}_n'(x^*) = \tau).$$

Clearly, the Nash–Equilibrium configuration $\tilde{v}_1, \ldots, \tilde{v}_n$ to this game differs, in general, from the original $v_1, \ldots, v_n$. The *realized* public decision $\tilde{x}^* (= x^*(\tilde{v}))$ is thus distorted $(\tilde{x}^* \neq x^*)$ and a welfare loss results. Denote it by $L(n) \equiv w(x^*, n) - w(\tilde{x}^*, n)$.

To illustrate these ideas, consider the following numerical example. There are n individuals each with valuation $v_i(x) = v(x) = \sqrt{x}$. The per unit cost of public services is unity, $c = 1$. As one can easily establish, the solution to the social planner's problem is $x^*(n) = (n/2)^2$. Thus maximal *potential* welfare is $w(x^*, n) = n^2/4$. On the other hand, a symmetric Nash–Equilibrium of the information transmission game is $\tilde{v}_i(x) = \tilde{v}(x) = 2\sqrt{x}/(n+1)$. At this equilibrium the quantity of public services is $\tilde{x}^*(n) = (n/(n+1))$. Therefore, *realized* welfare is $w(\tilde{x}^*, n) = (n/(n+1))^2$ while welfare loss is $n^2[\frac{1}{4} - (n+1)^{-2}]$. Note that in the limit as $n \to \infty$, the entire surplus, $w(x^*, n)$, is dissipated. More precisely,

$$\lim_{n \to \infty} \frac{L(n)}{w(x^*, n)} = 1.$$

This is so since as the number of individuals increases their ability to avoid paying taxes without appreciably affecting the level of public services provided is improved. Thus the inducement to free-ride is enhanced and all potential welfare gains are lost.

2. The Demand Revealing Mechanism

The fundamental reason for the above market breakdown is the discrepancy between the social goal (6.1) and the individual objectives, (6.4). Considering those expressions we see that agents can do better by falsely reporting to the center. Alternatively, given the $x - \tau$ tradeoff they are facing, they would choose a suboptimal level of public services. Under these circumstances, it would be ill-advised for the center to maximize social welfare using *reported* valuation. What is needed instead is an appropriate tax scheme, $\{t_i\}_{i=1}^n$, guaranteeing that it is in the best interest of individuals to correctly transmit their characteristics. Equivalently, we must design a suitable $x - \tau$ tradeoff inducing all agents to select the socially optimal level $-x^*(v)$. In short, we should realign their objectives with the social objective.

Consider then the Vickery–Clarke–Groves (VCG hereafter) tax scheme:

$$t_i(\tilde{v}) = cx^*(\tilde{v}) - \sum_{j \neq i} \tilde{v}_j(x^*(\tilde{v})) + h_i(\tilde{v}_{-i}), \tag{6.5}$$

where $h_i(\cdot)$ is an arbitrary function subject only to the condition that it is independent of $\tilde{v}_i$ and where $\tilde{v}_{-i} = (\tilde{v}_1, \ldots, \tilde{v}_{i-1}, \tilde{v}_{i+1}, \ldots, \tilde{v}_n)$. This mechanism collects from individual i the difference between the total cost of the project $(cx^*(v))$ and the sum of benefits to the remaining $(n-1)$ members. In addition a constant lump sum tax $h_i(\cdot)$ is levied. Note that $h_i(\cdot)$ has no effect on i's strategy since it can affect neither his tax liabilities nor the quantity of public services. The role of h_i will become apparent as we proceed.

Writing the ith individual maximand under this incentive structure we have:

$$\underset{\tilde{v}_i}{\text{Max}}\, v_i(x^*(\tilde{v})) + \sum_{j \neq i} \tilde{v}_j(x^*(\tilde{v})) - cx^*(\tilde{v}) - h_i(\tilde{v}_{-i}). \tag{6.6}$$

The above is manifestly equivalent to program (6.1). Given $\tilde{v}_{-i}$, (6.6) is x-maximized at $x^*(\tilde{v}_{-i}, v_i)$. But reporting $\tilde{v}_i = v_i$ enforces this x^*. Thus honesty is the best policy for individual i. Moreover, this is true for *any* $(n-1)$ tuple of valuations $\tilde{v}_1, \ldots, \tilde{v}_{i-1}, \tilde{v}_{i+1}, \ldots, \tilde{v}_n$ (sincere or otherwise). We conclude that truthful revelation is not just an equilibrium response but is, in fact, a *dominant strategy*. That is, it is the best one can do regardless of what others are doing. Summarizing, we have

THEOREM 1 (GROVES–LOEB, 1975). *Under the Vickery–Clarke–Groves mechanism*

$$x^*(v), \qquad t_i(v) = cx^*(v) - \sum_{j \neq i} v_j(x^*(v)) + h_i(v_{-i}),$$

reporting the true valuation $(\tilde{v}_i = v_i)$ *is a dominant strategy.*

This gives us one family of successful schemes (parameterized by h_i). Are there any other, perhaps more attractive, mechanisms? Green and Laffont [1979] provided a complete answer. It is given by the following

THEOREM 2 (GREEN–LAFFONT, p. 60). *Any dominant-strategy, truth-revealing scheme is a member of the VCG family.*

The planner's "opportunity set" is thereby delineated. Moreover, it is known that even if we restrict ourselves to a narrower family of valuations, the class of VCG mechanisms are still the only available schemes at our disposal. More specifically, assume that all conceivable valuations are of the following functional form: $v_i(x) = \theta_i x - x^2/2$ where θ_i is a positive constant, known only to the ith agent. The mechanism design problem is to construct a tax scheme inducing individuals to correctly transmit their θ_i values. This one-parameter family of valuations is substantially smaller than the set of all potential valuations. Thus, the mechanism is supposed to work only over a reduced domain. One would conjecture that the design task is easier, i.e., that there are many more revelation schemes. While highly plausible, this conjecture turns out to be false.

THEOREM 3 (GREEN–LAFFONT, p. 63). *Over the restricted domain of quadratic valuations, there are no other dominant strategy, truth revealing schemes except for the family of DRM's.*

To interpret the VCG incentive scheme (6.5), observe that each individual is offered a transfer $(-t_i)$ equaling the social surplus accruing to the rest of the group. Adding to this one's own benefit his objective function, (6.6), coincides with the center's maximand (6.1) (modulo the neutral term h_i). The wedge between the two objectives is thereby removed and the problem of adverse incentives is overcome.

Let us return now to our numerical example, set $h_i \equiv 0$, and examine the outcomes induced by the DRM. Computing, one obtains $x^*(v) = (n/2)^2$, $t_i(v) = (n/2)(1 - n/2)$. We see that the quantity of the public good produced is indeed "first-best." Disturbingly, though, the incentive taxes collected turn out to be negative. That is, the rules of the game dictate that we *transfer* money to the individual participants. Therefore, the problem of *financing* the project remains to be solved.

At our disposal there is one more "degree of freedom" we have thus far not exploited: namely, the h_i functions. As mentioned, we can adjust these tax components (so long as h_i does not depend on v_i) without destroying the truthtelling incentives. It turns out that the following particular choice solves the financing problem

$$h_i(v_{-i}) = \operatorname*{Max}_{x} \sum_{j \neq i} \left[v_j(x) - \frac{x}{n} \right]. \tag{6.7}$$

To verify this claim, insert the above expression into (6.5):

$$t_i(v) = \frac{c}{n} x^*(v)$$

$$+ \left\{ \underset{x}{\text{Max}} \sum_{j \neq i} \left[v_j(x) - \frac{c}{n} x \right] - \sum_{j \neq i} \left[v_j(x^*(v)) - \frac{c}{n} x^*(v) \right] \right\}. \tag{6.8}$$

(6.8) tells us that each individual pays an equal share, $(1/n)$, of the cost of the project *plus* the nonnegative term in the { } brackets (it is the definition of the Max operator which makes this term nonnegative).

Total taxes collected, $\Sigma_{i=1}^n t_i(v)$, are thus sufficient to cover the cost of producing $x^*(v)$. The bracketed term in (6.8) has an economically appealing interpretation. By participating in the decision-making process, the ith individual inflicts an externality on the remainder of the group. This externality is the result of i's impact on the group's choice. That is, the switch from Argmax $\{\Sigma_{j \neq i}[v_j(x) - cx/n]\}$ — the best choice of the other $(n-1)$ individual to $x^*(v)$ — the public choice including i's opinion. The bracketed term captures this "revision effect." For that reason, this particular version of the DRM (first proposed by Clarke [1971]) is often referred to as the *pivotal* mechanism. The tax liabilities of agent i are thus his proportional share $(1/n)$ *plus* the cost he imposes on others by expressing his preferences. Clearly, this extra term is smaller the lesser is the impact of individual i. It is paid only to the extent that his "vote" makes a difference. Finally note that there is nothing special about the equal $(1/n)$ tax shares. The pivotal mechanism would still work if we substitute in any set of *preassigned* weights $\{\theta_i\}_{i=1}^n, \Sigma_{i=1}^n \theta_i = 1$. Therefore, if the planner wishes to discriminate between individuals (on the basis of some prior information, for example) he could do so and still be able to finance the acquisition of the project.

Returning once again to our numerical example, one can verify that the inclusion of any individual does not change the decision. No extra payments (over the equal shares, that is) are generated and the government budget is exactly balanced. Note, however, that this happy occurrence is the result of the perfect symmetry imposed on the example at hand.

3. The Problem of Budget Balancing

While the above example gave rise to a zero budget surplus, the pivotal mechanism does, in general, collect excessive taxes. Looking at (6.8), again, the total surplus is

$$\sum_i \left\{ \underset{x}{\text{Max}} \sum_{j \neq i} \left[v_j(x) - \frac{c}{n} x \right] - \sum_{j \neq i} \left[v_j\left(x^*(v)\right) - \frac{c}{n} x^*(v) \right] \right\}. \tag{6.8'}$$

What should the center do with these excessive payments? One's natural tendency is to commend that the amount be split up in some manner among participants. Acceptable though the idea may be, nevertheless it is not easily implemented. The basic reason is that any set of "surplus refund rules" is going to destroy the truthtelling incentives. If participants receive the extra revenues and if they grasp the distribution rules, the possibility of increasing one's own gain (by lying) opens up. This is so because the reimbursement is driving a wedge between the private and social objectives. We now face a new dilemma. If the center is to retain no surplus, an efficient decision *and* the assurance of sufficient revenues are impossible. Yet, if it disposes of the extra money (giving it to nonparticipants or foreign countries, for example) an inefficiency in the form of waste is introduced.

In light of the characterization results (theorems 2 and 3) the only hope for remedying the problem is via a different choice for the h_i terms. Since the pivotal scheme collects, as we just saw, excessive taxes we should try to adjust the h_i functions so as to eliminate the imbalance (for *every* admissible n-tuple of valuations). Unfortunately, Green and Laffont have shown that so long as we want our mechanism to operate over a sufficiently broad domain, that is impossible.

THEOREM 4 (GREEN–LAFFONT).   *For the class of increasing concave valuations there is no balanced (i.e., such that $\Sigma_{i=1}^n t_i(v) \equiv 0$) VCG mechanism.*

One way around this is what is known as "domain restrictions." The idea is to confine individual valuations to a restricted (possibly parametric) family of utility functions. It is quite analogous to the single-peakedness condition of Social Choice Theory. The intuition behind such restriction is to rule out "badly behaved" configuration of preferences. Namely, avoid potential preference configurations giving rise to budget imbalances. Groves and Loeb [1975, p. 219–220] have shown that it is possible to do so for the quadratic family we have previously introduced (see p. 8). More specifically, they have shown that

$$h_i(\theta_{-i}) = -\frac{1}{2n^2} \sum_{j \neq i} \theta_j^2 - \frac{1}{n^2(n-2)} \sum_{\substack{j,k \neq i \\ j \neq k}} \theta_j \theta_k \qquad (6.9)$$

will result in a balanced budget (BB hereafter). Pursuing this line of attack, Green and Laffont characterized all parametric families for which BB is feasible. Their results allow us to check whether zero revenues is an attainable goal without having to explicitly construct the appropriate h_i functions. The example below shows how their criterion may be invoked.

THEOREM 5 (GREEN–LAFFONT, p. 96). *Let $[v(x, \theta)\}$ be a class of utility functions such that θ lies in an open interval R and x^* $(\theta_1, \ldots, \theta_n)$ is continuously differential. There exists a balanced DRM for this class if and only if:*

$$\sum_{i=1}^{n} \frac{\partial^{n-1}}{\partial \theta_{-i}} \left[\frac{\partial v_i}{\partial x} \bigg|_{x^*(\theta)} \cdot \frac{\partial x^*}{\partial \theta_i} \right] \equiv 0.$$

As an example, let us apply this test to the family $v_i(x, \theta_i) = \theta_i \sqrt{x}, \theta_i \geq 0$. It is straightforward to establish that:

$$\frac{\partial v_i}{\partial x} = \frac{\theta_i}{2\sqrt{x}}, \qquad x^*(\theta_1, \ldots, \theta_n) = \left(\frac{\Sigma \theta_i}{2} \right)^2,$$

$$\frac{\partial x^*}{\partial \theta_i} = \frac{\Sigma \theta_i}{2} = \sqrt{x^*(\theta_1, \ldots, \theta_n)}.$$

Thus,
$$\frac{\partial v_i}{\partial x} \bigg|_{x^*} \frac{\partial x^*}{\partial \theta_i} = \frac{\theta_i}{2}.$$

BB is thus possible for this particular class of preferences. On the other hand, Green and Laffont have shown that no balanced DRM can be designed for certain parametric examples (see page 96).

Many practitioners are skeptical about "domain restrictions". The reason is twofold. First, all domain limitations are quite restrictive. In other words, they narrow down the class of admissible valuations to a considerable degree. The disadvantage, of course, is that the scheme is operational only over a meager set of cases. Second, restricting oneself to a particular family is customarily justified on the grounds of prior information. Namely, that the planner knows (beforehand) that all potential valuations belong to the family in question (or, at least, can approximated by its members). Remember, however, that it is the planner's *ignorance* which originally motivated us to look into the design problem. Thus, the assumption of partial information is somewhat contrary to the spirit of the original formulation.[2]

A second line of attack on the zero excess-revenue problem is to require that the budget be balanced only *on average* (see Groves [1976]). To be specific, assume that the n-tuple of utilities $(v_1, \ldots, v_n)$ is the realization of some fixed probability law. Further assume that the center knows the probability distribution governing these "random draws." Given this law the design problem is to select h_i functions in such a way that the *expected* net surplus equals zero. That is,

$$E \sum_{i=1}^{n} t_i(v) = 0. \qquad (6.10a)$$

Groves [1976, p. 76] has shown that the following particular choice for h_i accomplishes the *expected* BB goal:

$$h_i(v_{-i}) = \sum_{j \neq l} E[v_j(x^*(v))|v_{-i}] \tag{6.10b}$$

But expected zero revenues still leaves something to be desired. In common with the previous approach it relaxes the assumption of the center's perfect ignorance. The only difference is that prior information is expressed as a probability assessment over potential valuations. Such representation is more flexible than the restricted domain assumption. A second shortcoming is that taking expectations would be most relevant to repetitive and independent choices. However, if the public decision is "once and for all" (and that is often the case) then an *expected* balanced budget is a relatively insignificant feature of the mechanism.

Motivated by the dissatisfaction with the first two lines of attack, we are led to the asymptotic approach. Our discussion so far suggests that imbalance is an unavoidable problem. The natural question that arises then is: How severe is it? Our investigation will focus on the sizable community case, i.e., where n is a large number. This is motivated by the great difficulty in agreeing on and executing a joint course of action by large groups. Thus, free rider problems and the design of collective decision schemes are most germane in such environments. A second advantage is that meaningful comparisons can be made to the Walrasian theory. As it is well known, the latter is founded on the assumption of a nonatomic environment.

Having justified the approach, a word about the methodology is in order. As things stand, the size of the imbalance is an ambiguous concept. It clearly depends on the particular realization of preferences, $v = (v_1, \ldots, v_n)$. Thus an aggregation issue arises. We shall tackle this problem using probabilistic methods. To be specific, we conceive of a space, V, of valuation endowing it with a certain probability distribution. A specific n-tuple v (and the associated surplus/deficit) is to be thought of as a random draw from this distribution. Employing such structure the concept of the *expected* budget surplus, S_n, can be meaningfully defined. (S_n pertains to a size n community.) Moreover, we can investigate the behavior of S_n for large n's.

Green and Laffont pioneered this line of research. They have treated the case of a choice between two options, i.e., where the decision is whether to adopt or reject a public project. In that case each individual may be characterized by a single scalar—his incremental willingness to pay for project A over project B. The probability law we have mentioned is then the c.d.f., F, of those valuations. It was shown that the budget imbalance for large n's is negligible in the following sense:

THEOREM 6 (GREEN–LAFFONT, p. 172).   *Assume the distribution function F is absolutely continuous with mean m and bounded variance.*

(a) *If, for $m = 0$, F has a continuous density f with a unique mode equal to zero, then*

$$\lim_{n \to \infty} \frac{S_n}{\sqrt{n}} = \frac{1}{2\sqrt{2\pi}}$$

(b) *If $m \neq 0$ and $n^\alpha f_n(x)$ converges uniformly to zero for all $\alpha > 0$ then*

$$\lim_{n \to \infty} n^\alpha S_n = 0, \quad \text{for all } \alpha > 0.$$

The only limitation of theorem 6 is the set of distributional assumptions underlying it. As mentioned, this contrasts somewhat with the original intent. That is, with the idea that the planner is perfectly ignorant. In this light, the advantage of distribution-free results paralleling the assertions of theorem 6 is clear. Optimality would then be assured without having to assume any prior information. That this is indeed the case (for the two alternatives model) has been demonstrated by the author.

THEOREM 7 (ROB [1982]).   *Assume that v_i's are independent draws from a common distribution with mean m. Then*

(a) The probability that any person pays excessive taxes converges to zero as the number of participants increases indefinitely.

(b) If $m \neq 0$, $\lim_{n \to 0} S_n = 0$.

(c) If $m = 0$, $\lim_{n \to 0} \dfrac{S_n}{n} = 0$.

Using a topological structure the above positive results were extended to the case of a continuous project space (i.e., where there is an infinite number of alternatives).

THEOREM 8 (MITSUI [1982]).   *Assume that Y is a compact metric space and that V is a closed, bounded, convex, and equicontinuous subset of valuations on Y. Let $\{v_i\}_{i=1}^\infty$ be Cesaro summable then $\lim_{n \to \infty} t_i^n(v) = 0$.*

Finally, we should remark that approximate optimality is associated with an undesirable feature of the mechanism. Remember that excessive revenues are collected only to the extent that individuals have an impact on the decision. Note also that the larger is the group the smaller is this individual impact. It follows that little, if any, excessive revenues are generated for large groups. This simple observation is the intuition behind the proof of the asymptotic efficiency theorems 6–8. However, this is unfortunate since optimality is achieved at the cost of participants' indifference. Surely, if an individual's vote can hardly influence the outcome, participants would be undermotivated to invest time and effort in a comparative evaluation of the alternatives (see Tideman–Tullock [1976, p. 146]).

All things considered, though, that state of affairs is more or less characteristic of all voting schemes (see Downs [1957]). On that account, it is clear that voters' indifference is no worse of a handicap for the DRM than it is for an ordinary voting procedure.

4. Limitations of the DRM

In this section we briefly list some of the shortcomings of the VCG mechanisms.

(1) Coalitional manipulability — one major advantage of the Groves scheme is that reporting one's true valuation is a dominant strategy. Thus, if individuals act in isolation, their true characteristics are revealed. What if a subgroup somehow managed to reach a cooperative agreement? It is not hard to show that by coordinating actions ($\equiv$ reports) they could all benefit. The DRM, in other words, is not immune to coalitional maneuvers. More generally

THEOREM 9 (GREEN–LAFFONT, p. 116). *No truthful mechanism can prevent cheating by coalitions of members.*

Observe, however, that coalitional manipulation requires the formation, agreement and enforcement of concerted actions by colluding participants. From Oligopoly theory we know that coalitions are subject to internal instabilities. Greedy coalition members can benefit by cheating on the cooperative agreement. It is these defections which threaten the existence of coalitions and which initially led us to the mechanism design problem. Therefore, the ability of a coalition to maintain an agreement is questionable.

In addition, any agreement between coalition members should depend on their individual characteristics-valuations. But if those characteristics are only privately known, and that is the essence of the present formulation, then the feasibility of attaining an agreement is very much in doubt. Finally, Green and Laffont have shown ([1979, p. 194]) that the potential gains from collusion shrink as the size of the community increases. Summarizing, we conclude that severe obstacles may very well prevent the realization of coalitional gains. Therefore, Coalitional manipulability seems to be a very slight defect of the DRM.

(2) Separability — the postulated form of utility functions, namely, $u_i(x, m_i) = m_i + v_i(x)$, precludes the existence of income effects. Clearly, it would be desirable to eliminate the assumption of additive separability. That would enlarge the domain over which our scheme is allowed to operate. Unfortunately, Green and Laffont have shown that such generalization is impossible.

THEOREM 10 (GREEN–LAFFONT, p. 83). *Assume that the class of admissible valuations includes all constant functions, one strictly monotone function, $\bar{v}$, and shifts of $\bar{v}$ by a constant. Then there exists no dominant-strategy, truth-revealing mechanism.*

(3) Voluntary Participation — Assume that initially no public goods are available. So at the initial state individual utilities are simply m_i^0. Since the decision $x^*(v)$ maximizes social welfare given true preferences, the utility of participants is expected to rise on the whole. Nonetheless, any one agent might be worse off participating in the mechanism than he was in the status quo. Consider, for example the case of two individuals with

$$u_i(x) = m_i^0 + \theta_i \sqrt{x}, \qquad i = 1, 2 \tag{6.11}$$

and where the pivotal mechanism is implemented with equal $(1/2)$ tax shares. Assume that production costs are unitary. One can easily establish that:

$$x^*(\theta_1, \theta_2) = \left(\frac{\theta_1 + \theta_2}{2}\right)^2;$$

$$t_i(\theta_1, \theta_2) = \frac{1}{2} x^*(\theta_1, \theta_2) + h_i(\theta_{-i}) = \left(\frac{\theta_1 + \theta_2}{2}\right)^2, \quad i = 1, 2.$$

That is, each individual is charged the *full* cost of the project. Thus the benefit to person i exceeds his cost (i.e., he is better off participating) if and only if

$$\theta_i\left(\frac{\theta_1 + \theta_2}{2}\right) > \left(\frac{\theta_1 + \theta_2}{2}\right)^2 \quad \text{or} \quad \theta_i > \theta_j.$$

We see that the pivotal mechanism penalizes individuals whose willingness to pay for public projects is low. Given the choice, those individuals would prefer no-participation. On the other hand, the exit of individuals reduces attained welfare because of the assumed no-congestion character of public goods. Thus, from the standpoint of *aggregate* welfare it would pay to maximize participation.

Assume that coercion is unacceptable on ethical grounds. Can we design a (necessarily nonpivotal) scheme which induces individuals to voluntarily participate? The key to the answer is given by the following:

THEOREM 11 (GREEN–LAFFONT, p. 122). *The set of individually rational VCG mechanisms is characterized by* $h_i(v_{-i}) \leq 0$ *for all i and all* $(n-1)$ *tuples* v_{-i}.

This condition makes it impossible to design such schemes. As we have already shown, the $h_i \equiv 0$ mechanism generates a budget deficit. Clearly, the revenue performance of schemes with $h_i < 0$ is even worse. Thus, individual rationality and project financing are incompatible goals.

As with budget balancing, one possible way around this problem is to invoke a weaker voluntary participation concept. A close examination of the individual rationality condition reveals that it is a kind of unanimity or veto power constraint. In other words, it is required that *all* individuals accept the decision making process. Certainly, this requirement is rather stringent. For example, none of the political processes in the real world satisfy it. Therefore, it would seem reasonable to invoke a weaker individual rationality constraint.

One possibility is *ex ante* voluntary participation. Ex ante means that the participation decision is made before the individual knows his type or valuation, v_i. Thus, the acceptance decision is based on *expected* gains where the expectation is taken over all the possible valuations an individual might possess. The similarity between this and Rawls [1977] "veil of ignorance" construct should be apparent. The only difference is that Rawls uses a Minimax rather than an expected value criterion. Groves [1976, pp. 77–78] has shown that the following particular choice for h_i

$$h_i(v_{-i}) = -E\left[v_i(x^*(v)) + \frac{n-1}{n} \sum_{j \neq i} v_j(x^*(v)) \middle| v_{-i} \right]$$

makes the DRM ex ante individually rational.

5. Alternative Equilibrium Concepts

We have discussed several of the limitations of the DRM as well as the ways to tackle them. One extension we have thus far not described is a weaker equilibrium concept. There are many options (Minmax and Nash to name just two) to consider; however, I shall confine the discussion below to the family of Nash–Bayesian mechanisms. For those truth is an equilibrium point (as opposed to a dominant strategy). Using this weaker equilibrium concept enlarges the set of feasible schemes. It is thus at least conceivable that we could overcome some of the alluded to limitations.

We have also mentioned the fact that prior information about participants' valuations allows us to attain certain goals that are otherwise unattainable. The Bayesian structure postulates such prior beliefs at the outset. Thus information is built into the structure. The superiority of analyzing the role of prior information in a model where information is an integral part gives us another reason to favor this approach.

Third, invoking prior information does not look so bad if we recall that both perfect ignorance and perfect knowledge are included as special cases (diffused and point priors, respectively). In between we have a whole spectrum parameterized by the degree of uncertainty. Thus, the Bayesian model is quite flexible in terms of what it can cover. Let us now look at what it has to offer.

Before we do that, let us briefly outline the structure of the Bayesian framework. It is assumed that agent i has a utility function of the form $u_i(x; \theta_i)$ + (other income) where $\theta_i \varepsilon R^k$ is a finite-dimensional taste parameter. The functional *form* of u_i is known to all but only agent i knows his own θ_i. In addition, agent i possesses a probability distribution over the parameters $\theta_1, \ldots, \theta_{i-1}, \theta_{i+1}, \ldots, \theta_n$ which is independent of his own parameter value (θ_i). As a matter of convention, we call this distribution — his prior. The center employs a decision rule $\hat{x}(\theta_1, \ldots, \theta_n)$ where $\theta = (\theta_1, \ldots, \theta_n)$ is the vector of *reported* characteristics. Regarding agents' choice of what to report we suppose that they act as Bayesian decision makers employing their priors and knowing the center's decision rule $\hat{x}$. This methodology was first introduced by Harsanyi [1967–68]. For a fuller description of the working of such models the reader is referred to Myerson [1984].

In a pioneering paper, Arrow [1979] exploited the above structure to show that zero excess revenues are possible. (Much in the same spirit is the independent work of C. d'Aspremont and L. A. Gérard-Varet [1979].) Unlike the Groves-type averaging condition, it is demonstrated that budget balancing can actually be attained pointwise, i.e., for every realization, θ, of valuations. A second feature of the Arrow mechanism is that it is applicable to a broad class of welfare criteria. Those include (but are not limited to) the Utilitarian sum of valuations on which we have so far focused. For example, redistributional considerations could be accommodated by a proper assignment of welfare weights. The class of admissible objectives covered under the Arrow scheme should only satisfy a responsiveness condition. Namely, that the marginal utility and the quantity of public goods change (on average) in the same direction as the individual varies his valuation parameter. Mathematically, it is required that

$$E_{-i}[u_x^i(\hat{x}(\theta_{-i}, \theta_i), \theta_i)\hat{x}_{\theta_i}(\theta_{-i}, \theta_i)] > 0.$$

Analyzing this Bayesian model Arrow has shown that the following tax structure implements $\hat{x}$ and balances the budget

$$t_i(\theta_i) = \sum_{j \neq i} t_{ji}(\theta_i) = t_i(-\infty) + \int_{-\infty}^{\theta_i} E_{\theta_{-i}}[u_x^i(\hat{x}(s, \theta_{-i}), s)\hat{x}_s(s, \theta_{-i}) \, ds,$$

where t_{ji} is the amount of money transferred from individual i to individual j.

One desideratum missing from the above model is a no-coercion or voluntary participation requirement. In an attempt to remedy this situation, the author introduced individual rationality constraints into a somewhat specialized structure. In my model the collective decision is of the zero-one variety. That is, $\hat{x}$ takes on only two values: accept (one) and reject (zero) the construction of a pollution-generating plant. Output levels are thus not a choice variable. If the plant is constructed, a firm will receive a benefit (profits) of $R > 0$ dollars where R is assumed common knowledge. The taste parameter, θ_i, is interpreted as the loss sustained by individual i, if the plant operates. Thus, a first-best decision would be "operate if and only if $\sum_{i=1}^n \theta_i \leq R$." Since $\theta_i's$ are private information a mechanism must be designed. This mechanism is *defined* as an $(n+1)$-tuple, $p(\theta), x_1(\theta), \ldots, x_n(\theta)$, of decision rules. $p(\theta)$ is the probability of operating the plant while $x_i(\theta)$ is the expected compensation to individual i. These decision rules are selected by a profit-maximizing firm which is subject to individual rationality (IR) and incentive constraints. More specifically, it is assumed that the initial state is one where no plant is operating and that individuals are entitled to maintain this status quo ("clean air"). IR means that a mechanism is admissible only if *all* individuals prefer participation to abstention (receiving their status quo utility levels). The incentive constraints, on the other hand, insure that revealing one's true damage, θ_i, is an equilibrium strategy.

With the "rules of the game" so specified, I have shown that the first best outcome-realizing a point on the Pareto frontier — is unachievable. Moreover, the welfare loss increases rapidly with the number of participants. In the limit, as $n \to \infty$, the entire potential surplus is dissipated. Clearly, these results run counter to the aymptotic efficiency theorems 6–8. The lesson to be learned from this is that the present form of IR is much too strong in terms of the welfare loss it imposes. It calls into question the reformulation of the appropriate voluntary participation conditions. One obvious possibility would be a majority rule instead of a person-by-person IR.

Notes

1. Assuming sufficient smoothness to warrant the use differential methods.
2. The two are not entirely contradictory since ignorance and perfect information are only two extreme cases. In between them lies a whole spectrum of cases differentiated by the degree of uncertainty. We shall shortly explore this idea.

References

Arrow, K. J., "The Organization of Economic Activity: Issues Pertinent to the Choice of Market versus Nonmarket Allocation." In *U. S. Congress Joint Economic Committee, 91st Congress, 1st Session*, 1969.

——, "The Property Rights Doctrine and Demand Revelation Under Incomplete Information." In *Economics and Human Wealth*, M. Boskin (ed.), New York: Academic Press, 1979.

Clarke, E. H., "Multipart Pricing of Public Goods." *Public Choice* 8 (1971), 19–33.

Downs, A., *An Economic Theory of Democracy*. New York: Harper and Row, 1957.

D'Aspremont, C. and L. A. Gerard-Varet, "Incentives and Incomplete Information." *Journal of Public Economics* 11 (1979), 25–45.

Green, J. and J. J. Laffont, *Incentives in Public Decision Making*. Amsterdam-New York: North-Holland, 1979.

Gresik, T. A. and M. A. Satterthwaite, "The Number of Traders Required to Make a Market Competitive: The Beginning of a Theory." Discussion Paper No. 651, Northwestern University, February 1983.

Groves, T., "Incentives in Teams." *Econometrica* 41 (1973), 617–31.

——, "Information, Incentives and the Internalization of Externalities." In *Theory and Measurement of Economic Externalities*, S. A. Lin (ed.), Academic Press, 1976.

Groves, T. and M. Loeb, "Incentives and Public Inputs." *Journal of Public Economics* 4 (1975), 211–226.

Harsanyi, J. C., "Games with Incomplete Information Played by Bayesian Players." *Management Science* 14 (1967–68), 159–189; 320–334; 486–502.

Mitsui, T., "Asymptotic Efficiency of the Pivotal Mechanism with General Project Space." Working Paper #105, Department of Economics, University of Kansas, March 1982.

Myerson, R., "An Introduction to Game Theory." Discussion Paper No. 623, CMSEMS, Northwestern University, September 1984.

Rawls, J., *A Theory of Justice*. Cambridge, Mass.: Harvard University Press, 1977.

Rob, R., "Asymptotic Efficiency of the Demand-Revealing Mechanism." *Journal of Economic Theory* 28 (1982), 208–220.

——, "The Coase Theorem: An Informational Perspective." University of Minnesota, IMA Reprint Series #60, February 1984.

Samuelson, W., "A Comment on the Coase Theorem." Mimeo, Boston University.

Tideman, T. and G. Tullock, "A New and Superior Process for Collective Choice." *Journal of Political Economics* 84 (1976), 1145–1159.

Vickrey, W., "Counterspeculation, Auctions, and Competitive Sealed Tender." *Journal of Finance* 16 (1961), 8–37.

Wilson, R., "A Bidding Model of Perfect Competition." *Review of Economic Studies* 44 (1977), 511–518.

———, "Double Auctions." Technical Report # 391, IMSSS, Stanford University, December 1982.

7 THE DESIGN
OF EFFICIENT RESOURCE
ALLOCATION MECHANISMS

Parkash Chander

A major part of the classical welfare economics is devoted to a study of a particular resource allocation mechanism, viz. perfect competition. Classical welfare theorems of Kenneth Arrow, Gerard Debreu, and Tjalling Koopmans show that in classical economies (those in which preferences and production possibilities have suitable convexity and continuity properties) the competitive mechanism may be expected to function satisfactorily in the sense that it would produce allocations that are Pareto optimal. Similarly, attempts have been made to characterize Pareto optimal allocations in nonclassical economies (those involving indivisibilities, increasing returns, or public goods). Mechanisms, which are quite different from the competitive one, have been designed which would compute these allocations. See, for example, Hurwicz [1959] and Hurwicz, Radner, and Reiter [1975]. Designing such mechanisms would of course be a trivial matter if the optimality of the resulting allocations were the only performance requirement. But as may be seen from the early debates over the feasibility of central planning in socialist economies, there are other important characteristics of mechanisms that also need to be taken into account. Among them are the amount of information processing required by the mechanism, and the extent to which the rules prescribed by it are compatible (or incompatible) with the natural incentives of the economic agents. Processing of information uses resources (the operating cost) and alternative mechanisms may be more or less demanding in this respect. Similarly, if the rules of the mechanism are in conflict with the private incentives, it may be necessary to have an external control system (for example, policing) in operation and resources to administer it.

We may thus view the resource allocation problem more generally as one in which the mechanism is an unknown. The designer's task is to choose only those mechanisms which in addition to computing (Pareto or related welfare criterion) optimal allocations would perform well in terms of their informational efficiency and incentive compatibility. But how may we evaluate and compare alternative mechanisms in terms of these criterion?

Work in this direction was began in earnest by Leonid Hurwicz, who along with others has developed a theory for the comparative study of resource allocation mechanisms. We shall not attempt to review that theory here. Instead, we shall illustrate how certain tools of this theory can help in analyzing the properties of resource allocation mechanisms alluded to above. We shall do this by studying a specific mechanism.

The mechanism we study produces Pareto optimal and individually rational allocations in certain economies with public goods. It was proposed independently by Drèze and de la Vallée Poussin and Malinvaud at the beginning of the seventies and has come to be called the MDP process. We shall focus on its informational properties. First, its incentives properties are more or less already well known. Second, the problem of incentives and public goods is analyzed by Rafael Rob separately in a paper that appears in this volume.

It will be shown that the MDP process is informationally the maximally efficient mechanism among a certain class of resource allocation mechanisms.

1. The Resource Allocation Problem

We shall study the problem of resource allocation for economies involving $l + 1$ commodities and $n + 1$ agents. Among the commodities the first l are public goods and the $(l + 1)$th commodity is the only private good. Each agent i, $i = 1, \ldots, n$, is a consumer and the $(n + 1)$th agent is the sole producer. All the public goods are produced by using the private good which is the only input.

Each agent i is described by his economic characteristics, to be denoted by e^i. For consumer i, these are his utility function u^i and initial resource endowment w^i of the private good. Thus, $e^i = (u^i, w^i)$, $i = 1, \ldots, n$. For the producer (the $(n + 1)$th agent), these are his (convex) cost function c and an n-tuple $\theta = (\theta^1, \ldots, \theta^n)$ satisfying $\theta^i \geq 0$ for all i and $\Sigma_j \theta^j = 1$. It is known that under certain convexity assumptions on the cost function, the marginal-cost-pricing rule would lead to a surplus in terms of the private good, which is the only input. The n-tuple $(\theta^1, \ldots, \theta^n)$ specifies the rule followed by the producer to distribute its surplus among the consumers. Thus, $e^{n+1} = (c, \theta)$.

We shall assume that the whole economy can be completely described in terms of the characteristics $e^1, \ldots, e^{n+1}$ of the agents and we shall regard the economy as the $(n+1)$-tuple of characteristics $e = (e^1, \ldots, e^{n+1})$. The characteristics $e^1, \ldots, e^{n+1}$ determine which resource allocations are feasible or optimal. It is the function of a mechanism to guide the economy to the optimal resource allocations.

We now fully specify the class of economies for which the MDP process computes the optimal resource allocations. We shall denote the kth public good quantity by x_k, and the private good quantity by y. Let[1]

$U = \{u\colon R_+^{l+1} \to R^1\colon$ (1) u is strictly quasiconcave and at least twice differentiable; (2) $\partial u(x, y)/\partial x_k \geq 0$ for each k $(= 1, \ldots, l)$ and $\partial u(x, y)/\partial y > 0$ for all $(x, y) \in R_+^{l+1}$; and (3) $\partial u(x, 0)/\partial x = 0$ for all $x \in R_+^l \}$[1];

$C = \{c\colon R_+^l \to R_+^1\colon$ (1) c is convex and at least twice differentiable; (2) $c(0) = 0$ and $\partial c(x)/\partial x_k \geq 0$ for all $x \in R_+^l$; and (3) there exists a positive constant K such that $x_k > K$ for any $k \Rightarrow c(x) > \Sigma w^i \}$;

$$\Delta = \{(\theta^1, \ldots, \theta^n) \in R_+^n \colon \Sigma \, \theta^i = 1\};$$
$$E^i = U \times R_{++}^1 \qquad (i = 1, \ldots, n);$$
$$E^{n+1} = C \times \Delta;$$

and
$$E^o = E^1 \times E^2 \times \cdots \times E^{n+1}.$$

Then, E^i is the *space of characteristics* of agent i, and E^o the *space or class of economies*. A generic element of E^o is denoted by $e = (e^1, \ldots, e^{n+1})$ or by $((u^1, w^1), \ldots, (u^n, w^n), (c, \theta)) = (\langle (u^i, w^i) \rangle, (c, \theta))$.

The *set of feasible programs* for each $(\langle (u^i, w^i) \rangle, (c, \theta)) \in E^o$ is given by

$$P(\langle (u^i, w^i) \rangle, (c, \theta)) = \{(\langle (x^i, y^i) \rangle, (x, y))\colon x^i = x \text{ and } w^i + y^i \geq 0$$
$$\text{for } i = 1, \ldots, n, \Sigma \, y^i = y \text{ and } c(x) + y = 0\}$$

and the set of *Pareto optimal programs* by

$$F(\langle (u^i, w^i) \rangle, (c, \theta)) = \{(\langle (x^i, y^i) \rangle, (x, y)) \in F(\langle (u^i, w^i) \rangle, (c, \theta)\colon$$
$$\sum_k \left(\sum_i \frac{\partial u^i(x^i, w^i + y^i)/\partial x_k^i}{\partial u^i(x^i, w^i + y^i)/\partial y^i} - \frac{\partial c(x)}{\partial x_k} \right) x_k = 0\}$$

Here y^i denotes the contribution of consumer i towards the cost of production of public goods, and the expression

$$\frac{\partial u^i (x^i, w^i + y^i)/\partial x^i_k}{\partial u^i (x^i, w^i + y^i)/\partial y^i}$$

is the marginal rate of substitution between the kth public good and the private good of consumer i. The expression $\partial c(x)/\partial x_k$ is the marginal cost of the kth public good production.

We shall adopt the following definitions. Let X and Y be two nonempty sets. A *correspondence F of X into Y* written $F: X \rightarrow Y$ is a rule which associates with each element x of X a (possibly empty) subset $F(x)$ of Y. A correspondence $F: X \rightarrow Y$ is *single valued* if $F(x)$ is a singleton for every $x \in X$, and in that case F is identified with the function $f: X \rightarrow Y$ such that $F(x) = \{ f(x) \}$ for every $x \in X$. Given a nonempty subset A of X, the *image $F(A)$ of A* under $F: X \rightarrow Y$ is defined by $F(A) = \{ y \in Y : y \in F(x) \text{ for some } x \in A \}$. The *domain and range of $F: X \rightarrow Y$* are defined as follows: dom $F = \{ x \in X : F(x) \neq \varnothing \}$ and range $F = F(X)$. The *lower inverse* of $F: X \rightarrow Y$ is a correspondence $F^{-1}: Y \rightarrow X$ defined by $F^{-1}(y) = \{ x \in X : y \in F(x) \}$. If A and B are subsets of X and Y, then $F: A \rightarrow B$ denotes the correspondence defined by $F(x) = F(x) \cap B$ for each $x \in A$.

Let $\Theta: E^o \rightarrow \Theta(E^o)$ be the correspondence such that

$$\Theta(\langle (u^i, w^i) \rangle, (c, \theta)) = \left\{ (\langle (x^i, y^i) \rangle, (x, y)) \in P(\langle u^i, w^i \rangle), (c, \theta)): \right.$$

$$\sum_k \frac{\partial u^i (x^i, w^i + y^i)/\partial x^i_k}{\partial u^i (x^i, w^i + y^i)/\partial y^i} x^i_k + y^i$$

$$\left. = \theta^i \left(\sum_k \frac{\partial c(x)}{\partial x_k} x_k - c(x) \right) \quad \text{for } i = 1, \ldots, n \right\}.$$

We shall refer to Θ as the *optimality correspondence*. Since c is convex, the allocations specified by Θ are *individually rational* in the sense that $u^i (x^i, w^i + y^i) \geq u^i (0, w^i)$ for each $(\langle (x^i, y^i) \rangle, (x, y)) \in \Theta(\langle (u^i, w^i) \rangle, (c, \theta))$.

The class E^o and the optimality correspondence Θ describe the basic data or the givens. The problem is one of devising a mechanism that would compute the allocations $\Theta(e)$ for each $e \in E^o$.

2. The MDP Process

It was mentioned in the introduction that we shall focus on the informational aspect of resource allocation mechanisms. The issue underlying this is that no one has complete information about the economy e. Each agent knows about his own characteristics but is totally unaware of the characteristics of the other agents, that is, agent i knows e^i but does not know anything about e^j for every j different from i. Since the optimal allocations would in general depend on the characteristics of more than one agent, no agent by himself can figure out the optimal allocations $\Theta(e)$. Some form of communication or information exchange among the agents is necessary.

The idea underlying resource allocation mechanisms is that instead of transmitting huge amounts of information (such as a complete description of the characteristics $e^1, \ldots, e^{n+1}$), the agents may exchange small amounts of information among them in an iterative fashion till they find the information which is sufficient to determine an optimal allocation. This may be expected to be more economical in terms of the costs of information transmission. We shall illustrate this issue by studying a specific resource allocation mechanism viz. the MDP process.

We first give a formal description of the process. Although it is a continuous time process, in order to understand clearly the nature of the information exchange it envisages, we shall state it as a discrete-time process.

Let $(\langle (u^i, w^i) \rangle, (c, \theta))$ be some economy belonging to the class E^o. The MDP process is formally described by the following system of temporally homogeneous first order difference equations:

$$x_k(t+1) = f_k^{n+1}(c, \theta, x(t), \langle y^j(t) \rangle, \langle \pi^j(t) \rangle) \qquad (k = 1, \ldots, l); \quad (7.1)$$

$$y^i(t+1) = f_{l+i}^{n+1}(c, \theta, x(t), \langle y^j(t) \rangle, \langle \pi^j(t) \rangle) \qquad (i = 1, \ldots, n); \quad (7.2)$$

$$\pi^i(t) = f^i(u^i, w^i, x(t), \langle y^j(t) \rangle) \qquad (i = 1, \ldots, n), t \geq 0; \quad (7.3)$$

where $x(0) = 0$, $y^j(0) = 0$ $(j = 1, \ldots, n)$,

$$f_k^i(u^i, w^i; x, \langle y^j \rangle) = \frac{\partial u^i(x, w^i + y^i)/\partial x_k}{\partial u^i(x, w^i + y^i)/\partial y^i} \qquad (k = 1, \ldots, l; i = 1, \ldots, n),$$

$$f_k^{n+1}(c, \theta; x, \langle y^j \rangle, \langle \pi^j \rangle)$$

$$= x_k + \begin{bmatrix} \Sigma_j \pi_k^j - (\partial c(x)/\partial x_k) & \text{if } x_k > 0, \\ \max\{0, \Sigma_j \pi_k^j - (\partial c(x)/\partial x_k)\} & \text{if } x_k = 0 \end{bmatrix}$$

and

$$f_{l+i}^{n+1}(c, \theta; x, \langle y^j \rangle, \langle \pi^j \rangle) = y^i - \sum_{k=1}^{l} \pi_k^i (f_k^{n+1} - x_k) + \delta^i \sum_{k=1}^{l} (f_k^{n+1} - x_k)^2$$

$$(i = 1, \ldots, n)$$

where $(\delta^1, \ldots, \delta^n) \in \Delta$ are some exogenously given constants.

At any time τ, $(x(\tau), \langle y^j(\tau) \rangle) \in R_+^{l+n}$ (which can be equivalently written as $(\langle x(\tau), y^j(\tau)) \rangle, (x(\tau), \Sigma y^j(\tau)))$ denotes the proposed (feasible) program and $\pi^i(\tau) \in R^l_+$, the vector of marginal rates of substitution between each public good and the private good of consumer i.

Difference equations (7.1), (7.2), and (7.3) formalize the following type of information exchange. At any time τ, given the program $(x(\tau), \langle (y^j(\tau)) \rangle)$ the message of consumer i to the producer is $\pi^i(\tau)$. Given the information about $\langle \pi^j(t) \rangle$ and the program $(x(\tau), \langle y^j(\tau) \rangle)$, the producer raises (lowers) the output of any public good for which the aggregate marginal value is greater (less) than the marginal cost and revises the contribution of each consumer according to (7.2). (For an interpretation of the rule specified by (7.2), see Drèze and de la Vallée Poussin [1981].) The message of the producer to the consumers is then the revised program $(x(\tau+1), \langle y^j(\tau+1) \rangle)$. The vector $(x(\tau), \langle y^j(\tau) \rangle, \langle \pi^j(\tau) \rangle) \in R^{l+n+ln}$ will be referred to as the *message vector* at time τ.

The MDP process is *temporally homogeneous* in the sense that the size and nature of the message vector at any time τ is the same, that is, each function f^i is independent of τ. Moreover, it is *informationally decentralized* in the sense that for each agent i the "response function" f^i does not depend on the characteristics of the other agents, acknowledging thereby that each agent knows only about his own characteristics, but is ignorant of the characteristics of the other agents.

It may be worth noting that the first order difference equations (7.1), (7.2), and (7.3), which describe the MDP process, can be transformed into those of second order by permitting the agents to have memory. But this will lead to certain rather unrewarding complications, since we shall have to deal with two concepts of informational capacity: memory and message size. The present formulation treats them both as one.

The stationarity condition for the system of equations (7.1), (7.2), and (7.3) is

$$(\bar{x}, \langle \bar{y}^j \rangle, \langle \bar{\pi}^j \rangle) = f(\langle (u^i, w^i) \rangle, (c, \theta); \bar{x}, \langle \bar{y}^j \rangle, \langle \bar{\pi}^j \rangle), \qquad (7.4)$$

where $f = (f^1, \ldots, f^{n+1})$.

The time path of the dynamic process described by (7.1), (7.2), and (7.3) depends on the values of the parameters $\delta^1, \ldots, \delta^n$. Drèze and de la Vallée Poussin [1981] show that for each $(\delta^1, \ldots, \delta^n) \in \Delta$ the process converges to a stationary point which is such that the corresponding program is Pareto optimal. Champsaur [1976] and Cornet [1983] show that the process can be made to converge to any given individually rational Pareto optimal program by a suitable choice of the parameters $\delta^1, \ldots, \delta^n$. In particular, the values of these parameters can be chosen such that at the stationary point

$$(\bar{\pi}^i \bar{x} + \bar{y}^i)/(\sum_j \bar{\pi}^j \bar{x} + \Sigma \bar{y}^j) = \theta^i \qquad (i = 1, \ldots, n), \qquad (7.5)$$

which means that the MDP process is a method for implementing the programs specified by Θ. This is, in fact, the interpretation that we shall adopt, i.e., we shall restrict only to the case when the values of the parameters $\delta^1, \ldots, \delta^n$ are fixed such that (7.5) is satisfied.

Let $\mu: E^o \to R^{l+n+ln}$ be the correspondence such that

$$\mu(\langle (u^j, w^j) \rangle, (c, \theta)) = \{(x, \langle y^j \rangle, \langle \pi^j \rangle): (x, \langle y^j \rangle, \langle \pi^j \rangle)$$
$$= f(\langle (u^j, w^j) \rangle, (c, \theta); x, \langle y^j \rangle, \langle \pi^j \rangle) \text{ and}$$
$$(\pi^i x + y^i)/(\Sigma \pi^j x + \Sigma y^j) = \theta^i, i = 1, \ldots, n\}.$$

We shall refer to μ as the *equilibrium message correspondence* of the MDP process. The twin properties of temporal homogeneity and informational decentralization are inherited by the correspondence μ in the following manner.

Let N denote the set $\{1, \ldots, n+1\}$. For any two $(n+1)$-tuples $\bar{a} = (\bar{a}^1, \ldots, \bar{a}^{n+1})$ and $\tilde{a} = (\tilde{a}^1, \ldots, \tilde{a}^{n+1})$, let $\bar{\tilde{a}}(i), i \in N$, denote the $(n+1)$-tuple $(\bar{a}^1, \ldots, \bar{a}^{i-1}, \tilde{a}^i, \bar{a}^{i+1}, \ldots, \bar{a}^{n+1})$.

PROPOSITION 1. *For every* $\bar{e}, \tilde{e} \in E^o, \mu(\bar{e}) \cap \mu(\tilde{e}) = \mu(\bar{\tilde{e}}(i)) \cap \mu(\tilde{\bar{e}}(i))$ *for every* $i \in N$.

Proof. If $(x, \langle y^j \rangle, \langle \pi^j \rangle) \in \mu(\bar{e}) \cap \mu(\tilde{e})$, then

$$(x, \langle y^j \rangle, \langle \pi^j \rangle) = f(x, \langle y^j \rangle, \langle \pi^j \rangle, \bar{e}) = f(x, \langle y^j \rangle, \langle \pi^j \rangle, \tilde{e}).$$

Which implies

$$(x, \langle y^j \rangle, \langle \pi^j \rangle) = f(x, \langle y^j \rangle, \langle \pi^j \rangle, \bar{\tilde{e}}(i))$$
$$= f(x, \langle y^j \rangle, \langle \pi^j \rangle, \tilde{\bar{e}}(i)) \quad \text{for } i \in N.$$

That is, $(x, \langle y^j \rangle, \langle \pi^j \rangle) \in \mu(\bar{\tilde{e}}(i) \cap \mu(\tilde{\bar{e}}(i))$. Similarly, if $m \in \mu(\bar{\tilde{e}}) \cap \mu(\tilde{\bar{e}})$, then $m \in \mu(\bar{e}) \cap \mu(\tilde{e})$. Hence the proposition. $\square$

Let $g: \mu(E^o) \to R^{(n+1)(l+1)}$ be the function defined by

$$g(x, \langle y^j \rangle, \langle \pi^j \rangle) = (\langle (x^j, y^j) \rangle, (x, y)),$$

where $x^i = x \ (i = 1, \ldots, n)$ and $y = \Sigma y^j$. We shall call g the *outcome function* and the pair $[\mu, g]$ the *static representation of the MDP process* or simply the *MDP process*. Clearly, $g \circ \mu = \Theta$, that is, the pair $[\mu, g]$ implements Θ.

The maximal informational efficiency of the MDP process refers to the following question. Is it possible to design a temporally homogeneous and informationally decentralized mechanism which would 'implement' the optimality correspondence Θ and in which the message vectors are of smaller dimensionality?[2] Results below show that the answer is no.

Although the MDP process is an iterative one, we shall only prove the minimality of the dimension of its equilibrium message vectors as characterized by the correspondence μ. Because of the temporal homogeneity restriction, this is equivalent to proving the minimality of the dimension of the message vectors in general.

The basic idea underlying the notion of informational efficiency adopted above is that the cost of transmission increases with the dimensionality of the message vectors. However, there is a technical problem with this, which is due to the possibility that a single real number can be used to convey information about two or more numbers simultaneously. Such a possibility exists because there exist bijective maps from the unit square $[0, 1] \times [0, 1]$ to the unit interval $[0, 1]$. The possibility of such maps is seen as follows. Let $h_1 : [0, 1] \to [0, 1] \times [0, 1]$ be the map defined by

$$h_1(x) = (x, 0) \quad \text{for all } x \in [0, 1].$$

Clearly, h_1 is an injection. On the other hand, let $h_2 : [0, 1] \times [0, 1] \to [0, 1]$ be the map defined by

$$h_2(x, y) = 0 \cdot x_1 y_1 x_2 y_2 x_3 y_3 \cdots \quad \text{for all } (x, y) \in [0, 1] \times [0, 1],$$

where $0 \cdot x_1 x_3 \cdots$ and $0 \cdot y_1 y_2 y_3 \cdots$ are the decimal representations of x and y which do not consist of nines from a certain point onwards. Clearly, h_2 is also an injection.

It follows from the Schroeder–Bernstein theorem (see, e.g., Munkres [1975]) that there exists a bijective map h from $[0, 1] \times [0, 1]$ to $[0, 1]$.

Observe that h cannot be a continuous map. Since if it were so, then by proposition 9.5 in Royden [1968] it would be a homeomorphism, which is absurd.

If every agent knows about the map h and, therefore, h^{-1}, then a mechanism in which the message vectors are of dimension two or more can be transformed into another in which they are of lesser dimension. Therefore, dimensionality can be a "genuine" measure of informational efficiency only so long as such "encoding" maps are not used. We show that they are not used in the case of the MDP process at least for a certain subclass of economies, which is as described below. Let

$$U^* = \{u \in U : \text{there is some } \alpha \in R_{++}^l \text{ such that } u(x, y) = y x_1^{\alpha_1} x_2^{\alpha_2} \cdots x_l^{\alpha_l} \text{ for each } (x, y) \in R_+^{l+1}\};$$

$$C^* = \{c \in C : \text{there is some } a \in R_{++}^l \text{ and } \lambda \in R^l, \ 1 < \lambda \leq 2, \text{ such that } c(x) = \sum_{i=1}^l a_i x_i^\lambda \text{ for each } x \in R_+^l\};$$

$$E^{*i} = U^* \times R_{++}^1 \quad (i = 1, \ldots, n);$$

$$E^{*n+1} = C^* \times \Delta \quad \text{and} \quad E^* = E^{*1} \times \cdots \times E^{*n+1}.$$

Define a metric d on U^* by $d(\bar{u}, \tilde{u}) = |\bar{\alpha}, \tilde{\alpha}|$ for each $\bar{u}, \tilde{u} \in U^*$, where $\bar{u}(x, y) = y \Pi_k \chi_k^{\bar{\alpha}_k}$ and $\tilde{u}(x, y) = y \Pi_k \chi_k^{\tilde{\alpha}_k}$ for each $(x, y) \in R_+^{l+1}$, and $|\cdot|$ is the usual (Euclidean) distance. Similarly, define a metric b on C^* by $b(\bar{c}, \tilde{c}) = |(\bar{a}, \bar{\lambda}), (\tilde{a}, \tilde{\lambda})|$, where $\bar{c}(x) = \Sigma \bar{a}_i x_i^{\bar{\lambda}}$ and $\tilde{c}(x) = \Sigma \tilde{a}_i x_i^{\tilde{\lambda}}$ for each $x \in R_+^l$. Give each E^{*i}, $i \in N$, and E^* the product topology, where R_{++}^1 and Δ have the relative topologies of R^1 and R^n, respectively. This gives a topological structure to E^*.

It may be worth noting that the class E^o can be endowed with a topology which is such that the relative topology for E^* will coincide with the topology given to it in the above. In particular, U and C can both be given the topology of closed convergence (see Hildenbrand [1970]), since with each $u \in U$ and $c \in C$ we can associate closed sets of $R_+^{l+1} \times R_+^{l+1}$ and $R_+^l \times R_+^l$, respectively.

Given two topological spaces X and Y, a correspondence $F: x \to Y$ is said to be *uniformly locally threaded* if for every $x_o \in X$ and $y_o \in F(x_o)$ there exists an open neighborhood U_o in X of x_o and a continuous function $s_o: U_o \to Y$ such that $s_o(x_o) = y_o$ and $s_o(x) \in F(x)$ for every $x \in U_o$. Note that the restriction of a uniformly locally threaded correspondence is also uniformly locally threaded, and a function is continuous if and only if it is uniformly locally threaded.

PROPOSITION 2. *The correspondence* $\mu: E^* \to \mu(E^*)$ *is single valued and continuous and* $\mu^{-1}: \mu(E^*) \to E^*$ *is uniformly locally threaded.*

Proof. A generic element $(\langle (u^i, w^i) \rangle, (c, \theta))$ of E^* will be denoted by $(\langle (\alpha^i, w^i) \rangle, (a, \lambda, \theta))$, where

$$u^i(x, y) = y \prod_k x_k^{\alpha_k^i} \quad \text{for all } (x, y) \in R_+^{l+1} \text{ and } i \in \{1, \ldots, n\}, \text{ and}$$

$$c(x) \quad = \sum_k a_k x_k^{\lambda} \quad \text{for all } x \in R_+^l.$$

We first prove that $\mu: E^* \to \mu(E^*)$ is single valued. Let $(\langle (\alpha^i, w^i) \rangle, (a, \lambda, \theta))$ be some element of E^*. Then $(\bar{x}, \langle \bar{y}^j \rangle, \langle \bar{\pi}^j \rangle) \in \mu(\langle (\bar{\alpha}^j, \bar{w}^j) \rangle, (\bar{a}, \bar{\lambda}, \bar{\theta}))$ if and only if

$$
\begin{bmatrix}
1 + \sum_j \bar{\alpha}_j^1 \\
+ \bar{\theta}^1(\bar{\lambda}-1), & \bar{\theta}^1(\bar{\lambda}-1), & \ldots, & \bar{\theta}^1(\bar{\lambda}-1) \\
\bar{\theta}^2(\bar{\lambda}-1), & 1 + \sum_j \bar{\alpha}_j^2 & \ldots, & \bar{\theta}^2(\bar{\lambda}-1) \\
& + \bar{\theta}^2(\bar{\lambda}-1), & & \\
& & \ldots, & \\
\bar{\theta}^n(\bar{\lambda}-1), & \ldots \ldots & \bar{\theta}^n(\bar{\lambda}-1), & 1 + \sum_j \bar{\alpha}_j^n \\
& & & + \bar{\theta}^n(\bar{\lambda}-1)
\end{bmatrix}
\begin{bmatrix}
-\bar{y}^1 \\
-\bar{y}^2 \\
\\
\\
-\bar{y}^n
\end{bmatrix}
=
\begin{bmatrix}
\bar{w}^1 \sum_j \bar{\alpha}_j^1 \\
\bar{w}^2 \sum_j \bar{\alpha}_j^2 \\
\\
\\
\bar{w}^n \sum_j \bar{\alpha}_j^n
\end{bmatrix}
\quad (7.6)
$$

$$
\begin{bmatrix}
\bar{\alpha}_1^1, \bar{\alpha}_1^2, \ldots, \bar{\alpha}_1^n \\
\bar{\alpha}_2^1, \bar{\alpha}_2^2, \ldots, \bar{\alpha}_2^n \\
\vdots \qquad \vdots \\
\bar{\alpha}_l^1 \, \bar{\alpha}_l^2, \ldots, \bar{\alpha}_l^n
\end{bmatrix}
\begin{bmatrix}
\bar{w}^1 + \bar{y}^1 \\
\bar{w}^2 + \bar{y}^2 \\
\vdots \\
\bar{w}^n + \bar{y}^n
\end{bmatrix}
=
\begin{bmatrix}
\bar{\lambda} \, \bar{a}_1 \, \bar{x}_1^{\bar{\lambda}} \\
\bar{\lambda} \, \bar{a}_2 \, \bar{x}_2^{\bar{\lambda}} \\
\vdots \\
\bar{\lambda} \, \bar{a}_l \, \bar{x}_l^{\bar{\lambda}}
\end{bmatrix}
\tag{7.7}
$$

$$
\bar{\pi}_k^j = (1/\bar{x}_k)\,(\bar{w}^j + \bar{y}^j)\,\bar{\alpha}_k^j. \tag{7.8}
$$

The coefficient matrix in the system of equalities (7.6) is nonsingular, since it has a dominant diagonal (cf. Mckenzie [1974a, theorem 1]). This means (7.6) has a unique solution. Moreover, as may easily be checked $\Sigma_j\,\bar{y}^j < 0$, and $\bar{w}^i + \bar{y}^i > 0$ for every i. This means that the system of equations (7.7) and (7.8) also have unique positive solutions. This proves that μ is single valued. It is evident that it is also continuous.

We now prove that $\mu^{-1}: \mu(E^*) \to E^*$ is uniformly locally threaded. Given any arbitrary $(\bar{x}, \langle \bar{y}^j \rangle, \langle \bar{\pi}^j \rangle) \in \mu(E^*)$ and

$$
(\langle \bar{\alpha}^j, \bar{w}^j) \rangle, (\bar{c}, \bar{\lambda}, \bar{\theta})) \in \mu^{-1}(\bar{x}, \langle \bar{y}^j \rangle, \langle \bar{\pi}^j \rangle) \cap E^*,
$$

we must show that there exists an open neighborhood $\bar{V}$ in $\mu(E^*)$ of $(\bar{x}, \langle \bar{y}^j \rangle \langle \bar{\pi}^j \rangle)$ and continuous function $\bar{s}: \bar{V} \to E^*$ such that

$$
\bar{s}(x, \langle y^j \rangle, \langle \pi^j \rangle) \in \mu^{-1}(x, \langle y^j \rangle, \langle \pi^j \rangle) \cap E^*
$$

for every $(x, \langle y^j \rangle, \langle \pi^j \rangle) \in \bar{V}$ and that $\bar{s}(\bar{x}, \langle \bar{y}^j \rangle, \langle \bar{\pi}^j \rangle) = (\langle (\bar{\alpha}^j, \bar{w}^j) \rangle,$ $(\bar{a}, \bar{\lambda}, \bar{\theta}))$. Since $(\bar{x}, \langle \bar{y}^j \rangle, \langle \bar{\pi}^j \rangle) = \mu(\langle (\bar{\alpha}^j, \bar{w}^j) \rangle, (\bar{a}, \bar{\lambda}, \bar{\theta})), \Sigma \bar{y}^j < 0, \bar{w}^i + \bar{y}^j > 0,$ $\bar{x}_k > 0$, and $\bar{\pi}_k^j > 0$ for every j and k. We can find a small neighborhood $\bar{V}$ of $(\bar{x}, \langle \bar{y}^j \rangle \langle \bar{\pi}^j \rangle)$ in $\mu(E^*)$ such that $\Sigma y^j < 0, \bar{w}^j + y^j > 0, x_k > 0$, and $\pi_k^j > 0$ for every j and k and each $(x, \langle y^j \rangle, \langle \pi^j \rangle) \in \bar{V}$. Let $\bar{s}: \bar{V} \to E^*$ be the function such that

$$
\bar{s}(x, \langle y^j \rangle, \langle \pi^j \rangle) = (\langle (\alpha^j, \bar{w}^j) \rangle, (a, \lambda, \theta)),
$$

where

$$
\alpha_k^i = (1/(\bar{w}^i + y^i))\,\pi_k^i x_k \qquad (k = 1, \ldots, l; \ i = 1, \ldots, n),
$$

$$
\lambda = (\sum_j \pi^j x / (-\Sigma y^j)),
$$

$$
a_k = \left(\sum_j \pi_k^j / \lambda x_k^{\lambda - 1} \right) \qquad (k = 1, \ldots, l),
$$

$$
\theta^i = (\pi^i x + y^i)/(\Sigma \pi^j x + \Sigma y^j) \qquad (i = 1, \ldots, n).
$$

Then $\bar{s}: \bar{V} \to E^*$ is clearly a continuous function such that $\bar{s}(x, \langle y^j \rangle,$ $\langle \pi^j \rangle) \in \mu^{-1}(x, \langle y^j \rangle, \langle \pi^j \rangle) \cap E^*$ and $\bar{s}(\bar{x}, \langle \bar{y}^j \rangle, \langle \bar{\pi}^j \rangle) = (\langle (\bar{\alpha}^j, \bar{w}^j) \rangle,$

$(\bar{a}, \bar{\lambda}, \bar{\theta}))$, i.e., $\bar{s}: \bar{V} \to E^*$ is a continuous thread of μ^{-1} passing through $(\langle(\bar{\alpha}^j, \bar{w}^i)\rangle, (\bar{a}, \bar{\lambda}, \bar{\theta}))$. This completes the proof. $\square$

Let E be a subset of E^o. For each $i \in N$, let

$$L^i(E) = \{e^i \in E^i: (e^1, \ldots, e^{i-1}, e^i, e^{i+1}, \ldots, e^{n+1}) \in E$$
$$\text{for some } (e^1, \ldots, e^{i-1}, e^{i+1}, \ldots, e^{n+1}) \in E^1$$
$$\times \cdots \times E^{i-1} \times E^{i+1} \cdots E^{n-1}\}$$

and let

$$L(E) = L^1(E) \times \cdots \times L^{n+1}(E).$$

A subset E of E^o will be said to have the *asymmetry property* with respect to a function f if (1) f is a function such that dom $f \subset E$ and $L(\text{dom } f) \subset E$, and (2) for every $\bar{e}$ and $\tilde{e}$ (in dom f), if there are $(n+1)$-tuples $\bar{z}, \tilde{z}$, and $\bar{z}(i)$ $(i \in N)$ such that $\bar{z} \in \Theta(\bar{e})$, $\tilde{z} \in \Theta(\tilde{e})$, and $\bar{\bar{z}}(i) \in \Theta(\bar{\bar{e}}(i))$ for every $i \in N$, then $f(\bar{e}) = f(\tilde{e})$.

Let

$$E^{**^i} = U^* \times \{1\} \qquad (i = 1, \ldots, n)$$

and

$$E^{**} = E^{**^1} \times \cdots \times E^{**^n} \times E^{*^{n+1}}.$$

PROPOSITION 3. *The subclass E^* has the asymmetry property with respect to the identity function on E^{**}.*

Proof. For any

$$(\langle(\alpha^i, w^i)\rangle, (a, \lambda, \theta)), (\langle(x^i, y^i)\rangle, (x, y)) \in \Theta \ (\langle(\alpha^i, 1)\rangle, (a, \lambda, \theta))$$

if and only if

(a) $x^1 = x^2 = \cdots = x^n = x$ and $\Sigma y^j = y$,
(b) $\Sigma_j(1 + y^j) \alpha_k^j = \lambda a_k x_k^2$ $(k = 1, \ldots, l)$, and
(c) $(1 + y^i) \Sigma_k \alpha_k^i x_k + y^i = -\theta^i(\lambda - 1) y$ $(i = 1, \ldots, n)$.

Let f denote the identity function on E^{**}. Then dom $f = E^{**} = L(\text{dom } f)$. Let $\bar{e} = (\langle(\bar{\alpha}^i, 1)\rangle, (\bar{a}, \bar{\lambda}, \bar{\theta}))$ and $\tilde{e} = (\langle(\tilde{\alpha}^j, 1)\rangle, (\tilde{a}, \tilde{\lambda}, \tilde{\theta}))$ be some elements of E^{**}. Then $\bar{\bar{e}}(i)$ belongs to E^{**} for every $i \in N$. Let there be some $\bar{z}, \tilde{z}$, and $\bar{\bar{z}}(i)$ $(i = 1, \ldots, n)$ such that $\bar{z} \in \Theta(\bar{e})$, $\tilde{z} \in \Theta(\tilde{e})$, and $\bar{\bar{z}}(i) \in \Theta(\bar{\bar{e}}(i))$ $(i = 1, \ldots, n)$. Then we must show that $\bar{\alpha}^i = \tilde{\alpha}^i$ for $i = 1, \ldots, n$, $\bar{a} = \tilde{a}$, $\bar{\theta} = \tilde{\theta}$, and $\bar{\lambda} = \tilde{\lambda}$.

Let $\bar{z} = (\langle(\bar{x}^j, \bar{y}^j)\rangle, (\bar{x}, \bar{y}))$, $\tilde{z} = (\langle(\tilde{x}^i, \tilde{y}^i)\rangle, (\tilde{x}, \tilde{y}))$. Since by hypothesis $\bar{\bar{z}}(i) \in \Theta(\bar{\bar{e}}(i))$ for $i \in N$, definition of $\bar{\bar{z}}(i)$ and conditions (a) and (b) imply that

$$\bar{x} = \tilde{x}, \ \bar{y}^i = \tilde{y}^i, \text{ and } \bar{\alpha}_k^i = \tilde{\alpha}_k^i \quad \text{for } i = 1, \ldots, n; k = 1, \ldots, l. \qquad (7.9)$$

But (7.9) along with condition (c) and that $\tilde{\bar{z}}(i) \in \Theta(\tilde{\bar{e}}(i))$ for $i \in N$ implies

$$\bar{\theta}^i = \tilde{\theta}^i \, (i = 1, \ldots, n) \quad \text{and} \quad \bar{\lambda} = \tilde{\lambda}. \tag{7.10}$$

It follows from (7.9), (7.10), condition (b), and that $\tilde{\bar{z}}(n+1) \in \Theta(\tilde{\bar{e}}(n+1))$ that

$$\bar{a}_k = \tilde{a}_k \quad (k = 1, \ldots, l).$$

This completes the proof. $\square$

PROPOSITION 4. *The correspondence* $\mu^{-1} \colon \mu(E^{**}) \to E^{**}$ *is single valued and continuous.*

Proof. It is clear from the last part of the proof of proposition 2 that $\mu^{-1} \colon \mu(E^{**}) \to E^{**}$ is single valued and continuous.

3. Allocation Machanisms and Informational Efficiency

Given a subset E of E^o, an ordered pair $[v, h]$ of a correspondence v and a function h is a *resource allocation mechanism* for E, if (1) $E \subset \text{dom } v$, and (2) $\{(m, e) \in v(E) \times E : m \in v(e)\} \subset \text{dom } h$ such that for every $e \in E$, $h(m, e) \in F(e)$ for every $m \in v(e)$. The correspondence v is called the *equilibrium message correspondence*, the function h the *outcome function*, and $v(E)$ the *message space* of the mechanism.

A mechanism $[v, h]$ is said to be nonparametric if for every $m \in v(E)$, $h(m, e) = h(m, \bar{e})$ for every $e, \bar{e} \in E$, that is, h is independent of e so that given the equilibrium message, an outside agency with no knowledge about the economy could determine the outcome. A mechanism $[v, h]$ is said to be *decisive* for E, if $v(e) \neq \varnothing$ for every $e \in E$, $[v, h]$ is said to be *nonwasteful* or *implement* Θ for E if for every $e \in E$, $h(m, e) \in \Theta(e)$ for every $m \in v(e)$; $[v, h]$ is said to be *privacy preserving* for E if (1) there is a $(n+1)$-tuple $(v^1, \ldots, v^{n+1})$ of correspondences such that $L^i(E) \subset \text{dom } v^i$ for every $i \in N$ and $v(e) = \bigcap_{i \in N} v^i(e^i)$ for every $e \in E$, and (2) the outcome function h is privacy preserving in the sense that $h = (h^1, \ldots, h^{n+1})$ such that dom $h^i = v(E) \times L^i(E)$ $(i \in N)$ so that for every $e \in E$, $h(m, e) = (h^1(m, e^1), \ldots, h^{n+1}(m, e^{n+1}))$ for every $m \in v(e)$.

The MDP process $[\mu, g]$ is nonparametric, decisive, and nonwasteful. It is also privacy preserving as proposition 1 and the following lemma (see Mount and Reiter [1974a] show.

LEMMA 1. *A resource allocation mechanism* $[v, h]$ *for a subclass* $E \, (\subset E^o)$, *which is such that* $L(E) = E$, *is privacy preserving for* E *if and only if for every* $\bar{e}$, $\tilde{e} \in E$, $v(\bar{e}) \cap v(\tilde{e}) = v(\tilde{\bar{e}}(i)) \cap v(\tilde{\bar{e}}(i))$ *for every* $i \in N$.

Proof. First suppose that $[v, h]$ is privacy preserving. Then

$$v(\bar{e}) \cap v(\tilde{e}) = v^1(\bar{e}^1) \cap \cdots \cap v^{n+1}(\bar{e}^{n+1}) \cap v^1(\tilde{e}^1) \cap \cdots \cap v^{n+1}(\tilde{e}^{n+1})$$
$$= [v^1(\bar{e}^1) \cap \cdots \cap v^{i-1}(\bar{e}^{i-1}) \cap v^i(\bar{e}^i) \cap v^{i+1}(\bar{e}^{i+1})$$
$$\cap \cdots \cap v^{n+1}(\bar{e}^{n+1})] \cap [v^1(\tilde{e}^1) \cap \cdots \cap v^{i-1}(\tilde{e}^{i-1}) \cap v^i(\tilde{e}^i)$$
$$\cap v^{i+1}(\tilde{e}^{i+1}) \cap \cdots \cap v^{n+1}(\tilde{e}^{n+1})]$$
$$= v(\bar{e}(i)) \cap v(\tilde{e}(i)).$$

Conversely, suppose that $v : E \to v(E)$ is a correspondence which satisfies the condition that for every $\bar{e}$, $\tilde{e} \in E$, $v(\bar{e}) \cap v(\tilde{e}) = v(\bar{e}(i)) \cap v(\tilde{e}(i))$ for every $i \in N$. By hypotheses $E = L^1(E) \times \cdots \times L^{n+1}(E)$. If $e^i \in L^i(E)$, then set

$$v^i(e^i) = \bigcup_{\bar{e} \in E} v(\bar{e}^1, \ldots, \bar{e}^{i-1}, e^i, e^{-i+1}, \ldots, \bar{e}^{n+1}),$$

that is, $v^i(e^i)$ is the union of all the values of v at the points of E which have the ith coordinate e^i. Thus, if we set $\bar{e} = (\bar{e}^1, \ldots, \bar{e}^{n+1})$, then

$$\bigcap_{i \in N} v^i(\bar{e}^i) = \bigcap_{i \in N} \left[\bigcup_{\tilde{e} \in E} v(\tilde{e}(i)) \right] \subset \bigcup_{\tilde{e} \in E} \left[\bigcap_{i \in N} v(\tilde{e}(i)) \right]$$

$$\subset \bigcup_{\tilde{e} \in E} (v(\bar{e}) \cap v(\tilde{e})) = v(\bar{e}).$$

On the other hand, $v^i(\bar{e}^i) \supset v(\bar{e})$ for each $i \in N$. Thus, $v^1(\bar{e}^1) \cap \cdots \cap v^{n+1}(\bar{e}^{n+1}) \supset v(\bar{e})$. This completes the proof. $\square$

Observe that the pair $[I, \Theta]$, where I is the identity map on E^o, is also a nonparametric, decisive, nonwasteful, and privacy preserving mechanism for E^o with message space E^o.

We shall restrict to resource allocation mechanisms whose message spaces are Hausdorff and prove the minimality of the dimension of the message space of the MDP process among the message spaces for the general class of decisive, nonwasteful, and privacy preserving mechanisms. Similar results will obtain if we consider mechanisms with general topological (message) spaces. We first prove a fundamental lemma (see Chander [1983]).

LEMMA 2. *Let E be a subset of E^o, and let $[v, h]$ be a decisive, nonwasteful, and privacy preserving mechanism for E. If E has the asymmetry property with respect to a one–one function f, then v is injective over* dom f.

Proof. We have to show that given two arbitrary elements $\bar{e}$, $\tilde{e} \in$ dom f, $v(\bar{e}) \cap v(\tilde{e}) \neq \varnothing$ implies $\bar{e} = \tilde{e}$. Let $m \in v(\bar{e}) \cap v(\tilde{e})$, and let $h(m, \bar{e}) = \bar{z}$ and $h(m, \tilde{e}) = \tilde{z}$. Then

$$\bar{z} = (\bar{z}^1, \ldots, \bar{z}^{n+1}) = (h^1(m, \bar{e}^1), \ldots, h^{n+1}(m, \bar{e}^{n+1}))$$

and

$$\tilde{z} = (\tilde{z}^1, \ldots, \tilde{z}^{n+1}) = (h^1(m, \tilde{e}^1), \ldots, h^{n+1}(m, \tilde{e}^{n+1})).$$

Because $[v, h]$ is given to be privacy preserving for E and L (dom f) $\subset E$ (by the definition of asymmetry), therefore, (A) if $m \in v(\bar{e}) \cap v(\tilde{e})$, then $m \in v(\bar{e}(i))$ for every $i \in N$ (by lemma 1), and (B) if $m \in v(\bar{e}(i))$ for every $i \in N$, $\bar{z} = h(m, \bar{e})$, and $\tilde{z} = h(m, \tilde{e})$, then $\tilde{\tilde{z}}(i) = h(m, \tilde{\tilde{e}}(i))$ for every $i \in N$, where $\tilde{\tilde{e}}(i)$ and $\tilde{\tilde{z}}(i)$ are as defined in the definition of the asymmetry property. Statements (A) and (B) together imply that $\bar{z} \in \Theta(\bar{e})$, $\tilde{z} \in \Theta(\tilde{e})$, and $\tilde{\tilde{z}}(i) \in \Theta(\tilde{\tilde{e}}(i))$ for every $i \in N$, since we are given that $[v, h]$ is nonwasteful for E and that dom $f \subset L$ (dom f) $\subset E$. The fact that $\bar{z} \in \Theta(\bar{e})$, $\tilde{z} \in \Theta(\tilde{e})$, and $\tilde{\tilde{z}}(i) \in \Theta(\tilde{\tilde{e}}(i))$ for every $i \in N$, together with the fact that E has the asymmetry property with respect to f, implies that $f(\bar{e}) = f(\tilde{e})$. Since f is one–one, $\bar{e} = \tilde{e}$. This completes the proof. $\square$

Given two topological spaces X and Y, a correspondence $F : X \to Y$ is said to be *locally threaded* if for every $x_o \in X$ there exists an open neighborhood U_o in X of x_o and a continuous function $s_o : U_o \to Y$ such that $s_o(x) \in F(x)$ for every $x \in U_o$ (see Mount and Reiter [1974a]. Note that every continuous function is locally threaded.

Let X be a topological space. We shall say that dim $X \geq m$ if some subspace Y of X is homeomorphic to R^m, where "dim" stands for dimension.

THEOREM. *Let E be a subset of E^o — such that (a) there is a function f such that*

(a.1) *f is one–one*

(a.2) *E has the asymmetry property with respect to f, and*

(a.3) *μ is single valued over dom f and μ(dom f) contains an open subset of R^{l+n+ln},*

and (b) E can be given a topology such that

(b.1) *$\mu : E \to \mu(E)$ is locally threaded, and*

(b.2) *$\mu^{-1} : \mu$ (dom f) $\to$ dom f is uniformly threaded.*

If $[v, h]$ is a decisive, nonwasteful, and privacy preserving mechanism for E such that $v : E \to v(E)$ is locally threaded and $v(E)$ is Hausdorff, then dim $(v$ (dom $f))$ $\geq$ dim $(\mu(\text{dom } f))$, and hence dim $v(E) \geq l + n + ln$.

Hypothesis (a) and (b) of the theorem require that the mechanisms should cover at least a similar if not the same subclass of economies. In proposition 5 below we show that the theorem is nonvacuous.

Proof of the theorem. Since $E \subset E^o$, $[\mu, g]$ is decisive, nonwasteful, and privacy preserving for E. Since E has the asymmetry property with respect to f

(by (a.2)) and f is one-one (by a.1), lemma 2 above implies that $\mu: \text{dom } f \to \mu$ (dom f) is injective. Since by definition dom $f \subset E$ and μ is single-valued over dom f (by (a.3)), μ is one-one over dom f. Thus, hypothesis (b.2) implies $\mu^{-1}: \mu \, (\text{dom } f) \to \text{dom } f$ is a continuous injection.

Let a^o be a point in the interior of $\mu (\text{dom } f)$ and let $e^o = \mu^{-1}(a^o) \cap \text{dom } f$. Since v is locally threaded on E, there exists an open set B_o in E of e^o and a continuous function $r: B_o \to v(E)$ such that $r(e) \in v(e)$ for every $e \in B_0$. Let $C_o = B_o \cap \text{dom } f$ and $r_o: C_o \to v(E)$ be the restriction of r to C_o. Then C_o is an open set of dom f and $r_o: C_o \to v(E)$ is continuous. Since E has the asymmetry property with respect to the one-one function f, and $[v, h]$ is decisive, nonwasteful, and privacy preserving process for E (by hypothesis), lemma 2 implies again that v is injective over dom f. Since $r_o(e) \in v(e)$ for every $e \in B_o$ and v is injective over dom $f \subseteq C_o$, $r_o: C_o \to v\,(\text{dom } f)$ must be one-one. Thus, $r_o: C_o \to v\,(\text{dom } f)$ is a continuous injection.

Let $A_o = \mu(C_o)$ and $\mu^{-1}: A_o \to C_o$ be the restriction of $\mu^{-1}: \mu\,(\text{dom } f)$ $\to \text{dom } f$. Then A_o is an open set containing a_o and $\mu^{-1}: A_o \to C_o$ is a continuous injection. Let $s_o: A_o \to v\,(\text{dom } f)$ be the composition of $\mu^{-1}: A_o \to C_o$ and $r_o: C_o \to v\,(\text{dom } f)$. Then $s_o: A_0 \to v\,(\text{dom } f)$ is a continuous injection.

Since A_o is an open set of the Euclidean space $\mu\,(\text{dom } f)$ containing a_o, there exists a compact set $\bar{A}_o \subset A_o$ such that $\dim \bar{A}_o = \dim A = l + n + ln$ (by (a.3) and that a_o is an interior point of $\mu\,(\text{dom } f)$). Let $\bar{s}_o$ be the restriction of s_o to A_o. Then $\bar{s}_o: \bar{A}_o \to \bar{s}_o(\bar{A}_o)$ is a continuous bijection. In fact, $\bar{s}_o$ is bicontinuous, i.e., a homeomorphism, since $\bar{A}_o$ is compact and $\bar{s}_o(\bar{A}_o) \subset v(E)$ is Hausdorff (by proposition 9.5 in Royden [1968]). Thus, $\dim \bar{s}_o(\bar{A}_o) \geq \dim \bar{A}_o$. But since $\dim \bar{A}_o = l + n + ln$ and $\bar{s}_o(\bar{A}_o) \subset v(E)$, $\dim v(E) \geq l + n + ln$. This completes the proof of the theorem. □

PROPOSITION 5. *There is a subclass $E \subset E^o$ which satisfies hypothesis (a) and (b) of the theorem.*

Proof. Let $E = E^*$ and let f be the identity function on E^{**}, where E^* and E^{**} are as defined above. Then in view of propositions 2, 3, and 4, the hypothesis (a) and (b) of the theorem are satisfied. □

Notes

1. R^m denotes the m-dimensional Euclidean space, $R_+^m = \{x \in R^m: x_i \geq 0$ for all $i\}$, and $R_{++}^m = \{x \in R^m: x_i > 0$ for each $i\}$.

2. In a complete analysis one may also like to take into account the speed of convergence of the processes. But it is generally not possible to compare alternative processes in terms of their speeds of convergence.

References

Aoki, Masahiko, "Increasing Returns to Scale and Market Mechanisms." Technical Report No. 6, Institute for Mathematical Studies in the Social Sciences, Stanford University, 1967.

————, "Two Planning Algorithms for an Economy with Public Goods." Discussion Paper No. 029, Kyoto Institute for Economic Research, Kyoto University, 1970.

Arrow, Kenneth J., "An Extension of the Basic Theorems of Classical Welfare Economics." In *Proceedings of the Second Berkeley, Symposium on Mathematical Statistics and Probability* (J. Neyman, ed.), U. Calif. Press, Berkeley, 1951, pp. 507–532.

Arrow, Kenneth J. and Gerard Debreu, "Existence of an Equilibrium for a Competitive Economy." *Econometrica* 22, 265–290.

Arrow, Kenneth J. and Leonid Hurwicz, "Decentralization and Computation in Resource Allocation." In *Essays in Economics and Econometrics*, (R. W. Pfouts, ed.), UNC Press, Chapel Hill, 1960, pp. 34–104.

Calsamiglia, Xavier, "Decentralized Resource Allocation and Increasing Returns." *Journal of Economic Theory* 14 (1977), 263–283.

Champsaur Paul, "Neutrality of Planning Procedures in an Economy with Public Goods." *Review of Economic Studies* 43 (1976), 293–299.

Chander, Parkash, "On a Planning Process due to Taylor." *Econometrica* 46 (1978), 761–777.

————, "Informational Requirements for Efficient Resource Allocation Processes." Paper presented at the Econometric Society World Congress, Aix France, 1980.

————, "Informational Decentralization and Production Economies involving Externalities." Discussion Paper No. 8103, Indian Statistical Institute, June 1981.

————, "On the Informational Size of Message Spaces for Efficient Resource Allocation Processes." *Econometrica* 51 (1983), 919–938.

————, "On the Informational Efficiency of the Competitive Resource Allocation Process." *Journal of Economic Theory* 31 (1983), 54–67.

————, "Surplus-sharing Rules and Incentives in Planning Procedures for Public Goods." mimeo, Indian Statistical Institute, 1984.

Cornet, B., "Neutrality of Planning Procedures." *Journal of Mathematical Economics* 11 (1983), 141–160.

Debreu, Gerard, *Theory of Value*. New York: Wiley, 1959.

Drèze, J. H. and D. de la Vallée Poussin, "A Tatônnement Process for Public Goods." *Review of Economic Studies* 46 (1981), 473–486.

Fugigaki, Y. and R. Sato, "Incentives in the Generalized MDP Procedure for the Provision of Public Goods." *Review of Economic Studies* 46 (1981), 473–486.

Gibbard, A., "Manipulation of Voting Schemes: A General Result." *Econometrica* 41 (1973), 587–601.

Groves, Theodore and John Ledyard, "Optimal Allocation of Public Goods: A Solution to the 'Free Rider' Problem." 45 (1977), 783–807.

Green, Jerry and J. Laffont, *Incentives in the Public Decision Making*. Amsterdam: North-Holland, 1979.

Guesnerie, R., "Pareto Optimality in Non-Convex Economies." *Econometrica* 43 (1975), 1–29.

Von Hayek, Fredrich A., "The Present State of the Debate." In *Collectivist Economic Planning*, London, 1935, pp. 201–243.

——, "The Use of Knowledge in Society." *American Economic Review* 35 (1945), 519–530.

Heal, Geoffrey, "Planning, Prices and Increasing Returns." *Review of Economic Studies* 38 (1971), 281–294.

——, *The Theory of Economic Planning*, Amsterdam: North-Holland, 1973.

Hildenbrand, Werner, "On Economies with Many Agents." *Journal of Economic Theory* 3 (1970), 161–188.

Hurwicz, Leonid, "Theory of Economic Organization." (abstract), *Econometrica* 19 (1951), 54.

——, "Optimality and Informational Efficiency in Resource Allocation Processes." In *Mathematical Methods in the Social Sciences*, Stanford University Press, Stanford, 1959, pp. 27–46.

——, "Conditions for Economic Efficiency of Centralized and Decentralized Structures." In *Value and Plan*, (G. Grossman, ed.), University of California Press, Berkeley, 1960, pp. 162–183.

——, "On the Dimensional Requirements of Informationally Decentralized Pareto Satisfactory Processes." mimeo presented at the Conference Seminar on Decentralization, Northwestern University, February 1972, reproduced in *Studies in Resource Allocation Processes*, (K. J. Arrow and L. Hurwicz, eds.), Cambridge University Press, Cambridge, 1977.

——, "On Informationally Decentralized Systems." In *Decision and Organization* (C. B. McGuire and R. Radner, eds.), North-Holland, Amsterdam, 1972, pp. 297–336.

Hurwicz, Leonid, Roy Radner and Stanley Reiter, "A Stochastic Decentralized Resource Allocation Process: Part I." *Econometrica* 43 (1975), 187–221; 363–393.

Hurwicz, Leonid, "On Allocations Attainable through Nash Equilibria." *Journal of Economic Theory* 21 (1979), 171–194.

Jordan, James, "Expectations Equilibrium and Informational Efficiency of Stochastic Environments." *Journal of Economic Theory* 16 (1977), 354–372.

——, "The Competitive Process is Informationally Efficient Uniquely." *Journal of Economic Theory* 28 (1982), 1–18.

Koopmans, Tjalling, *Three Essays on the State of Economic Science*. New York: Mc Graw Hill, 1957.

Kornai, J. and T. Liptak, "Two Level Planning." *Econometrica* 33 (1965), 141–169.

Laffont, J. J. and E. Maskin, "A Characterization of Strongly Locally Incentive Compatible Planning Procedures with Public Goods." *Review of Economic Studies* 50 (1983), 187–195.

Lange, Oskar, "On the Economic Theory of Socialism." In *Economic Theory of Socialism* (B. E. Lippincott, ed.), University of Minnesota Press, Minneapolis, 1938, pp. 57–141.

Ledyard, John O., "A Convergent Pareto-Satisfactory Non-Tatonnement Adjustment Process for a Class of Unselfish Exchange Environments." *Econometrica* 39 (1971), 467–499.

Malinvaud, Edmond, "Procedures for the Determination of a Program of Collective Consumption." *European Economic Review* 2 (1970)·187–217.

———, "A Planning Approach to the Public Goods Problem." *Swedish Journal of Economics* 73 (1971), 96–112.

———, "Prices for Individual Consumption, Quantity Indicators for Collective Consumption." *Review of Economic Studies* 39 (1972), 385–405.

———, "Decentralized Procedures for Planning." in *Activity Analysis in the Theory of Growth and Planning* (M. O. L. Bacharach and E. Malinvaud, eds.), Macmillan, London, 1967, pp. 170–208.

Mckenzie, L., "Matrices with Dominant Diagonals and Economic Theory." In *Mathematical Methods in Social Sciences* (K. J. Arrow, S. Karlin, and P. Suppes, eds.), Stanford University Press, Stanford, 1959, 47–62.

Mount, K. and Stanley Reiter, "The Informational Size of Message Spaces." *Journal of Economic Theory* 8 (1974a), 161–191.

———, "Economic Environments for which there are Pareto Satisfactory Mechanisms." *Econometrica* 45 (1977), 821–840.

Munkres, James R., *Topology: A First Course.* Englewood Cliff, New Jersey: Prentice-Hall, 1975.

Osana, Hiroaki, "On the Informational Size of Message Spaces for Resource Allocation Processes." *Journal of Economic Theory* 17 (1978), 66–78.

Reiter, Stanley, "The Knowledge Revealed by an Allocation Process and the Informational Size of the Message Space." *Journal of Economic Theory* 8 (1974a), 389–394.

———, "Informational Efficiency of Iterative Processes and the Size of the Message Space." *Journal of Economic Theory* 8 (1974b), 193–205.

Roberts, J., "Incentives in Planning Procedures for the Provision of Public Goods." *Review of Economic Studies* 46 (1979), 283–292.

———, "Incentives, Information, and Iterative Planning." Stanford University, August 1983, Festschrift for Leonid Hurwicz (to appear).

Royden, H. L., *Real Analysis.* London: Macmillan, 1968.

Samuelson, Paul, "The Pure Theory of Public Expenditure." *Review of Economics and Statistics* 36 (1954), 387–389.

Sato, F., "On the Informational Size of Message Spaces for Resource Allocation Processes in Economies with Public Goods." *Journal of Economic Theory* 24 (1981), 48–69.

Sonnenschein, Hugo, "An Axiomatic Characterization of Price Mechanism." *Econometrica* 42 (1974), 425–434.

Taylor, F. M., "The Guidance of Production in a Socialist State." *American Economic Review* 19 (1929), 1–8; reproduced in *Economic Theory of Socialism* (B. E. Lippincott, ed.), University of Minnesota Press, Minneapolis, 1938.

Tulkens, Henry, "Dynamic Processes for Public Goods." *Journal of Public Economics* 9 (1978), 163–201.

Tulkens, Henry and S. Zamir, "Surplus-sharing Local Games in Dynamic Exchange Processes." 46 (1979), 305–313.

Walker, M., "On the Informational Size of Message Spaces." *Journal of Economic Theory* 15 (1977), 366–375.

B. Ward, *The Socialist Economy*. New York: Random House, 1967.

8 THE THEORY OF BARGAINING

Kalyan Chatterjee

The standard microeconomics text employs a model of perfect competition (based either on a price taking assumption or on free entry) to explain the allocation of resources in the economy. While models of this type continue to be popular as an idealized limiting case, theoretical attention has increasingly shifted to the study of thin markets and other structures that appear to represent more closely the reality of economic life. The price and the quantity produced and exchanged in such a market are determined by a bargaining process. The study of bargaining is then a necessary complement to the study of perfect competition.

In addition to its relevance for understanding markets, the theory of bargaining has been recognized as interesting in its own right. It has relevance for understanding negotiations between nations, between management and labor, and between buyer and seller. The last ten years have accordingly seen substantial work on the theory of bargaining. We shall discuss recent developments in the study of bargaining in this chapter.

I am grateful to the editor of this book for helpful comments and suggestions.

An extreme case of thin markets is that of bilateral monopoly, where a single buyer of a commodity confronts a single seller. This provides an exceptionally tractable bargaining problem. For the sake of exposition, we concentrate on this two agent problem in this chapter, as has much of the bargaining literature. Studying this case provides qualitative insights that may translate into a workable understanding of situations with a number of bargainers.

A Simple Bargaining Problem

We will use a simple bargaining problem in this chapter to illustrate the various theoretical approaches which appear in the literature. Suppose that a seller (s) and a buyer (b) must negotiate the price of an object owned by the seller. The seller's valuation of the object, or the price at which the seller would be just indifferent between selling and not selling, is called the seller's reservation price. A similar reservation price can be defined for the buyer. If the seller's reservation price is lower than the buyer's, a "zone of agreement" exists. Equivalently, we can say that potential gains from trade exist. If the seller's reservation price and the buyer's reservation price are commonly known, we have a situation of complete information. Incomplete information arises when the seller, for example, knows the seller's reservation price, but has only (commonly known) probabilistic information about the buyer's. The buyer might similarly be uncertain as to the seller's reservation price. If so, we have two-sided incomplete information; if only the seller or only the buyer is disadvantaged by a lack of knowledge, we have a one-sided incomplete information case. The bargaining problem, informally stated, is to determine the allocation of the gains from trade betweeen the two parties.

We shall work in terms of this example throughout the chapter, in order to present the various results in a common framework. However, the theories described here are capable of being applied in much more complex contexts.

Approaches to the Bargaining Problem

There are two major approaches to the bargaining problem, both originating in the work of Nash [1950, 1953]. The first approach abstracts from specific descriptive models (or "extensive forms") of the process by which bargaining proceeds. Instead, this approach identifies principles that are considered reasonably descriptive of the outcome of bargaining processes, and that can be expected to hold regardless of the specific extensive form used to model the process. As we shall see, a small number of such principles serves to characterize completely the bargaining outcome in the special case of complete information. This axiomatic approach has accordingly proved to be very useful in complete information cases. The following section examines this axiomatic method.

We then turn to the second approach, which analyzes specific noncooperative game models of bargaining. An extensive form for the game is chosen that presumably captures the essence of the process by which bargaining proceeds, and the equilibrium outcomes of the game are examined. We shall consider three such complete information models as well as discuss incomplete information models.

The penultimate section describes recent work in the theory of mechanism design. This line of inquiry combines features of both the axiomatic and noncooperative approaches to bargaining. It has the potential to yield a welfare economics of bargaining. The last section concludes.

1. Axiomatic Bargaining Models

Nash's Axiomatic Solution

We begin by presenting an extremely simple version of Nash's analysis. Suppose the seller's reservation price is s and the buyer's reservation price is b, where s and b are common knowledge. If a price x is agreed upon by the buyer and the seller, the seller's profit is

$$x - s \qquad (8.1)$$

and the buyer's profit is

$$b - x. \qquad (8.2)$$

If no agreement is reached, the profit to each player is zero.

The seller and buyer have commonly known and continuously differentiable von Neumann–Morgenstern utility functions, denoted $u_s(\cdot)$ and $u_b(\cdot)$, so that their payoffs for an agreement of price x are

$$u_s(x - s) \quad \text{and} \quad u_b(b - x). \qquad (8.3)$$

The failure to achieve an agreement gives the bargainers utilities of $u_s(0)$ and $u_b(0)$. For convenience, we normalize the bargainers' utility functions so that $u_s(0) = 0 = u_b(0)$.[1]

It is intuitively obvious that the bargainers would come to an agreement if and only if $b \geq s$, so that gains from bargaining are available, and we restrict considerations to such cases. Furthermore, if both bargainers are risk neutral, one plausible outcome is that the bargainers settle on a price halfway between b and s.[2] However, other plausible outcomes may also arise. In addition, if the assumption of risk neutrality is relaxed, the problem of determining a reasonable solution to the bargaining problem becomes more complex.[3] Whatever the solution is, however, one generally finds agreement that it should be efficient and, in some sense, equitable.

Suppose the seller's profit from the bargaining outcome is R_s, and the buyer's profit is R_b. From (8.1) and (8.2), we have the expected restriction that total profit cannot exceed the gains from trade, or:

$$R_s + R_b \leq b - s. \tag{8.4}$$

An efficient choice of R_s and R_b must satisfy ·

$$\max_{R_s, R_b} \lambda_s u_s(R_s) + \lambda_b u_b(R_b), \tag{8.5}$$

subject to (8.4), where λ_s and λ_b are some positive constraints.

Differentiating the appropriate Lagrangean and solving, we get

$$\frac{\lambda_s}{\lambda_b} = \frac{u_b'(R_b^*)}{u_s'(R_s^*)}, \qquad R_b^* + R_s^* = b - s, \tag{8.6}$$

where starred quantities refer to solution values.

Thus, if R_s^* and R_b^* represent an efficient distribution of profits between the buyer and seller, they must satisfy expression (8.6) for some λ_s and λ_b. The interpretation of (8.6) is that for some weights λ_s and λ_b attached to the utilities of the two bargainers, the solution should maximize the resulting weighted utility sum. Without some guide as to the choice of λ_s and λ_b, however, this formulation reveals no useful information. We invoke an equity principle to guide the choice of λ_s and λ_b, and such a choice allows (8.6) to be interpreted meaningfully as the requirement that whatever weighting of the two agents is provided by the equity consideration, an efficient solution for that weighting is achieved.

The formulation of equity that we shall choose has two components.[4] For convenience, let us refer to the utility function $\lambda u(\cdot)$ as a λ-transformation of utility function $u(\cdot)$. Our first equity principle is that for some λ-transformations of the utility functions, the solution should give the bargainers equal increments of utility over their disagreement levels. Hence, there should exist λ_s' and λ_b' such that

$$\lambda_s' u_s(R_s^*) - \lambda_s' u_s(0) = \lambda_b' u_b(R_b^*) - \lambda_b' u_b(0)$$

or, recalling our normalization,

$$\lambda_s' u_s(R_s^*) = \lambda_b' u_b(R_b^*). \tag{8.7}$$

We can characterize (8.7) as the requirement that the weighted utility increments of the two bargainers be equal, for some weights. The second requirement, which is one of consistency, is that the weights used in the efficiency and equity calculations be equal. This gives $\lambda_s = \lambda_s'$ and $\lambda_b = \lambda_b'$, and allows us to solve (8.6) and (8.7) for

$$u_b(R_b^*)u_s'(R_s^*) + u_b'(R_b^*)u_s(R_s^*) = 0. \qquad (8.8)$$

Equation (8.8) identifies a solution consistent with our efficiency and equity principles. The solution is the pair of values of R_s and R_b that maximize the product of utilities (see figure 8-1):

$$u_s(R_s) \cdot u_b(R_b).$$

This is then the only pair of payoffs (and hence of weights) consistent with equity and efficiency.

As is often the case with axiomatic bargaining models, seemingly innocuous axioms produce very strong results. Notice that the solution given in (8.8)

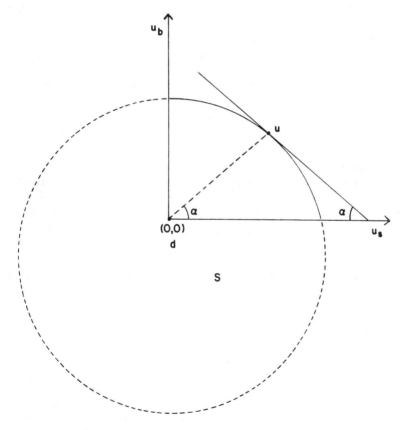

Figure 8-1. The Nash Solution[5]

features a reassuring property: λ-transformations of the utility functions simply cause a similar transformation in the equilibrium utilities. The violation of this property would be troubling, since a λ-transformation of a von Neumann–Morganstern utility function does not affect the information contained in that function, and hence presumably ought not to have any other effect on the solution.

Nash [1950] derives the result presented in (8.8) in a much more general way. His model consists of a utility possibility set, S, which identifies the utility payoffs from all possible feasible agreements; and a disagreement point, d, that gives the bargainers' utility payoffs in the event of disagreement. The set S is assumed to be compact, convex, and nonempty; and d is an element of S. In order to make the problem nontrivial, we assume that there is at least one point in S that makes both players strictly better off than at d.

A solution to this bargaining problem is a rule $f(S, d)$. This rule assigns a pair of feasible utility values (u_s^*, u_b^*) to every (S, d) pair; i.e., associates a pair of utility payoffs with every utility possibility set and disagreement point. Nash argued that an acceptable solution should satisfy the following four properties.

Independence of Equivalent Utility Representations. Since the model uses von Neumann–Morgernstern utility functions (which are unique up to a choice of origin and scale), information about the origin and scale of any individual's utility function should be irrelevant in the bargaining process. If the origin and scale of a utility function are changed, the solution should give each player essentially the same utility payoff as before the change, but expressed in terms of the new utility scale and origin. An alternative way of stating this principle is to note that the actual physical agreement reached should not be affected by strategically equivalent (affine) utility transformations, even though the utilities of this agreement to the bargainers will change to take the new origins and units into account.

Pareto Optimality. This principle requires that no joint gains from bargaining remain unexploited. Thus, in figure 8-1, the solution will lie on the frontier $u_b = \phi(u_s)$. This assumption does not appear to be consistent with such phenomena as strikes and bargaining breakdowns, but appears plausible in the context of a complete information bargaining model.

Symmetry. This is the only ethical axiom appearing in Nash's scheme, and imposes a seemingly weak equity requirement. Formally, if $d_s = d_b$ and if S is symmetric (i.e., if $u_s = u_1$ and $u_b = u_2$ being in S implies that $u_s = u_2$ and $u_b = u_1$ is also in S), then the solution should give equal utilities (measured as increments over the disagreement utility levels) to each bargainer. In other words, if the players are indistinguishable in terms of the utility possibility set and the disagreement point, the solution should not distinguish between them.

Independence of Irrelevant Alternatives Other than the Status Quo Point. This principle states that if S and T are two utility possibility sets with the same disagreement point, if S is a subset of T, and if the bargaining solution for the set T is an element of S, then this bargaining solution is also the solution for S. The independence of irrelevant alternatives is not as intuitively plausible as Nash's other axioms, and has been criticized in the literature (see Luce and Raiffa [1957]). Roth [1979, p. 7] interprets the condition as "expressing the kind of bargaining that Nash's solution is intended to model. In particular, [it] models a bargaining process which can proceed by first narrowing down the original set T of feasible alternatives to some small set S, without changing the outcome." It is not immediately obvious that bargaining would proceed in this way, so the intuitive status of the argument is questionable. An alternative argument for adopting the independence of irrelevant alternatives is that it is a consequence of certain types of collective optimizing behavior. If the bargaining solution is found by maximizing some function of the individual utilities (a "social welfare" function), then the independence of irrelevant alternatives would hold.

Nash showed that these axioms completely characterize a unique solution.[6] The solution is the one we obtained in the simpler formulation.

PROPOSITION 1 (NASH, 1950).   *The preceding four properties characterize a unique solution to the bargaining game. The bargaining outcome is the feasible point that maximizes the product of the utilities (normalized so that each player's disagreement outcome yields zero utility).*

In order to interpret an axiomatic approach to bargaining, we must examine the role each axiom plays in sustaining a given result. In a series of papers summarized in his 1979 book, Roth has taken several important steps in answering this question for Nash's axiom scheme. His findings can be stated briefly as:

PROPOSITION 2 (ROTH, 1979).

1.   *If Pareto optimality is replaced by an individual rationality requirement, stating that the solution must give each bargainer at least as much as his disagreement utility, there are precisely two solutions that satisfy the other axioms and individual rationality. These are the Nash solution and the disagreement outcome.*

2.   *If the symmetry axiom is replaced by the requirement that bargainers receive positive (but not necessarily equal) increments of utility in a symmetric game, then there is a unique solution that satisfies the axioms. This solution is the one that maximizes a weighted geometric average of utilities (normalized so that the disagreement outcome yields zero utility).*

These results suggest that Pareto optimality and symmetry are relatively innocuous requirements, and hence that the assumption driving the Nash result is axiom 4, the independence of irrelevant alternatives.[7] This principle has been criticized, and recent work has attempted to replace it. One of the most popular alternatives is individual monotonicity, propounded by Kalai and Smorodinsky [1975]. This axiom would replace the independence of irrelevant alternatives with:

Monotonicity.   If two bargaining problems (S_1, d) and (S_2, d) have the same disagreement point d, if S_1 is a subset of S_2, and if $\max_{u_s \in S_1} u_s = \max_{u_s \in S_2} u_s$, then the buyer B must obtain as much in the S_2 game as in the S_1 game. An intuitive interpretation of this condition is that if the utility possibilities available to the buyer improve (and the maximum utility available to the seller does not increase), then the utility secured by the buyer in the bargaining solution should not decrease.

Kalai and Smorodinsky show that this axiom, in connection with Nash's other principles, also provides a unique solution to the Nash bargaining problem. This solution is obtained by constructing the line segment joining the disagreement point to the "Utopia point" (given by $(\max_S u_b, \max_S u_s)$) and picking out the intersection of this segment with the Pareto frontier. This point will be the Kalai–Smorodinsky solution.[8] This is illustrated in figure 8-2. Suppose that D is the Nash and Kalai and Smorodinsky solution for the utility possibility set given by OAB in figure 8-2. The Nash solution for OADC remains D, by the independence of irrelevant alternatives axiom. However, the Kalai and Smorodinsky solution changes. The maximum value of u_s is the same for both sets, and the buyer receives higher utility in S_2 than in S_1.

These results allow us to interpret the role played by the various axioms. The interpretation attached to axiomatic bargaining approaches in general is often controversial. The axioms could be regarded as principles that would be followed by an impartial arbitrator. However, it is not clear that an arbitrator would behave in such a way. In particular, an arbitrator may not be as influenced by the status quo or disagreement point as many axiomatic approaches would suggest. Another interpretation, suggested by Roth [1979], regards these axioms as principles describing certain bargaining processes. Hence, it is suggested that the axioms describe the outcome of some class of

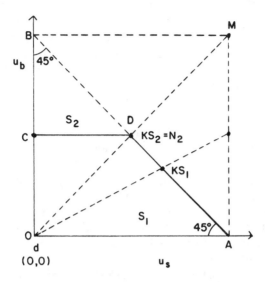

Figure 8-2. The Nash and the Kalai–Smorodinsky Solutions

bargaining procedures. The difficulty in this interpretation lies in identifying the class of bargaining procedures or extensive forms in question. Other than the obvious statement that other extensive forms are those that do not satisfy the axioms, the answer to this question has been elusive.

Risk Aversion in Nash Bargaining

In our discussion of the simplest bargaining model, we suggested that the attitude of the players toward risk might be expected to influence the bargaining outcome. This raises the question of the effect of risk attitudes on the Nash solution. The following result obtains.[9]

PROPOSITION 3. *The utility assigned to a player in a two person bargaining game by Nash's solution increases if the player's opponent is replaced by a more risk averse player.*

This result is significant for several reasons. First, it involves the properties of a von Neumann–Morgenstern utility function in a somewhat more essential way than the independence of origin and scale axiom invoked in Nash's original model. Second, proposition 3 demonstrates the difficulty in using the

Nash solution as a "fair" arbitration scheme. If the arbitrator is unaware of the bargainers' utility functions and attempts to elicit these utilities, it is to a player's advantage to misrepresent his utility function as being less risk averse than it really is. Even if the utility functions are known, it may not seem fair or ethical to give more utility to a less risk-averse person. This last criticism especially suggests that Nash bargaining may not be an acceptable normative theory.

The reader may suspect that there is a close link between the result obtained in proposition 3 and Nash's axiom of independence of equivalent utility representations. To illuminate this link, let any bargaining solution that features the property described in proposition 3 be described as satisfying risk sensitivity. We might then explicitly impose risk sensitivity as an axiom in constructing a bargaining solution. It can be shown that risk sensitivity, coupled with the axioms of symmetry, Pareto efficiency, and the independence of irrelevant alternatives, yields the Nash solution. Hence, given the other Nash axioms, risk sensitivity and the independence of equivalent utility representations are interchangeable. Peters [1983] constructs axiomatic models involving risk sensitivity.

We offer a heuristic argument supporting proposition 3. We construct our argument in the context of the differentiable, concave Pareto frontier of figure 8-1. We first clarify what is meant by "more risk-averse." Pratt [1964, theorem 1], and Kihlstrom and Mirman [1974] show that a utility function $w(x)$ is more risk-averse than a utility function $u(x)$ if $w(x)$ is an order preserving strictly concave transform of $u(x)$. Hence, we must have

$$w(x) = v(u(x)), \qquad (8.9)$$

where $v(\cdot)$ is increasing and strictly concave. Without loss of generality, we take $v(0) = 0$.

In the single dimension case, examined by Pratt [1964], this characterization is equivalent to the requirement that the local risk aversion measure be uniformly larger for $w(x)$ than for $u(x)$. In the multidimensional case examined by Kihlstrom and Mirman [1974], this is equivalent to the requirement that the acceptance set for lotteries for the more risk averse player (characterized by $w(x)$) be contained in the acceptance set of the less risk averse player (characterized by $u(x)$).

In the bargaining model shown in figure 8-1, with the utility functions normalized to equal 0 at the disagreement point, we get the Nash solution x_i^* by maximizing $u_s u_b = u_s \phi(u_s)$. The necessary conditions for this maximization include

$$u_s \phi'(u_s) + \phi(u_s) = 0, \qquad (8.10)$$

or

$$u_{s1}^* = - \frac{\phi(u_{s1}^*)}{\phi'(u_{s1}^*)}, \tag{8.11}$$

where u_{s1}^* is the utility the seller obtains in the Nash solution.

Now suppose the buyer is replaced by a more risk averse agent. The latter's utility function is given by $w_b(x) = v(u_b(x)) = v(\phi(u_s(x)))$, where $v(\cdot)$ is concave and differentiable. The Pareto frontier is now given by

$$v(\phi(u_s)). \tag{8.12}$$

The Nash solution for this new game is obtained by maximizing $u_s v(\phi(u_s))$. The necessary conditions for this maximization include

$$u_s(v'(\phi(u_s))\phi'(u_s) + v(\phi(u_s)) = 0, \tag{8.13}$$

or

$$u_{s2}^* = - \frac{v(\phi(u_{s2}^*))}{v'(\phi(u_{s2}^*))\phi'(u_{s2}^*)}. \tag{8.14}$$

Since $v(\cdot)$ is concave and $v(0) = 0$, we must have

$$v(y) \geq v'(y)y. \tag{8.15}$$

From (8.15) we obtain

$$\frac{v(y)}{v'(y)} \geq y, \tag{8.16}$$

or on substituting $y = \phi(u_s)$, we have

$$\frac{v(\phi(u_{s2}^*))}{v'(\phi(u_{s2}^*))} \geq \phi(u_{s2}^*). \tag{8.17}$$

Combining (8.14) and (8.17) we obtain

$$u_{s2}^* \geq \frac{\phi(u_{s2}^*)}{-\phi'(u_{s2}^*)}, \tag{8.18}$$

or

$$u_{s2}^* \phi'(u_{s2}^*) + \phi(u_{s2}^*) \leq 0. \tag{8.19}$$

Finally, we investigate the function $g(u) = u\phi'(u) + \phi(u)$. Differentiating $g(u)$ with respect to u, and noting that $\phi'' \leq 0$ (by virtue of the concavity of the utility function) and $\phi' < 0$ (since the Pareto frontier is negatively sloped), we obtain

$$g'(u) = u\phi''(u) + 2\phi'(u) \leq 0. \tag{8.20}$$

Comparing (8.19) and (8.11), we see that

$$u_{s2}^* \geq u_{s1}^*. \tag{8.21}$$

We can conclude that the seller is better off playing against a more risk averse buyer. This finding reinforces the tendency to interpret the Nash solution as a description of the outcome of a bargaining procedure, since one intuitively suspects that it is to one's advantage to face a relatively risk averse opponent.

2. Noncooperative Bargaining Models

Noncooperative Bargaining Models with Complete Information

The alternative to an axiomatic approach to bargaining is to construct a model of the process by which bargaining occurs, and then to ascertain both the (optimal) behavior of agents faced with such a procedure as well as the outcome induced by this behavior. This approach has the advantage of revealing the connection between the bargaining process and the resulting outcome. It also may appear more realistic, as one can directly check how well the proposed process corresponds with actual bargaining. It has the disadvantage of failing to explain how the bargaining procedure was obtained. We return to this point in the next section.

The notion of equilibrium employed in noncooperative bargaining models is the familiar game theoretic concept of a Nash equilibrium. The concept of a Nash equilibrium must not be confused with the Nash bargaining solution we have discussed in the last section. To avoid ambiguity, we explicity present the Nash equilibrium idea. Given strategy sets X_s and X_b for players s and b and payoff functions $u_s(x_s, x_b)$ and $u_b(x_s, x_b)$, where $x_s \in X_s$ and $x_b \in X_b$, a pair of strategies (x_s^*, x_b^*) is a Nash equilibrium iff [10]

$$u_s(x_s^*, x_b^*) \geq u_s(x_s, x_b^*), \qquad x_s \in X_s, \tag{8.22}$$

$$u_s(x_s^*, x_b^*) \geq u_b(x_s^*, \qquad x_b), x_b \in X_b. \tag{8.23}$$

As with axiomatic models, noncooperative approaches to bargaining have their origins in the work of Nash [1953]. Nash attempted to justify explicitly the interpretation of his axiomatic solution as a description of the outcome of a bargaining process by constructing a process that would yield such an outcome. We examine Nash's model, and then turn to two more recent formulations.

Nash. Nash proposed the following bargaining procedure. The buyer and seller simultaneously identify numbers x_b and x_s. These might be interpreted as utility demands made by the two agents, in the sense that each player can be described as demanding the solution yield a level of utility equal to x. If (x_s, x_b)

belongs to the utility possibility set, then Nash's procedure allocates these utilities to the agents. If not, each player receives the disagreement outcome.

A Nash equilibrium for this noncooperative game is given by the axiomatic Nash bargaining solution. This suggests that some credence can be attached to the interpretation of the Nash bargaining solution as describing the outcome of a noncooperative game. However, the noncooperative game allows a multitude of other equilibria. Any Pareto efficient point is a possible Nash equilibrium outcome, as is the disagreement outcome.[11] This multiplicity of equilibria calls into question the ability of the noncooperative game to rationalize the Nash bargaining solution. Only if the Nash bargaining solution can be shown to be a special (in some sense) Nash equilibrium of the noncooperative game does the latter provide some rationalization for the axiomatic bargaining approach.

Nash approaches this difficulty by suggesting that the noncooperative Nash equilibrium that yields the axiomatic Nash bargaining solution does have special properties. His analysis, which has been considerably sharpened by Binmore [1980, 1981], depends upon the concept of a smoothed game. Following Binmore, let (x_s^*, x_b^*) be the Nash bargaining solution. Let $p(x_s, x_b)$ be a function describing the probability that two agents making utility demands x_s and x_b will achieve these utilities. With probability $1 - p(x_s, x_b)$, the players receive the disagreement outcome. In the noncooperative game described by Nash, we have

$$p^*(x_s, x_b) = \begin{array}{ll} 1 & \text{if } (x_s, x_b) \text{ is feasible,} \\ 0 & \text{otherwise.} \end{array}$$

In a smoothed game, the function $p(x_s, x_b)$ is taken to be continuous. Hence, a sudden jump of the probability of receiving one's utility demands (from 0 to 1) at the edge of the feasible set does not occur. Instead, $p(0, 0)$ is taken to be unity, and $p(x_s, x_b) = 0$ for infeasible (x_s, x_b); but the function decreases as the utility demands increase. Notice that as a result, there is some probability that even if a pair of feasible utility offers is made, the disagreement outcome will be obtained.

To reveal the special properties attached to the noncooperative Nash equilibrium which yields the Nash bargaining solution, we first examine a typical smoothed game. Our analysis follows Binmore [1981]. Suppose the seller is interested in maximizing his expected utility, given that the buyer's strategy is held fixed at x_b^o. Then the seller will choose x_s to maximize $x_s \cdot p(x_s, x_b^o)$. The necessary conditions for the maximization include

$$x_s \frac{\partial p(x_s, x_b^o)}{\partial x_s} + p(x_s, x_b^o) = 0. \tag{8.24}$$

An analogous condition must hold for the buyer. The conditions for (x_s^o, x_b^o) to be a Nash equilibrium are then

$$x_s^o \frac{\partial p(x_s^o, x_b^o)}{\partial x_s} = 0, \qquad x_b^o \frac{\partial p(x_s^o, x_b^o)}{\partial x_b} = 0. \tag{8.25}$$

A simple calculation reveals that the Nash bargaining solution for a game with the utility possibility set given $\{x_s, x_b | p(x_s, x_b) \geq p(x_s^o, x_b^o)\}$ also satisfies (8.25).[12] It is this observation which allows the key relationships to be derived.

We can now put these results together. Consider a sequence of smoothed games, defined by a sequence of functions $p_n(\cdot, \cdot)$. Let these functions approach the function $p^*(\cdot, \cdot)$, which gives the original noncooperative game posed by Nash, which we might refer to as Nash's simple demand game. We then have

PROPOSITION 4.   *If the functions $p_n(\cdot, \cdot)$ are differentiable, quasiconcave, and strictly decreasing, then every sequence of Nash equilibria of approximating smoothed games tends in the limit (as $p_n(\cdot, \cdot)$ approaches $p^*(\cdot, \cdot)$) to the equilibrium of Nash's simple demand game which coincides with the Nash bargaining solution.*

It is easy to see why this result obtains. Every noncooperative Nash equilibrium in the sequence of smoothed games is also the axiomatic Nash bargaining solution to some hypothetical bargaining problem. The limit of the noncooperative Nash equilibria in the smoothed games will then be the axiomatic Nash bargaining solution to a bargaining problem which is the limit of the hypothetical bargaining problems associated with each smoothed game. This limiting bargaining problem is the original bargaining problem posed by Nash. Hence, the limit of the noncooperative Nash equilibria of the smoothed games is that noncooperative Nash equilibrium of the original game which coincides with the Nash bargaining solution to that game.

This argument, based on the concept of a smoothed game, demonstrates that of all the Nash equilibria in Nash's noncooperative bargaining game, special properties can be attached to the equilibrium which yields an outcome equivalent to the Nash bargaining solution. However, these special properties are presumably significant only if some economic interpretation can be attached to the smoothed games. One possibility, suggested by Binmore, is that errors are attached to the utility demands made by the players. A feasible pair of observed offers then produces some uncertainty as to whether the actual offers are feasible, and hence may introduce some uncertainty as to whether the actual offers or the disagreement point should be awarded to the bargainers. This suggests some economic rationale for the smoothed game, and hence potentially for the Nash solution of the original game.

Harsanyi–Zeuthen.   A second noncooperative bargaining theory is offered by Harsanyi, formalizing earlier work by Zeuthen, (see Harsanyi [1956] and the references therein). In Harsanyi's model, the bargainers begin by making presumably incompatible offers, with the seller offering utilities (x_s, x_b) and the buyer offering (y_s, y_b). The bargaining proceeds by having the two agents make concessions. A concession for the seller is a revision of the seller's offer, decreasing y_s and increasing y_b. A buyer's concession is an increase in x_s and decrease in x_b. Concessions of any magnitude and timing are allowed.

Suppose the current (incompatible) offers are (x_s, x_b) (from the seller) and (y_s, y_b) (from the buyer). As usual, we let the disagreement utilities be $(0, 0)$. Suppose the seller believes that with probability p_s, the buyer will never alter the buyer's offer, and that with probability $1 - p_s$, the buyer will accept the seller's offer. Then the seller will find it optimal to maintain the seller's current offer rather than accept the buyer's offer if

$$p_s \cdot 0 + (1 - p_s)x_s > y_s, \tag{8.26}$$

while a failure of (8.26) may induce the seller to concede. Rewriting (8.26), we find that the seller will not offer a concession if

$$p_s < \frac{x_s - y_s}{x_s} = \bar{p}_s. \tag{8.27}$$

A similar calculation for the buyer suggests that the buyer will not concede if

$$p_b < \frac{y_b - x_b}{y_b} = \bar{p}_b. \tag{8.28}$$

Harsanyi next asserts that if $\bar{p}_s < \bar{p}_b$, the seller can be expected to make the first concession, while $\bar{p}_s > \bar{p}_b$ leads to an expectation of the buyer's making the first concession. This implies that a seller concession is expected if

$$\frac{x_s - y_s}{x_s} < \frac{y_b - x_b}{y_b} \tag{8.29}$$

or

$$x_s y_b - y_s y_b < x_s y_b - x_s x_b, \tag{8.30}$$

$$y_s y_b > x_s x_b. \tag{8.31}$$

Thus, if the seller concedes first, the agreed offers will be (y_s, y_b) instead of (x_s, x_b); in other words, the concession by the seller will increase the product of the utilities. We state this as a proposition.

PROPOSITION 5. (HARSANYI–ZEUTHEN).   *Concessions will occur in the Harsanyi–Zeuthen bargaining model so as to increase the value of the product of utilities (measured incrementally from the disagreement point). This concession process accordingly leads toward the Nash bargaining solution.*

Harsanyi's work represents one of the earliest attempts to construct a noncooperative model of an iterated bargaining process. Such models are important, since one's intuition readily suggests that bargaining processes often take an iterated form. However, the version of Harsanyi's model presented here encounters several difficulties. It fails to provide an explicit account of the time structure of the bargaining process, and fails to explain the magnitude of the concessions made by the players. The optimization process on the part of the bargainers which produces the behavior described by Harsanyi is accordingly unclear. However, his work has provided the foundations of the noncooperative approach.

Rubinstein.   Rubinstein constructs a model of an iterated bargaining process under complete information which explicitly addresses the various omissions cited above. The model again involves a risk neutral buyer and seller. Let the units of measurement be chosen so that the potential gains from bargaining are 1. We can follow Rubinstein in thinking of this as a problem of dividing a "pie" of size 1 between the two agents.

The game begins at time 0, with the buyer making an offer. This offer is either accepted or rejected by the seller. If the seller accepts, the pie is divided as specified by the offer, and the game ends. If the seller rejects the offer, the seller makes a counter offer at time $t = 1$. This offer is either accepted or rejected by the buyer. An acceptance again ends the game. If the buyer rejects the offer, the buyer makes a counter proposal at time $t = 2$, and the game continues in this fashion. This process is illustrated in the game tree shown in figure 8-3. The discount factors for the seller and buyer are given by D_s and D_b. The seller's payoffs are listed first in each case, and the buyer's second.

It is clear that Nash equilibria exist in this game that yield any possible division of the pie between the two players. Hence, a Nash equilibrium may allocate all of the pie to the seller; all to the buyer; or may produce any intermediate outcome. This is a disconcerting result. A bargaining analysis under which any outcome is possible is clearly of limited interest.

Some of the Nash equilibrium outcomes in Rubinstein's model do not appear to be plausible. Consider the Nash equilibrium that allocates all of the pie to the seller. This outcome occurs if the seller demands all of the pie each time the seller makes an offer, and rejects any offer of less than all of the pie from the buyer. Faced with such intransigence, the buyer has no possibility of securing any of the pie. It is then an optimal strategy for the buyer to simply accede to the seller's demand and offer all of the pie to the seller (since no other strategy can secure a better outcome for the buyer).

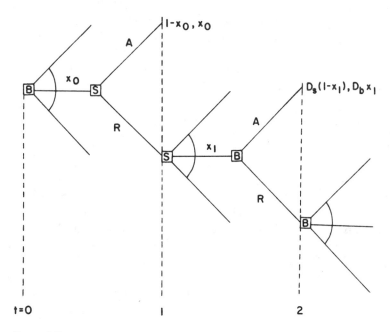

Figure 8-3

The difficulty is that the seller's strategy does not appear to be credible in this case. A strategy for the seller is a rule which associates with any t the offer the seller will make if stage t is reached (if it is the seller's turn to offer) or the response the seller will make to various buyer's offers in stage t. The strategy described above commits the seller to demanding all of the pie and refusing any lesser offer no matter what stage is reached. One suspects, however, that if the buyer were to consistently refuse the seller's demands, so that some advanced stage of the game were actually achieved, then the seller would eventually moderate those demands. Doing so would allow some agreement to be obtained, while refusing to do so would risk further disagreement. The seller thus achieves all of the pie by adopting a strategy which lacks credibility. Hence, Nash equilibria support any outcome, but many such equilibria do not yield plausible descriptions of bargaining behavior.

The difficulty, as recognized by Rubinstein, is that the Nash equilibrium concept is not a sufficiently powerful equilibrium requirement in many cases. Rubinstein accordingly invokes a strengthening of the Nash concept, requiring that the game exhibit a sequential equilibrium. Intuitively, a sequential equilibrium is a pair of Nash equilibrium strategies with the additional requirement that if any point on the game tree is reached, the continuation of the strategies in question must still be optimal.[13] This property is not satisfied by the Nash equilibrium described above, which allocates all of the pie to the seller. There is some stage of the process which, if it is reached, will presumably induce the seller to alter the seller's offer.

Rubinstein finds that requiring the equilibrium to be sequential has powerful implications. In particular:

PROPOSITION 6 (RUBINSTEIN). *In the alternating offers game under complete information, there is a unique sequential equilibrium.*

We briefly describe how this result is obtained, and reveal some properties of the sequential equilibrium. (See also Shaked and Sutton [1984].)

Let an offer of x denote an offer to provide x of the pie to the buyer and $1 - x$ to the seller. If the game reaches stage $t = 2$, let the undiscounted optimal expected payoff to the buyer of the remainder of the game be denoted as V_b. The seller's undiscounted expected payoff from the remainder of the game at stage $t = 2$ is then at most $1 - V_b$, and may be lower. At $t = 1$, the buyer's decision to accept or reject the seller's period one offer (x_1) will accordingly be governed by:

$$\text{accept } x_1 \quad \text{if } x_1 \geq D_b V_b, \qquad \text{reject } x_1 \quad \text{if } x_1 < D_b V_b. \qquad (8.32)$$

For the seller, an offer of $x_1 > D_b V_b$ in stage $t = 1$ is then clearly suboptimal, since a lower offer will be accepted by the buyer and will provide the seller with a higher payoff. The seller's choice is accordingly to offer $x_1 = D_b V_b$ or $x_1 < D_b V_b$. If $x_1 = D_b V_b$, the offer is accepted and the seller's payoff (discounted back to $t = 0$) is

$$D_s(1 - D_b V_b). \qquad (8.33)$$

If $x_1 < D_b V_b$, the buyer rejects the offer, and the $t = 0$ payoff to the seller is at most

$$D_s^2(1 - V_b). \qquad (8.34)$$

It is clear that (8.33) exceeds (8.34), since $0 < D_s, D_b < 1$. Therefore, the optimal period one offer for the seller to make is

$$x_1 = D_b V_b. \qquad (8.35)$$

We now consider the decision problem at $t = 0$. It is known that if period 1 is reached, equilibrium strategies involve the seller offering $D_b V_b$ and the buyer accepting. An argument analogous to that constructed for $t = 1$ then reveals the seller will accept a buyer's stage $t = 0$ offer of x_0 if

$$1 - x_0 \geq D_s(1 - D_b V_b) \qquad (8.37)$$

and reject it otherwise. The buyer will not offer an x_0 which satisfies (8.37) with strict inequality, since a larger offer would also be accepted and would yield a higher payoff to the buyer. If the buyer offers x_0 such that

$$x_0 = 1 - D_s(1 - D_b V_b), \tag{8.38}$$

then the offer is accepted and the right side of (8.38) gives the buyer's payoff. If the buyer makes an offer x_0 which is greater than this, the offer is rejected, and the buyer's payoff (from our period one calculations), is

$$D_b^2 V_b. \tag{8.39}$$

At $t = 0$, the game facing the buyer is identical to the game the buyer faces at $t = 2$. Therefore, the value of the buyer from the game's continuation in period $t = 2$ must equal the value at $t = 0$. The latter value must be the larger of (8.38) and (8.39), so we have

$$V_b = \max\{1 - D_s(1 - D_b V_b), D_b^2 V_b\}. \tag{8.40}$$

It is clear that $V_b > D_b^2 V_b$. Therefore, (8.40) yields

$$V_b = 1 - D_s(1 - D_b V_b), \tag{8.41}$$

or

$$V_b = \frac{1 - D_s}{1 - D_s D_b}. \tag{8.42}$$

The unique sequential equilibrium allocates a payoff to the buyer given by (8.42). It can be shown that the seller will achieve the residual payoff (one minus the sum given by (8.42)). From (8.42), we see that the key elements in determining the gains from bargaining are the discount factors of the two agents. This is not surprising. The means by which an agent potentially extracts a more favourable outcome from the bargaining process is to prolong the process, rejecting existing offers in hope of securing a more favourable outcome. The higher is an agent's discount rate (the lower is D) the more costly is this technique, and the less able is the agent to secure a high payoff.

There initially appears to be an impossibly complicated collection of possible offers and counter offers in Rubinstein's bargaining model. It is an indication of the power of the sequential equilibrium concept that in spite of this complexity, the game exhibits a unique sequential equilibrium. The analysis also provides a potential characterization of bargaining power and the allocation of the gains from bargaining, based upon the discount factors of the bargainers. These results provide a sophisticated *theory* of bargaining. Attention accordingly turns to the sensitivity of the results of the specification of the bargaining model. Of particular interest is the amount of information the bargainers are presumed to have.

Noncooperative Bargaining Models with Incomplete Information

The models discussed in the previous section assume that the bargainers have complete information. In particular, each bargainer is assumed to know the opponent's reservation price. In practice, such complete information is unlikely to be available. This possibility is addressed by examining noncooperative bargaining models with incomplete information.

The first requirement in constructing a model of bargaining under incomplete information is to specify the nature of the incomplete information.[14] Suppose that the seller is uncertain as to the buyer's reservation price. We first identify the values which this price might take. We then refer to each of the possible buyer's reservation prices as a type of buyer. Hence, if the buyer's reservation price may take on one of two values, we say that there are two types of buyer. We must then specify the seller's belief as to how likely the buyer is to be of each possible type. This is accomplished by introducing a probability distribution on the potential buyer's types, with this distribution describing the seller's expectation of the likelihood of the various types.

We can think of the game of incomplete information as being a game in which a third player (generally called "nature") makes the first move. This move consists of choosing a type for the buyer (or for any bargainer about whose type there is uncertain information), with this choice governed by the probability distribution describing the uncertain information. The results of this choice are concealed from the players who have uncertain information, though the probability distributions describing the uncertain information are assumed to be common knowledge.

The equilibrium concept in such games is often referred to as a Bayesian Nash equilibrium. Because one or more agent is uncertain about the type of the agent's opponent, an equilibrium strategy for each possible type of the latter must be calculated, so that the uncertain agent can anticipate all possible types of opponents' behavior. We can then think of a strategy as a rule associating a course of action with each possible agent type.

One of the first bargaining models with incomplete information was examined by Harsanyi and Selten [1972]. In their framework, there are m possible types for the buyer and n possible types for the seller. Different types of buyers or sellers are characterized by different payoff functions. To describe the incomplete information, we assume that there exist probabilities q_i and r_i indicating the likelihood of the buyer or seller being of a particular type. Hence, bargainer type i of the m buyer typeset has a chance q_i of being "chosen" by Nature to play, bargainer type j of the n seller types has a chance r_j of being chosen. Strategies in this game consist of rules describing what actions each of the m possible buyer types will take and what actions each of the n possible seller types will take.

The difference in types is reflected only in differing payoff functions, caused by differences in disagreement payoffs and in utility functions. The total size of the gains from trade (or, more generally, the set of feasible agreements) remain fixed and known. Under these assumptions, the Harsanyi and Selten bargaining solution is an asymmetric Nash procedure. Each type of player's incremental utility payoff is raised to the power of the marginal probability of that type (in this case q_i for buyer type i, r_j for seller type j) occurring, and the product of these utilities maximized. Harsanyi and Selten also examine a multistage noncooperative game with multiple equilibria and offer their axioms as principles for choosing one of these equilibria.

A slightly different approach to bargaining under incomplete information is taken by Chatterjee and W. Samuelson [1983]. In this model, uncertainty arises concerning the reservation prices of the agents. The incomplete information is two sided, in that each agent is uncertain about the other's reservation price. To describe the uncertainty, the reservation prices, b and s, are assumed to be drawn from independent, continuous probability distributions. The following demand game is examined. The players make offers simultaneously. If the buyer's offer is greater than the seller's, an agreement takes place at a value which is a convex combination of the offers (for example, midway between them). If the buyer's offer is less than the seller's, there is no agreement and the bargaining ends.

Chatterjee and W. Samuelson characterized the equilibria of this game for several specific ways of splitting the difference between the offers. For the case where both b and s are drawn from uniform distributions on $[0, 1]$, the following results are derived:

PROPOSITION 7. *Let the seller's offer be a_s and the buyer's offer a_b.*

(1) *If the agreed price (when $a_b \geq a_s$) is*

$$x = \frac{a_b + a_s}{2} \tag{8.43}$$

then the optimal offers are (recall that b and s are the buyer and seller reservation prices):[16]

$$a_b = \frac{2}{3}b + \frac{1}{12} \quad and \quad a_s = \frac{2}{3}s + \frac{1}{4}. \tag{8.44}$$

(2) *If the agreed price (when $a_b \geq a_s$) is $x = a_s$, then the optimal seller offer is*

$$a_b^* = b \quad and \quad a_s^* = \frac{1+s}{2}. \tag{8.45}$$

(3)   *If the agreed price (when $a_b \geq a_s$) is $x = a_b$, then the optimal offers are*

$$a_b^* = \frac{b}{2} \quad and \quad a_s^* = s. \qquad (8.46)$$

The first result corresponds to a·procedure in which the bargainers split the difference between offers. The second can be viewed as a procedure in which the seller makes a single offer and the buyer either accepts or rejects the offer. The third result reverses the roles of the agents in this procedure.

Chatterjee and W. Samuelson also derive some general characteristics of equilibrium strategies, which do not depend upon the method of splitting the difference between offers. The important finding, illustrated by the special cases described above, is that the bargaining procedure is not efficient. It is said to lack efficiency because cases arise in which $b > s$, so that gains from trade are possible, but in which trade does not occur. Such cases arise because the buyer generally makes an offer lower than the buyer's reservation price, and the seller generally makes an offer higher than the seller's reservation price. By securing more desired outcomes in most cases, these manipulations secure higher expected payoffs for the players. The cost, however, is that some cases arise in which gains from trade exist and are not exploited.

Chatterjee [1982] has shown that this potential failure of efficiency is characteristic of any incomplete information bargaining process that satisfies certain innocuous assumptions. The most important of these assumptions is that of "responsiveness" to the offers of the players. This assumption requires that variations in players' offers produce variations in the final outcome.

Recent research has extended the Chatterjee and W. Samuelson model. The primary difficulty with the latter is that the bargaining is restricted to a single period. This restriction implies that if no agreement is reached in the initial stage, the bargainers will cease negotiations, even though there remains some possibility of gains from bargaining. It may be advantageous for a bargainer to promise to behave in this way. The threat to bargain no further if an agreement is not reached may induce one's opponent to make a more generous offer, so as to enhance the probability of reaching an agreement. However, such a threat does not appear to be credible. If no agreement is reached in the first stage, but gains from bargaining are still possible, then one would expect the bargainers to resume negotiations. Any promise or commitment to cease negotiations is likely to be broken. The bargaining process is then actually a multistage process, with myriad possibilities for offers and counter-offers. The question arises of whether Chatterjee and W. Samuelson's results continue to hold in this larger game.

Multistage bargaining models generally make two simplifying assumptions. Incomplete information is generally presumed to arise on only one side of the market. One of the bargainers (the informed bargainer) thus has complete information about the other. The other (uninformed) bargainer does not know the reservation price of the informed bargainer. In addition, the uninformed bargainer is conventionally the only one permitted to make offers. The remaining player is confined to accepting or rejecting offers. Hence, in each period the uninformed player makes an offer, which is accepted or rejected by the opponent. Delayed payoffs are subject to discounting. Examples include Sobel and Takahashi [1983] and Fudenberg, Levine, and Tirole [1984]. The major results of these models can be summarized as:

PROPOSITION 8. *In infinite horizon bargaining problems with one-sided incomplete information and successive offers made by the uninformed player:*

(1)   *The bargaining procedure is inefficient, in that some of the potential gains from trade are not realized by the bargainers. The inefficiency takes the form of a delay in achieving agreement rather than complete failure to agree. Intuitively, this delay occurs because prolonging the game provides an opportunity for the uninformed player to infer information about the opponent, or for the opponent to conceal such information.*
(2)   *In a sequential equilibrium, the uninformed player makes offers which allocate successively more of the gains from trade to the opponent.*
(3)   *Other equilibria exist which are Nash but not sequential equilibria. These include "commitment" equilibria, in which the agent making the offers fulfills a commitment to make no offer more favorable to the opponent than the original offer.*

The crucial feature which produces these results is what Fudenberg, Levine, and Tirole [1984] call the "successive skimming lemma." The informed player merely accepts or rejects an offer at each stage, and does not make counter offers. Each rejection reveals to the uninformed player that the range of the opponent's possible reservation prices is smaller than previously surmised. The uninformed player accordingly updates the player's probabilistic beliefs at each stage by truncating the previously held probability distribution describing the informed player's suspected reservation price.[17] This truncation induces a concession in the offer made by the uninformed player.

A multistage game with known gains from trade has been examined by Rubinstein [1983]. In Rubinstein's model, the uninformed bargainer does not know the discount rate of the informed bargainer. The agents' reservation prices are all common knowledge. As we have seen, discount rates are of crucial importance in Rubinstein's complete information model. The unknown discount rate may take on two possible values, so that two possible types of one bargainer exist. Rubinstein finds that in this case of one sided incomplete information, multiple sequential equilibria appear (so opposed to the uniqueness obtained by Rubinstein with complete information). The outcome again may not be efficient (i.e., the payoffs may sum to less than the gains from bargaining). Intuitively, the inefficiency again occurs because some potential bargaining gains are expended in attempts to discern or conceal information.

While these are intriguing results, the presumption of one completely informed bargainer may be unrealistic, and the generalization of these models to encompass two sided incomplete information accordingly poses interesting issues. Fudenberg and Tirole [1983] examine a two stage, two-sided incomplete information game with two types for each bargainer and with offers being restricted to one of the players. Uncertainty again arises concerning reservation prices. They show that the strategy of concessions (obtained with one sided incomplete information) is not necessarily optimal in this setting. A potential difficulty with this model is the restriction to two bargaining stages. This restriction encounters the criticisms levelled at the Chatterjee and W. Samuelson one stage model. The criticism can be avoided only by allowing a potentially unlimited number of stages.

Two recent papers, Cramton [1984] and Chatterjee and L. Samuelson [1984], examine two-sided incomplete information games with infinite horizons. Cramton examines a continuous model in which a continuum of types (reservation prices) for each player exists. In this framework a player could apparently choose to make any offer at any time. Cramton restricts his attention to equilibria in which players' strategies consist of the choice of time to reveal their actual types of reservation prices. Such equilibria are sustained by conjectures by one player that make it unprofitable for the other to consider any partially revealing offer. Once one type is revealed, the game becomes a continuous time, one sided incomplete information problem, while the revelation of both players' types leads to the complete information world of Rubinstein [1982]. Chatterjee and L. Samuelson's paper is a descendant of Fudenberg and Tirole [1983], and also shares some features with Cramton's approach. In order to illustrate the reasoning involved in determining a sequential equilibrium, we describe this paper.

The Chatterjee and L. Samuelson model is an infinite horizon model with two-sided incomplete information and two sided offers. The seller and buyer alternate in making offers. The model is summarized in table 8.1. There are two possible types for each bargainer, referred to as a hard and soft type. Mutually beneficial trade is possible unless both players are hard. Each player is uncertain as to the type of the other player. This uncertainty is described by the following common knowledge probabilities:

π_s^1—the initial probability that the seller is soft;

π_b^1—the initial probability that the buyer is soft. $\qquad$ (8.47)

Table 8-1. Two-sided Incomplete Information Reservation Prices

Type	Reservation Price		Discount Factor	
	Seller	Buyer	Seller	Buyer
Hard	$\bar{s}$	$\underline{b}$	D_s	D_b
Soft	$\underline{s}$	$\bar{b}$	D_s	D_b

where $\underline{s} \leq \underline{b} < \bar{s} < \bar{b}$

The bargaining proceeds as follows. In each period, the seller makes an offer. The buyer either accepts this offer or makes a counter offer. In the former case, the bargaining is completed. In the latter, the process proceeds to the next period. Discounting occurs, and the process continues with the seller either accepting the buyer's offer (ending the process) or rejecting the buyer's offer and making a new offer. Equivalently, we could say that at each stage, the seller makes an offer, and the buyer responds with a counter offer. If offers allow a mutually acceptable trade, trade occurs and the game ends. If not, the game proceeds to the next stage. For convenience, the agents' offers are restricted to be either $\underline{b}$ or $\bar{s}$.[18] This restriction significantly simplifies the analysis, but retains the strategic aspects of the game. Given these possible offers, the payoffs if trade occurs are given in table 8-2. As shown in table 8-2, we find it convenient to characterize offers as tough or weak. In the most interesting case, in which both agents are soft, there are potential gains from trade of $\bar{s} - \underline{b}$ to be allocated by the bargaining.

If the seller was known to be soft, a Nash equilibrium strategy for the soft buyer would be to commit to playing tough (i.e., offering $\underline{b}$) for a large number of periods (in the Harsanyi–Zeuthen framework, this strategy would constitute not conceding). The soft seller then has no better strategy available than to

Table 8-2. Two-sided Incomplete Information Payoffs

Strategy		Payoffs			
Seller	Buyer	Seller		Buyer	
		Soft	Hard	Soft	Hard
$\underline{b}$ (weak)	$\underline{b}$ (tough)	$\underline{b} - \underline{s}$	<0	$\bar{b} - \underline{b}$	0
$\bar{s}$ (tough)	$\bar{s}$ (weak)	$\bar{s} - \underline{s}$	0	$\bar{b} - \bar{s}$	<0

accede to the buyer's offer immediately, and this pair of strategies yields a Nash equilibrium. With two-sided incomplete information, however, such Nash equilibria no longer exist. The buyer cannot be certain that the seller is soft, and the strategy of repeatedly playing tough risks delaying an agreement for a suboptimally long time.

The bargaining ends (with an agreement) whenever an agent plays weak, while a tough offer always prolongs the bargaining. Notice, however, that playing weak is equivalent to surrendering any of the gains from bargaining. The agent is then faced with a choice between playing weak to achieve an early but small payoff; or playing tough, which prolongs the game and subjects the eventual payoff to heavier discounting.

Given this structure for the game and our restrictions on offers, a strategy for a soft agent can be entirely described as a choice of period in which to play weak. A pure strategy is then a choice of a particular period in which to play weak with probability one (if the opponent has not already played weak). A mixed strategy consists of a probability distribution over periods, describing the likelihood that each of the periods is the one selected for playing weak. An inspection of the payoffs indicates that hard agents will always play tough, while soft agents have a potentially complex optimization problem to solve in selecting offers.

We can now describe the equilibrium of this game.

PROPOSITION 9 (CHATTERJEE AND L. SAMUELSON).

(1)   *Pure strategy equilibria exist only if one or both of the initial probabilities is below a threshold value, denoted $\bar{\pi}_s$ for the seller and $\bar{\pi}_b$ for the buyer.*
(2)   *A Nash equilibrium exists, and is generically both unique and sequential.*
(3)   *The bargaining always ends with an agreement after a finite number of periods. This number is endogenously determined, and depends upon the specifications of the game's parameters.*
(4)   *The bargaining process is in general inefficient, in that some of the gains from trade are dissipated in the bargaining process.*
(5)   *The distribution of the expected gains from bargaining depends upon the bargainer's characteristics (reservation prices and discount rates) and upon the initial probabilities that the agents are hard. A characterization of agents' bargaining strength in terms of these values can be constructed, with relatively strong bargainers expecting a relatively large share of the gains from bargaining.*

To provide an intuitive idea of the origin of these results, we illustrate how the sequential equilibrium strategies can be determined. Suppose π_s^t and π_b^t are the period t expectations or probabilities of a soft seller or buyer. These are obtained from the initial probabilities by a consistent, Bayesian updating. Let h_b^t be the probability that a soft buyer plays weak in period t, and let V_s^{t+1} be the optimal expected payoff for the soft seller if the game continues to period $t+1$. If the seller plays weak in period t, the game ends with a trade and the seller's payoff is

$$\underline{b} - \underline{s}. \tag{8.48}$$

If the seller plays tough, the soft buyer may play weak (with probability h_b^t) and end the game, or may play tough (with probability $1 - h_b^t$) and prolong the bargaining. The hard player will certainly play tough. The seller's expected payoff, after some simplification, is then

$$\pi_b^t h_b^t \, (\bar{s} - s) + (1 - \pi_b^t h_b^t) D_s V_s^{t+1} \tag{8.49}$$

The soft seller will play weak only if the value given by (8.48) exceeds that given by (8.49). This requires that π_b^t be sufficiently small. Chatterjee and L. Samuelson demonstrate that soft agents will never play tough with probability one (with the possible exception of the seller in period one). Intuitively, playing tough is to a soft player's advantage only if doing so can induce the opponent to increase the estimated probability that the agent in question is hard. This information revision can occur only if the soft player randomizes between weak and tough, since otherwise the strategies of hard and soft agents are identical, and no information is revealed. Hence, soft agents play only random strategies or play weak with probability one. This allows us to make two inferences. First, the equilibrium strategies must give

$$\underline{b} - \underline{s} \geq \pi_b^t h_b^t (\bar{s} - \underline{s}) + (1 - \pi_b^t h_b^t) (D_s V_s^{t+1}), \tag{8.50}$$

since otherwise playing tough would be optimal for a soft agent, which contradicts the results just reported. In addition, we have

$$V_s^{t+1} = \underline{b} - \underline{s}. \tag{8.51}$$

This last result obtains because if the game reaches period $t + 1$, the soft seller either plays weak, with a payoff of $\underline{b} - \underline{s}$; or randomizes. In the case of a mixed strategy, it is well known that the randomizing agent must be indifferent between the possible outcomes of the randomization. Hence, a soft seller randomizes only if the expected returns from playing tough and weak are equal. The expected return from randomization thus equals the return from playing weak, or $\underline{b} - \underline{s}$. The latter is then the expected return from any period $t + 1$ action (playing weak or randomizing), allowing us to conclude the relationship given in (8.51).

If the inequality in (8.50) is strict, the soft seller plays weak and the game ends. The soft seller randomizes, and the game potentially continues, only if equality obtains in (8.50), or only if

$$\pi_b^t \, h_b^t = \frac{(\underline{b}-\underline{s})(1-D_s)}{\bar{s}-\underline{s}-D_s(\underline{b}-\underline{s})}. \tag{8.52}$$

Hence, as long as the game continues, the soft buyer's strategy must satisfy (8.52). A similar condition can be developed for the soft seller. It is the necessity of these conditions in equilibrium that yields the generic uniqueness of equilibrium, since these conditions (along with some initial condition considerations) determine the strategies of the soft agents in each period. The game thus continues along the unique sequential equilibrium path described by (8.52) (and the counterpart of (8.52) derived from examining the buyer) until one of the equalities cannot be maintained. A strict inequality then appears, inducing an agent to play weak and ending the game. A pure strategy equilibrium arises only if this last sequence of events appears in the first stage of the game, which generally does not occur.

This motivates the uniqueness of a sequential equilibrium, but not of a Nash equilibrium. Notice, however, that the difference between a sequential and Nash equilibrium is that only credible strategies or threats are allowed in the former. In the two-sided incomplete information game, any strategy or threat will be tested if one's opponent is hard. Since this possibility always remains, all strategies are potentially tested. This forces the agents to play only credible strategies, and forces the Nash equilibria to be generally sequential.

It will be useful to close this section by comparing the results of the Chatterjee and L. Samuelson incomplete information game with Rubinstein's complete information game described in the previous section. Three differences arise. First, the incomplete information game is inefficient, as we have observed in connection with a one sided incomplete information game. The inefficiency again takes the form of a delayed agreement, with this delay prompted by attempts to ascertain or conceal information. Second, the distribution of the gains from bargaining depend not only upon the player's characteristics (including discount factors), as in the complete information case, but upon the uncertainty about players' types. An agent who is more likely to be hard can expect to secure a larger share of the gains from bargaining. Finally, a property which distinguishes the two sided incomplete information game from both complete information and one sided incomplete information games is the uniqueness of the Nash equilibria in the former. Additional work must be done, however, before it can be determined how robust these findings are to the specification of the model.

3. Mechanism Design

The previous sections have described the two primary approaches to the theory of bargaining. The first specifies a set of properties or axioms which a bargaining outcome might or should satisfy, and attempts to characterize the solutions which feature these properties. The disadvantage of this approach is that no insight is provided into the bargaining processes that yield such an outcome. The second approach addresses this issue directly by postulating the existence of an extensive form game or bargaining process and examining the outcome of this game. The disadvantage in this case is that the properties of the outcome are not always revealed. Further, the question is not addressed of how the extensive form bargaining process is determined.

Recent work in bargaining theory combines these two approaches.[19] This work can be described as study of the design of bargaining processes or mechanisms, and is accordingly often referred to as the study of mechanism design. The basic procedure in the study of mechanism design is to examine the set of all bargaining solutions which could be realized as the equilibrium of an extensive form game or bargaining process. This set of bargaining outcomes is then examined for the presence of solutions which satisfy certain interesting properties.

The mechanism design approach shares with the axiomatic approaches, discussed previously, an interest in the properties of the bargaining solution. It differs in that interest is specifically restricted to bargaining solutions which could be achieved as Nash equilibria of noncooperative games. This restriction does not appear in traditional axiomatic approaches. The mechanism design approach shares with the noncooperative approaches, discussed previously, an interest in the outcomes of extensive form bargaining processes. The difference is that by revealing the properties of various equilibria, the mechanism design analysis provides some basis for examining the choice or origins of various extensive forms. In particular, the potential may exist to identify some extensive forms as being better than others.

It may initially appear that in resolving to consider only bargaining solutions which are potential outcomes of noncooperative games, an impossible task has been proposed. How is the set of such solutions to be identified? It is clearly impossible to actually examine all extensive form games. Fortunately, a more manageable approach can be constructed, and is based on the "revelation principle," discovered by Myerson [1979]. The revelation principle states that corresponding to an equilibrium outcome of any extensive form game there exists an incentive compatible direct mechanism that will generate the same outcome. We can accordingly restrict attention to incentive compatible direct revelation mechanisms, which is a manageable inquiry, and be assured that the class of outcomes we are examining is the class of all extensive form bargaining equilibria.

A direct revelation mechanism is a one stage game. The players announce their private information (in our framework, this private information consists of reservation prices). An outcome function associates a bargaining outcome with each possible pair of private information announcements. To see how the revelation principle is obtained, we note that in any extensive form game, the equilibrium strategy a player chooses will depend on the player's information (and perhaps upon information inferred from the actions of others, which in turn depends upon the information of these other players). Given the players' information values, one can then infer the equilibrium of the extensive form game. By choosing the outcome function of the one stage game to associate the appropriate equilibrium of the extensive form game with each set of private information values, the equilibrium of the latter can be achieved in the direct revelation mechanism. We can accordingly duplicate in a one stage game the correspondence between player types and equilibrium outcomes induced by any extensive form game. If the outcome mapping is further suitably designed, players will find it optimal in the direct revelation game to announce true values of their private information. A mechanism with this property is referred to as an incentive compatible mechanism. We can accordingly restrict attention to incentive compatible direct revelation mechanisms, and be confident that we are effectively examining all Nash equilibria of extensive form games.

Within the class of incentive compatible direct revelation mechanisms, we now turn to the search for bargaining mechanisms which possess certain desirable properties. Two properties immediately suggest themselves. First, we would like the bargaining mechanism to be ex post efficient, in that no outcome should arise which does not allocate all of the potential gains from bargaining to the bargainers. In addition, the mechanism should be individually rational, in that the expected payoff to each bargainer from participating in the process should exceed the payoff from not participating. Notice that this is a weak individual rationality requirement. We might ask that any possible realized outcome allocate a payoff to each bargainer which exceeds the payoff from not entering the process, rather than that the expected payoff exceed the latter value. However, the following result (from Myerson and Satterthwaite [1983]) reveals that we already have requirements which are too strong:

PROPOSITION 10. *No incentive compatible, individually rational solution with a balanced budget (i.e., whose payoffs sum to the potential gains from trade in the event of an agreement) exists that is ex post Pareto efficient.*

This suggests that incomplete information bargaining models may be able to explain such phenomena as disagreement when agreement would be mutually beneficial. One's initial reaction is that a bargaining process should be able to avoid such inefficient outcomes, but this conflicts with the results of proposition 10. Under incomplete information, there is no individually rational bargaining process that can always avoid such inefficient outcomes.

Perhaps ex post efficiency is too strong to require of a bargaining mechanism. We might replace it with the weaker requirement of interim incentive efficiency. A bargaining mechanism is interim incentive efficient if there is no other mechanism that does at least as well (produces at least as high a payoff) for all possible types of the players, and produces a higher payoff for at least one type. Hence, interim incentive efficiency insists not that a mechanism achieve Pareto efficiency, but only that no other mechanism comes closer to Pareto efficiency (in the sense just defined). While this is an intuitively desired property, it provides us with little power to discriminate between bargaining mechanisms. Instead, too many mechanisms satisfy the property. Formally

PROPOSITION 11. *Incentive compatible direct revelation mechanisms exist which are individually rational and interim incentive efficient. Such mechanisms are not unique.*

As proof of the proposition, we need only observe that all three of the Chatterjee and W. Samuelson mechanisms described in proposition 6 satisfy the conditions of proposition 11.

If the study of mechanism design is to allow a relatively small class of bargaining mechanisms to be identified as desirable, an efficiency criterion weaker than ex post efficiency and stronger than interim incentive efficiency must be invoked. Myerson and Satterthwaite [1983] suggest the concept of an ex ante optimal mechanism. Suppose that bargaining proceeds by nature first choosing a type for the buyer and seller, with this choice being governed by commonly known probability distributions. The bargainers then participate in a bargaining process given by a direct revelation mechanism. The ex ante payoff to the buyer is the expected payoff to the buyer before nature has drawn the buyer's type. Equivalently, we could say that we are interested in the buyer's expected payoff before the buyer learns the buyer's type. This payoff would be calculated by summing (integrating), over all possible buyer types, the product of the probability of that type occurring and the expected payoff of the type from the bargaining mechanism. We can similarly calculate the ex ante expected sum of payoffs to the two bargainers. A mechanism is ex ante optimal if it maximizes this expected sum.

Myerson and Satterthwaite have shown that, in at least one special case, the concept of ex ante optimality is very powerful.

PROPOSITION 12 (MYERSON AND SATTERTHWAITE [1983]). *The ex ante optimal mechanism for the symmetric uniform trading problem (the case where the buyer and seller have reservation prices drawn from a uniform distribution on* [0, 1]), *is to let each agent make a single offer, and to split the difference if the buyer's offer exceeds the seller's.*

This is a powerful result. Unfortunately ex ante optimality is not as intuitively obvious a condition as one would like, since agents are assumed to be ignorant of their types when selecting a bargaining mechanism. If agents know their types, their preferences over bargaining mechanisms are not likely to coincide with the recommendations made by an ex ante optimality calculation. Hence, the suggestion that agents will employ ex ante optimal mechanisms is unlikely to produce a useful descriptive theory of bargaining. It may, however, serve as a palatable normative recommendation if one is willing to impose a mechanism choice in conditions reminiscent of Rawls' initial position.

It is apparent that additional work is required before the theory of mechanism design will allow bargaining mechanisms to be ranked in terms of some desirability criteria. However, work in this area has already provided several useful concepts with which to compare mechanisms. Additional work is also continuing. Myerson [1984a] offers a general axiomatic approach to choosing a bargaining mechanism. His approach differs from the axiomatic approaches, discussed previously, in that Myerson addresses cases of incomplete information, and restricts attention to incentive compatible direct revelation mechanisms. Myerson (1984b) constructs a mechanism satisfying these axioms for the symmetric uniform trading problem. This is a combination of procedures (2) and (3) of proposition 7, with the player with greater 'bargaining strength' (that is, with a reservation price closer to the respective extreme 1 for the seller and 0 for the buyer) making a take-it or leave-it offer.

The revelation principle, and the work on mechanism design it has made possible, has provided valuable insights into the theory of bargaining. It has permitted the development of a welfare analysis of bargaining mechanisms. This suggests that bargaining theory may yield useful normative statements about the relative merits of various bargaining procedures. This is an encouraging possibility, since the theory of bargaining (especially axiomatic bargaining approaches) was initially criticized for being too abstract to yield insights about the actual practice of bargaining.

A potential difficulty is that the revelation principle refers only to Nash equilibria. Hence, direct revelation mechanisms allow us to study the class of Nash equilibria of extensive form games. In light of our previous discussion, this may be considered too broad an inquiry, with the analysis being more useful if it is limited to sequential equilibria. It is not immediately obvious how this limitation can be accomplished, and additional work is required in this area.

4. Conclusion

The field of two agent bargaining has progressed rapidly in the last few years, and has attracted interest among practitioners, economists and decision analysts.[20] Recent work has provided a clearer understanding of the limitations of axiomatic theories of bargaining and of noncooperative theories which presume complete information. Many of these limitations are addressed by recent and continuing work on incomplete information models and mechanism design.

Studies of bargaining are also beginning to make the transition from theory to practice. We have mentioned that recent work in mechanism design suggests the possibility of a welfare analysis of bargaining processes. Space limitations have prevented us from mentioning a growing collection of experiments designed to test bargaining theories. Finally, while we have presented our analysis in terms of bargaining between a buyer and seller, there is active interest in the application of bargaining theory to a host of other bargaining situations.

It is clear that the theory of bargaining will continue to be an area of active research. The two agent theories we have constructed will serve as building blocks for analyses of multiagent bargaining. Work can also be expected on enriching the institutional descriptions provided in the theory of bargaining. The expectation is that bargaining theory will continue to offer insights into the behavior of agents in thin markets.

Notes

1. We restrict the discussion to games in which the profits in the event of no agreement are fixed, often called "fixed threat" games. Nash [1953] also considered "variable threat" games, in which an auxiliary game is first played to determine the payoffs which appear in the event of no agreement in the primary game.

2. It is possible, of course, that a player who expects to engage in repeated bargaining processes might consider the effects of current bargaining on future bargains. Such an effect might arise if a bargainer can, by adopting aggressive positions in initial bargains, acquire a reputation as a tough

bargainer. Hence, a bargainer may refuse to accept any settlement that does not allocate to the bargainer three fourths (for example) of the gains from trade. While initial bargains may then end in disagreement, the bargainer might establish a reputation for toughness and thus obtain enough more favorable agreements in the future to compensate for these initial disagreements.

3. In the absence of risk neutrality, utility is no longer transferable from one player to another at a $1:1$ ratio.

4. This formulation is a loose statement of what Shubik [1982, p. 191] calls Shapley's Principle of Equivalence. Yaari [1981] uses essentially the same principle in demonstrating the equivalence of the Nash solution and a reformulated Rawlsian theory that does not assume interpersonal comparisons.

5. If (u_b, u_s) are chosen to maximize $u_b \cdot u_s$, the solution x is the point on the Pareto frontier for which the two angles shown are equal. Equivalently, the line joining x to the origin has the same magnitude of the slope as the tangent at x, but with opposite sign. This follows because u_s maximizes $u_s \phi(u_s)$, so that $u_s^* \phi'(u_s^*) + \phi(u_s^*) = 0$, or $u_b^* = \phi(u_s^*) = -\phi'(u_s^*) u_s^*$.

6. Nash's result can be generalized to include n-player unanimity games, where an agreement is reached if and only if all n players consent to it.

7. We identify the independence of irrelevant alternatives and not the independence of equivalent utility representatives as the key remaining axiom because the latter is a minimal requirement given von Neumann–Morgenstern utility functions. See, however, Roth and Malouf [1979].

8. Raiffa [1953] and Maschler and Perles [1978] examine variants of Kalai-Smorodinsky type solutions. Roth [1979] and Peters [1983] offer surveys of axiomatic approaches to bargaining.

9. This section is based on the work of Kihlstrom, Roth and Schmeidler [1981] and Roth [1979].

10. Nash equilibria have been shown to exist in a variety of games. The conditions of recurring importance in establishing the existence of a Nash equilibrium are compactness of the strategy sets and continuity of the payoff functions.

11. This last point is obtained as a Nash equilibrium because one of the best responses to an exceptionally high offer from the seller is an equally unreasonable offer from the buyer, giving the disagreement point as an outcome. Notice that the Nash bargaining solution is one of the Nash equilibria of the noncooperative game.

12. This Nash bargaining solution will exist as long as the utility possibility set in question is convex which requires the quasiconcavity of p.

13. See Kreps and Wilson [1982] for a rigorous formulation of the sequential equilibrium concept. Rubinstein actually examined a sub-game perfect equilibrium which is a special case of a sequential equilibrium.

14. Harsanyi [1967, 1968a, 1968b] developed techniques for examining games of incomplete information. In specifying the nature of the incomplete information, we are actually transforming the game from one of incomplete to one of imperfect information.

15. Binmore [1981] has applied a smoothed game argument to Harsanyi and Selten's model, and obtains convergence of the smoothed game equilibria if the latter are nonrevealing. A nonrevealing equilibrium is one in which all types of buyers (sellers) play identical strategies.

16. For values of the reservation prices such that the probability of agreement is zero, any strategy that does not disturb this equilibrium probability of agreement is permissible.

17. A similar updating technique appears in Cramton [1983], who has a two sided incomplete information model, but restricts the incomplete information over reservation prices to be given by uniform distributions and again restricts offers to one of the two bargainers.

18. This restriction is motivated and the implications of its relaxation are explored in Chatterjee and L. Samuelson [1984].

19. See Myerson [1979, 1984a, 1984b], Myerson and Satterthwaite [1983], and Holmstrom and Myerson [1984].
20. See Raiffa [1982] for accounts and analyses of many negotiation settings.

References

Aumann, Robert, "Agreeing to Disagree." *Annals of Statistics* 4 (1976), 1236–1239.

Binmore, K. G., *Nash Bargaining Theory* II. International Center for Economics and Related Disciplines Discussion Paper, London School of Economics, 1980.

Binmore, K. G., *Nash Bargaining and Incomplete Information.* Department of Applied Economics, Cambridge University, 1981.

Chatterjee, K. "Incentive Compatibility in Bargaining Under Uncertainty." *Quarterly Journal of Economics* 97 (1982), 717–726.

Chatterjee, K. and L. Samuelson, *Infinite Horizon Bargaining with Alternating Offers and Two-sided Incomplete Information.* The Pennsylvania State University Working Paper, 1984.

Chatterjee, K. and W. F. Samuelson, "Bargaining Under Incomplete Information." *Operations Research* 31 (1983), 835–851.

Cramton, Peter C., "Bargaining with Incomplete Information: An Infinite Horizon Model with Continuous Uncertainty. "Mimeo, Stanford University and Yale University, 1983.

Cramton, Peter C., "The Role of Time and Information in Bargaining." Mimeo, Stanford University and Yale University, 1984.

Fudenberg, Drew, David Levine, and Jean Tirole, "Infinite Horizon Models of Bargaining with One-Sided Incomplete Information." In *Game Theoretic Models of Bargaining*, (A. E. Roth ed.) Cambridge, Cambridge University Press, forthcoming, 1984.

Fudenberg, Drew and Jean Tirole, "Sequential Bargaining with Incomplete Information." *Review of Economic Studies* 50 (1983), 221–248.

Harsanyi, John C., "Approaches to the Bargaining Problem Before and After the Theory of Games." *Econometrica* 24 (1956), 144–157.

Harsanyi, John C., "Games of Incomplete Information Played by 'Bayesian' Players." *Management Science* 14 (1967, 1968a, 1968b), 159–183, 320–334, 486–502.

Harsanyi, John C. and Reinhard Selten, "A Generalized Nash Solution for Two-Person Bargaining Games with Incomplete Information." *Management Science* 18 (1972), 80–106.

Holmstrom, Bengt and Roger B. Myerson, "Efficient and Durable Decision Rules with Incomplete Information." *Econometrica* 51 (1983), 1799–1820.

Kalai, Ehud and Meir Smorodinsky "Other Solutions to Nash's Bargaining Problem." *Econometrica* 43 (1975), 413–418.

Kihlstrom, Richard and L. J. Mirman, "Risk Aversion with Many Commodities." *Journal of Economic Theory* 8 (1974), 361–388.

Kihlstrom, Richard, Alvin E. Roth, and David Schmeidler, "Risk Aversion and Nash's Solution to the Bargaining Solution." In *Game Theory and Mathematical Economics*, (O. Moeschlin and D. Pallaschke, eds.) North-Holland, Amsterdam, 1981.

Kreps, David M. and Robert B. Wilson, "Sequential Equilibria." *Econometrica* 50 (1982), 863–894.

Luce, R. D. and H. Raiffa, *Games and Decision.* New York: John Wiley, 1957.

Maschler, M. and M. Perles, "A Superadditive Solution to Nash Bargaining Games." Report to Fourth International Conference on Game Theory, Cornell University, Ithaca, New York, 1978.

Myerson, Roger B., "Incentive Compatibility and the Bargaining Problem." *Econometrica* 47 (1979), 61–73.

Myerson, Roger B. and Mark Satterthwaite, "Efficient Mechanisms for Bilateral Trading." *Journal of Economic Theory* 29 (1983), 265–281.

Myerson, Roger B., "Two Person Bargaining Problems with Incomplete Information." *Econometrica* 52 (1984a), 461–488.

Myerson, Roger B., "Analysis of Two bargaining Problems with Incomplete Information." In *Game Theoretic Models of Bargaining,* (Alvin E. Roth, ed.), Cambridge, Cambridge University Press, forthcoming, 1984b.

Nash, John F., "The Bargaining Problem." *Econometrica* 18 (1950), 155–162.

Nash, John F., "Two Person Cooperative Games." *Econometrica* 21 (1953), 128–140.

Peters, H. J. M., "Some Axiomatic Aspects of Bargaining." Mathematics Department, University of Nijmegen Report 83–11, The Netherlands, 1983.

Pratt, John W., "Risk Aversion in the Small and In the Large." *Econometrica* 32 (1964), 122–136.

Raiffa, Howard, "Arbitration Schemes for Generalized Two-Person Games." In *Contributions to the Theory of Games* II (A. W. Kuhn and A. W. Tucker, eds.) Annals of Mathematics Studies, No. 28, Princeton University Press, 1953, pp. 361–387.

Raiffa, Howard, *The Art and Science of Negotiation.* Harvard University Press, Cambridge, Mass., 1982.

Roth, Alvin E. and M. W. K. Malouf, "Game Theoretic Models and the Role of Information in Bargaining." *Psychological Review* 86 (1979), 574–594.

Roth, Alvin E., *Axiomatic Models of Bargaining.* Springer-Verlag: Berlin and New York, 1979.

Rubinstein, A., "Perfect Equilibrium in a Bargaining Model." *Econometrica* 50 (1982), 97–110.

Rubinstein, A., "A Bargaining Model with Incomplete Information." Hebrew University of Jerusalem, working paper, 1983.

Selten, Reinhard, "Reexamination of the Perfectness Concept for Equilibrium Points in Extensive Form Games." *International Journal of Game Theory* 4 (1975), 25–55.

Shaked, A. and J. Sutton, "Involuntary Unemployment as a Perfect Equilibrium in a Bargaining Model." *Econometrics* 52 (1984), 1351–1364.

Shubik, M., *Game Theory for the Social Sciences.* MIT Press: Cambridge, 1982.

Sobel, Joel and I. Takahashi, "A Multistage Model of Bargaining." *Review of Economic Studies* 50 (1983), 411–426.

Yaari, Menahem, "Rawls, Edgeworth, Shapley, Nash: Theories of Distributive Justice Reconsidered." *Journal of Economic Theory* 24 (1981), 1–39.

9 THE ELEMENTS OF FIXPRICE MICROECONOMICS

Joaquim Silvestre

"I shall argue that the postulates of the classical theory are applicable to a special case only, and not to the general case, the situation which it assumes being a limiting point of the possible positions of equilibrium."

J. M. Keynes, *General Theory* . . . , Chapter 1.

"Allegiance to rigor dictates the axiomatic form of analysis where the theory, in the strict sense, is logically entirely disconnected from its interpretations."

G. Debreu, *Theory of Value*, preface.

1. Introduction

1.1. Two Ideas

Two main ideas will be developed here. First, that fixprice analysis is not a negation of the competitive equilibrium model, but rather a more general framework which includes perfect competition as a special case. It is a study of markets in a wider sense. It concerns "prices" more than "fixity": it abstracts from specific features of market behavior and analyzes general properties of allocation mechanisms where market prices play a fundamental role. Second, that fixprice analysis has two main interpretations (logically distinct but related in a subtle way, see Arrow [1959]): the *monopolistic competition* interpretation, which views economic agents as having differing degrees of monopoly (or monopsony) power (competitive equilibrium being the special case where monopoly is nil) and the *competition in the short run* interpretation, which views

The author has benefited from comments by J.-P. Benassy, O. Hart, A. Mas-Colell, J. Roemer and S. Sheffrin. Of course, they share no responsibility for any errors, and the opinions expressed in the text reflect solely the author's view. The assistance of C. Berrade, C. Greene and R. Torres, and support from the *Comisión Asesora de Universidades* (Spanish Ministry of Education) are gratefully acknowledged.

the economy as perfectly competitive but assumes that it takes time for prices and quantities to adjust to their competitive equilibrium levels (competitive equilibrium being the only relevant situation in the special case where adjustment is very fast).

Thus, fixprice analysis is presented here as an organizing tool rather than a completely determined economic model. It does not choose a particular behavioral model of monopolistic or perfect competition, or a specific dynamic path for prices and quantities out of equilibrium—the present state of economic theory makes such choices very hard or impossible to justify. It rather derives properties of the price quantity pairs which may obtain in a market economy from a few basic principles common to a variety of specifications. It then classifies the possible states of the economy in a way potentially useful for empirical analysis and for policy recommendations. Finally, by explicitly analyzing generic market economies, it throws new light on competitive theory as a particular model of the operation of markets.

1.2. The Limited Scope of the Competitive Equilibrium Model

The competitive equilibrium model (perhaps under the intertemporal, perfect foresight interpretation) is the center of present economic theory. The model is certainly inadequate for environments for which no competitive equilibrium exists, e.g., technologies with economies of scale.

But the issue of adequacy is deeper. As Mas-Colell [1980, p. 121] noted, competitive equilibrium theory is more concerned with examining the consequences of the hypothesis of perfect competition than with giving a theoretical explanation of the hypothesis itself. Some important work has addressed this issue both from the cooperative (core equivalence theory) and, more recently, from the noncooperative viewpoint (see, e.g., Mas-Colell [1980]). Both approaches suggest that the hypothesis of perfect competition can be justified only as a limit when the number of agents of each type (say, buyers and sellers of any given commodity) tends to infinity. Rival theories for the case where this fails have been present since Bertrand's [1883] criticism of Cournot [1838]. Some recent work (see, e.g., Vives [1983]) has offered insights on their adequacy to alternative structural conditions. But no systematic results exist for the justification of the diverse theories of imperfect competition.

Thus, we have a set of economic environments for which a well-determined economic model, namely, the competitive equilibrium model, is adequate. But this model has nothing to say for (empirically relevant) environments with economies of scale or with relatively few decision-makers of a certain type (say, sellers of a given commodity). Moreover, we do not know which behavioral models are adequate for environments in this class.

1.3. Competitive Economies Out of Equilibrium

Consider a set of economic environments for which the competitive model is adequate, and assume, for the sake of the argument, that equilibrium is unique. The model singles out an allocation, namely the competitive equilibrium corresponding to a given environment, as the only possible state of rest of the system. But economic environments are not stationary. A change in the environment will change the equilibrium position. If the state variables do not adapt instantaneously to the new equilibrium position, then the system will be, at least temporarily, out of equilibrium. The empirical relevance of the equilibrium allocation depends on whether and how fast the system converges to it.

Economic theory has been so far unable to provide a satisfactory answer to the question of convergence, let alone that of the speed of adjustment. Empirical evidence moreover suggests that in modern market economies prices fail to fall rapidly when their equilibrium values fall. Hence, disequilibrium situations may very well be empirically important, and the competitive equilibrium model is inherently unable to contemplate economic activity out of equilibrium.

1.4. Partial Versus General Equilibrium

The competitive equilibrium model comes in two varieties: partial and general equilibrium. The partial equilibrium model studies an isolated market, i.e., an institution where a good is exchanged against money in a uniform, impersonal manner.

The general competitive equilibrium (also Walrasian or Arrow–Debreu) model considers a world with n goods: it is, in this sense, more general than the two good partial equilibrium model. But it is undefined as far as trading institutions are concerned. The theoretical model is compatible, from its high level of abstraction, with a variety of trading forms. The question: "How many markets in the Arrow–Debreu model?" does not have a unique answer. Perhaps n (one for each good, with the interpretation that in market j good j is exchanged against an unlisted $(n+1)$th good which disappears after the execution of the exchanges), or possibly $(n-1)$ (with the interpretation that one of the goods, say good n, is a means of payment exchanged against good j in market j), or maybe $n(n-1)/2$ markets, one for each pair of goods, or even zero markets (with the interpretation that the equilibrium allocation is implemented by means other than trading). And other possibilities are imaginable. Arrow–Debreu's model is hence a theory of markets only in a remote sense: it could also be considered a theory of planning (see Lange and Taylor [1938]). But the institutional framework has to be explicit as soon as trade at non-Walrasian prices is admitted. And, in a parallel manner, one cannot be precise about the notion of "market power" without formalizing the idea of "market" first.

We shall assume here that, in each market, a commodity is exchanged against a common medium of exchange (money). Thus, there are $(n + 1)$ goods, one of them being the medium of exchange, in the case of n markets. We shall study the cases of one market and several markets, but the expressions "partial" and "general equilibrium" will be avoided.

1.5. The Logic of the Fixprice Method

Fixprice theory addresses two questions. (I) Given a price vector p (not necessarily a competitive equilibrium one), what allocations are compatible with it? (II) Consider a given p and an allocation σ which is compatible with it; what are the characteristics of each market at (p, σ)? The answers are derived from three basic principles: *voluntary trading, absence of market frictions,* and *effective demand.* The principle of effective demand concerns the interaction among different markets. Those of voluntary trading and absence of market frictions already appear in the case of one market.

For clarity, the cases of one and of several markets will be considered separately. Section 2 below presents the principles of voluntary exchange and of absence of market frictions within the context of one market. The interpretations of monopolistic competition and of short run competition are presented first in this simple context.

1.6. Competition in the Short Run

Section 3 below considers the case of several markets within the context of the popular model with three goods studied, among others, by Barro–Grossman [1971, 1974, 1976], Benassy [1977a, 1982], and Malinvaud [1977]. The principle of effective demand is first illustrated for the short run competitive interpretation (as in the original formulation by Clower [1965]), and the classification of the short run disequilibrium states is derived. Section 3.3.2 below analyzes (following Malinvaud [1977]) the consequences of assuming slow and asymmetric (in the sense of faster upwards) price adjustments in the presence of observed shocks, and suggests that, disequilibrium situations of the

Keynesian type (i.e., with unemployment and prices higher than marginal cost) are more likely to persist.

1.7. The Monopolistic Competition Interpretation

Sections 3.4–5 below present the interpretation of fixprice theory as not necessarily perfect competition in a multimarket economy. Its essential features are that, in a given market, only agents on one side of the market may have market power (i.e., at least one side treats prices parametrically), and that an agent may be a price taker in one market and a price setter in another market. Thus, his price taking supply or demand schedule in one market must reflect his power in other markets. This is the translation of the "principle of effective demand" into the monopolistic competition version of the fixprice model.

The analysis in Section 3.4. is rather general: it considers all possible distributions of market power and compares (following Benassy [1973, 1977a]) the resulting market types with the typology of the short run interpretation. It is in the tradition of the "perceived demand curve" approach, pioneered by Bushaw–Clower [1957] and Negishi [1961], and incorporated into fixprice analysis by Benassy [1973, 1976, 1977a] (see also Grandmont–Laroque [1976], Hahn [1977a, 1978] and Negishi [1974, 1976, 1977, 1979]). Market power is translated as the elasticity of the demand (or supply) curves on which price setters base their decisions. Such curves may be viewed as the result of a learning process (see e.g., Benassy's [1973, 1976] explicit dynamics), but formally very few restrictions are placed on them.

One can say, paraphrasing Mas-Colell's quotation in p. 196 above, that the perceived demand approach is more concerned with examining the consequences of a particular hypothesis of imperfect competition (i.e., a particular set of postulated perceived demand curves) than with giving a theoretical explanation of the hypothesis itself. Section 3.5 below presents one such explanation due to Hart [1982]: the perceived demand curves depend on structural variables, namely the degree of concentration in the markets. He obtains allocations of the Keynesian type, but his method can prove useful for a variety of other forms of imperfect competition. We call it the objective demand function approach.

1.8. Extensions

This chapter is solely concerned with the microeconomic elements of fixprice analysis. Section 4 below offers some notes on the large and growing literature on fixprice microeconomics.

Benassy's book [1984] provides an excellent general treatment of fixprice macroeconomics.[1] Fixprice econometrics are presented in Quandt [1982] and Ito [1980a]. Laffont [1985] surveys recent empirical work.

2. One Market

2.1. Introduction

Consider an isolated market, where a commodity — output — is exchanged against another one — money. The aggregate level of output transacted is denoted by Y.

The data of the model are a social marginal cost curve $C'(Y)$ (stating the minimum amount of dollars which compensates sellers for aggregately furnishing an extra unit of output) and a social marginal value curve $V'(Y)$ (stating the maximum amount of dollars that buyers, in the aggregate, can part with in exchange for an extra unit of output). For concreteness, let $C'(Y) = Y$ (with the interpretation that sellers are firms which produce output according to the aggregate cost function $C(Y) = (1/2)Y^2$) and let the social marginal value curve be: $V'(Y) = 1 - Y$ (with the interpretation that buyers are consumers for whom the aggregate dollar value of Y is $V(Y) = Y - (1/2)Y^2$). These curves are represented in figure 9-1. Under perfect competition, $V' = C'$, i.e., the total quantity is $Y^* = 1/2$, and the competitive price is $p^* = V'(Y^*) = C'(Y^*) = 1/2$.

The perfectly competitive model will be adequate if there is a large number of sellers and a large number of buyers.

Suppose that the number of human beings in the society is indeed very large, but that in order to make buying and selling decisions individuals associate in groups. An association formed with the objective to sell will be called a "seller" or a "firm." One formed with the objective to buy will be called a "buyer" or a "consumer union," or, for short, a "consumer."

If there are N identical firms, the curve $C'(Y)$ can be viewed as the horizontal aggregation of N individual marginal cost curves: $\hat{C}'(y) = Ny$ (the individual total cost function is $\hat{C}(y) = (1/2)Ny^2$, satisfying $N\hat{C}(y) = C(Ny)$). Similarly, if there are M consumers, the curve $V'(Y)$ can be viewed as the horizontal aggregation of M individual marginal value curves: $\hat{V}'(y) = 1 - My$ (the individual total value function is $\hat{V}(y) = y - (1/2)My^2$, and satisfies: $M\hat{V}(y) = V(My)$).

2.2. Oligopoly

Suppose that the number of sellers N is small, and the number of buyers M is large. Then the market structure will typically be oligopolistic. Microeconomic textbooks offer a variety of oligopolistic models, each of them presumably

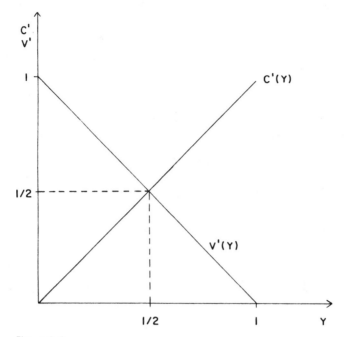

Figure 9-1

valid for a certain range of structural conditions. For a particular condition in this range, the oligopoly model determines an equilibrium price-quantity pair.

We shall keep in this section as maintained hypothesis the time honored Cournot model, and consider the number of sellers N as representing the structural conditions of the market. For $N = 1$ we have the pure monopoly model. Equilibrium is then given by $(p^M, Y^M) = (2/3, 1/3)$ (see figure 9-2). For a given N, the price-quantity pair is given by: $(p, Y) = ((N + 1)/(2N + 1), N/(2N + 1))$. This expression always satisfies the condition $p = V'(Y)$ (since $V'(Y) = 1 - N/(2N + 1) = (N + 1)/(2N + 1) = p$, i.e., we are always on the demand curve); it gives, for $N = 1$, (p^M, Y^M); as $N \to \infty$, it tends to the Walrasian point $(p^*, Y^*) = (1/2, 1/2)$. These facts are illustrated in figure 9-2.

Summarizing, under Cournot conditions we have that $p = V'(Y) > C'(Y)$. The precise (p, Y) equilibrium point will depend on the specific structural condition N. These conclusions obtain also for a variety of oligopoly models besides Cournot's.

2.3. Oligopsony

Imagine now that the number M of buyers is small, whereas there is a large number of sellers, and consider a Cournot type model of a Nash nonco-

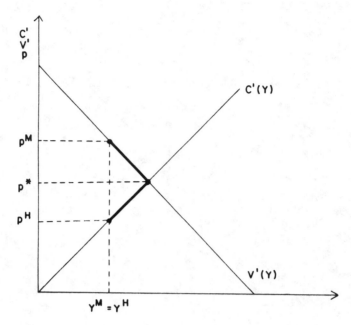

Figure 9-2

operative equilibrium in quantities among buyers (see, e.g., Henderson and Quandt [1971, section 6.5]). For $M = 1$ we have the pure monopsony solution $(p^H, Y^H) = (1/3, 1/3)$. For a given finite M, the oligopsonistic equilibrium solution is given by: $(p, Y) = (M/(2M + 1), M/(2M + 1))$, and always satisfies the condition $p = C'(Y)$. It tends to the Walrasian point $(1/2, 1/2)$ as $M \to \infty$ (see figure 9-2). Here, we have that $p = C'(Y) < V'(Y)$. Again, the precise (p, Y) equilibrium point will depend on the specific structural conditions. These conclusions will also obtain for a variety of oligopsony models.

2.4. Perfect Competition, But With Transactions Out of Equilibrium

Assume that prices are fixed by decree, say at $\bar{p}$ in figure 9-3. Or, less demandingly, assume that prices are, at $\bar{p}$, temporarily away from their competitive equilibrium levels, but that transactions take place at them. What will be the aggregate quantity transacted? We submit that it cannot be larger than $\bar{Y} = (V')^{-1}(\bar{p})$, since for any vector of individual purchases $(y_1, \ldots, y_M)$ such that $\sum_{i=1}^{M} y_i > \bar{Y}$ there would be some i such that $y_i > \bar{Y}/M$, i.e.,

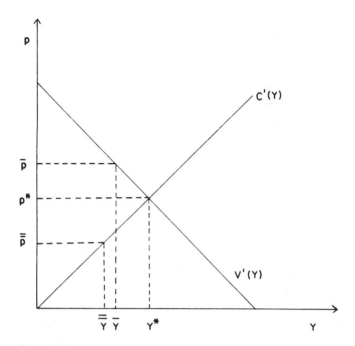

Figure 9-3

$\hat{V}'(y_i) < \hat{V}'(\bar{Y}/M) = V'(\bar{Y}) = \bar{p}$. This implies that agent i would be better off buying, at $\bar{p}$, less than y_i. To the extent that this is an impersonal market with terms of trading equal to $\bar{p}$, agent i should be able to do so. Hence, a level of transactions greater than $\bar{Y}$ is ruled out.

A different argument rules out aggregate transactions less than $\bar{Y}$. First, any $Y < \bar{Y}$, with $Y = \Sigma_{i=1}^{M} y_i^B = \Sigma_{i=1}^{N} y_i^S$ (where y_i^B (resp. y_i^S) is the individual quantity bought by buyer i (resp. sold by seller i)) would be such that for some buyer i, $y_i < \bar{Y}/M$, i.e., $\hat{V}'(y_i) > \hat{V}'(\bar{Y}/M) = V'(\bar{Y}) = \bar{p}$, and for some seller j, $y_j < \bar{Y}/N$, i.e., $\hat{C}'(y_j) < \hat{C}'(\bar{Y}/N) = C'(\bar{Y}) < V'(\bar{Y}) = \bar{p}$. If this is a well-organized market, buyer i and seller j will meet and engage in further trading. Hence, transactions smaller than $\bar{Y}$ can be ruled out.

It follows that $\bar{Y}$ will be the quantity transacted at $\bar{p}$. A similar argument shows that (see figure 9-3) $\bar{Y}$ will be the quantity transacted at $\bar{\bar{p}}$. We have that the quantity transacted at any p will be given by min $\{(V')^{-1}(p), (C')^{-1}(p)\}$. For $p > p^*$, $p = V'(Y) > C'(Y)$, i.e., competitive buyers satisfy their demand and (at least some) competitive sellers are constrained to sell less than their supply. The converse situation obtains when $p < p^*$.

*2.5. Comparing Imperfect Competition With Trading at
Non-Walrasian Prices. The Principles of Voluntary Trading
and of Absence of Market Frictions*

We observe that, under either interpretation, any allocation compatible with p must satisfy the following conditions:

Voluntary trading. For $i = 1, \ldots, M$, $p \leq \hat{V}'(y_i)$, which implies that: $p \leq V'(Y)$. For $j = 1, \ldots, N$, $p \geq \hat{C}'(y_j)$, which implies that $p \geq C'(Y)$.

Frictionless market. One cannot find a buyer i and a seller j such that $\hat{C}'(y_j) < p < \hat{V}'(y_i)$.

These two conditions imply that the admissible pairs (p, Y) satisfy:

$$Y = \min \{(V')^{-1}(p), (C')^{-1}(p)\}, \tag{9.1}$$

and, hence, that three basic types of situations may appear depending on whether $p = V' > C'$, $p = C' < V'$, or $p = C' = V'$. The imperfect competition models and the short run competitive model can be viewed as alternative interpretations of the theory embodied in (9.1). Table 9-1 presents the dual interpretations of the three basic types of price-quantity pairs.

These interpretations are logically independent but related in a not totally understood way. Consider the observed reluctance of prices to fall under excess supply. This can be viewed as the appearance of (temporary) oligopolistic

Table 9-1.   Interpretations of Price–Quantity Pairs

	Interpretation I: Not necessarily perfect competition	Interpretation II: Competitive trading at any given price
$p = V' > C'$ $(p < p^*)$	oligopoly (sellers have market power)	*(Some) competitive sellers are quantity constrained. *There is excess supply. *It is a buyers' market.
$p = V' = C'$ $(p = p^*)$	perfect competition (nobody has market power)	*Nobody is quantity constrained. *The market is balanced.
$p = C' < V'$ $(p > p^*)$	oligopsony (buyers have market power)	*(Some) competitive buyers are quantity constrained. *There is excess demand. *It is a sellers' market.

power (see Arrow [1959]). Conversely, typical industrial firms engage in efforts to expand sales at the going price, even though the price has been determined by the firm itself (this point has been forcefully presented by Weitzman [1984]). One can then say that firms are constrained by demand, but analytically this simply means that demand is satisfied at prices which exceed marginal costs, the expected outcome of an oligopolistic situation.

The list of interpretations given in table 9-1 is by no means exhaustive. As another example, trade can take place at non-Walrasian prices for a variety of institutional reasons. The prices of some commodities may be controlled or fixed by the government. Or prices may result from a negotiation between representatives of buyers and sellers: the representatives agree on a price, and then individual sellers (resp. buyers) are not forced to sell (resp. buy) amounts with marginal cost higher (resp. marginal value lower) than the price[2]. The same allocations will appear. Again, the interpretations may be related. As an illustration, suppose that the price is fixed by government decree at $p > p^*$. Then the government is in some sense implementing an oligopolistic situation: the power of the government is used as oligopolistic power.

3. Several Markets

3.1. Introduction: The Principle of Effective Demand

The isolated market analysis of Section 2 presented the principles of "voluntary trading" and "absence of market frictions" in terms of the given marginal cost and value functions. But these functions can no longer be taken as data of the model when markets are not isolated.

Perfect competition theory deals with this issue by assuming that agents take all prices as given, and conjecture that any exchange of two commodity bundles worth the same at the given prices can be realized — this is the competitive conjecture. The conjecture defines objective functions and constraint sets for each price vector (the objective function or the constraint set may be constant relative to the price vector), and constrained maximization of the objective function defines the Walrasian supply and demand functions which have the price vector as only argument. At equilibrium, supply and demand for each commodity are equal. It is then possible to reinterpret the general equilibrium allocation as a situation where several markets are in equilibrium, although such an interpretation is neither required by the theory nor unique.

But the Walrasian supply and demand functions (called "notional" by Clower [1965]), based as they are on the competitive conjecture, are of little help when the competitive conjecture is contradicted, as is the case when transactions are made at non-Walrasian prices.

This leads to the principle of effective demand (see Clower [1965] and Leijonhufvud [1968]), which has different interpretations depending on whether we view the economy as basically competitive but with trade out of equilibrium or as monopolistically (or monopsonistically) competitive. Consider the competitive case with trade out of equilibrium. Then the principle of effective demand states that the marginal value or cost functions in a market depend on the (price and) quantity constraints observed in other markets. For instance, a competitive consumer who sells labor has a marginal value curve in the market for output which depends on the amount of labor he is able to sell in the labor market. Or the cost function of a firm may reflect the impossibility of buying more than a certain quantity of inputs.

Second, consider the monopolistic competition interpretation. With several markets, an agent may have market power in market A and act as a price taker in market B. Then his (price taking) reaction to prices in market B (say, his supply function there) depends on his power in market A. Consider, for concreteness, a firm which is a price taker in the output market (B) but which has monopsonistic power in the labor market (A). Then its supply function in the output market will not equate the wage/price ratio to the marginal physical product of labor. If, say, this firm is selling to a monopsonist in market B, then the supply function faced by the monopsonist is not the Walrasian supply of its suppliers — despite the fact that these suppliers are price takers in market B. It rather is an "effective" supply function which incorporates the market power held in other markets by the suppliers in market B. These ideas will be made precise within the context of a specific model.

3.2. The Model

Let there be three goods: money (denoted by k), which is a nonproduced good initially available in K_0 units, labor, initially available in L_0 units, and output which is initially nonavailable and is produced using labor as the only input. Aggregate amounts of output (resp. labor) are denoted by Y (resp. L).

There are two markets: a labor market, where labor is exchanged against money (consumers — resp. firms — being sellers — resp. buyers) and an output market, where output is exchanged against money (consumers — resp. firms — being buyers — resp. sellers). The money wage (resp. price) will be denoted by w (resp. p). Only strictly positive pairs (p, w) will be considered.

The aggregate production function $Y = f(L)$ is assumed differentiable, with $f'' < 0$ and $\lim_{L \to 0} f'(L) = \infty$. It corresponds to the sum of the technologies of

N firms, each with production function $\hat{f}$, where $f(L) = N\hat{f}(L/N)$. All profits are distributed to consumers.

There are M consumers, with positive money endowments adding up to K_0. They all have the same utility function[3] $U(y, k)$ (where y denotes consumption of output by a consumer) which does not have leisure as an argument. We assume that U is differentiable, strictly quasi-concave, and homothetic. Thus, the marginal rate of substitution depends only on the ratio k/y, i.e., $(\partial U/\partial y)/(\partial U/\partial k) = \phi(k/y)$, where ϕ is an increasing function. We shall assume that $\lim_{\xi \to \infty} \phi(\xi) = \infty$ and $\lim_{\xi \to 0} \phi(\xi) = 0$. The equation "$\phi(\xi) = p$" has then a unique, positive solution for all $p > 0$.

We shall obtain an abstract formulation of the admissible price-quantity pairs in each market based on the principles of voluntary trading and absence of market frictions. An expression like (9.1) will result. But now the marginal cost and marginal value curves for a market are no longer data of the model: they must rather be derived from the original data (utility functions, production functions, and initial endowments) and must take into account the interdependence between markets.

First, the marginal value curve for output (derived from the utility function) must reflect the fact that the marginal rate of substitution depends also on K. Here we define: $V'(Y) = \phi(K_0/Y)$ (if, for instance, the utility function is $U(y, k) = y^\beta k^{1-\beta}$, then $\phi(K_0/Y) = (\beta/(1 - \beta))(K_0/Y)$). This curve is represented in figure 9-4 and plays the role of the V' curve in figure 9-1.

Second, the marginal cost curve depends on the wage rate w. Instead of a single aggregate marginal cost curve, we have a family of aggregate marginal cost curves $C'_w(Y) = w(f^{-1})'(Y)$, one for each wage rate w. This is illustrated in figure 9-5 where $\bar{\bar{w}} > w^* > \bar{w}$.

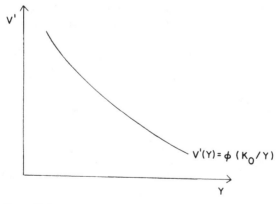

Figure 9-4

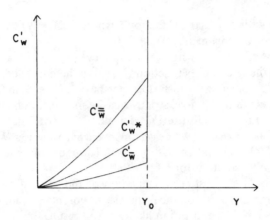

Figure 9-5

Third, the total amount of labor L_0 available in the economy puts an absolute bound of $Y_0 = f(L_0)$ units of output, and the cost function must reflect the impossibility of producing more than Y_0 units. Figure 9-5 depicts this impossibility as a vertical continuation of the cost curves at the Y_0 level.[4]

Combining the V' and C'_w curves so obtained, we observe that, depending on w, three types of complete pictures appear: these are illustrated in figures 9-6 (a)–(c). The V' curve and the vertical line "$Y = Y_0$" are the same in the three graphs, but the C'_w curves are drawn for three different levels of w. In figure 9-6(a) (resp. (c)), w is high (resp. low). In figure 9-6(b) the wage rate w^* exactly puts the C'_{w^*} curve at the intersection of the V' curve and the vertical line "$Y = Y_0$": w^* can be recognized as the competitive equilibrium (Walrasian) wage rate.

The admissible price–quantity pairs in the output market are depicted as the solid lines in figures 9-6(a)–(c). Formally, the admissible combinations (p, w, Y) are given by:

$$Y = \min\{(V')^{-1}(p), (C'_w)^{-1}(p), Y_0\}, \tag{9.2}$$

which translates (9.1) into the present two market setup.[5]

We shall now typify the admissible combinations according to the comparison between prices and marginal values and costs, and according to the presence or absence of unemployment. Seven types will result.[6] Their description will include the relevant area of the (p, w) plane as partitioned in figure 9-7, which partition is to be justified later. The regions K, C, and E are understood as closed. Intersections "$\cap$" indicate common boundaries, the symbol "$\circ$" denotes the interior of the relevant region, and "$\setminus$" indicates set subtraction.

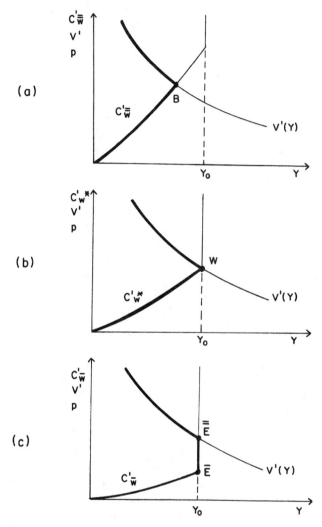

Figure 9-6

Type I *situations: prices equal marginal values and are greater than marginal costs; there is unemployment.* This corresponds to price–quantity pairs on the V' curve above point B (resp. W, resp. $\bar{\bar{E}}$) in figure 9-6(a) (resp. (b), resp. (c)). The price–wage pair belongs to area $\mathring{K}$ in figure 9-7 below.

Type II *situations: prices equal marginal costs and are less than marginal*

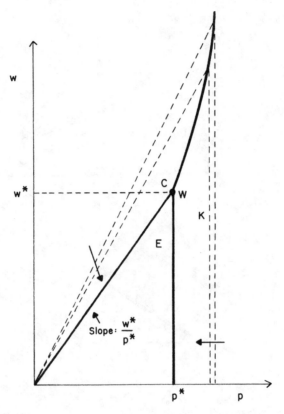

Figure 9-7

values; there is unemployment. This corresponds to price-quantity pairs on the C'_w curve below point B (resp. W, resp. $\bar{E}$) in figure 9-6(a) (resp. (b), resp. (c)). The price–wage pair is in area $\overset{\circ}{C}$ of figure 9-7.

Type III *situations: prices are higher than marginal costs and lower than marginal values; there is full employment.* This corresponds to points on the "$Y = Y_0$" line in figure 9-6(c) between points $\bar{E}$ and $\bar{\bar{E}}$ ($\bar{E}$ and $\bar{\bar{E}}$ not included). The price–wage pair is in area $\overset{\circ}{E}$ of figure 9-7.

Type IV *situations: prices equal both marginal costs and marginal values. There is unemployment.* This is point B in figure 9-6(a). The price–wage pair belongs to the curve $K \cap C \setminus \{W\}$ of figure 9-7.

Type V *situations: prices equal marginal values and are greater than marginal costs; there is full employment.* This is point $\bar{E}$ in figure 9-6(c). The price–wage pair belongs to the segment $K \cap E \setminus \{W\}$ of figure 9-7.

Type VI *situations: prices equal marginal costs and are lower than marginal values; there is full employment.* This is point $\bar{E}$ of figure 9-6(c). The price–wage pair belongs to the segment $C \cap E \setminus \{W\}$ of figure 9-7.

Type VII *situation: prices equal both marginal values and marginal cost. There is full employment.* This is point W in figure 9-6(b). The price–wage pair is in the singleton $\{W\}$ (or $K \cap C \cap E$) of figure 9-7.

Figure 9-7 is based on the standard division of the (p, w) plane into the full employment region E, the "price equals marginal utility" region K (for Keynesian) and the "price equals marginal cost" region C (for Classical or Full Capacity). The reader may work out the derivation of the regions — or consult any of the multiple references on the two market model, e.g., Benassy [1982]. The Walrasian price p^* is given by the equation: $(V')^{-1}(p) = Y_0$; graphically, it is the vertical coordinate of the point of intersection between the V' curve and the vertical line "$Y = Y_0$" in figures 9-6(a)–(c). See figure 9-6(b) for the representation of the Walrasian wage w^*. The ratio w^*/p^* gives the slope of the boundary $C \cap E$: it is the Walrasian real wage and the maximal real wage compatible with full employment. The equation of the boundary $C \cap K$ is obtained (together with the associated levels of output Y) from the system of equations in (p, Y, w): $p = C'_w(Y) = V'(Y)$. Two iso-output lines have been drawn as dashed lines; arrows indicate the directions of increasing output: there is full employment in E.

For an illustration, assume a Cobb–Douglas utility function $U(y, k) = y^\beta k^{1-\beta}$ and suppose that the aggregate production function is given by: $Y = (\gamma L)^{1/\alpha}$, where $\alpha > 1$ and $\gamma > 0$. The curve $V'(Y)$ (see Section 3.2 above) is thus: $V'(Y) = (\beta/(1-\beta))(K_0/Y)$, and the curve C'_w is: $C'_w = \alpha Y^{\alpha-1} w/\gamma$. The Walrasian equilibrium price of output p^* is given by the equation: $(V')^{-1}(p) = Y_0$, i.e.,

$$p^* = \frac{\beta}{1-\beta} \frac{K_0}{(\gamma L_0)^{1/\alpha}},$$

and the Walrasian real wage w^*/p^* is given by the equation: $p = C'_w(Y_0)$, i.e., $p = \alpha[\gamma L_0]^{\frac{(\alpha-1)}{\alpha}} w\gamma^{-1}$, which yields: $w^*/p^* = \alpha^{-1}\gamma^{1/\alpha}L_0^{(1-\alpha)/\alpha}$.

3.3. The Short Run Competitive Interpretation

3.3.1. Characterization of the Regime. We shall consider first the short run interpretation of the theory presented, for the one market case, in Sections 2.4–5 above. To recall, all markets are perfectly competitive, but there are transactions out of equilibrium. Thus, this is a short run framework in the sense that prices do move according to competitive excess demand, but at a finite speed so that, at any given instant (short run), there is production and trade. This is Interpretation II in table 9-1.

This interpretation makes the model comparable to the textbook Keynesian multiplier model.[7] The homogeneity of U implies that demand for output, as a function of price p and wealth I, can be written: $h(p)I$. The function $h(p)$ satisfies: $h(p) < 1$ and $ph(p) < 1$, and is related to the function $\phi(k/y)$ by the equality: $\phi((1 - ph(p))I/h(p)I) = p$ (e.g., $h(p) = \beta/p$ for the Cobb–Douglas utility function $U(y, k) = y^\beta k^{1-\beta}$). Aggregate wealth is the sum of the initial holdings of money K_0 and the value of production at p, pY. Hence, demand c (i.e., effective demand, since it embodies the process of income determination) is given by:

$$c = h(p)[K_0 + pY] = K_0 h(p) + ph(p)Y.$$

This can be viewed as the Keynesian consumption function, where $ph(p) < 1$ is the marginal propensity to consume (see figure 9-8) (in the Cobb-Douglas case, $ph(p) = \beta$.) At a point where effective demand equals output (as $\bar{Y}$ in figure 9-8), $Y = (h(p)/(1 - ph(p)))K_0$, i.e., $\phi(K_0/Y) = V'(Y) = p$. Effective demand is thus satisfied at $\bar{Y}$.

Amounts of output greater than $\bar{Y}$ cannot be sold at the given price because of insufficient demand. On the other hand, depending on the values of p and w, it may happen that $\bar{Y} > f(L_0)$ (in which case it is physically impossible to

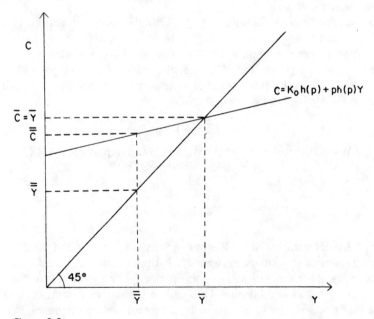

Figure 9-8

produce $\bar{Y}$) or that $p < C'_w(\bar{Y})$, in which case to produce $\bar{Y}$ some firm would be forced to sell at a price below marginal cost. In either case, production will take place at a level lower than $\bar{Y}$, say $\bar{\bar{Y}}$ in figure 9-8, where $\bar{\bar{Y}} = \min\{Y_0, (C'_w)^{-1}(p)\}$ and where demand is unsatisfied, i.e., $\bar{\bar{Y}} < K_0 h(p) + ph(p)\bar{\bar{Y}}:= \bar{c}$, or equivalently, $V'(\bar{\bar{Y}}) > p$.

We now ask the question: When can we say that there is excess supply or demand? When are sellers (or buyers) constrained? In other words, how can the seven types of situations identified in Section 3.3 be interpreted from the "competition in the short run" view (i.e., in terms of column two of table 9-1)? We shall first consider the issue of which side is constrained. The results are displayed in table 9-2.

The criterion is quite clear for *sellers of labor*: unconstrained if there is full employment and constrained if there is employment. This allows us to fill the entries in the last column of table 9-2. It is also clear for *buyers of output*, constrained if $p < V'$ and unconstrained if $p = V'$ (first column in table 9-2). Moreover, it is natural to say that if $p = C'_w$ then both *sellers of output* and *buyers of labor* are unconstrained. This allows us to fill the corresponding entries in rows II, IV, VI, and VII, but their entries for the cases where $p > C'_w$ (rows I, III, and V) remain to be filled.

Next, impose the condition "at most one side constrained in a given market," i.e., in no market may both buyers and sellers be simultaneously constrained. This is a natural version of the "absence of market frictions" idea. Under this condition, buyers of labor are unconstrained in Type I situations (since sellers of labor are constrained) and sellers of output are unconstrained in Type III situations (since buyers of output are constrained). Last, it is also natural to say that, if $p > C'_w$ and sellers of output (resp. buyers of labor) are unconstrained. then buyers of labor (resp. sellers of output) must be constrained. This justifies the "constrained" label for sellers of output in Type I and for buyers of labour in Type III. But the blanks in row five remain.

We now define the sign of excess demand in each market as positive if buyers are constrained, negative (or excess supply market) if sellers are constrained and zero (or balanced market) if nobody is constrained. This is given in table 9-3.

The question marks in row five reflect those in table 9-2. No straightforward answer exists for these (see Silvestre [1978a, 1982b] and Weddepohl [1983]). Moreover, Type V disappears in models where output is durable and firms keep inventories.[8]

We feel that the disequilibrium element present in Type V situations is best understood as being internal to the firm (excess capacity) and generating pressures for the adjustment of the capital stock of the firm instead of market pressures on prices.[9]

Table 9-2. Pattern of Constrained Traders

Type of Allocation	Agents	Buyers of Output	Sellers of Output	Buyers of Labor	Sellers of Labor
I. $(C'_w < p = V'; L < L_0)[\mathring{K}]$		unconstrained	constrained	unconstrained	constrained
II. $(C'_w = p < V'; L < L_0)[C]$		constrained	unconstrained	unconstrained	constrained
III. $(C'_w < p < V'; L = L_0)[E]$		constrained	unconstrained	constrained	unconstrained
IV. $(C'_w = p = V'; L < L_0)[K \cap C \setminus \{W\}]$		unconstrained	unconstrained	unconstrained	constrained
V. $(C'_w < p = V'; L = L_0)[K \cap E \setminus \{W\}]$		unconstrained	?	?	unconstrained
VI. $(C'_w = p < V'; L = L_0)[C \cap E \setminus \{W\}]$		constrained	unconstrained	unconstrained	unconstrained
VII. $(C'_w = p = V'; L = L_0)[W]$		unconstrained	unconstrained	unconstrained	unconstrained

Table 9-3.   Pattern of Excess Demand

Type of allocation	Market Output	Labor
I. $(\mathring{K})$	excess supply	excess supply
II. $(\mathring{C})$	excess demand	excess supply
III. $(\mathring{E})$	excess demand	excess demand
IV. $(K \cap C \, \imath\{W\})$	balanced	excess supply
V. $(K \cap E \, \imath\{W\})$	?	?
VI. $(C \cap E \, \imath\{W\})$	excess demand	balanced
VII. (W)	balanced	balanced

3.3.2. Shocks and Asymmetric Speeds of Adjustment.   An economy subject to a shock altering its environment is temporarily out of equilibrium. Transactions are realized out of equilibrium and prices adjust at finite speed to their new equilibrium values. Prices change according to the characteristics of the disequilibrium situation, e.g., according to the sign of excess effective demand[10] discussed in the previous section (See, e.g., Veendorp [1975], Honkapohja [1979], Eckalbar [1980], Laroque [1978b, 1981b] and Honkapohja and Ito [1983].)

If prices adjust according to the sign of excess demand, then region $\mathring{K}$ of figure 9-7 is a deflationary region (both p and w tend to go down), region $\mathring{E}$ is inflationary, and in region $\mathring{C}$ prices will tend to go up and wages will tend to go down.

Situations of unemployment, where prices exceed marginal costs while demand is satisfied (i.e., region $\mathring{K}$ in figure 9-7) are observed more frequently in modern market economies than price-wage pairs in the other regions of figure 9-7. This observation is consistent with an asymmetry in the speed of price adjustment, i.e., with the notion that prices respond more quickly to upward pressure (excess demand) than to downward pressure (excess supply)[11]. The economy will converge to its equilibrium values relatively fast after shocks which temporarily locate it in regions C and E.

We shall consider now, following Malinvaud [1977], the effects of different types of shocks. We shall see that shocks which affect the parameters of demand will lead to region K (and have relatively persistent effects, under the asymmetry hypothesis) while shocks which affect the productivity of labor will lead to region C, and will therefore generate a more ephemeral disequilibrium situation. For concreteness, assume the specification presented in Section 3.2: a Cobb–Douglas utility function $U(y, k) = y^\beta k^{1-\beta}$, and a production function $Y = (\gamma L)^{1/\alpha}$, where $\alpha > 1$ and $\gamma > 0$.

Consider first shocks in the demand parameters, say a contraction of demand caused by a decrease in β (the marginal propensity to consume) or K_0 (the money stock). Since the Walrasian price is given by $\beta K_0/(1-\beta)(\gamma L_0)^{1/\alpha}$ the Walrasian price will go down, but the Walrasian real wage (given by $\alpha^{-1}\gamma^{1/\alpha}L_0^{(1-\alpha)/\alpha}$) will be unaffected. Figure 9-9 superimposes the maps of figure 9-7 above corresponding to high and low demand. After the contraction of demand, prices and wages stay temporarily close to their previous equilibrium levels ($W_{\text{HIGH DEMAND}}$), which now is a disequilibrium situation of Type I ($\mathring{K}$ region), i.e., with general excess supply.

Consider now an expansion of demand. Now prices stay temporarily close to the $W_{\text{LOW DEMAND}}$ point, which is now a disequilibrium situation of Type VI, i.e., with excess demand for output (See table 9-3). If prices react fast to excess demand, the disequilibrium will be short lived.

The implications for a business cycle caused primarily by fluctuations in demand are: (1) the economy will fluctuate between Type I (unemployment with prices higher than marginal costs) and Type VI (full employment with unsatisfied demand) situations; and (2) to the extent that the adjustment speed is asymmetric, the unemployment phase will be more persistent than the full employment one.

Next, we analyze shocks in the productivity of labor represented by changes in the parameter γ. Suppose that γ decreases, i.e., there is a deterioration in productivity. Now the Walrasian price goes up and the Walrasian real wage goes down (see figure 9-10; the Walrasian nominal wage, given by $w^* = \beta K_0/(1-\beta)\alpha L_0$, remains unchanged). The price wage pair stays temporarily close to its (high productivity) previous Walrasian value, and we are now in a Type II disequilibrium situation (region $\mathring{C}$) with excess demand for output and excess supply of labor (see table 9-3). The price wage pair will tend to move southeastward.

With an increase in productivity, the price-wage pair will temporarily stay close to its previous (low productivity) equilibrium levels, which now is a disequilibrium situation of Type I ($\mathring{K}$ region) with general excess supply. The (presumably slow) adjustment will move the price-wage pair southwestwards.

Summarizing, a business cycle driven by productivity shocks will fluctuate between Type I (Keynesian) and Type II (Classical) situations (with perhaps other types appearing in the process). To the extent that adjustment speed is asymmetric, the phase with unemployment of the Keynesian type will be relatively more persistent.

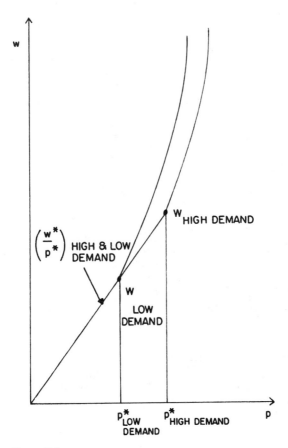

Figure 9-9

The reader is referred to Malinvaud [1977, chapter III] for a more detailed analysis, where he argues that the type of unemployment of the late seventies may be characterized as one of "Keynesian unemployment with Classical contamination" (p. 110). A more disaggregated model is required to capture disequilibrium regimes where, say, industrial markets are partially isolated and some of them are in excess demand while some others are in excess supply. Some interesting applied work has followed this approach (see Laffont [1985] for an exposition). As Laffont [1985] notes, the disaggregated approach may

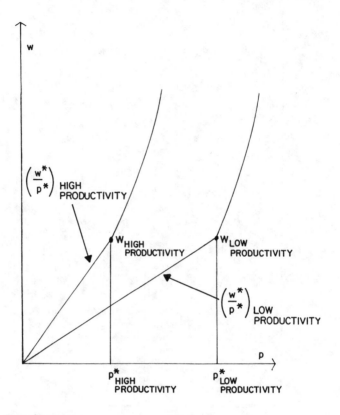

Figure 9-10

determine the relative shares of Classical and Keynesian unemployment, and it also may attempt to explain why a given sector is in one type of unemployment or the other. Both issues are highly relevant for the purposes of economic policy.

3.4. The Monopolistic Competition Interpretation: Perceived Demand and Supply Curves

3.4.1. Perceived Curves. This interpretation of the fixprice model is given in Benassy [1976, 1977a] (see also Negishi [1974, 1976, 1977, 1979], Grandmont–Laroque [1976], and Hahn [1977a, 1978]). It is based on the perceived demand curve approach to imperfect competition pioneered by

Bushaw–Clower [1957] and developed by Negishi [1961] (see Hart [1985] for a recent survey of the area).

We shall assume, for the remainder Section 3, symmetry in the endowments (i.e., each consumer is endowed with $K_0/M := k_0$ units of money and $L_0/M := l_0$ units of labor) and profits shares, and we shall only consider symmetric fixprice allocations (each consumer will consume $Y/M := y_C$ units of output, will work $L/M := l_C$ hours and will end up with k_0 units of money; each firm will use $L/N := l_f$ units of labor and will produce $Y/N := y_f$ units of output).

The data of the model include, for each agent, a family of perceived (conjectured or subjective) demand curves (for the commodity he sells) and one of perceived supply curves (for the commodity he buys), parametrized by a vector $\bar{z}$ interpreted as the "current conditions," "state of the market," or "status quo." Prices for all commodities and consumption (resp. production) vectors for all consumers (resp. firms) may in principle be components of the status quo vector $\bar{z}$. But here we shall consider only symmetric status quo vectors, i.e., of the form: $\bar{z} = (\bar{p}, \bar{y}_f, \bar{y}_C, \bar{w}, \bar{l}_f, \bar{l}_C) \in R_+^6$. We interpret $\bar{p}$ (resp. $\bar{w}$) as the "current" price of output (resp. wage), $\bar{y}_f$ (resp. $\bar{y}_C$) as the "current" amount of output sold (resp. bought) by a firm (resp. consumer), and $\bar{l}_f$ (resp. $\bar{l}_C$) as the "current" amount of labor bought (resp. sold) by a firm (resp. consumer). Some components of $\bar{z}$ may be irrelevant for a given perceived curve.

An individual firm faces perceived demand curves for output written (in indirect form) $\tilde{p}_d(y_f | \bar{z})$, and perceived supply curves for labor, written $\tilde{w}_s(l_f | \bar{z})$. The value $\tilde{p}_d(y_f | \bar{z})$ is interpreted as the price at which a firm thinks it can sell the quantity y_f when the state of the market is the vector $\bar{z}$. The function $\tilde{w}_s(l_f | \bar{z})$ is interpreted in a similar way. All firms have the same family of perceived demand curves. Similarly, $\tilde{p}_s(y_C | \bar{z})$ (resp. $\tilde{w}_d(l_C | \bar{z})$) denotes the supply of output (resp. demand for labor) curve perceived by a consumer. The profit income perceived by a consumer is also a function of $\bar{z}$. It is given, in our symmetric world, by:

$$\Pi(\bar{z}) = (N/M)(\bar{p}\bar{y}_f - \bar{w}\bar{l}_f).$$

This approach leaves the perceived demand curves largely unrestricted. They may, in particular, have a kink at the state of the market price-quantity pair. For instance, the slope of the function $\tilde{p}_d(y_f | \bar{z})$ may be lower on the left of the state of the market point $(\bar{p}, \bar{y}_f)$ than on the right, as in the time honored (see Sweezy [1939]) oligopoly model of the kinked demand curve. The reader is referred to the book by Negishi [1979] (see also Negishi [1974, 1977], Trujillo [1985], and Woglom [1982]) for a general treatment of the kinked demand function approach in disequilibrium analysis.

We assume in what follows that the perceived demand and supply curves are differentiable, and, hence, that the (inverse) demand and supply elasticities are well defined. They will be denoted by

$$e_d^p(y_f \mid \bar{z}) = \tilde{p}_d' \cdot y_f / \tilde{p}_d, \qquad e_s^w(l_f \mid \bar{z}) = \tilde{w}_s' \cdot l_f / \tilde{w}_s,$$
$$e_s^p(y_C \mid \bar{z}) = \tilde{p}_s' \cdot y_C / \tilde{p}_s, \qquad e_d^w(l_C \mid \bar{z}) = \tilde{w}_d' \cdot l_C / \tilde{w}_d.$$

Two assumptions usually postulated in the perceived demand literature (see Hart [1985]) will be imposed here.

Nonincreasing Demand Assumption: $e_d^p \leq 0$, $e_d^w \leq 0$, $e_s^p \geq 0$, $e_s^w \geq 0$.

No Bilateral Monopoly Assumption: $e_d^p \cdot e_s^p = 0$, $e_d^w \cdot e_s^w = 0$.

Of course, price taking (competitive) behavior is represented by a zero (inverse) elasticity of the perceived curve. The assumption of no bilateral monopoly requires that at least one side of the market (buyers or sellers) be price takers.

3.4.2. Optimal Actions and Imperfectly Competitive Equilibrium.

Given a state of the market $\bar{z}$, a firm chooses a point $(\hat{y}_f(\bar{z}), \hat{p}_f(\bar{z}))$ on its perceived demand curve for output, and a point $(\hat{l}_f(\bar{z}), \hat{w}_f(\bar{z}))$ on its perceived supply curve of labor in order to maximize profits.

Formally,

$$\hat{p}_f(\bar{z}) = \tilde{p}_d(\hat{y}_f(\bar{z}) \mid \bar{z}), \quad \hat{l}_f(\bar{z}) = \hat{f}^{-1}(\hat{y}_f(\bar{z})), \quad \hat{w}_f(\bar{z}) = \tilde{w}_s(\hat{l}_f(\bar{z}) \mid \bar{z}),$$

where $\hat{y}_f(\bar{z})$ solves:

$$\text{Max}_{y_f} \, \tilde{p}_d(y_f \mid \bar{z}) y_f - \tilde{w}_s(\hat{f}^{-1}(y_f) \mid \bar{z}) \cdot \hat{f}^{-1}(y_f). \tag{9.3}$$

Similarly, a consumer chooses $(\hat{y}_C(\bar{z}), \hat{p}_C(\bar{z}), \hat{l}_C(\bar{z}), \hat{w}_C(\bar{z}))$ in order to maximize utility subject to the budget constraint. Since leisure does not enter the utility function, the point $(\hat{l}_C(\bar{z}), \hat{w}_C(\bar{z}))$ on the perceived demand curve for labor must maximize wage income, i.e., $\hat{w}_C(\bar{z}) = \tilde{w}_d(\hat{l}_C(\bar{z}) \mid \bar{z})$ and $\hat{l}_C(\bar{z})$ solves:

$$\max_{l_C} \, \tilde{w}_d(l_C \mid \bar{z}) l_C \quad \text{subject to: } l_C \leq l_0, \tag{9.4}$$

and $\hat{p}_C(\bar{z}) = \tilde{p}_s(\hat{y}_C(\bar{z}) \mid \bar{z})$, where $\hat{y}_C(\bar{z})$ solves:

$$\max_{y_C} \, U(y_C, k_0 + \hat{w}_C(\bar{z})\hat{l}_C(\bar{z}) + \Pi(\bar{z}) - \tilde{p}_s(y_C \mid \bar{z}) y_C). \tag{9.5}$$

An imperfectly competitive equilibrium (relative to the families of perceived curves $(\tilde{p}_d, \tilde{p}_s, \tilde{w}_d, \tilde{w}_s)$) is a z^* such that

(i) $y_f^* = \hat{y}_f(z^*)$, $l_f^* = \hat{l}_f(z^*)$, $p^* = \hat{p}_f(z^*)$, $w^* = \hat{w}_f(z^*)$.

(ii) $y_C^* = \hat{y}_C(z^*)$, $l_C^* = \hat{l}_C(z^*)$, $p^* = \hat{p}_C(z^*)$, $w^* = \hat{w}_C(z^*)$.

(iii) $Ny_f^* = My_C^* := Y^*$, $Nl_f^* = Ml_C^* := L^*$.

3.4.3. Characterization of Imperfectly Competitive Equilibria.

We shall now classify imperfectly competitive equilibria according to the elasticities of the (indirect) perceived supply and demand functions — a zero elasticity meaning competitive behavior in the corresponding market.

From (9.3) we obtain the first order condition for a firm:

$$\tilde{p}'_d \cdot y^*_f + \tilde{p}_d - \tilde{w}'_s \cdot (\hat{f}^{-1})' \cdot \hat{f}^{-1} - \tilde{w}_s \cdot (\hat{f}^{-1})' = 0.$$

Since at equilibrium $(\tilde{p}_d(y^*_f|z^*), \tilde{w}_s(\hat{f}^{-1}(y^*_f)|z^*)) = (p^*, w^*)$, we have that:

$$p^*(1 + e^p_d) - w^*(\hat{f}^{-1})'(1 + e^w_s) = 0,$$

where, by the assumption of nonincreasing demand, $e^p_d \le 0$ and $e^w_s \ge 0$. Thus, using symmetry, we have that

- If both $e^p_d = 0$ and $e^w_s = 0$, then $p^* = C'_{w^*}(Y^*)$.
- If either $e^p_d < 0$ or $e^w_s > 0$ (or both), then $p^* > C'_{w^*}(Y^*)$.

(9.6)

Similarly, from (9.5) and (9.4) we obtain the first order conditions for a consumer:

$$\frac{\partial U}{\partial y} - \frac{\partial U}{\partial k} \cdot (\tilde{p}'_s \cdot y_c + \tilde{p}_s) = 0; \tag{9.7}$$

$$\tilde{w}'_d \cdot l_c + \tilde{w}_d \ge 0, \ (l_c - l_0)(\tilde{w}'_d \cdot l_c + \tilde{w}_d) = 0. \tag{9.8}$$

Since at a symmetric imperfectly competitive equilibrium $k = k_0$ for each consumer, and hence $(\partial U/\partial y)/(\partial U/\partial k) = \phi(k_0/y^*_c) = \phi(K_0/Y^*)$, (9.7) implies:

- If $e^p_s > 0$, then $p^* > V'(Y^*)$,
- If $e^p_s = 0$, then $p^* = V'(Y^*)$;

(9.9)

whereas from (9.8) we obtain:

- if $e^w_d = 0$, then $L^* = L_0$ (full employment)
  [if $e^w_d < 0$, then $L^* \le L_0$ (unemployment or full employment)] (9.10)

Using the assumption of absence of bilateral monopoly, the admissible sign combinations for the elasticities of the perceived demand and supply curves are:

LABOR MARKET

- $e^w_s = 0$ and $e^w_d < 0$ (oligopoly);
- $e^w_s = 0$ and $e^w_d = 0$ (competition);
- $e^w_s > 0$ and $e^w_d = 0$ (oligopsony);

OUTPUT MARKET

- $e_d^p < 0$ and $e_s^p = 0$ (oligopoly);
- $e_d^p = 0$ and $e_s^p = 0$ (competition);
- $e_d^p = 0$ and $e_s^p > 0$ (oligopsony).

We have nine combinations. Using (9.6), (9.9), and (9.10), we observe that, if the price-wage pair of the imperfectly competitive equilibrium is (p^*, w^*), then aggregate output Y^* satisfies:

$$Y^* = \min \{ (V')^{-1}(p^*), (C'_{w^*})^{-1}(p^*), Y_0 \},$$

in accordance with (9.2). The correspondence between the imperfect competition combinations and the types of Section 3.2 above (see tables 9-2 and 9-3) can be established as in table 9-4 below.

3.5. The Monopolistic Competition Interpretation: Objective Demand and Supply Curves in Hart's Model

3.5.1. Objective Curves. The analysis in the previous section relates non-competitive behavior — defined as nonzero elasticity of the perceived demand or supply curve — to the type of resulting allocation. But it does not justify the slopes of the perceived supply and demand curves. In Hart's [1982, p. 111] words, this approach "does not distinguish between small and large economies. In particular, a highly monopolistic outcome can be sustained in a large economy if agents are given appropriate conjectures and a competitive outcome can be sustained in a small economy with different conjectures."

There is no general theory of which demand and supply curves are correct for each economic environment. Quoting Hart [1985, p. 13], "It is impossible to construct a completely general 'objective' model of imperfect competition." We shall now present Hart's [1982] particular but illuminating model of "objective" supply and demand curves.

Consider the economy of the previous sections, but with the interpretation that decisions regarding the sale of labor are not made by individual workers, but by trade unions or syndicates (decisions to buy output are still made individually). As before, N denotes the number of firms. The number of human beigns is mN (both m and N are viewed as large numbers), and that of syndicates will be written $N/q\rho$ ($mq\rho$ persons in each syndicate). It will be convenient to identify the consumer of the previous sections not with an individual person but with the "syndicate" of this one. Thus, $M = N/q\rho$, and l_c

Table 9-4. Imperfect Competition Combinations and Types of Allocation

Labor Market → / Output Market ↓	Oligopoly $(e_d^w < 0 = e_s^w)$	Competition $(e_d^w = 0 = e_s^w)$	Oligopsony $(e_d^w = 0 = e_s^w)$
Oligopoly $(e_d^p = 0 = e_s^p)$	• $C'_w < p = V'$ • unemployment or full employment TYPE I or TYPE V $(\mathring{K}$ or $K \cap E \upharpoonright \{W\})$	• $C'_w < p = V'$ • full employment TYPE V $(K \cap E \upharpoonright \{W\})$	• $C'_w < p = V'$ • full employment TYPE V $(K \cap E \upharpoonright \{W\})$
Competition $(e_d^p = 0 = e_s^p)$	• $C'_w = p = V'$ • unemployment or full employment TYPE IV or TYPE VII $(K \cap C)$	• $C'_w = p = V'$ • full employment TYPE VII (W)	• $C'_w = p < V'$ • full employment TYPE V $(K \cap E \upharpoonright \{W\})$
Oligopsony $(e_d^p = 0 < e_s^p)$	• $C'_w = p < V'$ • unemployment or full employment TYPE II or TYPE VI $(\mathring{C}$ or $C \cap E \upharpoonright \{W\})$	• $p = C'_w < V'$ • full employment TYPE VI $(C \cap E \upharpoonright \{W\})$	• $C'_w < p < V'$ • full employment TYPE III $(\mathring{E})$

(resp. y_C, resp. l_0, resp. k_0) will be interpreted here as the amount of labor sold (resp. output bought, resp. leisure owned, resp. money owned) by a group of $mq\rho$ identical persons.

There is a large number N/q (resp. θN) of identical and isolated labor (resp. output) markets. Each output market contains $1/\theta$ firms (perhaps a small number) and m/θ persons (a large number). Firms may have oligopoly power in output markets: the given number θ can be viewed as an index of monopoly in the typical output market. In each labor market there are $1/\rho$ syndicates (each with $mq\rho$ persons): altogether there are mq persons in each labor market and a large number q of firms. Syndicates may have oligopoly power in labor markets. The number ρ can be viewed as an index of monopoly in labor markets.

Hart [1982, p. 113] assumes

A.1. Any two firms in the same product market are also in the same labor market. This guarantees that all firms in any output market face the same wage rate.

A.2–3. Persons from a given labor market are distributed uniformly across different product markets, and each person owns a fraction $1/mN$ of every firm. This guarantees that the price and quantities of a given market have negligible effect on the wealth of buyers in that market.

We shall now describe the demand and supply curves perceived by each agent in this economy, and justify their objectiveness.

Decisions to buy output are made by persons, who have negligible influence on the price of output. Thus, they perceive a market price independent of the amount y bought, i.e.,

$$\tilde{p}_s(y|\bar{z}) = \bar{p}. \qquad (9.11)$$

Decisions to sell output are made by firms, which may have oligopolistic power. Denote by $I(\bar{z})$ the aggregate wealth of the buyers in a given output market.[12] The demand curve faced by a firm when the state of the market is $\bar{z}$ is postulated to be given, in direct form, by:

$$\tilde{y}_d(p|\bar{z}) = h(p)I(\bar{z}) - [(1/\theta) - 1]\bar{y}_f \qquad (9.12)$$

Its indirect form $\tilde{p}_d(y_f|\bar{z})$ is simply the inverse of the expression in (9.12), i.e., $\tilde{p}_d(y_f|\bar{z})$ satisfies: $\tilde{y}_d(\tilde{p}_d(y_f|\bar{z})|\bar{z}) = y_f$, for all $y_f \geq 0$.

The objectiveness of the curve in (9.12) is justified in two steps.

Step 1. By A.2-3, what happens in one of the output markets has negligible influence on the wealth of the buyers in that market. Thus, $I(\bar{z})$ should be taken as given by firms in the market and, at $I(\bar{z})$, total demand addressed to that market by price taking buyers is $h(p)I(\bar{z})$. This is, in a very natural sense, the true demand curve that a monopolist in that market would face.

Step 2. But output markets are oligopolistic instead of monopolistic. Expression (9.12) embodies Cournot behavior: each firm takes the "status quo" joint output of the other firms Y' as given. In our symmetric setup, $Y' = (1/\theta - 1)\bar{y}_f$, where $\bar{y}_f$ is the status quo output of a single firm. It follows that the objectiveness of the perceived demand function given in (9.12) is not absolute, but rather conditional to the objectiveness of the Cournot conjecture (see Hart [1985, section 5] for a discussion).

We turn now to the labor markets, where any firm has a negligible influence in the market wage, i.e.,

$$\tilde{w}_s(l_f|\bar{z}) = \bar{w}. \tag{9.13}$$

Decisions to sell labor are made by syndicates, and their perceived demand curves will be presented next. Under some assumptions (see Hart [1982, section III]), given w and a market demand curve $h(p) \cdot I$, a unique and symmetric Cournot equilibrium for $1/\theta$ firms with cost functions $w\hat{f}^{-1}(y)$ exists. Denote by $\hat{y}_f(w, I)$ the output of a firm at such a Cournot solution. Write: $\hat{l}_f(w, I) := \hat{f}^{-1}(\hat{y}_f(w, I))$ and: $\hat{l}(w, I) := q\hat{l}_f(w, I)$. In words, $\hat{l}(w, I)$ is the quantity of labor that q firms want to employ when their level of output is that of the Cournot solution in their respective output markets, which solution depends on w and I. The assumptions in Hart [1982] guarantee that $\hat{l}(w, I)$ is decreasing in w.

The demand-for-labor curve perceived by a syndicate is defined, in its direct form, as:

$$\tilde{l}_d(w|\bar{z}) = \hat{l}(w, I(\bar{z})) - ((1/\rho) - 1)\bar{l}_C, \tag{9.14}$$

and its inverse is denoted by $\tilde{w}_d(l_C|\bar{z})$. As before, this curve is justified in two steps.

Step 1. By A.2-3, what happens in one of the labor markets has negligible influence on the wealth of the customers of the firms that buy labor in that labor market. Hence, $I(\bar{z})$ should be taken as given by syndicates. If output markets are true Cournot oligopolies, it is justified to choose the Cournot solution $\hat{l}(w, I(\bar{z}))$ as the demand for labor addressed to that market by wage taking (but Cournot-oligopolistic in their output markets) buyers. The curve $\hat{l}(w, I(\bar{z}))$ is, in a natural sense, the true demand curve that a monopolistic syndicate would face in that labor market.

Step 2. As before, (9.14) assumes that the $1/\rho$ syndicates are themselves Cournot oligopolists in their labor markets.

3.5.2. Optimal Actions and Imperfectly Competitive Equilibrium in the Sense of Hart.
The maximization problem of firms is (9.3) for the perceived

curves given in (9.12) and (9.13). Here, decisions to sell labor are made by syndicates in order to maximize wage receipts. The maximization problem generating labor supply is (9.4) for the perceived curve given in (9.14).

Decisions to buy output are made by (price and wealth) taking persons, but given the homogeneity of U, the quantity demanded by a group of $mq\rho$ persons can be viewed as the solution to the maximization problem in (9.5) for the perceived curve given in (9.11).

Hart [1982] shows that, under some assumptions, an imperfectly competitive equilibrium (as defined in Section 3.4) $z^* := (p^*, y_f^*, y_C^*; w^*, l_f^*, l_C^*)$ exists. We shall call it HICE (for Imperfectly Competitive Equilibrium in the Sense of Hart). Of course, the HICE depends on the values of the parameters, in particular, on θ and ρ.

The conclusions derived for subjective demand and supply (Section 3.4) apply here, since the assumptions of nonincreasing demand and of the absence of bilateral monopoly are satisfied. In particular, if the price-wage pair at the HICE is (p^*, w^*), then aggregate output $Y^* = Ny_f^*$ satisfies:

$$Y^* = \min\{(V')^{-1}(p^*), (C'_{w^*})^{-1}(p^*), Y_0\},$$

again agreeing with (9.2). But here the classification of the resulting allocation ultimately depends on more primitive data, namely on the "degree of monopoly" parameters ρ and θ.

3.5.3. Characterizing Imperfectly Competitive Equilibria in the Sense of Hart.
The elasticity of the direct demand curve faced by a firm at the HICE is:

$$(e_d^p)^{-1} = h'(p^*)I(z^*)\frac{p^*}{\theta h(p^*)I(z^*)} = h'(p^*)\frac{p^*}{\theta h(p^*)},$$

which is negative as long as $\theta > 0$ and tends to $-\infty$ as $\theta \to 0$. Thus, the elasticity e_d^p of the indirect demand curve tends to 0 as $\theta \to 0$. Since firms are wage takers, from (9.6) we obtain

$$p^* > C'_{w^*}(Y^*) \quad \text{if } \theta > 0,$$

$$\lim_{\theta \to 0}(p^* - C'_{w^*}(Y^*)) = 0.$$

A parallel argument gives a negative elasticity of demand for labor if $\rho > 0$ and limit zero elasticity as $\rho \to 0$. From (9.10) we have

$$\lim_{\rho \to 0} L^* = L_0 \quad \text{and} \quad L^* \le L_0 \quad \text{for } \rho > 0.$$

Hence, there is full employment for $\rho = 0$ and possibly for some positive values of ρ. These results can be summarized in table 9-5, which is identical to the northwest four entry region of Table 9-4.

Table 9-5. "Degree of Monopoly" Parameters and Type of Allocation

Reciprocal of the Number of Firms per Output Market	Reciprocal of the Number of Syndicates per Labor Market	
	$\rho > 0$	$\rho = 0$
$\theta > 0$	• $C'_w < p = V'$ • unemployment or full employment TYPE I or TYPE V $(\mathring{K}$ or $K \cap E \setminus \{W\})$	• $C'_w < p = V'$ • full employment TYPE V $(K \cap E \setminus \{W\})$
$\theta = 0$	• $C'_w = p = V'$ • unemployment or full employment TYPE IV or TYPE VII $(K \cap C)$	• $C'_w = p = V'$ • full employment TYPE VII (W)

The reason why the remaining entries of table 9-4 do not appear in Hart's model is clear. Hart's [1982] maintained hypothesis is that the number of buyers is everywhere large, and therefore monopsonistic power in either market is ruled out (i.e., the last row and last column of table 9-4 cannot apply). Thus, only allocations in region K can result (as indicated by the four northwestern entries of table 9-4).

But Hart's formulation of objective demand functions could be applied to other distributions of market power. Leisure does not enter the utility function in the economy studied here, and therefore it is hard to imagine oligopsony in the labor market with firms facing "true" supply functions for labor and with a positive wage at equilibrium (although this could be imaginable if leisure entered the utility function). Hence, no natural modification of Hart's assumptions would yield equilibria of the types described in the last column of table 9-4.

But we conjecture that it is possible to modify Hart's framework to accommodate oligopsony in the output market with competition or oligopoly in the labor market. The number of firms in each labor market should be large, and consumers should, in each output market, form consumer cooperatives (say, such that there are $1/\lambda$ cooperatives in each output market) with possible monopsony power. One could then construct a model of "objective" perceived supply functions of output yielding allocations in region C of figure 9-7 (two first entries of the last row in table 9-4).

We are not suggesting that consumer cooperatives have been historically as important as labor unions. On the contrary, casual empiricism suggests that typical markets are oligopolistic or competitive, and therefore that region K is empirically more relevant than region C (or E). As noted in Section 3.3.2, the alternative interpretation of the model as competition in the short run also assigns greater empirical relevance to region K. Our point is rather that Hart's method of embedding partial equilibrium noncompetitive analysis in a multimarket framework may be fruitful elsewhere.

Notes on the Literature

Three independent formulations (Drèze [1975], Benassy [1973, 1975, 1976], and Younès [1975]) are the core of the fixprice model for economies with many agents and markets.[13] Their definitions are equivalent under some conditions, in particular for the economies studied here[14] (see Silvestre [1982a, 1983]). They all prove existence of fixprice equilibria in general settings. The structure of the set of fixprice equilibria is studied in Laroque [1978a, 1981a], Laroque–Polemarchakis [1978], and Böhm [1982], Schulz [1983]. The phenomenon of fixprice disequilibrium allocations at Walrasian prices (a case of non-uniqueness of fixprice equilibrium) is analyzed in Hahn [1977b], Ito [1979], Heller–Starr [1979], and Silvestre [1980]. The multiplicity of Pareto-ranked equilibria generates a pecuniary externality analyzed in Heller [1984]. Multiplier-type adjustment processes are studied in Böhm [1978], Honkapohja [1980] and Eckalbar [1981]. Dynamic models for economies where output is storable and firms hold inventories are presented in Honkapohja and Ito [1980], Ito [1980b], and Green and Laffont [1981].

Non-Walrasian fixprice allocations are typically Pareto inefficient (Nayak [1980], Madden [1982], Silvestre [1985]). Alternative notions of efficiency are analyzed in Benassy [1973, 1975, 1982], Younès [1975], Böhm–Müller [1977], Grandmont–Laroque–Younès [1978], Drèze–Müller [1980], Silvestre [1982c], Balasko [1982], Benassy [1975, 1982], Müller [1983], and Maskin–Tirole [1984].

The fixprice model is often embedded in a temporary equilibrium framework (see Benassy [1973, 1975], Grandmont [1977, 1981], Grandmont–Laroque [1976]). The role of expectations in this context is emphasized in Benassy [1973, 1984], Hildenbrand–Hildenbrand [1978] and Ellis [1983]. Models of perfect foresight in disequilibrium are offered in Heller [1981], Neary–Stiglitz [1983] and Benassy [1984]. They illustrate the notion (see Tobin [1980]) that rational expectations and market clearing are logically independent hypotheses.

Notes

1. See also Barro–Grossman [1976] and Muellbauer–Portes [1978].

2. See Silvestre [1982c].

3. It should be viewed as an indirect utility function in a temporary equilibrium context, where money is a proxy for future consumption. See Hart [1982] for an alternative interpretation of the nonproduced good k.

4. For given w, the aggregate cost curve of figure 9-5 (including the vertical line at Y_0) is the horizontal aggregation of N curves, each with a vertical line at $\hat{f}(L_0/N)$ and, to its left, equal to $\hat{C}'_w = w(\hat{f}^{-1})'$. It corresponds to uniform rationing in the demand for labor.

5. Note that (9.2) is expressed in aggregate terms: it is independent of M and N, and it does not rule out asymmetric allocations. See note 14.

6. Since $p \leqslant V'(\bar{Y})$, $p \geqslant C'_w(\bar{Y})$, $\bar{Y} \leqslant Y_0$ and at least one of the weak inequalities must be an equality.

7. See Barro–Grossman [1976], Hool [1980], and Benassy [1983, 1984] for an extension of this analysis to cover a third market (bonds) as in the standard IS–LM model. This allows for the explicit formulation of monetary and fiscal policies. Benassy's graphical presentation (under the hypothesis that the bond market clears, that $p = V'(Y)$ and that the supply of labor is constant) is very similar to figures 9-6 and 9-7 above.

8. See Muellbauer–Portes [1978] and Honkapohja–Ito [1985]. Three new types appear instead: one with excess demand for labor and excess supply of output, one with excess supply of output and balanced labor market, and one with excess demand for labor and balanced output market. The same phenomenon appears if firms hold money balances (Gourieroux–Laffont–Montfort [1980]) or if the employment of labor is subject to adjustment costs (Ito [1980a]).

9. Such a criterion for classifying disequilibrium regimes is presented in Silvestre [1978b, section 4]. It may be derived from Malinvaud–Younès' [1977b] fixprice notion.

10. Even when such signs are well defined [see Silvestre [1982b, 1983]] it may be difficult to construct reasonable indices of the magnitude of excess demand.

11. Some recent papers (Van der Laan [1980], Kurz [1982], and Dehez–Drèze [1984]) formalize the view that the only relevant situations are those where demand is not rationed.

12. Explicitly,

$$I(\bar{z}) = \frac{1}{\theta}\left(\frac{K_0}{N} + \frac{\bar{w}\bar{l}_C}{q\rho} + \bar{p}\bar{y}_f - \bar{w}\bar{l}_f\right).$$

This expression is computed as follows: there are mN human beings, each with an initial endowment of K_0/mN units of money, with a profit income of $(N/mN)(\bar{p}\bar{y}_f - \bar{w}\bar{l}_f)$, and with a wage income of $\bar{w}\bar{l}_C/mq\rho$ (where $\bar{l}_C$ is the amount of labor sold by a syndicate); this individual wealth must be multiplied by m/θ, the number of persons in each output market.

13. See Silvestre [1982a, 1983]. Younès [1975] is generalized in Malinvaud–Younès [1977a, b]. Böhm–Lévine [1979] and Heller–Starr [1979] offer alternative notions based on the Nash noncooperative solution.

14. One can show that the three formulations generate expression (9.2) if demand for labor is uniformly rationed, i.e., each firm employs L_0/N units whenever aggregate employment is L_0. For a sketch of proof, rule out the case $Y > \min\{(V')^{-1}(p), (C'_w)^{-1}(p), Y_0\}$ by the first argument in Section 2.4 above (p. 202–203); if $Y < \min\{(V')^{-1}(p), (C'_w)^{-1}(p), Y_0\}$, then $L < L_0$ (since $L = L_0$ implies that each firm employs L_0/N units of labor and thus $Y = N\hat{f}(L_0/N) = f(L_0) = Y_0$), i.e., some consumer is constrained in his sales of labor. Thus, no firm may be constrained in its purchase of labor. But then, at $Y < (C'_w)^{-1}(p)$, some firm must be constrained in its sales of output,

and thus no consumer can be constrained in its purchases of output, contradicting the fact that $Y < (V')^{-1}(p)$. Notice that this argument requires no symmetry besides the uniform rationing of labor demand.

References

Arrow, K. J., "Towards a Theoby of Price Adjustment." In *The Allocation of Economic Resources* (M. Abramowitz, ed.), Stanford: Stanford University Press, 1959.

Arrow, K. J. and S. Honkapohja, eds. *Frontiers of Economics.* Oxford: Basil Blackwell, 1985.

Balasko, Y., "Equilibria and Efficiency in the Fix-price Setting." *Journal of Economic Theory* 28(1) (1982), 113–27.

Barro, R. J. and H. I. Grossman, "A General Disequilibrium Model of Income and Employment." *American Economic Review* 61 (1971), 82–93.

Barro, R. J. and H. I. Grossman, "Suppressed Inflation and the Supply Multiplier." *Review of Economic Studies* 41 (1974), 87–109.

Barro, R. J. and H. I. Grossman, *Money, Employment and Inflation.* Cambridge: Cambridge University Press, 1976.

Benassy, J. P., 'Disequilibrium Theory," Unpublished Ph.D. Dissertation, University of California, Berkeley, 1973.

Benassy, J. P., "Neo-Keynesian Disequilibrium Theory in a Monetary Economy." *Review of Economic Studies* 42(4) (1975), 503–23.

Benassy, J. P., "The Disequilibrium Approach to Monopolistic Price Setting and General Monopolistic Equilibrium." *Review of Economic Studies* 43(1) (1976), 69–81.

Benassy, J. P., "A Neokeynesian Model of Price and Quantity Determination in Disequilibrium." In (G. Schwödiauer, ed.), 1977a.

Benassy, J. P., *The Economics of Market Disequilibrium.* New York: Academic Press, 1982.

Benassy, J. P., "The Three Regimes of the IS-LM Model: A Non-Walrasian Analysis." *European Economic Review* 23(1) (1983), 1–18.

Benassy, J. P., *Macroéconomie et théorie du déséquilibre.* Paris: Dunod (English translation: *Non-Walrasian Macroéconomics*, New York: Academic Press, forthcoming), 1984.

Bertrand, J., Book review of 'Théorie mathématique de la richesse sociale' and 'Recherches sur les principes mathématiques de la theorie des richesses', by A. Cournot, *Journal des savants* (1883) 499–508.

Böhm, V., "Disequilibrium dynamics in a Simple Macroeconomic Model." *Journal of Economic Theory* 17(2) (1978), 179–99.

Böhm, V., "On the Uniqueness of Macroeconomic Equilibria with Quantity Rationing." *Economics Letters* 10(1–2) (1982), 43–48.

Böhm, V. and P. Lévine, "Temporary Equilibria with Quantity Rationing." *Review of Economic Studies* 46(2) (1979), 361–77.

Böhm, V. and H. Müller, "Two Examples of Equilibria under Price Rigidities and Quantity Rationing," *Zeitschrift für Nationalökonomie* 37 (1–2) (1977), 165–173.

Bushaw, D. W. and R. W. Clower, *Introduction to Mathematical Economics.* Homewood, Illinois: Richard D. Irwin, 1957.

Clower, R. W., "The Keynesian Counter-revolution: a Theoretical Appraisal." In *The Theory of Interest Rates*, (F. H. Hahn and Brechling, eds.), London: Macmillan, 1965; originally published in German in *Schweizerische Zeitschrift für Volkswirtschaft und Statistic*, 1963; Reprinted in *Monetary Theory* (R. W. Clower, ed.), Penguin Modern Economics Readings, 1969.

Cournot, A. A. *Recherches sur les principes mathématiques de la théorie des richesses.* Paris: Librairie des sciences politiques et sociales, M. Rivière & Cie. 1838.

Debreu, G., *Theory of Value.* New York: Wiley, 1959.

Dehez, P. and J. Drèze, "On Supply-constrained Equilibria." *Journal of Economic Theory* 33(1) (1984), 172–182.

Drèze, J. H., "Existence of an Exchange Equilibrium under Price Rigidities." *International Economic Review* 16(2) (1975), 301–20.

Drèze, J. H. and H. Müller, "Optimality Properties of Rationing Schemes." *Journal of Economic Theory* 23 (1980), 131–149.

Eckalbar, J. C., "The Stability of Non-Walrasian Processes: Two Examples." *Econometrica* 48(2) (1980), 371–86.

Eckalbar, J. C., "Stable Quantities in Fixed-price Disequilibrium." *Journal of Economic Theory* 25(2) (1981), 302–13.

Ellis, C. J., "A Note on Walrasian Equilibria in Non-Walrasian Models." *European Economic Review* 23(1) (1983), 55–58.

Gourieroux, C., J. J. Laffont and A. Monfort, "Disequilibrium Econometrics in Simultaneous Equation Systems." *Econometrica* 48 (1980), 75–96.

Grandmont, J. M., "The Logic of the Fix-price Method." *Scandinavian Journal of Economics* 79(2) (1977), 169–86.

Grandmont, J. M., "Temporary General Equilibrium Theory." In *Handbook of Mathematical Economics*, (K. J. Arrow and M. D. Intriligator, eds.), North-Holland, Amsterdam, 1981.

Grandmont, J. M. and G. Laroque, "On Temporary Keynesian Equilibria." *Review of Economic Studies* 43(1) (1976), 53–67.

Grandmont, J. M., G. Laroque and Y. Younès, "Equilibrium with Quantity Rationing and Recontracting." *Journal of Economic Theory* 19(1) (1978), 84–102.

Green, J. and J. J. Laffont, "Disequilibrium Dynamics with Inventories and Anticipatory Price-setting." *European Economic Review* 16(1) (1981), 199–221.

Hahn, F. H., "Exercises in Conjectural Equilibria." *Scandinavian Journal of Economics* 79(2) (1977a), 210–224.

Hahn, F. H., "Unsatisfactory Equilibria." Technical Report 247, IMSSS, Stanford, 1977b.

Hahn, F. H., "On Non-Walrasian Equilibria." *Review of Economic Studies* 45(1) (1978), 1–17.

Hart, O., "A Model of Imperfect Competition with Keynesian Features." *Quarterly Journal of Economics*, February (1982), pp. 109–138.

Hart, O., "Imperfect Competition in General Equilibrium: an Overview of Recent Work." In Arrow–Honkapohja, eds. 1985.

Heller, W. P., "Disequilibrium Rational Expectations." *Economics Letters* 7 (1981), 17–24.

Heller, W. P., "Coordination Failure with Complete Markets in a Simple Model of Effective Demand." Working Paper 84–16, University of California, San Diego, 1984.

Heller, W. P. and R. M. Starr, "Unemployment Equilibrium with Myopic Complete Information." *Review of Economic Studies* 46(2) (1979), 339–59.

Henderson, J. M. and R. F. Quandt, *Microeconomic Theory*. (2nd ed.), New York: McGraw-Hill, 1971.

Hildenbrand, K. and W. Hildenbrand, "On Keynesian Equilibria with Unemployment and Quantity Rationing." *Journal of Economic Theory* 18(2) (1978), 255–77.

Honkapohja, S., "On the Dynamics of Disequilibrium in a Marco Model with Flexible Wages and Prices." In *New Trends in Dynamic System Theory and Economics*, (M. Aoki and A. Marzollo, eds.), New York: Academic Press, 1979.

Honkapohja, S., "The Employment Multiplier after Disequilibrium Dynamics." *Scandinavian Journal of Economics* 82(1) (1980), 1–14.

Honkapohja, S. and T. Ito, "Inventory Dynamics in a Simple Disequilibrium Macroeconomics Model." *Scandinavian Journal of Economics* 82(2) (1980), 184–98.

Honkapohja, S. and T. Ito, "Stability with Regime-Switching." *Journal of Economic Theory* 29 (1983), 22–48.

Honkapohja, S. and T. Ito, "On Macroeconomic Equilibrium with Stochastic Rationing," *Scandinavian Journal of Economics* (1985).

Hool, R. B., "Monetary and Fiscal Policies in Short Run Equilibria with Rationing." *International Economic Review* 21(2) (1980), 301–16.

Ito, T., "An Example of Non-Walrasian Equilibrium with Stochastic Rationing at the Walrasian Equilibrium Prices." *Economics Letters*, 1979.

Ito, T., "Methods of Estimation in Multimarket Disequilibrium Models," *Econometrica* 48 (1980a), 97–126.

Ito, T., "Disequilibrium Growth Theory." *Journal of Economic Theory* 23(3) (1980b), 380–409.

Keynes, J. M., *The General Theory of Employment, Interest and Money*. Harcourt Brace, 1936.

Kurz, M., "Unemployment Equilibrium in an Economy with Linked Prices." *Journal of Economic Theory* 26(1) (1982), 100–123.

Laffont, J. J., "Fixprice Models: A Survey of Recent Empirical Work." In Arrow–Honkapohja, eds. 1985.

Lange, O. and F. M. Taylor, *On the Economic Theory of Socialism*. Minneapolis: University of Minnesota Press, 1938.

Laroque, G., "The Fixed Price Equilibria: Some Results in local Comparative Statics." *Econometrica* 46(5) (1978a), 1127–54.

Laroque, G., "On the Dynamics of Disequilibrium: A Simple Remark." *Review of Economic Studies* 45(2) (1978b), 273–78.

Laroque, G., "On the Local Uniqueness of the Fixed Price Equilibria," *Review of Economic Studies* 48(1) (1981a), 113–129.

Laroque, G., "Stable Spillover among Substitutes: A Comment." *Review of Economic Studies* 48 (1981b), 355–61.

Laroque, G. and H. Polemarchakis, "On the Structure of the Set of Fixed Price Equilibria." *Journal of Mathematical Economics* 5(1) (1978), 53–69.

Leijonhufvud, A., *On Keynesian Economics and the Economics of Keynes*, London: Oxford University Press, 1968.

Madden, P., "Efficiency of Non-Walrasian Equilibria: A Note." *Econometrica* 50(3) (1982), 755–76.

Malinvaud, E., *The Theory of Unemployment Reconsidered*. Oxford: Basil Blackwell, 1977.

Malinvaud, E. and Y. Younès, "Some New Concepts for the Microeconomic Foundations of Macroeconomics." In *The Microeconomic Founations of Microeconomics*, (G. Harcourt, ed.), London: Macmillan, 1977a.

Malinvaud, E. and Y. Younès, "Une nouvelle formulation générale pour l'étude de certains fondements microéconomiques de la macroéconomie." *Cahiers du Séminaire d'Économétrie*, C.R.N.S., Paris 18 (1977b), 63–109.

Mas-Colell, A., "Non-Cooperative Approaches to the Theory of Perfect Competition: Presentation." *Journal of Economic Theory* 22(2) (1980), 121–135.

Maskin, E. and J. Tirole, "On the Efficiency of Fixed-price Equilibrium." *Journal of Economic Theory* 32(2) (1984), 317–327.

Muellbauer, J. and R. Portes, "Macroeconomic Models with Quantity Rationing." *Economic Journal* 88 (1978), 788–821.

Müller, H., *Fiscal Policies in a General Equilibrium Model with Persistent Unemployment*. Lecture Notes in Economics and Mathematical Systems, Berlin: Springer-Verlag, 1983.

Nayak, P. R., "Efficiency of Non-Walrasian Equilibria." *Econometrica* 48(1) (1980), 127–134.

Neary, J. P. and J. E. Stiglitz, "Towards a Reconstruction of Keynesian Economics: Expectations and Constrained Equilibria." *Quarterly Journal of Economics* 98(3) (1983), 199–228.

Negishi, T., "Monopolistic Competition and General Equilibrium." *Review of Economic Studies* 28 (1961), 196–201.

Negishi, T., "Involuntary Unemployment and Market Imperfection." *Economic Studies Quarterly* 25 (1974).

Negishi, T., "Unemployment, Inflation and the Microfoundations of Macroeconomics." In *Essays in Economic Analysis: Proceedings of the 1975 AUTE Conference*, (M. J. Artis and A. R. Nobay, eds.), Cambridge: Cambridge University Press, 1976.

Negishi, T., "Existence of an Under-Employment Equilibrium." In G. Schwödiauer 1977.

Negishi, T., *Microeconomic Foundations of Keynesian Macroeconomics*. Amsterdam: North Holland, 1979.

Quandt, R., "Econometric Disequilibrium Models." *Econometric Reviews* 1 (1982), 1–63.

Schulz, N., "On the Global Uniqueness of Fix-price Equilibria." *Econometrica* 51(1) (1983), 47–68.

Schwödiauer, G., ed., *Equilibrium and Disequilibrium in Economic Theory*. Boston: Reidel, 1977.

Silvestre, J., "Fixprice Analysis: A Synopsis of Three Solution Concepts." Working Paper IP-270, CRMS, University of California, Berkeley, 1978a

Silvestre, J., "Fixprice Analysis: The Classification of Disequilibrium Regimes." Working Paper IP-271, CRMS, University of California, Berkeley, 1978b.

Silvestre, J., "Continua of Hahn-Unsatisfactory Equilibria." *Economics Letters* 5(3) (1980), 201–208.

Silvestre, J., "Fixprice Analysis in Exchange Economies." *Journal of Economic Theory* 26(1) (1982a), 28–58.

Silvestre, J., "Ambiguities in the Sign of Excess Effective Demand by Firms." *Review of Economic Studies* 49 (1982b), 645–651.

Silvestre, J., "Negotiable Prices and Wages in a Disequilibrium Model." Working Paper 82–37, University of California, San Diego, 1982c.

Silvestre, J., "Fixprice Analysis in Productive Economies." *Journal of Economic Theory* 30(2) (1983), 401–09.

Silvestre, J., "Voluntary and Efficient Allocations are Walrasian." *Econometrica*, 53(4) (1985), 807–816.

Sweezy, P. M., "Demand under Conditions of Oligopoly." *Journal of Political Economy* 47 (1939), 568–573.

Tobin, J., *Asset Accumulation and Economic Activity*. Oxford: Basil Blackwell, 1980.

Trujillo, J., "Rational Responses and Rational Conjectures." *Journal of Economic Theory*, forthcoming, 1985.

Van der Laan, G., "Equilibrium under Rigid Prices with Compensation for the Consumers." *International Economic Review* 21(1) (1980), 63–73.

Veendorp, E. C. H., "Stable Spillovers among Substitutes." *Review of Economic Studies* 42 (1975), 445–56.

Vives, X., "Capacity pre-commitment, Technology, Flexibility and Oligopoly Outcomes," CARESS W. P. 83–12, University of Pennsylvania, 1983.

Weddepohl, C., "Fixed Price Equilibria in a Multi-Firm Model," *Journal of Economic Theory* 29(1) (1983), 95–108.

Weitzman, M., *The Share Economy*. Cambridge MA: Harvard University Press, 1984.

Woglom, G., "Underemployment Equilibrium with Rational Expectations." *Quarterly Journal of Economics* 97(1) (1982), 89–107.

Younès, Y., "On the Role of Money in the Process of Exchange and the Existence of a Non-Walrasian Equilibrium." *Review of Economic Studies* 42(4) (1975), 489–501.

10 POSSIBILITY THEOREMS, INCENTIVES, AND PROGRESS IN ECONOMIC THEORY

Barry W. Ickes

One of the most exciting areas in economic theory is the study of incentives. Within this rubric a broad range of problems are currently being addressed. They range from the problems of social choice, to the economics of planning, to the character of labor contracts. The central theme of the research agenda concerns how the incentive structure affects the quality of information agents are willing to communicate. The principal question concerns how truthful revelation of information can be induced.[1] Such questions are important whenever agents can profit from distorting information. The problem thus arises in all sorts of guises in economics. The purpose of this essay is to illustrate this point by focusing on three distinct areas, social choice, public finance, and economic planning.

Equilibrium theory in its classical form — formalized in Arrow–Debreu — is a theory of how the actions of individuals are coordinated through markets. Implicit in the work on coordination via markets is the problem of how information that is decentralized is communicated to the proper agents. In the standard analysis this communication occurs via the *tâtonnement*. Agents

Thanks to the editor of this book for his comments on an earlier draft of this chapter.

respond to vectors of relative prices that are announced to them by the auctioneer. In a market with many agents there is no incentive to distort information about preferences or possibilities; there is no gain to be had from such misrepresentation. Our market coordination stories can thus proceed without explicit consideration of the incentives to communicate. But in markets where agents are not small, or where all goods are not private, the problem is more complex. One must study the incentives to reveal information in a truthful manner. Economic analysis has always been concerned with incentives. But as we leave the world of Arrow–Debreu, economics becomes, to a large extent, the study of incentives to tell the truth.

Three distinct literatures intersect at the modern frontier of incentive theory (and are joined by others as well). The economics of planning has long been concerned with how decentralized information can be acquired by a planning agency from subordinates whose welfare is affected by what they communicate. In public finance the problem is how to obtain a truthful revelation of preferences for public goods, given the free rider problem. And social choice theory is concerned with procedures for constructing a representation of social preferences based on individual preference orderings. In each case the problem is how to get the possessors of information to accurately reveal it to some other body. Though starting from very different problems these three areas of research have progressed in a common direction. The paths they have taken provides a reflection on progress in these areas of economic theory, and demonstrates how the theory of incentives has become a central organizing theme. A review of these paths illuminates the real progress that has been made.

We begin with social choice. A common theme in welfare economics (at least since Robbins) has been the effort to purge the subject of inter-personal utility comparisons. Such desires led to the debate on compensation criteria. The hope was that welfare judgments could be made without the resort to some prior notions about equity, etc. Instead economists hoped to build up representations of social preference solely on the basis of individual preferences. This goal received a severe jolt when Arrow proved his Impossibility Theorem (see the Chapter by Blair and Pollak). His theorem demonstrated that such an effort could not succeed. That is, given certain desired properties of any social choice rule (unanimity, unrestricted domain, independence of irrelevant alternatives, and transitivity) no nondictatorial rule could exist. Any social choice rule that satisfies these seemingly minimal requirements turns out to be a dictatorship.

This is a striking, and unsettling, result. It tells us that no matter how imaginative we are, we cannot construct a rule that derives social preferences from individual ones without lessening our (already fairly weak) standards. As one would expect, efforts to weaken the assumptions followed Arrow's proof.

But as both Blair and Pollak (in general) and Bandyopadhyay (with particular reference to the independence axiom) demonstrate, these efforts have been unsuccessful in restoring the viability of the program. Constructing social preferences solely from information about the ordinal rankings of individuals seems hopeless.

But as Bandyopadhyay explains, the struggle over the independence axiom produced another significant negative result. The independence axiom restricts the social choice between two alternatives x and y solely to individuals' rankings of *these* alternatives. This precludes the use of any information that would cardinalize utility for interpersonal comparisons. Now suppose we drop the axiom and allow some system like vote-trading which would allow for such comparisons. We now can avoid Arrow-like paradoxes. But this opens up more problems. Our social choice rule is no longer strategy proof. For Gibbard and Satterthwaite have (independently) shown that all such procedures that drop the independence axiom are subject to the misrepresentation of preferences by individuals. When social choice is based solely on pairwise rankings individuals have no incentive to misrepresent their preferences. But if we drop independence to avoid dictatorial rules, we can no longer construct social choices that are "strategy proof." Arrow's theorem taught us that social choice would have to be based on information about cardinal preferences. But just when we became ready to accept this and proceed, Gibbard and Satterthwaite demonstrate that any such procedure may be plagued by incentives to misrepresent.

It is at this, somewhat depressing juncture, that progress in public finance becomes relevant to our story. For here we may obtain at least a partial escape from our dilemma. At least since Wicksell economists have worried about the free rider problem in the provision of public goods. Given the market's inability to provide the optimal amount of public goods, it rests to the collective choice of the society. But how can the state acquire the knowledge of the actual amount of such goods its citizens desire? If my share of the project's cost is related to my stated preference, then surely I will understate my true preference, and ride free on the community. But if my share is independent of my stated preference, I can insure the project's success (if I so desire) by overstating my true desire. Can we escape this dilemma?

This is where recent developments have signalled real progress. The Demand Revealing Mechanism (the DRM, see Rob's Chapter), which was suggested independently by Vickery [1961], Clarke [1971], and Groves [1973] is able to circumvent the free rider problem for public goods. Given the importance of this development let us briefly indicate how it works. The idea is to construct a mechanism which will induce individuals to communicate their true preferences about public projects, and at the same time produce the revenue to pay for them. The DRM is not addressed to the problem of selecting the optimal social state. We know from the Gibbard-Satterthwaite theorem that this is not possible without acceptance of some *prior ethical notions about* distribution.[2] What the DRM allows for is to decide whether a public project should be undertaken. It thus allows us to ascertain whether the project's approval is Pareto improving, even if we cannot determine whether it leads to the *best* social outcome.

Consider then the following tax schedule (retaining Rob's notation):

$$t_i(\tilde{v}) = cx^*(\tilde{v}) - \sum_{j \neq i} \tilde{v}_j [x^*(\tilde{v})] + h_i(\tilde{v}_{-i}). \qquad (10.1)$$

This schedule relates individual i's contribution towards a project to the difference between the cost of the project, $cx^*(\tilde{v})$, and the benefits to all other individuals given the amount of the project approved based on their choice, plus a term $h_i(\cdot)$, independent of i's choice.[3] This scheme has the property that the best individual i can do is report his truthful evaluation (see Rob's paper for a proof of this proposition). The reason is readily seen. The utility from the project that individual i reports $(\tilde{v})$ affects the likelihood that the project will be built and the tax i will pay. But since the tax depends only on the difference between the project's cost and *everyone else's* benefit, there is no gain to misrepresentation. If I overstate my benefit the cost of the project is increased. But it will not affect what other individuals report, so it will increase my tax by the amount it increases costs. By overstating $\tilde{v}$ the tax increases by the same amount as the cost. If I report $\tilde{v} > \tilde{v}$, then I pay more for the project than I believe it is worth to me. Consequently the truth is the best I can do. Honesty is not only an equilibrium strategy, but a *dominant* strategy.

Given the negative results in the social choice literature, the DRM is a striking success. It is thus important to step back and ask why this success is possible in the light of what we have learned. The goal of social choice theory is to find a mechanism that will base social rankings solely on individual's ordinal preferences. This goal, we have seen, is plagued either by Arrow's impossibility result or, if we drop the independence axiom, the problem of strategic manipulation. The revelation literature on the other hand, is concerned with the choice of efficient outcomes, not optimal ones. The idea is to find a procedure that will allow for an efficient decision about public goods. This is a difficult problem, but not nearly so difficult as choosing the best outcome. Now Groves and Ledyard [1977] have been able to construct a mechanism that will select any Pareto optimum given a suitable redistribution of endowments.[4] Thus the "Second Welfare theorem" is extended to a world with public goods. This is an important achievement, yet it is important to keep in mind that it does not solve the problem of *which* Pareto optimum is best. The revelation mechanisms make efficient choices. They do not identify *best* choices. The DRM succeeds because the problem it copes with is not as difficult as that of the social choice literature.

It would nonetheless be a mistake to minimize the importance of the DRM. To illustrate this point we turn to a problem that appears far removed from the issues of public finance. This is the problem of economic planning, the third area of economic theory we examine. Ever since the days of the "Socialist Controversy" economists have pondered the question of how a central planning board can acquire the relevant information to properly execute its task. The problem here (similar in form to those we have already discussed) is that most of this information is decentralized. In order for the planners to construct a feasible, let alone optimal, plan they must "tap" into this information. Much interesting work in this area has studied how these information flows can be effectively minimized. But experience (in the Soviet-type economies) has demonstrated that designing the proper incentives for honest reporting is the critical problem.

An important case in point is the design of a success indicator. This is the aspect of an enterprise's performance on the basis of which the manager is compensated. The typical practice is to base the manager's bonus on his performance relative to some target level. But to formulate the target the planners require information — about capacity, technology, etc. — that resides with the manager. There is thus an incentive for the manager to distort the true picture to obtain a target that will be easier to fulfill. The success indicator problem is to find a bonus function which will induce the manager to honestly report the situation.

The Soviets (and other planned economies) have experimented with many bonus functions, but the problem is a difficult one. The reason is that the information the enterprise reveals affects not only the enterprise's targets but also resource allocation in the economy. But these allocations in turn will affect the enterprise's performance (i.e., if capital allocations depend on the manager's responses). Under these circumstances it is very difficult to construct an indicator that will induce truthful revelation.[5] Utilizing the DRM, however, such an indicator can be designed. Consider the following bonus scheme:

$$\hat{S}_i \left(\pi_i^A, \pi^F \right) = \pi_i^A(\hat{K}_i) + \sum_{j \neq i} \pi_j^F(\hat{K}_j) - A_i, \qquad (10.2)$$

where π_i is the profit of enterprise i, the superscript A refers to actual values, and F to forecasts, $\hat{K}_j$ is the capital assigned to enterprise j, and A_i is any real value calculated independently of π^F (its importance will appear below). This indicator is just the DRM of (10.1) applied to the present problem. Its nature should thus be straightforward. Enterprise i's forecast affects its own success in two ways. First of all it affects the target it will receive. Secondly it affects capital allocation throughout the economy, and thus its own performance. But $\hat{S}_i$ depends on the profits of i, plus the *forecasted* profits of all other enterprises, *given their allocations based on i's forecast.* Since A_i is independent of π^F, enterprise i chooses π^F to maximize

$$\pi_i^A + \sum_{j \neq i} \pi_j^F(\hat{K}_j). \tag{10.3}$$

But π_i^F affects other enterprise allocations. If enterprise i attempts to acquire more capital than it deserves, it will lower profits elsewhere. By basing $\hat{S}_i$ on a system of joint profit maximization, this indicator induces the manager to report in a manner that allocates capital efficiently. Clearly truthful revelation will lead to a maximization of (10.3). Truth is now a dominant strategy for the manager.

What about the role of the A_i? It clearly parallels the $h_i(\cdot)$ of (10.1). But here its role is to insure a proper distribution of income across managers. Since the A_i are chosen independently of the managers responses they do not affect the incentive properties of (10.2). However, there are constraints to the values the A_i can take and maintain the efficiency of the system. If the productivity of a manager falls below the opportunity cost of his time, a proper incentive structure should induce him to quit (or so efficiency would seem to require). So the A_i cannot be chosen so large that they will maintain an inefficient manager in his place. This, however, introduces a relationship between the π^F and the A_i, which can reintroduce incentive problems (see Murrell and Miller [1984]). Nonetheless, the DRM is seen to provide an important practical improvement over common procedures in planned economies. This provides an interesting example of its utility.

Of course not all problems in incentive theory have been solved. One major complication arises when the group that is making a decision is not a "team" (i.e., an organization that shares common goals). If, for example, the planners and the managers have conflicting goals (say on how much effort should be provided) further problems arise. The planners may wish to encourage the managers to maximize their effort levels, while the managers naturally seek to minimize them. Such conflict over incentives complicates the search for an optimal indicator (Murrell and Miller [1984]).

This points, perhaps, to where future progress in the theory of incentives will lay. The problem of designing incentive compatible mechanisms in a team environment is but a prelude to understanding these issues when there exists a conflict of interest. Progress along these lines of research will have important implications for a host of important problems.

An important example would be in the area of labor contracts. The implicit contracts literature argues that employers offer insurance to their more risk averse employees against unforeseen fluctuations in the demand for labor. But between the employers and the employees there is asymmetric information about the marginal revenue product of labor. It is in the interests of the employers to misrepresent such information in order to pay lower wages. Such a threat, however, would vitiate the efficiency of the contract, causing both sides to lose. The question then becomes how to design incentive compatible contracts in this environment. This is, at present, an active area of research.

But wherever future progress takes us, the study of incentives has offered economists insights into a variety of economic problems. The neglect of incentives for truthful revelation could be safely ignored only as long as attention was confined to Walrasian models. But in richer environments it is precisely the incentive problems that condition economic outcomes. From designing rationing schemes for allocating a commodity in short supply, to assessing the desirability of a public project, to optimal behavior of a firm in a noncompetitive environment, the strategies and actions of agents will depend on the incentives for revealing information. As we have seen, various distinct literatures have converged on this theme. The fact that progress in this area has not come easily demonstrates that the problems are nontrivial. It also makes that progress all the more important.

Notes

1. Perhaps the most important contributor to this literature is Hurwicz [1977a and b]. In these essays the importance of incentive compatibility in the problem of mechanism design is clearly laid out. In that sense, Hurwicz defined the general problem in its most basic and general form. But as the present essay should illustrate, many aspects of this problem have a long history in economics.

2. As we noted above, the Gibbard–Satterthwaite theorem indicates that we cannot resort to cardinal utility information in the construction of social preferences. This arises because agents will have incentive to misrepresent their beliefs to affect social decisions. But it does not invalidate the resort to prior distributional judgments (utilitarian, Rawlsian, etc.) to judge outcomes of social choices.

3. What is the role of $h_i(\cdot)$? This is a lump sum unrelated to the $\tilde{v}$ individual i reports. It serves to raise revenue for the project. Without the $h_i(\cdot)$ the DRM leads to the proper amount of the public goods, but *not* the receipts with which to finance it. In order to raise revenue for the project, we add the $h_i(\cdot)$. Unfortunately, however, we cannot choose them so as to just balance the budget. Most rules for choosing $h_i(\cdot)$, the "pivot mechanism" (see Rob) for example, collect too much revenue. And any rule for distributing the surplus will vitiate the incentive properties of the model. One of the ways out of this dilemma is to require the budget to balance only on average. There is, obviously, still more work to be done here. Rob's paper discusses this problem at some length.

4. One element of Groves and Ledyard's success is to weaken the equilibrium concept from that of a dominant strategy to Nash. This requires agent's strategies to be optimal *given* the actions of other agents. The Nash assumption is not as appealing as a dominant strategy. The latter

requires the agent's strategy to be optimal independent of the actions of others. It thus poses minimal information requirements on agents. The Nash assumption, on the other hand, requires a good bit of information, since agents must calculate their strategies based on the actions — and thus preferences — of others. One might interpret Nash equilibria as the end point of a process of successive responses, as agents learn about others' actions. While restrictive, the Nash assumption has led to positive results, and may be realistic in environments where actual choices are observable. See Hurwicz [1977a] for a discussion of some of these issues.

5. The 1971 Soviet reforms introduced a new bonus function which appeared to be quite an improvement (see Weitzman's analysis). The bonus function consisted of a two step procedure, where the enterprise made a tentative forecast, and then was rewarded in terms of how close it came to this. The system had penalty coefficients for missing the target in either direction. If other resource decisions (i.e., capital allocations) are made independently of these forecasts, then this procedure has "nice" incentive properties (Weitzman [1976]). But if the forecasts are used to make allocative decisions, then there is an incentive to misrepresent Loeb and Magat [1978].

References

Arrow, K. J., *Social Choice and Individual Values*. Revised edition, New York: Wiley, 1963.

Clark, E. H., "Multipart Pricing of Public Goods." *Public Choice* 11, Fall 1971.

Gibbard, A., "Manipulation of Voting Schemes: A General Result." *Econometrica* 41 (1973) 587–602.

Groves, T., "Incentives in Teams." *Econometrica* 41(4) (1973).

Groves, T. and J. Ledyard, "Optimal Allocation of Public Goods: A Solution to the 'Free Rider Problem'." *Econometrica* 45 (1977) 783–810.

Hurwicz, L., "On Informationally Decentralized Systems." In *Studies in Resource Allocation Processes*, (K. J. Arrow and L. Hurwicz, eds.), Cambridge University Press, Cambridge, Mass., 1977a.

———, "The Design of Resource Allocation Mechanisms." In *Studies in Resource Allocation Processes*, (K. G. Arrow and L. Hurwicz, eds.), Cambridge University Press, Cambridge, Mass., 1977b.

Loeb, M. and W. Magat, "Success Indicators in the Soviet Union: The Problem of Incentives and Efficient Allocations." *American Economic Review* 68(1), March 1978.

Murrell, P. and J. Miller, "The Applicability of Information-Revealing Incentive Systems in Economic Organizations." *Journal of Comparative Economics* 8(3), September 1984.

Satterthwaite, M., "Strategy-proofness and Arrow's Conditions: Existence and Correspondence Thorems for Voting Procedures and Social Welfare Functions." *Journal of Economic Theory* 10 (1975) 187–217.

Vickery, W., "Counterspeculation, Auctions, and Competitive Sealed Tenders." *Journal of Finance*, 16, May 1961.

Weitzman, M., "The New Soviet Incentive Model." *Bell Journal of Economics* 7 Spring 1976.

11 INSTITUTIONS AS A SOLUTION CONCEPT IN A GAME THEORY CONTEXT

Philip Mirowski

". . . he believed that human beings, when it had been clearly explained to them what were their vital needs and necessities, would not only altrustically but selfishly become honest and reasonable: they would sacrifice what might be short term advantages for long term ends. What he never saw was that in politics as in other forms of human activity, human beings are for the most part interested in struggle, in manoeuvrings for power, in risks and even unpleasantnesses; and that there are often in direct opposition to what might reasonably be seen as their long term ends . . ."

"This was one reason why he could so often make rings around his opponents by reasoning: he believed in it; while they, although they said they did, ultimately did not. Yet what they felt instinctively, and might have answered [him] by, was traditionally unspoken. They could not say to him in effect – Look, in your reasoning you leave out of account something about human nature: you leave out the fact that human beings with part of themselves like turmoil and something to grumble at and perhaps even failure to feel comfortable in: your economic perfect blueprint will not work simply because people will not want it to."

—(Mosley, 1983, pp. 68–69)

I would like to thank Alex Field for the speedy comments and suggestions which I have yet to reciprocate, as well as Don Katzner for his overall influence.

In the history of neoclassical economic theory, there have been two major categories of rejoinders to critics of the theory: one, that the critics did not adequately understand the structure of the theory, and thus mistook for essential what was merely convenient; or two, that the criticism was old hat, and had been rendered harmless by recent (and technically abstruse) innovations with which the critic was unacquainted.[1] The freedom of passage between these defenses has proven to be the bane of not only those opposed to neoclassicism, but also to those who have felt the need for reform and reformulation of economic theory from within. It has fostered the impression that any arbitrary phenomenon can be incorporated within the ambit of conventional neoclassical theory with enough ingenuity, therefore rendering any particular change in "assumptions" as innocuous as any other, and thus rendering them all equally arbitrary.

Nowhere has this impasse been more evident than in the confrontations between the various partisans of an "institutional" economics and the adherents of neoclassical economic theory. The early Institutionalists, such as Thorstein Veblen, John R. Commons, and Wesley Clair Mitchell, mounted a scathing attack on neoclassical value theory in the first decades of the century, ridiculing the "hedonistic conception of man [as] that of a lightening calculator of pleasures and pains, who oscillates like a homogeneous globule of desire of happiness under the impulse of stimuli that shift him about the area but leave him intact."[2] The unifying principles of this movement were: (a) an assertion that neoclassical economists were the advocates of a spurious scientism which insisted upon imitating physics without understanding the implications of such mimesis; (b) an expression of an alternative to the above conception of society based upon a study of the working rules which structured collective action and going concerns, such as the corporation, the trade union, the bank and the state; (c) in conjunction with the construction of theories which took as their provenience the explanation of the evaluation of the working rules and then attendant institutions. Their writings on the vagaries of behavior, such as Veblen's book on "conspicuous consumption," were intended to show that theories based on individual psychologies were built upon shifting sands; and that, as Commons writes, "cooperation does not arise from a presupposed harmony of interests, as the older economists believed. It arises from the necessity of creating a new harmony of interests" (Commons [1934, p. 6]).

The initial rebuttal to the Institutionalists adopted the first tactic: to cite just are prominent example, Paul Samuelson insisted that nothing substantial would be lost if economists relinquished utility (Wong [1978]), and that institutions were effectively included in the assumptions of neoclassical economic theory (Samuelson [1965 p. 8]). When fully interpreted, this assertion meant that the study of institutions was *separable* from neoclassical economic theory, to the point of being independent of any particular institutional framework (Mirowski [1981]). Economics could cut itself free of the inessential institutional considerations, and preserve its core as the study of rational allocation of scarce means in a thoroughly abstract frame. Veblen and Commons were drummed out of the economists' camp, and exiled to the provinces of sociology or anthropology.

With the passage of time, this first rebuttal has fallen into disuse, and the second option has gained favor. Among a certain subset of theorists, it has become acceptable to admit that conventional neoclassical theory is "mechanistic," in the sense that it slavishly imitates certain procedures in physics, and that this might be undesirable in certain respects. In most cases, this admission is accompanied by an assertion that this flaw has been remedied by the development of new techniques in the theory of games, to such an extent that there is a "new mathematical institutional economics" which has incorporated the concerns of the earlier critics (Johansen [1983], Schotter [1981, 1983], Schotter and Schwodiauer [1980], Shubik [1975, 1976]).

It is a curious fact that the language of the critique of neoclassical theory of the game theorists is so close to that of the earlier Institutionalists as to be almost indistinguishable. For example: "The neoclassical agents are bores who merely calculate optimal activities at fixed parametric prices . . . No syndicates or coalitions are formed, no cheating or lying is done, no threats are made . . . The economy has no money, no government, no legal system, no property rights, no banks . . ." (Schotter, [1981, p. 150]). "The general equilibrium model is: (1) basically noninstitutional. (2) It makes use of few differentiated actors. (3) It is essentially static. No explanation of price formation is given. (4) There is no essential rule for money. (5) It is nonstrategic "(Shubik [1976, p. 323]). However, similarities in language can be misleading. How justified is the claim that Institutionalist concerns have been absorbed by game theorists?

For the purposes of this chapter, we shall choose to avoid discussion of the first variant of the neoclassical defense. We shall simply assume that the central concept of neoclassical economic theory is the application of a physics metaphor to the market.[3] This will allow us to concentrate our attention on the second variant: Are recent game theoretic models different in any substantial way from neoclassical theory? Do game theory models capture the concerns which Institutionalists believed were ignored in neoclassical economics? How can one judge the various claims made for the superior efficacy of game theory?

1. Game Theory and Institutional Analysis: Shubik and Schotter

It is a difficult task to discern the wood from the many trees that have passed through the pulper in the cause of game theory. Game theory burst upon the scene in 1944 with von Neumann and Morgenstern's book. The solutions of games were claimed to be isomorphic to "orders of society," "standards of behavior," "economic organizations"; and yet these models also claimed to be following "the best examples of theoretical physics" (von Neumann and Morgenstern [1966, pp. 43, ix]). Forty years of development have revealed that game theory is not the philosopher's stone which its progenitors had claimed: more than half of any competent textbook in game theory is occupied with developing taxonomies of the numerous variants of games — cooperative and noncooperative; constant or nonconstant-sum; static or sequential; extensive, strategic or characteristic forms; cardinal or noncardinal payoffs; various permutations of information sets and sequences of moves; small and large numbers of players; different conceptions of uncertainty; stationary versus nonstationary payoffs and/or strategies — so that the permutations and their attendant solution concepts have far outstripped any claims for generality or unity.

Doubts about the efficacy of game theory have begun to surface — sometimes during inauspicious occasions, such as Nobel Prize lectures (e.g., Simon [1982, pp. 486–7]). In this context, it is noteworthy that its most vocal defenders have chosen to reemphasize the potential of game theory to encompass institutional considerations. We shall therefore concentrate our initial attention (in this section) on the work of the two most prolific proselytizers for a "new institutional economics": Martin Shubik and Andrew Schotter.

Shubik has built an illustrious career upon the development of game theory in economics, providing many of the basic theorems and results in that literature, as well as writing the best introductory textbook (Shubik [1982]). In this respect, he is particularly well-qualified to judge which areas of game theory should be credited with having made substantial contributions and novel innovations, as well as revealing the motivations behind the prosecution of game theoretic research. In a series of journal articles, Shubik has been persistently critical of Walrasian general equilibrium because it does not explain price formation; it merely *assumes* it. The actors in a Walrasian world have no freedom to make errors or even choices about process, he says; and in this, he sounds very similar to Veblen. More unexpectedly, he is also critical of cooperative game theory: "As an early proponent of the core and of the replication process for studying mass economic behavior, I am completely willing to admit that to a great extent the results on the core have helped to

direct attention away from the understanding of the competitive process . . ."
(Shubik [1975, p. 560]; see also Shubik [1982, p. 286]). He believes that whole
other classes of games tend to be mere repetitions of pre-game-theoretic
models and add little insight to the corpus; for example, constant sum games
impose conservation rules which hinder the adequate description of process
(Shubik [1975A, p. 557]; Shubik [1972]; Mirowski [1984a]).

Where, then, does the advantage of game theoretic techniques lie? Shubik
claims that the future belongs to noncooperative nonconstant-sum games.
"Noncooperative game theory appears to be particularly useful for the study of
mass phenomena in which the communication between individuals must be
relatively low and individuals interact with a more or less faceless and
anonymous economy, polity or society" (Shubik [1982, p. 300]). Since strategic
considerations are linked to a perception of society as consisting of impersonal
social forces, and this conception informs Shubik's notion of "institutions," he
therefore proselytizes for the appearance of a "new mathematical institutional
economics": ". . . my basic approach to economics is through the construction
of mathematical models in which the 'rules of the game' derive not only from
the economics and technology of the situation, but from the sociological,
political and legal structure as well" (Shubik [1982, p. 10]).

Shubik's research program is not so very different from the 17th century
dream of Hobbes, that ". . . in the same way as man, the author of geometrical
definitions can, by starting from those arbitrary definitions, construct the
whole of geometry, so also, as the author of the laws which rule his city, he can
synthetically construct the whole social order in the manner of the geometers"
(Halevy [1972, p. 494]). Just as with Hobbes, there is some equivocation in
deciding what is *necessary* and what is *adventitious*; we are referring in this
case to the notion of social structures "external" to what is identified as the
"economy." Shubik has, in places, suggested that institutions are merely ad hoc
rules (Shubik [1975A, p. 558]), of which he is providing mathematical
descriptions. In other places, he suggests he is actively constructing optimal
rules with regard to various problems, such as the treatment of bankruptcy
(Shubik [1975B, p. 526]; Dubey and Shubik [1979]). In either event, Shubik's
claim to be including "sociological, political and legal structures" is, in practice,
reduced to the mathematical specification of rules which impinge upon the
operation of a market whose basic constituents — tastes, technologies and
endowments — are essentially the same as in the conventional Walrasian
models. These rules have a different analytical status than the tastes,
technologies and so forth, because they are not treated as "natural" or
fundamental givens, but rather as arbitrary intrusions from outside the sphere
of the economy.

The arbitrary character of the rules is only confronted once, to my knowledge, in the Shubik corpus. In (Shubik [1974, p. 383]) he asks the two revealing questions: "Should we assume that the laws and customs are to be modelled as rules of the game which are given and never broken? . . . Why should individuals accept fiat money or the laws and customs of trade in the first place?" Both questions are not answered: they are instead relegated to be outside the competence of the mathematical institutional economist, and by implication, outside of the sphere of the "economic."

It is possible to attempt a summary of Shubik's canonical institutional model. He distinguishes between "market games," which can be represented by a characteristic function, because the payoff of any subset of players is independent of the activities of the complement (i.e., all other traders); and a "strategic market game," in which the activities of all traders are linked by an explicit price formation mechanism and a distinct monetary system. One valuable insight of Shubik's work has been to show how the neoclassical economists' notion of "externalities" pervades the entire price system through a demonstration that realistic descriptions of the trading process preclude the possibility of treating traders' options and objectives as independent of one another. Nonetheless, he retains the neoclassical predisposition to see prices mainly as the means of conveyance of information. He writes: "The key aspect of many economic activities that differentiates them from the viewpoint of information processing and coding from, say, political or societal activities or from abstract games is that a natural metric exists on many of the strategies. In mass markets, for example, for wheat, the information that two million tons were produced last season is probably more useful to most buyers and sellers than is a detailed list of the quantities produced by each individual farmer" (Shubik [1975A, p. 560]).

A strategic market game is modelled as a noncooperative nonconstant sum game. It consists of a list of traders[4] and their endowments, the postulation of a market structure as a set of rules governing the process by which traders may convey information about bids and offers, as well as rules for the clearing of markets, and the utility functions of and strategies available to each player. The specification of market structure may become quite complicated, including the role of a bank, the rules for bankruptcy, and so on (Shubik and Wilson [1977]). A further assertion is that the specification of the generic types of strategies pursued by the traders captures the presence or absence of "trust" in the market. The predominance of historical strategies — i.e., where a player's move is conditional upon the past moves of a set of players — is said to represent a situation of low trust. On the other hand, the acceptance of state strategies, where a player's move depends solely upon the present state of the game, is said to represent a situation of widespread trust. There is a hint, but no more, of an evolutionary argument embedded in this distinction: as markets become more anonymous and threats, by their very nature, become less specific, state strategies slowly displace historical strategies. Shubik explicitly links this development to the spread of the use of money, which he calls "the symbol of trust" (Shubik [1974, p. 379]).

Perhaps the most striking characteristic of Shubik's published work is the relative unpretentiousness of the claims made for its efficacy. He admits that game theory enforces a symmetry upon the personalities of the players which belies any serious intrusion of personal detail, while also abstracting away from social conditioning and role playing; he also admits that game theory requires a fixed and well defined structure of payoffs. Even more significantly, he explains that "there is as yet no satisfactory blending of game theory with learning theory" (Shubik [1982, p. 358]). The impression conveyed is that game theory is one of many techniques of social analysis, with its own strengths and weaknesses; the matter of choice of analytical technique is left to the individual reader without any explicit discussion. This attitude is encouraged by statements that one should choose the solution concept to fit the preconceived objective: "The [Walrasian] price system may be regarded as stressing decentralization (with efficiency); the core shows the force of countervailing power; the value offers a "fairness" criterion; the bargaining set and Kernel suggest how the solution might be delineated by bargaining conditions . . ." (Shubik [1982, p. 382]). One cannot help, however, but receive a different impression from the collected body of his writings. There intermittent claims are made that game theoretic models are necessary prerequisites for the integration of macro- and Walrasian micro-economic theory and ironically, that Nash equilibrium points of strategic market games frequently include the conventional Walrasian general equilibrium (Dubey and Shubik [1979, p. 120]). It would appear that all the different solution concepts really are subordinate to the one "real" solution, the Walrasian general equilibrium.

Shubik's caution contrasts sharply with the claims made by the other prominent mathematical institutional economist, Andrew Schotter. (Schotter [1983, p. 692]) writes, "Game theory is the only tool available today that holds out hope for creating an institutionally realistic and flexible economic theory." Schotter reveals that he is aware that other economists such as John R. Commons also have tackled these issues, but apparently feels that such research can be written off as ineffectual without any discussion, simply because it is not phrased in game theoretic terms.

In certain respects Schotter resembles Shubik: he also disparages Walrasian theory for leaning on the *deus ex machina* of the auctioneer rather than directly confronting processes (Schotter [1983, p. 674]); as well as repudiating co-operative game theory and the solution concept of the core, because after limit theorems that showed the core converged to the Walrasian general equilibrium

(Debreu and Scarf [1963]; Aumann [1964]) "what we have left is an economy that is not any richer institutionally than the neoclassical analysis, which merely assumed that this degenerate set of market institutions existed at the outset" (Schotter [1983, p. 682]). Schotter gives voice to what may have been said privately: these results stole the thunder from game theory by demonstrating that it added little or nothing to the analytical content of Walrasian general equilibrium (Schotter [1981, p. 152]).

It is here that Schotter begins to diverge from Shubik. Whereas the latter seems to pursue a "live and let live" policy in the house of Neoclassicism, the former is critical of the modern general equilibrium trick of handling time, uncertainty, externalities and a host of other complications by the redefinition and expansion of the commodity space. (A Hershey bar at 6 P.M. on Tuesday on the Boston Common in the rain is different from a Hershey bar at 7 P.M. etc., etc.; and presumably is traded in a separate "market.") "When market institutions fail, as in the case of economies with uncertainty and externalities, the neoclassical economist does not, as he should, try to explain what alternative sets of institutions would be created to take their place" (Schotter [1981, p. 151]). It is the stress on the creation of institutions which Schotter believes sets him apart from Shubik and others. Shubik, as we have observed, has a tendency to define institutions as *ad hoc* rules which act to constrain or restrict the operation of the market; Schotter, on the other hand, insists that institutions are *solutions* to games. (Schotter [1981, p. 155]; Schotter [1983, p. 689].) Initially, the distinction might seem to be excessively subtle: although Shubik will not commit himself on where his "rules" come from, he is not hesitant to suggest bankruptcy rules as a reaction to a perceived market failure, and then examine the spectrum of possible rules to discover which are "optimal." But Schotter insists this conception is wrong because he does not believe institutions are consciously constructed; instead, behavioral regularities "emerge endogeneously" or "organically." In his book, he makes a preliminary attempt at developing a taxonomy of different kinds of institutions (Schotter [1981, p. 22]), but quickly abandons all but one category as not being sufficiently "organic." His rationale is worth quoting in its entirety: "If the social institutions we are investigating are created by a social planner, their design can be explained by maximizing the value of some objective function existing in the planners mind . . . On the other hand, if the form of social organization created is the outcome of a multilateral bargaining process, a bargaining theory would be required" (Schotter [1981, p. 28]). A number of references to the Austrian school, and particularly Hayek, are provided in support of this notion of an institution.

Again, appearances suggest an affinity with the stress of earlier Institutionalists on the unintended consequences of both conscious choices and evolutionary drift. For this reason, it is all the more important to be clear and precise about how Schotter conceptualizes an institution. In his scenario, institutions do not lead a separate or semiautonomous existence: "Social and economic institutions are informational devices that supplement the informational content of economic systems when competitive prices do not carry sufficient information to totally decentralize and coordinate economic activities" (Schotter [1981, p. 109]). Institutions are stopgaps or pis aller which evolve naturally whenever a market is not capable of producing a Pareto optimal outcome. The failure of the market to produce these outcomes is not explored in depth, nor are there any suggestions of ubiquity or the determinants of the presence or absence of failure; and in this it stands in contrast to the work of Shubik. Without any motivation, all market failures are attributed to the existence of prisoner's dilemma structures, given presumably by "states of nature." The overall picture is of a market which organically heals itself, with health defined as the conventional Walrasian general equilibrium.

Schotter has provided us with a canonical model which can be easily summarized. His model starts by *assuming* "that the only institution existing is the auctioneer-led market institution, whose origin is left unexplained by the model" (Schotter [1981, p. 120]). Schotter's "market" is not Shubik's "market": for all practical purposes it is not strategic; its only glitch is that it does not clear in any short sequence of "gropings" for the correct vector of Pareto-optimal prices, due to the fact that preferences are not strictly convex (Schotter [1981, p. 124]). Traders cannot communicate directly with each other, but must communicate through the "price system" by making *quantity* offers to the auctioneer. It is asserted (Schotter [1981, p. 125]) that this is isomorphic to a supergame played over individual component games which are both stationary, and of the form of the prisoner's dilemma. The purported reason the payoff is of prisoner's dilemma form is that it is assumed that if all parties cannot arrive at agreement upon the same aggregate quantity of the commodity both bid upon and offered, *no trades are executed.*

Before we summarize the technical details of the supergame, it will be instructive to examine the structure of one of these component "moves" or subgames. Table 11-1 is a presentation of the situation presented graphically in (Schotter [1981, p. 125]). Let us restrict our attention to two traders each with endowments of a single commodity. Because utility is not strictly convex, auctioneer-provided equilibrium prices are tangent to utility functions at more than one point: here, for simplicity's sake, let us assume there are only two possible trading points: A, where Trader 1 (seller of commodity X) ends up with less of his endowment, and B, where he ends up with more. Because utility is "flat" in this region, both traders end up with the same level of utility whichever quantity is traded at the fixed price. However, if no trade is executed (because the traders could not agree upon relative quantities), they would be stuck with their initial endowments, and their concomitant lower utility levels. It is a curiosity of Schotter's graph that he neglects to discuss the presence or absence of symmetry in the level of utility of the two traders, because as one can readily observe, this game is not of the prisoner's dilemma format. The problem here is not that the equilibrium point is sub-optimal: it is only that there are a *multiplicity of equally desirable equilibria* and that the game does not allow any external coordination to agree upon which of these indifferently acceptable equilibria will be settled upon. If utilities are not comparable and side payments are not allowed, there are only two possibilities as one adds more traders to the market: (i) everyone is psychologically identical up to a scalar multiple and the number of multiple equivalent equilibria proliferate; or (ii) people have different utility functions, and as the number of traders increases, the solution shrinks to a single Walrasian general equilibrium, which the auctioneer effectuates. Schotter seems not to have noticed that this is not an intrinsically noncooperative game, and that only in the most idiosyncratic of special cases of utility functions is there any problem of coordination.

Far from being a niggling criticism, this reveals that the "market model" is not isomorphic to the supergame model, because the latter model is predicated on the Nash equilibrium point solution concept applied to a sequence of generic prisoner's dilemma games, which the former clearly is not.

Let us assume that Schotter has found a way of recasting his model of the market process so that it is in the form of a prisoner's dilemma. From whence come his claims of "evolution" and "organic developments"? First he must postulate a fixed prisoner's dilemma situation which is repeatedly played over and over again by an identical set of players. Players are assumed to "learn" from past plays of the game, but this learning is constrained to a very small subset of experience: they are allowed neither threat strategies nor to be different from other players, and cannot 'remember' past the last immediate play of the game. Technically, allowable strategies are restricted to a mixed strategy over best responses in which the probabilities attached to each

Table 11-1. Component Trading Game

		Trader 2	
		A	B
Trader 1	A	10, 20	3, 6
	B	3, 6	10, 20

response are updated with a mechanical Bayesian procedure (Schotter [1981, p. 72]). The rule is so constructed that it will eventually converge to a pure strategy Nash equilibrium point if that strategy is played at some juncture in the game. For Schotter, an institution is any one such Nash equilibrium of a fixed game converged upon after repeated play. He does not claim to have identified the single unique institutional outcome of the situation: there are in general multiple Nash equilibria; all he can guarantee is that the Markov chain of mixed strategies will eventually converge upon one of the equilibrium points, which is an absorbing state.

One point needs elucidation which it does not receive in Schotter's book. The necessity for the single component subgame to be of the form of a prisoner's dilemma derives from the narrow conception of learning implied in the mechanical Bayesian updating rule. The question arises, as it does in all Austrian theory, how the institutional regularity is to be 'policed' if it is, in fact, 'organic' or 'evolutionary.' If the game is not of the prisoner's dilemma form, there is no longer any unique way for a player to 'punish' the others for behavior undesirable from his point of view (Schotter [1981, p. 83]). This can be easily observed by again looking at table 11-1. Suppose Trader 1 in the last round of play has chosen *A* while Trader 2 has chosen *B*. Clearly both of their situations could be improved, but how can he teach this to Trader 2? No message can be sent which would not involve the recall of the pattern of all plays previous to the last, and that is prevented by the Bayesian updating rule, due to the fact that mixed strategies are allowed. In other words, no strategy is explicitly identified as punishment by the structure of the game.

Schotter, like many other latter-day Austrians, shies away from explicitly discussing *learning*, as opposed to the transmission of a discrete and seemingly prepackaged commodity called *knowledge*, because the former suggests a social process, whereas the latter conjures up the grocer's dairy case (Field [1984]). This is done largely by mathematical sleight-of-hand: assuming that everyone's psychology is identical (Schotter [1981, p. 88]), and ruling out what he calls "disguised equilibria," that is, situations where the opponent's choice of strategy cannot be divined from the actual outcome or payoff. In effect, he defines the "problem" to be so straightforward and unambiguous that only one choice can be made: it is not so much learning as it is mechanism. Any discussion of the influence of history are rendered pointless, since only state strategies (in Shubik's terms) are allowed, or indeed, make any sense, given that the situation is so well defined. It should not surprise us, then, that at the end of the narrow corridor through which we are allowed to pass, we arrive at-voilà-a Walrasian general equilibrium (Schotter [1983, p. 685–6]). It is difficult to maintain that this model transcends the passive cooperation found in conventional neoclassical general equilibrium. The question posed at the beginning of this section remains: where has game theory gotten us?

2. Game Theory and Neoclassical Economics: The Rules of the Game

What is a game? It is, as quite correctly perceived by von Neumann, a set of rules, a set of objectives or payoffs, and a ranking of those objectives by the set of players. If all of these sets are *discrete* and well defined, they may be expressed in the format of mathematical formalism, and then further manipulation of the symbols can serve to suggest potential outcomes. However, it is also true, as Wittgenstein wrote in his *Remarks on the Foundations of Mathematics*, "A game, a language, a rule is an institution" (Wittgenstein [1978, vi. 32]). The copula "is" in this quote should not be confused with an equals sign, for the relationship is neither commutative nor symmetrical. To say that a game is an institution is not necessarily to say that an institution is a game (Field [1984]).

Game theory and neoclassical market theory start from an identical premise: market trades are not adventitious, but possess a regularity and stability which permits them to be causally explained. So what is the constancy postulated by game theory? The first, and least discussed postulate[5], is the persistence and constancy of the players (Heims [1980, p. 307]). Within a static one-shot game the persistence of the players' identities may be ignored; but with any repetition or learning this condition becomes critical. The constancy of humans, and therefore the putative constancy of human nature, is the key to the translation of any game into mathematical formalism. If humans are not to be treated with all their individual quirks and idiosyncracies (that is, to be the subject of generalization), then their communication and behavior must be treated symmetrically. If one merely assumes that language is always adequately shared, that the content of a transmitted message is identical to the content received, and that interpretation is not problematic, then the people who are the subject of the analysis must be substantially "the same," no matter what happens.

The second postulate of game theory is the assumed constancy of the rules. As we have observed, this appeared to be the bone of contention between Shubik and Schotter. Shubik seemed content to accept the rules as arbitrarily fixed; Schotter claimed that the rules were solutions to supergames. Some examination of Schotter's model revealed that the rules were no more flexible than in Shubik's models; if anything, Schotter mistakes arbitrary psychological rigidities for rule structure. As with the previous postulate, this problem is not apparent in one-shot games, but only attains importance upon repetition. The rules are what exist to be learned by the players, although this is often obscured by mathematically posing the game in strategic form.[6] We shall return to this issue shortly.

The third postulate of game theory is that relative stability of the objectives and the environment. Interestingly enough, this is not an endogenous outcome in game theory, but must be given *a priori* as part of the mathematical formalism. Many pages have been written about the necessity or expendability of cardinally measurable payoffs, and especially the requirement of cardinal utility, but few have realized that this is merely the tip of the iceberg. A game must have a single valued objective function which somehow summarizes the jumbled, confused and sometimes unconsciously contradictory desires and drives of human beings; and further, this index must generally conform to the axiom of Archimedes (Krantz et al. [1971, pp. 25–6]), which translates into requiring that all potential outcomes be comparable before the fact, or more prosaically, every man must have his price. It is of paramount importance that these rankings be stable,[7] for without them, there is no sense in which a game can be "solved."

Now, the most important aspect of these postulates is not their tenuous connection to "reality" (game theorists have been historically thick-skinned when it comes to empirical disconfirmation of solutions and/or assumptions), but rather what passes for analysis and explanation. Given the fixed actors with their fixed objectives and the fixed rules, the analyst (and *not the actors*) prereconciles the various sets, insists the prereconciled outcome is the one which will actually obtain, and calls this a "solution." The critical role of the three postulates of constancy becomes evident: without them, there is no preordained reconciliation to be discovered. The process in which the actors take part is irrelevant, because the deck has been stacked in a teleological manner. Insofar as the three postulates are 'naturally' given, equilibrium is identified with harmony and natural order, while conflict and disharmony can only be expressed as disequilibrium.

This caricature is crudely drawn, and the game theorists would surely complain (at least here, if not in their published work) that the world is not that simple. I should think they would aver that the distinction between cooperative and noncooperative games was invented precisely to conjure up a more subtle and penetrating analysis of harmony and conflict. I would like to suggest that the promise of game theory to encompass conflict and strategy in a rigorous manner is more than a little illusory, and is rooted in a confusion over the role of the analyst in the solution of games.

The clearest definition of a cooperative game has been provided by (Shubik [1981, p. 165]): Pareto optimality is taken as an axiom, sidepayments of utility or other payoff units are permitted outside of the actual structure of the game, and communications and bargaining of an unspecified nature are permitted and presumed to take place (at least virtually, in that the value of each potential coalition must be well defined). Cooperation is not modelled; it is subsumed in the various payoffs to coalitions. In the presence of the three postulates, the players know that the analyst knows, and both the players and the analyst "agree" upon the feasible and desirable outcomes. It is no surprise that early partisans of cooperative games have lately been repudiating their premature enthusiasm: in this scenario, "natural order" is imposed by the analyst.

The distinctive characteristic of noncooperative games is that the players and the analyst no longer "think" the same things: in essence, the analyst would like to impose a solution that the players would not choose as a result of obeying the rules. The conflict is not located amongst the players as much as it resides in the tension between the rule-governed situation and the Pareto optimum. The analyst, obeying his own self-denying ordinance, resists simply imposing the naturally given optimum (or optima), and then is challenged by the need to provide a description of simple rule-governed stability in the presence of infinite degrees of freedom. The analyst is faced with the prospect of constructing some definition of rationality which is not transparently a reflection of the natural givens.

This impasse has surfaced whenever someone tries to explain what a Nash equilibrium point means or signifies (Johansen [1982]; Harsanyi [1982]; Shubik [1981]; Friedman [1977]). Mathematically, the Nash EP is the maximum point or points on a compact convex set of the "best replies" of each player's strategy set. The Nash EP is often motivated by appealing to some lack of knowledge or ability to compare goals among players, but this is not strictly true. Each player knows all the relevant information about the other players, and has the ability to prereconcile the entire process in his own head. The only difference from a cooperative game is that the rules create the potentiality that rationality is indeterminate, in that the interpretation of strategy sets becomes an issue.

It is well known that every finite N-person game has at least one Nash EP if mixed strategies are allowed. This mathematical existence proof does us a disservice, however, once we realize that mixed strategies are only rational if deployed outside of a one-shot static game (Shubik [1981, p. 155]). Therefore, a noncooperative game can in most cases only be seriously discussed if it is repeated; more generally, after Wittgenstein, we can say that no one is capable of following a rule only once. Games, if they are to describe behavior rather than a set of prearranged natural conditions, must be repeated. But it is precisely in repetition that the notion of a fixed strategy set slowly unravels: more and more *ad hoc* assumptions must be made about how each player interprets the sequences of the other players' moves over time. In general, the solutions to a sequence of noncooperative games will not be the sequence of individual solutions to each of the component games (van Damme [1981]; Friedman [1971, p. 199]). It is in this sense that rationality, as conceived in game theory, is indeterminate.

At this juncture we once again return to the postulates of constancy. Shubik is right to point out that it is a misnomer to call the Nash solution concept "rational expectations," because there is no guarantee that the outcome will meet the *analysts'* criteria of rationality (i.e., Pareto optionality) (Shubik [1981, p. 153]). He suggests it is more appropriate to think of a Nash EP as displaying "consistent expectations," in that conjectures about players' behavior match *ex post* outcomes. However, the definition of consistency is a function of the time frame over which the Nash equilibrium is defined; once that is realized, it follows directly that all Nash EP require our three postulates of constancy. How else could we possibly "construct" consistency solely from the payoffs of the game, unless the players, the rules, and the objectives were identical through time?

Contrary to the claims often made in the literature on supergames, those models cannot encompass historical change. Works that claim to include change of players over time such as (Schotter [1981, pp. 127–139]) in fact specify the sequential agent characteristics so that they are functionally identical. In contrast, works such as (Friedman [1977]) which vary the payoffs over time, do so in such a way that the change can be specified independent of history (i.e., are stationary). If changes in strategy sets are allowed, they are restricted to stationary Bayesian revisions, by their very structure myopic and ahistorical. There is no published work which attempts to change all three postulates simultaneously. This poor showing cannot be excused as a temporary situation contingent upon further mathematical effort and virtuosity. It is a corollary of the neoclassical notion of rationality, which can only augment the psychological abilities of *homo rationalis* in order that all interactions must be virtually prereconciled in their heads, whether or not they actually occur. This conception, of course, is exactly what caused the older Institutionalist school to renounce neoclassical economics.

It is easy to be lulled by all the language of "conflict," "retaliation," and "enforcement" into believing the solvable supergames portray processes. (Harsanyi [1982]) and (Aumann [1981]) both define the Nash EP as a self-enforcing equilibria, but we should now understand this to mean that the solution would persist if the postulates of constancy held and if the analyst imposes an arbitrary set of rules governing how players interpret each others' moves. These requirements wreak havoc with any common sense notion of this enforcement of rules. The neoclassical economist wants to portray a world where there is no active coercion, because rationality polices itself. What causes this goal to elude their grasp is that there is no such thing as a self-justifying rule (Levison [1978]). Quoting Wittgenstein: "However many rules you give me—I give a rule which justifies *my* employment of your rules" (Wittgenstein [1978, I.113]). "The employment of the word 'rule' is interwoven with the employment of the word 'same'" (Wittgenstein [1978, VII.59]). The exercise of rationality, as opposed to the twitches of a zombie or a machine, depends upon active interpretation of whether the rule applies in the particular instance, and whether to regard anomalies as exceptions or failures to abide by the rule. Rationality is the deployment of judgment as a process, which cannot itself be justified by a rule at the risk of falling into an infinite regress[8] (Field [1979]).

This is nowhere better illustrated than in the proliferation of solution concepts and individual solutions in game theory. As soon as someone proposes a "rational" solution to a particular game someone else generates a counterexample which questions its rationality. For example (Morgenstern and Schwodiauer [1976]) criticize the core as being dominated by other imputations if the players are aware of the theory of the core. Or (Johansen [1982, p. 430]) points out that if player X knew player Y was experimenting with his options and had any basis for guessing the pattern of player Y's experiments, then player X would in general choose strategies outside of the Nash equilibrium. Van Damme [1981, p. 37] shows that in certain game structures, "A player can punish the other as badly as he wishes and therefore each player can force the other player to steer the system to any state he wishes. So all kinds of behavior (even rather foolish) can appear when one plays according to a history dependent EP." (Aumann [1981]) reports that the solution points of a supergame depend critically upon the discount rate used to calculate the present value of future payoffs; I believe no one has yet indicated how vulnerable these results are to the paradoxes arising out of the Cambridge capital controversy (Harcourt [1982, pt. V]). We have already noted that the Nash EP for a one-shot noncooperative game is not identical to a Nash EP for the same game repeated over and over again.

Game theorists have opened the Pandora's Box marked "Rationality," and do not know how to close it again. Walrasian general equilibrium was based upon a direct appropriation of a metaphor from physics, and this meant that the natural givens of the analysis would directly determine the optimal outcome (Mirowski [1984b]). Planets in motion are passive and do not talk back, and neither did the passive Walrasian trader. The natural world is stable and unchanging,[9] which allowed the postulations of laws which were independent of their spatial or temporal location. The Walrasian laws were also stationary and static. Then game theorists proposed to discuss bargaining, which led to cooperative games, which begat noncooperative games, which begat discussions of process, which allowed the transactors the freedom to differ in their interpretations of the roles of others and the constancy of the world, all of which is now undermining the older construct of mechanistic rationality. This is not happening because game theorists have willed it so—in fact, much effort is spent demonstrating that special sorts of solutions to special sorts of games converge to Walrasian equilibria. It is happening because game theory exposes the weaknesses of the physical metaphor that all the excessive mathematical formalism served to obscure. Game theory does not, however, suggest what to put in its place. It cannot conceptualize the reduction of a language or an institution to a game.

3. Rules are not Homogeneous

The word "institution" has been so far used loosely; the time has arrived to suggest a more precise definition. In view of the criticisms voiced in the previous sections of this chapter, it may prove illuminating to conceptualize institutions as consisting of three tiers of rules. The first tier is the rules most familiar to game theorists: these are rules grounded in stable, persistent, and independent givens of the analysis. These rules are in some sense "policed" by the stability of the environment. A good example of this type of situation is provided by prisoner's dilemma games describing the overgrazing of a commons or the depletion of a fish species. Insofar as the "payoff" is well defined and not socially defined (i.e., fish caught or animal fed), and the players are fairly homogeneous, Nash equilibria can explain certain regularities in behavior. We could refer to these situations as "natural" rules.

The second tier of rules is based upon the recognition that human rationality cannot be an algorithm, but must constantly be flexible and prepared for change. These rules are social, consciously constructed, and consciously policed. Into this category would fall property rights, money, religion, the family, and much else that comprises social order. This class of rules cannot be explained as the outcome of underlying natural forces, because their enforcement mechanisms are not "natural": they possess neither persistence nor independence from the phenomena. We could refer to those situations as "bootstrap" rules.

The third tier of rules derives from the recognition that the first two classes of rules must interact over time. For example, the overgrazing game will be influenced by the institution of money, and any natural regularity of behavior may be destabilized or redefined by the penetration of market relationships: here, the payoff itself becomes partly socially defined. The exercise of human rationality itself transforms the environment. The recognition that there may be temporal regularities to the relative dominance or importance of natural rules versus bootstrap rules leads to the meta-rationality of evolutionary regularities. Unlike the first two classes of rules, evolutionary regularities by their nature cannot be teleological: they reflect interactions of natural rules and bootstrap rules beyond the imagination of any player.

It should be clear from previous comments that most neoclassical econ-omists would insist that a scientific economics would only recognize expla-nations which linked any given social phenomenon to its natural rules (Mirowski [1981]). Explanation in this framework is satisfied to take as given tastes, technologies, and endowments, and to identify equilibrium with the extremum of some objective function. Why can't all social processes be reduced to their natural rules? To reiterate, this program leads to a logical contradic-tion. All natural rules must be subject to human interpretation. Natural constraints do not inexorably compel us to do anything, because human reason intervenes: it is this freedom which provides us with all the multiform variation which comprises the history of the human race. To put it in Wittgensteinian terms: a rule does not certify its own correct application. To pretend that it does so is to appeal to other rules, and can only lead in a circle. Whether a reason or an activity conforms to a rule in a particular case is a problem in reasoning and interpretation, having to do with judgments about when situations are "the same." We may feel compelled to follow a rule, but the rule itself cannot compel us.

There are also those who believe that the world is only comprised of bootstrap rules. Let us call this opinion "conventionalism." Why cannot all social phenomena be reduced to bootstrap rules? This position also meets an insuperable logical difficulty: knowledge of this theory of social phenomena tends to undermine its efficacy. To argue that all social regularities are consciously instituted is to argue that the only prerequisite for change is will; a society based upon this premise cannot ultimately enforce or maintain the stability required to define rules. In other words, just as the natural world is intrinsically incapable of defining the totality of social life, so too is the belief that might makes right. Even if the world of language, markets, and culture were ultimately organized by bootstrap rules, these rules would themselves be asserted by some actors to be grounded in natural rules, in order to provide stability and diffuse responsibility.

What then, is the function of the evolutionary regularities? These must be present because bootstrap rules influence natural rules, and vice versa. They are the locus of the understanding of change. The determination that a natural situation is producing regularities in behavior is itself a function of society's conception of science; and, as 20th century philosophers of science have come to argue, science consists largely of bootstrap rules. As our understanding of what is natural evolves, it cannot help but change the formal relations of bootstrap rules to natural rules in social life. These changes are not purely erratic: a good example of this is provided by Wesley Clair Mitchell in his "Role of Money in Economic History." He argues that money cannot be cogently explained by the prosaic notion that it made life naturally easier for traders.

"When money is introduced into the dealing of men, it enhances their freedom. For example, personal service is commuted into money payment . . . . Adam Smith's obvious and simple system of natural liberty seems obvious and natural only to the denizens of a money economy" (Mitchell [1953, p. 200]). More significantly, Mitchell proposes that the penetration of the money economy into social life altered the very configurations of rationality, to the extent of encouraging particular conceptions of abstraction, quantification, and thus ultimately, the ontology of modern Western science. Here we have socially constructed rules slowly transforming the understanding of natural constraints through the rational interpretative structure, finally changing the natural rules themselves.

What has all this to do with game theory and economic theory? It clearly and concisely provides a framework within which to evaluate the claims that there is a new mathematical institutional economics in the offing. Neoclassical economists will only sanction explanation in terms of natural rules. This is a reflection of their perennial search for a natural order, an invisible hand, and so forth. Since bootstrap rules and evolutionary regularities cannot be reduced to natural rules, their project is doomed to failure. One need only compare Schotter's "explanation" of the rise of money as a game theoretic solution to a naturally given problem of transactions costs to Mitchell's broad interpretation of the influence of money on economic life to see this failure.

There are other economists who believe that conscious and deliberate planning will solve all economic ills; they are partisans of the view that the world is nothing but a collection of bootstrap rules. Since neither natural rules nor evolutionary regularities can be fully reduced to bootstrap rules, this research project is also doomed to undermine itself.

Game theoretic explanations of human institutions fall into one of these two categories. Contrary to Schotter, all phenomenal rules cannot be reduced to their underlying natural rules. Contrary to Shubik, the postulation of rules as bootstrap or *ad hoc* leaves explanations without any firm foundations. A theory of institutions must operate simultaneously on all three levels. The mathematical formalism of game theory is best suited for the discussion of natural rules. It can be used to *describe* bootstrap rules; but it also reveals that notions of rationality and equilibrium are distorted beyond recognition in those models, to the point that neither the existence nor efficacy of those rules can be said to be illuminated by the analysis. Since evolutionary rules are not teleological, they are not suited to game theoretic structures.

In conclusion, game theory is not a substitute for a theory of institutions. It can only be one component of such a theory, a theory committed to the explanation of change as well as of complacency.

Notes

1. This history of the critique of the concept of the maximization of a clear example of the peripatetic migration between one defense and the other. For recent examples of the former, see (Boland [1981]); for the latter see (Wong [1978]).

2. The quote is from Veblen's "Why is Economics Not an Evolutionary Science?" reprinted in (Veblen [1919]). The best introduction and summary of the thought of the Institutionalists is still chapters 14 and 15 of (Mitchell [1950]).

3. Evidence for this statement is provided in (Mirowski [1984b]).

4. Sometimes there is postulated a continuum of traders, i.e., a nonatomic agglomeration who therefore cannot be subject to a discrete list. This assumption is often used to 'prove' that Nash equilibria converge to Walrasian competitive equilibria.

5. This absence of discussion may provide a counterexample to the common opinion that mathematical models, by their very nature, make assumptions more clear and transparent than common speech.

6. "There is a not completely innocent modelling assumption that any finite game in extensive form can be reduced to a game in strategic form, which is equivalent to the original description of the game from the viewpoint of the application of solution theory" (Shubik [1981, p. 157]).

7. We way "stable" and not "constant," because of the tradition of probabilistic concepts of utility dating back to the original work of (von Neumann and Morgenstern [1964]).

8. Perhaps this explains the final chapter of (Schotter [1981]) with its discussion of sociobiology. One way to short-circuit the infinite regress is to locate 'fundamental' rules in our genes.

9. At least until the 20th century, when physics left the economists behind.

References

Aumann, R., "Markets With a Continuum of Traders." *Econometrica* 32 (1964), 39–50.

Aumann, R., "Survey of Repeated Games." In *Essays in Game Theory and Mathematical Economics in Honor of Oskar Morganstern* B.I., Mannheim, 1981.

Boland, Lawrence, On the Futility of Criticizing the Neoclassical Maximizing Hypothesis." *American Economic Review*, Dec. 71 (1981) 1031–1036.

Commons, John R., *Institutional Economics*. Macmillan: New York, 1934.

van Damme, E. E., "History-Dependent Equilibrium Points in Dynamic Games." In *Game Theory & Mathematical Economics*, (O. Moeschlin and D. Pallaschke, eds.), North-Holland, Amsterdam, 1981.

Debreu, G. and H. Scarf, "A Limit Theorem of the Core of the Economy." *International Economic Review* 4 (1963), 243–246.

Dubey, Pradeep and Shubik, Martin, "Bankruptcy and Optimality in a Closed Trading Mass Economy Modelled as a Noncooperative Game." *Journal of Mathematical Economics* 6 (1979), 115–134.

Dubey, Pradeep and Shubik, Martin, "A Strategic Market Game with Price and Quantity Strategies." *Zeitschrift Für Nationalökonomie* 40 (1980), 25–34.

Field, Alexander, "On the Explanation of Rules Using Rational Choice Models." *Journal of Economic Issues*, 13 (1979), 49–72.

Field, Alexander, "Microeconomics, Norms and Rationality." *Economic Development and Cultural Change* 32 (1984), 683–711.

Friedman, James, *Oligopoly and the Theory of Games.* Amsterdam: North-Holland, 1977.

Halevy, Elie, *The Growth of Philosophical Radicalism.* London: Faber, 1972.

Harcourt, Geoffrey, *The Social Science Imperialists.* Routledge Kegan Paul: Boston, 1982.

Harsanyi, John, "Noncooperative Bargaining Models." In *Games, Economic Dynamics and Time Series Analysis*, (Deistler, M. E. Furst & G. Schwödiauer, eds.), Physica-Verlag, Wein, 1982.

Heims, Steve, *John von Neumann and Norbert Wiener.* Cambridge: MIT Press, 1980.

Johansen, Leif, "On the Status of the Nash Type of Noncooperative Equilibrium in Economic Theory." *Scandinavian Journal of Economics* 34 (1982), 421–441.

Johansen, Leif, "Mechanistic and Organistic Analogies in Economics: The Place of Game Theory." *Kyklos* 36 (1983), 304–307.

Krantz, D., R. Luce, P. Suppes and A. Tversky, *Foundations of Measurement.* New York: Academic Press, 1971.

Levinson, Arnold, "Wittgenstein and Logical Laws." In *Ludwig Wittgenstein: The Man and His Philosophy*, (K. T. Fann, ed.), Humanities, New York, 1978.

Mirowski, Philip, "Is There a Mathematical Neoinstitutional Economics?." *Journal of Economic Issues* 15 (1981), 593–613.

———, "The Role of Conservation Principles in 20th Century Economic Theory." *Philosophy of the Social Sciences* 14, (1984a), 461–473.

———, "Physics and the Marginalist Revolution." *Cambridge Journal of Economics* 8, (1984b), 361–379.

Mitchell, Wesley Clair, *The Backward Art of Spending Money.* New York: Kelley, 1950.

———, "The Role of Money in Economic History." In *Enterprise and Secular Change*, (Lane, F. & J. Riemersma, eds.), Irwin, Homewood, Ill., 1953.

Morgenstern, O. and Schwödiauer, G., "Competition and Collusion in Bilateral Markets." *Zeitscrift Für Nationalökonomie* 36 (1976), 217–245.

Mosley, Nicholas, *The Rules of the Game.* London: Fontana, 1983.

von Neumann, J. and Morgenstern, O., *The Theory of Games and Economic Behavior.* 3rd Ed., New York: Wiley, 1964.

Rosenberg, Alexander, "Can Economic Theory Explain Everything?" *Philosophy of the Social Sciences* 9 (1979), 509–529.

Samuelson, Paul, *Foundations of Economic Analysis.* New York: Atheneum, 1965.

Schotter, Andrew, *The Economic Theory of Social Institutions.* Cambridge Mass.; Cambridge University Press, 1981.

Schotter, Andrew, "Why Take a Game Theoretical Approach to Economics?" *Economie Appliquée* 36 (1983), 673–695.

Schotter, A. and Schwödiauer, G., "Economics and The Theory of Games: a Survey." *Journal of Economic Literature* 18, 1980.

Shubik, Martin, "Commodity Money, Oligopoly, Credit and Bankruptcy in a General Equilibrium Model." *Western Economic Journal* 11 (1972), 24–38.

————, "Money, Trust and Equilibrium Points in Games in Extensive Forms." *Zeitscrift Für Nationalökonomie* 34 (1974), 365–85.

————, "The General Equilibrium Model is Incomplete and Not Adequate for the Reconciliation of Macro and Micro Theory." *KYKLOS* 28 (1975A), 545–573.

————, "Mathematical Models for a Theory of Money and Financial Institutions." In *Adaptive Economic Models*, (Day, R. & T. Groves, eds.), New York: Academic Press, 1975B.

————, "A General Theory of Money and Financial Institutions." *Economie Appliquée* 29 (1976), 319.

————, "Perfect or Robust Noncooperative Equilibrium: A Search for the Philosopher's Stone? In *Essays in Game Theory and Economics in Honor of Oskar Morgenstern*, B.I., Mannheim, 1981.

————, *Game Theory in the Social Sciences.* Cambridge: MIT Press, 1982.

Shubik, Martin and Wilson, Charles, "Optimal Bankruptcy Rule in a Trading Economy Using First Money." *Zeitscrift Für Nationalökonomie* 37 (1977), 337–354.

Simon, Herbert, *Models of Bounded Rationality.* Cambridge: MIT Press, 1982.

Veblen, Thorstein, *The Place of Science in Modern Civilization*, New York: Huebsch, 1919.

Wittgenstein, Ludwig, *Remarks on the Foundations of Mathematics.* Revised Edition, Cambridge: MIT Press, 1978.

Wong, Stanley, *The Foundations of Paul Samuelson's Preference Theory.* Boston: Routledge and Kegan Paul, 1978.

Wright, Crispin, *Wittgenstein on the Foundations of Mathematics.* London: Duckworth, 1980.

12 THE STATE OF MICROECONOMICS:
An Historical Perspective

K. H. Hennings

The state of microeconomics is in many respects unsatisfactory. This is as it should be. Only a stagnant discipline does not present new problems that need to be solved by at least partial change. It is natural, therefore, to ask in what respect microeconomics as a discipline has been changing, and whether ideas have been cast away in the process which it might be worthwhile to take up again. I will indeed contend that microeconomic analysis has undergone important changes in the last hundred years, and that some of its aspects which are found wanting today are in fact the result of these changes. In particular, I will argue that some of the answers provided by modern microeconomics are unsatisfactory because the problems that are posed today differ from those posed a hundred years ago.

The development of microeconomic analysis is intimately tied to the development of neoclassical economic theory. It is true that there is hardly a textbook on microeconomic theory which does not invoke the name of Adam Smith. It is equally true that there are some pertinent truths about markets, about entrepreneural behavior, and about the force of competition in the *Wealth of Nations*, as there are in Richards Cantillon's *Essai sur la Nature du Commerce en Général* (written in the 1730s, published in 1755, and known to Adam Smith), and, it should be added, in John Stuart Mill's mid-19th century restatement of classical doctrines in his *Principles of Political Economy* (1848). On the whole, however, classical political economy had little to say about microeconomics if that term is taken to designate an analysis of the economic behavior of individual economic agents such as consumers, firms, or entrepreneurs, and especially their interaction in markets.[1] Microeconomic analysis in this sense came to the fore with the growth of neoclassical economic theory in the 1870s and 1880s. Indeed, between the 1880s and the 1930s microeconomic analyses were the very core of economic theory. This was so much the case that the term "microeconomics" became common only in the 1940s, when the Keynesian Revolution and the ascent of aggregative analyses made it necessary to distinguish between microeconomics and macroeconomics. Boulding's textbook on *Economic Analysis* (1948) was, as far as I am aware, one of the first to put these "two main branches to modern economic analysis" on an equal footing.[2] The distinction is older, and goes back at least as far as Wicksell, who devoted one half of his course on economics to microeconomic analyses, and the other half to monetary economics. Significantly, however, Wicksell subtitled the first half "theoretical economics," because to him and his contemporaries economic theory was almost synonymous with microeconomic analyses. One reason why macroeconomics came to acquire a standing equal to microeconomics in the 1940s was that the microeconomic analyses, which had been almost all there was to economic theory, had undergone changes which altered the questions asked and answers provided so much that it came to be thought that certain problems could not be analysed within the framework they provided.

In order to illuminate these changes, consider Alfred Marshall's *Principles of Economics* (1890),[3] and compare it to more recent microeconomic textbooks.[4] There is much in the moderns which is not in Marshall; and there is much in Marshall which is not in modern textbooks. In some cases old wood has been discarded, or uninteresting disquisitions put aside. In other cases important and interesting analyses have been changed almost out of recognition. Three examples should be singled out: Marshall's discussion of wants; his analysis of supply and the role of firms; and his concept of equilibrium.[5]

To Marshall, wants (or preferences, to use the modern term) are not exogenous: economic agents acquire them by virtue of social interaction, i.e., by participating in economic activity:

> Speaking broadly therefore, although it is man's wants in the earliest stages of his development that give rise to his activities, yet afterwards each new step upwards is to be regarded as the development of new activities giving rise to new wants, rather than of new wants giving rise to new activities (Marshall [1920, p. 76]).

Preferences change endogenously, and as Parsons [1931] was the first to emphasize, Marshall was deeply concerned with the interaction between economic progress, changing wants, and human behavior. Indeed, many of Marshall's detailed discussions of various forms of economic organization throughout the *Principles* can be understood as an attempt to go back to Adam Smith's concern with the way in which economic and social institutions shape and influence economic behaviors. He is at pains to point out that he does not deal with economic agents as "economic man," but wishes to consider "all motives the action of which is so far uniform in any class at any time and place, that it can be reduced to general rule" (Marshall [1920, v and vi]). Economic behavior, then, is based on observed regularities and motives, with the rational pursuit of gain as just one of many springs of human action. In another context, Marshall argued that "modern forms of industrial life" are characterized by three features: "a certain independence and habit of choosing one's own course for oneself," "a deliberation and yet a promptness of choice and judgement, and a habit of forecasting the future and of shaping one's course with reference to distant aims" (Marshall [1920, p. 4]). Nevertheless, "stress is laid on the fact that there is a continuous gradation from the actions of 'city men,' which are based on deliberate and far-reaching calculations, and are executed with vigour and ability, to those of ordinary people who have neither the power not the will to conduct their affairs in a business-like way" (Marshall [1920, vi]). All this is a far cry from the axioms of rational behavior to which the economic agents in modern textbooks are confined; and so Marshall's theory of demand is far richer in content than its anemic modern counterpart which has been emptied of almost all economic content to provide an axiomatic basis for the proposition that demand functions are downward sloping, and no more.

Similarly, Marshall's theory of supply is much richer in economic content than its modern counterpart, even though (or perhaps because?) it lacks the full apparatus of cost curve diagrams. It is well known that Marshall placed much emphasis on the time element in his supply analysis, and thus the differences in the adjustment of supply to changing conditions in the very short, the short and the long run; but it is not always realized that to Marshall the shape of supply functions depended not only on the scale of output normally produced but also on (among other things) the past history of output growth (Marshall [1920, p. 667]). Marshall thought increasing returns to scale were perfectly compatible with competition precisely because it was impossible for firms to expand output so rapidly as to monopolize the market (Marshall [1920, p. 381]). Because firms differ in their past histories, one cannot "regard the conditions of supply by an individual producer as typical of those which govern the general supply in a market" (Marshall [1920, p. 380]). Marshall's representative firm differs from the firm in modern textbooks not only because it has a past, but also because it is growing. Its managers have to make decisions in changing circumstances characterized by both technical progress and uncertainty about future developments; they can be lucky, and they can make mistakes; and they are subject to the restrictions which result from the fact that firms are organizations.[6] Compared to these considerations, the theory of the firm as it is expounded in modern textbooks has been streamlined so much that it is hardly more than an abstract entity which allows one to join together supply behavior on output markets and demand behavior on input markets in a static environment without much analysis of adjustment mechanisms.

In his theory of demand, Marshall emphasized the formation of preferences; in his theory of supply, he emphasized the adjustment of firm behavior over time. In his discussion of market equilibrium, Marshall was likewise much more interested in how equilibrium is attained than in its properties once it is attained. Temporary equilibria (and even more so short period and long period ones) depend on changing expectations; but "we cannot foresee the future perfectly. The unexpected may happen; and the existing tendencies may be modified" before equilibrium is attained (Marshall [1920, p. 289]). Hence the institutional framework of markets matters to Marshall, because it provides the environment within which economic agents can accumulate the experience and information they need in order for equilibria to be attained (Marshall [1920, pp. 277–8]). For similar reasons, Marshall worries about the effects of out-of-equilibrium trading (Marshall [1920, pp. 279–80]). More generally, Marshall does not have anything approaching perfect competition. His concept is "free competition" (Marshall [1920, p. 284]), by which he means a state of affairs which is much more akin to imperfect competition or oligopoly as described in modern textbooks. Both buyers and sellers know each other, and have (limited!) knowledge of bargains struck in other parts of the market, and related markets. Moreover, they have the confidence that all traders will adhere to rules and stick to established relationships.[7] When Marshall talks of business cycles, he emphasizes not only that "the chief cause of the evil is a want of confidence," but also that it is due to a cumulative "disorganization" of trade (Marshall [1920, p. 592]), or, in modern terms, a failure of information networks especially in the markets for capital goods. Similarly, when he defines the "famous fiction" of a stationary state, he assumes that "every business remained always of the same size, and with the same trade connection" (Marshall [1920, p. 305]).

In sum, then, Marshall's theory of equilibrium between demand and supply is not primarily a theory of static equilibria in the short and the long run. It does include them, but "it is especially needful to remember that economic problems are imperfectly presented when they are treated as problems of statical equilibrium" (Marshall [1920, p. 382]). Looking back after 30 years, in the preface to the eighth edition of his *Principles*, Marshall was at pains to stress that he was "concerned throughout with the forces that cause movement" (Marshall [1920, xiii]), and goes on to argue that when he speaks of "normal" conditions, reference is made to an unchanging environment as well as the time period required to attain short period equilibrium. In his view, "The main concern of ecnomics is thus with human beings who are impelled, for good or evil, to change and progress." The "central idea of economics . . . must be that of living force and movement." Hence the circumstances under which equilibrium is attained were of prime importance to him; among them, institutional arrangements and the informational and expectational structures they create (or help to establish) hold the first rank.

Marshall was not the only one in his generation to emphasize these matters. He certainly pushed these arguments further than anyone else, but similar ideas pervade the work of Carl Menger and other Austrians, notably Wieser and to some extent also Böhm–Bawerk. By contrast, very little of this emphasis can be detected in Walras or Pareto, or those economists working in their tradition. In their work, static equilibria rule supreme. Conditions are stationary, firms (if they are dealt with at all) are of equal size, and anonymous to other traders. Competition is perfect, and information requirements are rarely mentioned. In brief: what we find in Walras and Pareto is much more akin to what one finds in modern microeconomic textbooks than what is set out in Marshall and Menger. Modern microeconomic theory bears much more the imprint of the Walrasian general equilibrium tradition with its emphasis on static equilibrium conditions than the Marshallian or Mengerian concern for changing circumstances and the conditions under which equilibria are attained. That, indeed, is the main change in the development of neoclassical economic theory between the 1880s and the 1930s.[8]

There can be no question that this change has brought advantages. By concentrating rigorously on static conditions in a system of mutually interlocking markets much has been learned about the nature of equilibrium. Moreover, the theory has been extended: we can deal better with risky situations, and promising attempts have been made to apply the theory to noneconomic, or partly economic, behavior such as politics, marriage formation, procreation, and much else besides. More recently, we have learned, or perhaps better, are beginning to learn, how to handle transaction costs and property rights. The notion of choice has been extended from individual choice behavior to collective, or social choices, and it has become common to consider other mechanisms of resource allocation than the market as well. Finally, much advance has been made in analytical techniques, and much irrelevant detail has been cut out in the process.

All this is no mean achievement (as other contributions to this collection attest), and constitutes progress. But it should not blind us to the fact that it was achieved by posing in effect simpler problems than Marshall and Menger did. Perhaps the questions they asked were too difficult for their time; that at least is suggested by the fact that only some aspects of their work were taken up. Yet at the same time many of those aspects of their work that were not taken up are exactly those which nowadays cause unease with the present state of microeconomics. Changing preferences, the way in which supply is adjusted in situations of imperfect competition, the conditions in which equilibria are attained, and above all the institutional arrangements which shape economic behavior and ensure the required flow of information—these are aspects of market processes which still need to be analysed in detail. This is not to say of course that Marshall or Menger or other neoclassical authors such as Knight have the answers; they do not. What they have to offer are, I submit, "good" questions, and perhaps some suggestions about how to set about in answering them.

What I contend, then, is that we can still learn something from reading Marshall and Menger among other neoclassicals; in particular, we can find in their work ideas which, if refined and worked out with the help of modern analytical techniques, can remove some of the unease about the present state of microeconomics.

Notes

1.   Marx is an exception; but his work had almost no impact in the period here considered. For an analysis of what Smith and Mill had to say about firms, see Williams [1979].

2.   Boulding [1948, p. 439]; I have not been able to consult the first edition (1941). Neither term is listed in the index of the Ellis [1948] and Haley [1952] survey volumes, although at least one contributor used them; see Haley [1952, p. 439].

3.   All references will be to the eighth edition (1920).

4.   As there is no text comparable in stature to Marshall's *Principles*, none will be singled out. What I have in mind is an amalgam of such well-known textbooks (at various levels of rigor) as those of Alchian and Allen, Henderson and Quandt, and Hirshleifer. Note that the emphasis is on textbooks rather than the frontiers of research.

5.   For much of what follows, I am indebted to Loasby [1978].

6.   These ideas have been elaborated, in a Marshallian manner, by F. H. Knight [1921].

7.   It is in this context that one would have expected Marshall to discuss the importance of transactions costs.

8.   One aspect of this change is discussed in Hennings [1985].

References

Alchian, A. A. and W. R. Allen, *Exchange and Production*. Third edition, Belmont, CA: Wadsworth Publishing, 1983.

Böhm-Bawerk, E. von, *Capital and Interest* (translated by G. D. Huncke and H. F. Sennholz), South Holland, IL: Libertarian Press, 1959.

Boulding, K. E., *Economic Analysis*. Revised edition, London: Hamish Hamilton, 1948.

Cantillon, R., *Essai sur la Nature du Commerce en Général* (H. Higgs, ed.), London: Macmillan for the Royal Economic Society, 1931.

Ellis, H. S., *A Survey of Contemporary Economics, Vol. I* (ed. for American Economic Association), Homewood, IL: Irwin, 1948.

Haley, B. F., *A Survey of Contemporary Economics, Vol. II* (ed. for American Economic Association), Homewood, IL: Irwin, 1952.

Henderson, J. M. and R. F. Quandt, *Microeconomic Theory*. Third edition, New York: McGraw Hill, 1980.

Hennings, K. H., "The Exchange Paradigm and the Theory of Production and Distribution." In *Foundations and Dynamics of Economic Knowledge* (M. Baranzini and R. Scazzieri, eds.), Blackwell, Oxford, 1985.

Hirshleifer, J., *Price Theory and Applications*. Englewood Cliffs, NJ: Prentice-Hall, 1984.

Knight, F. H., *Risk, Uncertainty, and Profit*. Boston and New York: Houghton Mifflin, 1921.

Loasby, B. J., "Whatever Happened to Marshall's Theory of Value?" *Scottish Journal of Political Economy* 25 (1978), 1–12.

Marshall, A., *Principles of Economics*. London: Macmillan (eighth edition 1920), 1890.

Menger, C., *Principles of Economics* (translated by J. Dingwall and B. F. Hoselitz). Glencoe: Free Press 1950.

Mill, J. S., *Principles of Political Economy*. London: Longmans, 1848.

Pareto, V., *Manuel of Political Economy* (translated by A. S. Schwier; edited by A. S. Schwier and A. N. Pagel). Clifton, NJ: Augustus M. Kelley, 1971.

Parsons, T., "Wants and Activities in Marshall." *Quarterly Journal of Economics* 46 (1931), 316–347.

Smith, A., *An Inquiry into the Nature and Causes of the Wealth of Nations*. London: Strahan and Cadell, 1776.

Walras, L., *Elements of Pure Economics* (translated by W. Jaffé). Homewood, IL: Richard D. Irwin, Inc., 1954.

Wicksell, K., *Lectures on Political Economy* (translated by E. Classen), 2 vols. London: Routledge, 1934 and 1935.

Wieser, F. von, *Natural Value* (translated by C. A. Malloch, edited by W. Smart). London: Macmillan and Co., Ltd., 1893.

Williams, P. L., *The Emergence of the Theory of the Firm*. London: Macmillan, 1979.

INDEX